INSIGHT GUIDES

PERU

◎ Walking Eye App

YOUR FREE DESTINATION CONTENT AND EBOOK AVAILABLE THROUGH THE WALKING EYE APP

Your guide now includes a free eBook and destination content for your chosen destination, all for the same great price as before. Simply download the Walking Eye App from the App Store or Google Play to access your free eBook and destination content.

HOW THE WALKING EYE APP WORKS

Through the Walking Eye App, you can purchase a range of eBooks and destination content. However, when you buy this book, you can download the corresponding eBook and destination content for free. Just see below in the grey panels where to find your free content and then scan the QR code at the bottom of this page.

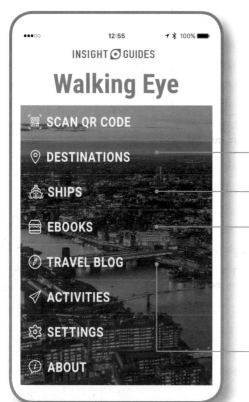

Destinations: Download your corresponding essential destination content from here, featuring recommended sights and attractions, restaurants, hotels and an A–Z of practical information, all for free. Other destinations are available for purchase.

Ships: Interested in ship reviews? Find independent reviews of river and ocean ships in this section, all available for purchase.

eBooks: You can download your free accompanying digital version of this guide here. You will also find a whole range of other eBooks, all available for purchase.

Free access to travel-related blog articles about different destinations, updated on a daily basis.

HOW THE DESTINATION CONTENT WORKS

Each destination includes a short introduction, an A–Z of practical information and recommended points of interest, split into 4 different categories:

- Highlights
- Accommodation
- Eating out
- What to do

You can view the location of every point of interest and save it by adding it to your Favourites. In the 'Around Me' section you can view all the points of interest within 5km.

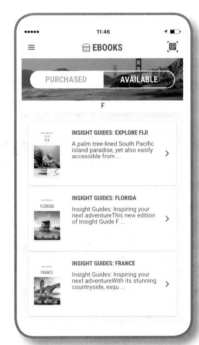

HOW THE EBOOKS WORK

The eBooks are provided in EPUB file format. Please note that you will need an eBook reader installed on your device to open the file. Many devices come with this as standard, but you may still need to install one manually from Google Play.

The eBook content is identical to the content in the printed guide.

HOW TO DOWNLOAD THE WALKING EYE APP

1. Download the Walking Eye App from the App Store or Google Play.
2. Open the app and select the scanning function from the main menu.
3. Scan the QR code on this page – you will then be asked a security question to verify ownership of the book.
4. Once this has been verified, you will see your eBook and destination content in the purchased ebook and destination sections, where you will be able to download them.

Other destination apps and eBooks are available for purchase separately or are free with the purchase of the Insight Guide book.

CONTENTS

Introduction

The Best of Peru 6
Ancient and Modern 19
Land of Extremes 21

History & Features

Decisive Dates 26
Lost empires: Peru before the Incas 31
The Incas 39
The Conquest 47
    🔎 Looking for the past 57
From Colony to Republic 59
    🔎 The covered ones 67
Democracy, Crises, and Resurgence 69
A Changing Society 79
Daily Life in the Andes 87
Peoples of the Amazon 91
How Crafts Have Adapted 97
    🔎 Pottery culture 101
Music and Dance 103
📷 Festivals and Fusion 108
Fusion of Flavors 111
Andean Adventures 117
    🔎 Running the Andes 125
Wildlife of the Sierra 127

Places

Introduction 139
■ LIMA 145
    🔎 Oasis of hope 156
■ THE NORTH COAST 161
    🔎 Witch doctor and wellness 168
📷 Buried Treasures 172
■ NORTHERN SIERRA 175
    🔎 Huallaga, Valley of Coca 178
■ CALLEJÓN DE HUAYLAS 185
    🔎 Cordillera Huayhuash 192
■ CENTRAL SIERRA 197
■ THE NORTHERN AMAZON 207
    🔎 The Amazon by riverboat 214
■ MANU TO MALDONADO 219
    🔎 Jungle lodges 220
📷 Birds of the Amazon 224
■ THE SOUTH COAST 227
■ AREQUIPA 243

◎ Colonial Art and Architecture **252**
■ CUSCO **255**
■ THE SACRED VALLEY **269**
■ MACHU PICCHU **277**
■ LAKE TITICACA **289**
◎ Taquile Island **298**

Travel Tips

TRANSPORTATION

Getting there **302**
Getting around **303**

A – Z

Accommodations **306**
Addresses **306**
Admission charges **306**
Budgeting for your trip **306**
Business travelers **306**
Children **306**
Climate **307**
Crime and security **307**
Customs regulations **308**
Disabled travelers **308**
Electricity **308**
Embassies and consulates **308**
Etiquette **309**
Health and medical care **309**
Internet **310**
LGBTQ travel **310**
Maps **310**
Media **310**
Money **310**
Opening hours **312**
Photography **312**
Postal services **312**
Public holidays **313**
Religious services **313**
Shopping **313**
Student travelers **313**
Telephones **313**
Time zones **314**
Toilets **314**
Tourist information **314**
Visas and passports **314**
Weights and measures **314**
Women travelers **314**

LANGUAGE

Language **315**
Pronunciation **315**
Basics **315**
Greetings **315**
Telephone calls **316**
Finding your way **316**
In the hotel **316**
In the restaurant **317**
Menu decoder **317**
Shopping **318**
Tourist attractions **318**
Airport/travel agency **318**
Transportation **319**
Driving **319**
Road signs **319**
Emergencies **320**
Health **320**
Months of the year **320**
Seasons **320**
Time **320**

FURTHER READING

General **321**
History **321**
Amazon Jungle **322**
Other Insight Guides **322**

Maps

Peru **140**
Lima **142**
North Coast **162**
Trujillo **164**
Northern Sierra **176**
Callejón de Huaylas **186**
Ayacucho **199**
Central Sierra **200**
Northern Amazon **208**
Manu to Maldonado **222**
South Coast **230**
Arequipa **245**
Around Arequipa **247**
Cusco **256**
The Sacred Valley **270**
Machu Picchu **282**
Lake Titicaca **290**
Inside front cover Peru
Inside back cover Lima

LEGEND

♀ Insight on
◎ Photo Story

THE BEST OF PERU: TOP ATTRACTIONS

△ **Colca Canyon.** Twice as deep as the Grand Canyon, Peru's Colca Canyon is one of the world's great natural wonders. From the Mirador del Condor, Andean condors can be seen gliding on the air currents high above the valley floor. See page 249.

▽ **Machu Picchu.** This ancient city lay hidden under jungle for centuries. Perched on a hilltop high in the Andes, it is an architectural marvel. See page 277.

△ **North Coast.** Home to Peru's best beaches, including Máncora, Punta Sal, Playa La Pena, and Huanchaco, famous for its *totora* reed boats. See page 161.

▽ **Cusco.** Known to the Incas as "the navel of the earth," the high-altitude city of Cusco is where you'll find some of colonial Peru's most impressive buildings, built directly on top of stones laid by the Incas. See page 255.

△ **Monasterio de Santa Catalina.** Cut off from the outside world until 1970, this is an oasis of calm amidst the hustle and bustle of Arequipa's busy streets. See page 246.

▽ **Nazca lines.** Giant etchings of animals and geometric figures created many thousands of years ago, the lines are one of the world's greatest archeological mysteries. See page 236.

△ **Cordillera Blanca.** The Cordillera Blanca mountain range offers some of the best trekking in South America. See page 185.

△ **Plaza Mayor, Lima.** Lima's main square lies at the heart of the "City of Kings" founded by Francisco Pizarro in 1535. It is overlooked by the Cathedral, the Archbishop's Palace, and the Government Palace. See page 149.

△ **Uros Islands.** The incredible floating islands of Uros on Lake Titicaca date back to pre-Inca times and are made of *totora* reeds, which must be continually replaced as they rot away. See page 293.

▷ **Cameloids.** Peru is home to four types of cameloid: llamas, alpacas, guanacos, and vicuñas. See page 127.

THE BEST OF PERU: EDITOR'S CHOICE

A canopy walkway above the Peruvian Amazon.

BEST NATURAL WONDERS

The rainforest. Covering some 50 million hectares (125 million acres), home to some of the greatest biodiversity on the planet, and storehouse of traditional medicine. See page 207.

The Andes. The highest mountain range outside the Himalayas, with some peaks eternally covered in snow. See page 117.

The volcanoes. Near Arequipa, many are over 6,000-meters (19,000ft) high, their craters filled with boiling mud. See page 243.

The northern beaches.

Girl from the highlands.

The northern beaches of Punta Sal, Máncora, and around Tumbes: sparkling clear water, white sands, and palm trees. See page 170.

Lake Titicaca. The highest navigable lake in the world. See page 289.

The Coastal Desert. The world's highest dunes and a stark coastline for adventure sports and to view Andean and ocean wildlife. See page 227.

The Cotahuasi Canyon. Like Colca but more remote, one of the deepest river canyons in the world. See page 250.

Hot springs. The Baños del Inca in Cajamarca and the hot springs at Chivay. See pages 180 and 249.

BEST ADVENTURE TOURISM

Trekking. The Cordillera Blanca and the Cordillera Huayhuash, near Huaraz, offer some of the best trekking in South America.

The Inca Trail. The hard – and scenic – way to reach Machu Picchu.

Climbing. Peru is home to some of the highest mountains in the world, such as Huascarán, at 6,760 meters (22,200ft).

Whitewater rafting. Rapids and beautiful stretches of river can be found on the Urubamba and Apurímac near Cusco.

Mountain biking. Classic biking destinations include the Cordillera Negra, the ranges near Cusco, or the trails of the Colca and Cotahuasi canyons near Arequipa.

Kayaking. Paddling the clear waters of Lake Titicaca and visiting its unique islands is an unmissable experience.

Surfing. The Pacific Ocean offers some of the best surf breaks in the world. See Andean Adventures, page 117, for details of adventure sports in Peru.

Royal Guardsman.

BEST NATIONAL PARKS

Macaws in Manu National Park.

340,000 hectares (850,000 acres) protect some of Peru's best high-altitude environments. See page 190.

Reserva Nacional Pacaya-Samiria. Two million hectares of lakes, rivers, and semi-submerged rainforest, territory of the rare manatee, pink dolphins, and giant anacondas. See page 215.

Parque Nacional del Manu. Covering 1,716,295 hectares (4,290,738 acres) of rainforest, this is the largest national park in Peru and one of the largest on the planet. It is home to 800 species of bird, 200 types of mammal, and seven distinct indigenous tribes. See page 219.

Parque Nacional Cordillera Azul. Protects the northern cloud forests between the Andes and the lowland rainforest. Little visited, home to indigenous communities. New species of birds are continuously discovered here. See page 179.

Parque Nacional Huascarán. Around

La Virgen de la Candelaria festival in Puno.

BEST FOR FAMILIES

Train to Machu Picchu. The passenger train from Cusco is a spectacular way to travel to Machu, especially for kids who are too young to walk the Inca Trail. See page 281.

Islas Ballestas. Take a boat out to the Islas Ballestas, Peru's answer to the Galápagos, to see penguins, sea lions, seals, and pelicans. See page 231.

Parque de las Leyendas. Lima's zoo in Pueblo Libre offers a great way to learn more about Peru's wildlife and is divided into coast, mountain, and jungle zones. It also has a children's playground. See page 155.

Circuito Mágico del Agua. Located in Lima's Parque de la Reserva, the Magic Water Circuit is composed of 13 fountains, with the largest shooting water to a height of 80 meters (262ft). Night-time light, sound, and water shows are amazing. See page 293.

BEST FESTIVALS

La Virgen de La Candelaria. In early February in Puno, thousands of people in traditional dress participate in dances, songs, parades, folkloric plays, and fireworks to celebrate the city's patron saint. See page 291.

Inti Raymi. The Festival of the Sun. This yearly occasion on June 24 in Cusco is perhaps the biggest and most colorful festival in Peru, and celebrates the return of the sun after the winter solstice. See page 264.

Carnival. Celebrated throughout Peru in mid-February, most wildly in Cajamarca. See page 177.

Semana Santa. This festival in March or April is marked with solemn religious processions in the streets. One of the best is in Ayacucho. See page 198.

Independence Day. Celebrated on July 28 and 29 throughout the country. See page 108.

El Señor de los Milagros. Held on October 18, 19, and 28 in Lima, a huge procession in honor of the city's patron saint. See page 153.

Marinera dancer.

BEST FOOD AND DRINK

Pisco. Peru's national drink is a powerful type of brandy. Pisco sour is the national cocktail, made with pisco, lemon juice, sugar syrup, and egg white.

Ceviche. Raw fish and mixed seafood marinated in lemon juice, garlic, and spices.

Anticuchos de corazón. Marinated beef-heart kebabs.

Humitas **and** *tamales.* Cornmeal dumplings cooked in corn or banana leaves, sometimes with a savory filling.

Pachamanca. An Andean specialty of spiced meat, potatoes, and corn, cooked in the ground on hot rocks.

Pollo a la brasa. Roast chicken is one of Peru's favorite meals and lip-smackingly good.

Potatoes. Peru has some 400 varieties of potatoes, or *papas*. They are the key ingredient for numerous dishes, including the delicious *papa a la huancaína*, a creamy dish with eggs.

Ají. A hot, spicy sauce made with chilis and garlic to accompany meals.

Chicha morada. A sweet, deep-purple non-alcoholic drink made from corn which is surprisingly refreshing.

Cuy. Although not to everyone's taste, roasted or fried guinea pig is a Peruvian specialty. See Fusion of Flavors, page 111, for more on Peru's food and drink.

Peruvian spirit.

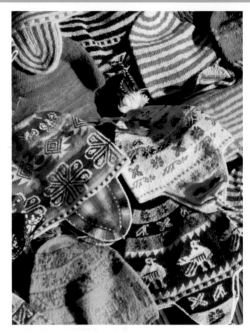

Traditional Peruvian hats made from llama wool.

BEST CULTURAL EXPERIENCES

The Island of Amantaní. On this island in Lake Titicaca, visitors can stay as guests in villagers' homes and share the meals they prepare. See page 294.

Ayacucho during Holy Week. As Peruvian festivals go, these *Semana Santa* celebrations are the ones to outdo all the rest. See page 198.

Handicraft shopping. Shop in one of Peru's many craft markets, such as Pisac near Cusco. See page 313.

Visiting a market. Food markets are found in larger towns and offer an impressive range of Peruvian produce, including unusual fruits and vegetables. See page 272.

Session with a shaman. Learn about your future or drink the powerful Ayahuasca in Chiclayo or the Amazon. See page 168.

Trekking with llamas. Walks organized by villagers from the Callejón de Huaylas that use llamas as pack animals. See page 194.

Moche statue.

BEST HISTORICAL SITES

Chavín de Huantar. Intricate carvings highlight this mysterious Andean cultural site, the greatest of the Cordillera Blanca. See page 191.
Kuélap. Little-visited ruined citadel in Peru's north, spectacular enough to rival Machu Picchu. See page 181.
Chan Chan. The ancient ruins of the Moche civilization, and the largest adobe city in pre-Columbian America. See page 166.
Caral. A circular court and pyramids in the desert reveal an ancient city. See page 161.

Cajamarca. This lovely colonial city is a relief after the crowds of Cusco. See page 175.
Huaca Pucllana. This well-preserved pre-Inca site in Miraflores, Lima, dates back to AD 400 and was the administrative center of the Lima culture. See page 158.
Huacas del Sol y de la Luna. Ancient temples just outside Trujillo were built over several generations of the Moche people and were once covered with brightly colored murals. See page 166.

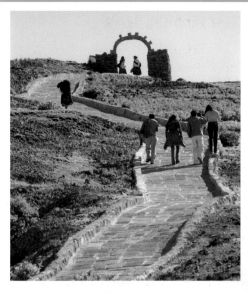
Isla Amantaní on Lake Titicaca.

Visiting the Huaca Pucllana in Lima.

BEST MUSEUMS AND GALLERIES

Museo de los Santuarios Andinos. In Arequipa, exhibits include a fascinating display on Inca human sacrifice, and a mummified body of one of the victims. See page 248.
Qoricancha. Now the Iglesia Santo Domingo, the Qoricancha or Temple of the Sun in Cusco was the Incas' most sacred building. See page 261.
Monasterio de San Francisco. In Lima, with its religious art and amazing skull-filled catacombs. See page 151.
Museo de Arte Precolombino. A wonderful collection of textiles, pottery, and gold in Cusco. See page 265.
Tumbas Reales. This world-class museum in Lambayeque contains gold treasures from the Tomb of Lord Sipán. See page 169.

TRAVELER'S TIPS

Go with the flow
Don't expect everything to go to plan. Things change with astounding frequency in Peru. Be flexible, and don't get angry when your plans need to be altered.

Keep your change
Always carry toilet paper, bottled water, and small change in Peru. Outside the biggest tourist spots, you can rarely pay small amounts with large-denomination notes.

Make friends
You might well have been warned to be careful, but don't let this stop you enjoying people's generosity and kindness. Peruvians are an endlessly friendly and hospitable people, and are always keen to communicate and make friends with visitors.

Travel light
Arrive with your suitcase half empty: you can buy almost anything you need here, and clothes are stylish and cheap.

¿Habla español?
Even if you aren't a linguist, be sure to learn a few phrases in Spanish. The effort will be appreciated and will make for a more fulfilling trip.

Coastal mist in Lima.

Sunset on the beach at Máncora.

A dancer in traditional dress at one of Peru's many festivals.

ANCIENT AND MODERN

Inca ruins, Amazon jungle, and fascinating tribal customs make Peru a top destination for travelers interested in landscape and culture. But it also has a modern, urban side that looks to the future rather than the past.

Stallholder in Lima.

Despite its rugged and often inhospitable landscape, Peru ranks among the world's great centers of ancient civilization. The sun-worshiping Incas are the last and most famous in a long line of highly developed cultures that thrived thousands of years before the arrival of Europeans. Their heritage fascinates travelers and archeologists alike. Along with the stunning Inca ruins near Cusco and the great city of Machu Picchu, Peru is home to the Nazca lines etched on its coastal deserts, the Colla burial *chullpas* near Lake Titicaca, the enormous adobe city of Chan Chan, the great Moche adobe pyramids and burial sites near Trujillo and Chiclayo, and the massive stone citadel of Kuélap near Chachapoyas. These cultures left no written records, just mysterious and beautiful works in gold, silver, textiles, and stone.

But ancient ruins are only a fraction of the story. Although the traditional American world was shattered by the bloody Spanish conquest in the 16th-century, the legacy of ancient cultures is very much alive. Roughly half of Peru's over 30 million people are of indigenous origin; often living in remote mountain villages, they still speak the Quechua or Aymara tongue of their ancestors, and many of their beliefs and customs are a mixture of traditional Andean ways and the culture imposed by the Spanish conquistadors. There are also more than 50 ethnic groups who live in Peru's Amazon region, some of whom still shun contact with the outside world.

On Pimental beach.

Peru is also one of the most spectacular countries on earth. Its variety is astonishing: scientists have ascertained that of 101 possible ecological zones, Peru has 84 within its borders. As a result, the country can offer virtually every conceivable scenic attraction: the Peruvian Andes draw trekkers and mountain climbers from all over the world, over half of Peru lies within the Amazon jungle, and the world's driest desert runs the entire length of its coast.

In the 21st century, Peru is still being formed as a modern nation. Separated by geographical differences and an often violent past, Peruvians today are justly proud of their heritage and their country's riches. Peru is one of the world's great travel destinations.

The Llaca Valley, near Huaraz.

LAND OF EXTREMES

Mountains, deserts, and jungle combine to make the
Peruvian landscape a varied and breathtaking one,
where nature is firmly in control.

Bordered to the north by Ecuador and Colombia, to the east by Brazil and Bolivia, to the south by Chile, and to the west by the waters of the Pacific, Peru is the third-largest country in South America. Ask Peruvians about their homeland and they will cut it into geographical slices – coastal desert, highlands, and jungle – pointing out that theirs is the only South American nation that contains all three. It is this challenging geography that has bequeathed Peru its variety of ethnic cultures, foods, music, and folklore.

Peruvians often use superlatives to describe the country's features. They include Lake Titicaca, the world's highest navigable lake at 3,850 meters (12,720ft) above sea level, and Mount Huascarán, Peru's tallest Andean peak and South America's fourth-highest mountain at 6,760 meters (22,200ft). The Amazon, the world's greatest river system, has its source at southern Peru's Mismi Volcano and, along with its rainforest namesake, makes up much of the country.

Settled among those wonders are over 31 million Peruvians, nearly 10 million of them crowded into Lima and the surrounding area. About 45 percent of the population is indigenous – mostly Quechua speakers, with a small proportion of Aymara-speaking peoples in the south and of Amazon tribes. Some 37 percent are mestizos (of mixed white and native blood), 15 percent are of European extract, and 3 percent are descendants of black slaves brought to work the cotton and sugar plantations, Chinese-indentured laborers shipped in during the 19th-century guano boom, or later waves of Japanese immigrants. Official languages include Spanish,

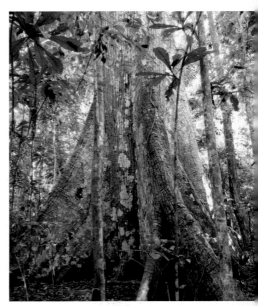

The dense Amazon rainforest.

Quechua, and Aymara, as well as other indigenous languages in the areas where they are predominant. Over 80 percent of the country's residents are Roman Catholic – although the religious rites they practice bear traces of pre-Christian religions – and close to 13 percent are now evangelical Christians.

BARREN BEACHES

The Spanish conquistadors' first glimpse of Peru was along its 2,500km (1,500-mile) coastal desert. Visitors familiar with South America's Caribbean coast find Peru's sandy beaches unsettling, with their harsh backdrop of dunes or cactus-covered cliffs. But when conquistador Francisco Pizarro arrived in

1532 the coast was less desolate. The native peoples had developed sophisticated irrigation systems, and fields of vegetables and grains were grown in the desert. Today, agricultural settlements still flourish around the oases formed by rivers running down from the Andean slopes, creating fertile valleys in the otherwise bare terrain.

At the southern end of the coast, Chile's appropriation of some of this desert land more than a century ago in the War of the Pacific (1879–83) meant the loss of a mineral treas-

Titicaca, the world's highest navigable lake.

ure – tracts rich in copper and the nitrates sought for fertilizers and explosives. Still, the coast has brought wealth to Peru despite its inhospitable landscape and dearth of water. Fish stocks are plentiful in the coastal waters, making Peru one of the world's foremost exporters of fishmeal, a livestock feed derived from anchovies.

It is the cold, fish-bearing current running along the hot coast from the south that keeps rain away from the desert. So little moisture accumulates above the Humboldt Current (named for the 19th-century German explorer Alexander von Humboldt) that ocean winds heading toward the mountains rarely carry condensation. What they do bring to the land,

however, is a thick, dense fog that causes havoc with air traffic and covers Lima for much of the year with a gloomy mist known as garúa. The exceptions to the rainless norm are the freak showers, and sometimes floods, caused by El Niño.

MOUNTAIN AND JUNGLE

Above all, it is the highlands that are associated with Peru. Here Quechua-speaking women weave rugs and garments, condors soar above the Andes, and wild vegetation

Peru is home to two of the world's deepest canyons, both near Arequipa. Twice as deep as the Grand Canyon, the Colca Canyon has a depth of 3,180 meters (10,600ft), while Cotahuasi is 3,500 meters (11,480ft) deep.

camouflages Inca ruins. Although breathtakingly beautiful, the Sierra seems brutally inhospitable: the thin, cold air here combines with a rugged landscape to make the Andes an obstacle to transportation, communication, and development.

Nevertheless, nearly half of Peru's population is scattered across the Sierra. Between the harsh mountain ranges where alpaca herders and potato farmers eke out a living lie warmer, fertile valleys where irrigated crop terraces have produced abundant corn and vegetable harvests since Inca times.

Three-fifths of Peru is jungle, divided into the hot, steamy Lower Amazon and the so-called High Jungle, or ceja de la selva (eyebrow of the jungle). The latter is the area where the mountains meet the Amazon, a subtropical expanse where coffee, tropical fruits, and coca are grown.

Peru has a policy of protecting the rainforest through legislation and by designating virgin areas as national parks. Extending from the Andean foothills to the east of Cusco into the low jungle is the Parque Nacional del Manu, which has one of the world's most impressive concentrations of wildlife; more than 850 bird species alone. A few hours away by river from Puerto Maldonado is the Reserva Nacional

Tambopata-Candamo, which contains more than 1,110 butterfly species.

The presence of oil and natural gas beneath the Peruvian rainforest, an ill-controlled influx of settlers, plus a Trans-Oceanic highway from Brazil through southeastern Peru, places protected areas under constant threat. In late 2007, conservationists succeeded in stopping a bill to shrink the Tambopata reserve by 20 percent. In 2014 a nationwide ban on illegal mining came into force, which allowed police to destroy several hundred pieces of heavy

100,000 homeless. A 7.0-magnitude earthquake which hit central Peru in August 2011 subsequently claimed the lives of three people, leaving another 50 wounded.

The broad range of weather conditions across the country makes labels such as "winter" and "summer" of little practical use. Lima residents refer to their hot sunny months (December to April) as summer, and the rest of the year, when the fog sets in, as winter. In the Sierra, winter is the rainy months (November to April). The jungle, meanwhile, is hot and humid all year.

Peru's arid coastline.

machinery used by illegal miners operating within the reserve. However, illegal gold mining continues to be a problem.

LAND OF EARTHQUAKES

Nature has dealt this country many cruel blows. Peru straddles the Cinturón del Fuego (the Ring of Fire), a geologic fault line running the length of the continent. The line passes along the coast, cutting directly through Arequipa, which, over the centuries, has borne the brunt of the seismic damage. In August 2007 a violent 8.0-magnitude earthquake struck the coast 160km (100 miles) south of Lima, causing massive damage in Pisco, Chincha, and Ica, killing more than 500 people, and leaving upwards of

⊘ EL NIÑO

Every few years around Christmas, a warm current known as El Niño (The Christ-Child) travels southward from the equator, displacing the cold Humboldt Current, with potentially destructive effects on Peru's climate. Centuries ago its disruptive effects brought down an entire civilization, the Moche. More recently, in 1983, 1997–8, and again in 2017, unusually fierce currents spread the effects globally and brought the phenomenon to international attention. Peru's northern coast in particular suffered very badly from floods and mudslides brought on by heavy rainstorms, which claimed over 100 lives and caused US$3billion worth of damage at the beginning of 2017.

Painted textile, Late Intermediate Period. The felines either side of the central figure may signify shaman or chieftain status.

DECISIVE DATES

Artifact from the tomb of the Lord of Sipán.

10000–3000 BC
Human settlement, based on marine resources and rudimentary floodplain agriculture, appears on the Peruvian coast.

COTTON PRECERAMIC PERIOD
3000–1800 BC
First known urban settlement of the Americas established on the coast at Caral. Simple cotton textiles appear.

INITIAL PERIOD
1800–800 BC
Irrigation agriculture appears on the coast, together with maize cultivation and pottery. Settlements move inland to control supply of water.

Huaca del Dragon.

EARLY HORIZON PERIOD
800–300 BC
Chavín culture rises on strategic trans-Andean trade route. Innovations in textiles, metallurgy, and stone carving appear.

EARLY INTERMEDIATE PERIOD
300 BC–AD 600
Nazca and Moche cultures flourish on the south and north coasts, developing distinctive ceramic styles. The Nazca lines are drawn on the southern desert and the Moche build huge adobe pyramids. El Niño weather events provoke collapse of the Moche civilization.

MIDDLE HORIZON PERIOD
AD 600–1000
Wari people initiate terrace agriculture in the central highlands, and the Tihuanaco develop intensive raised-field cultivation on the shores of Lake Titicaca. The Sicán culture thrives in the Lambayeque Valley, producing superb gold, silver, and copper objects.

LATE INTERMEDIATE PERIOD
c.1000–1470
Numerous regional cultures emerge; most important are the Chimú, the Chachapoyas, the Ica, the Huanca, and the Incas. The Chachapoyas people build the huge walled citadel of Kuélap; successive kings of Chimú build the adobe city of Chan Chan, the capital until the Inca conquest.

THE INCA EMPIRE
1438–1533
According to later Inca mytho-history, Pachacutec launches an imperial expansion across a vast swathe of the Andes. The Incas absorb the crafts and technologies of assimilated peoples, and deploy their own genius for agricultural engineering, architecture, and large-scale organization.

1527–32
The death of Huayna Capac leaves the empire divided between his sons, Huascar and Atahualpa. Civil war erupts, and Atahualpa emerges victorious.

Sechín mural.

THE SPANISH CONQUEST
1532
Spanish conquistadors arrive in Tumbes and march to meet Atahualpa at Cajamarca. The Inca emperor is tricked and captured, and offers a huge ransom in exchange for his life.

1533
The Spaniards execute Atahualpa, then march on Cusco and loot the city's treasures. Manco, another son of Huayna Capac, is installed as puppet ruler.

Atahualpa.

1535
Francisco Pizarro founds Lima, the future seat of the Spanish Viceroyalty.

1536
Manco rebels against the Spanish, but is defeated at Sacsayhuamán. The following year he retreats to Vilcabamba.

1538
Diego de Almagro, Pizarro's original partner, leads an opposing faction. Civil war breaks out. Almagro is defeated and garroted.

1541
Pizarro is assassinated by Almagro supporters.

Pre-Columbian vessel.

1544
Manco is murdered by Almagrist allies at Vitcos.

1570s
Viceroy Francisco de Toledo invades Vilcabamba and executes Manco's son, Tupac Amaru, ending Inca resistance. Toledo establishes *reducciones*, the forced resettlement of native populations, formalizes the *encomienda* system, whereby Indians provide tribute to their Spanish masters, and co-opts the *mita*, an Inca taxation-through-labor system.

Early 1600s
A Catholic campaign to stamp out native religions results in many indigenous beliefs and rites being given a Christian veneer.

1700–13
The War of the Spanish Succession in Europe sees the Habsburg dynasty replaced by the Bourbons, who try to improve the economy and reduce corruption.

1759
Charles III ascends the throne of Spain and opens up trade in Peru.

A Spanish stamp depicting Francisco Pizarro.

1767
The powerful Jesuit Order, influential in securing fairer treatment of natives, is expelled from the New World.

1780
Indigenous rebellion against the Spanish led by José Gabriel Condorcanqui, known as Tupac Amaru II, who is defeated and executed in 1781.

1784–90
Viceroy Teodoro de Croix institutes reforms, setting up a court to deal with indigenous claims.

1814
An indigenous uprising led by Mateo García Pumacahua captures Arequipa and wins Creole support before being put down by royalist troops.

1820
After liberating Chile, the Argentinian General José de San Martín invades Peru, helped by the recently formed Chilean navy under British command.

MODERN HISTORY

1821
San Martín enters Lima and proclaims Peruvian independence on July 28, although royalists still control most of Peru.

1824
Independence armies headed by General José de Sucre crush royalist forces at the Battle of Ayacucho.

1824–6
Bolívar presidency, after which a period of turmoil ensues, with 35 presidents in 40 years.

1840
First guano and nitrate fertilizer contracts with Britain, which come to control Peru's economy.

1851
Lima–Callao railroad inaugurated.

1854
President Ramón Castilla abolishes slavery and "Indian tribute" taxation.

1866
Spain attacks the port of Callao, failing in a bid to recover her strategic colony.

1869
Spain recognizes Peruvian independence.

1877
Foreign debts bankrupt Peru.

1879
War of the Pacific over nitrate deposits in southern Tarapacá province begins.

1880
Chile occupies the provinces of Tacna, Arica, and Tarapacá.

Hiram Bingham.

1881
Chileans sack Lima and occupy Peru.

1883
Treaty of Ancón cedes Arica and Tarapacá to Chile.

1911
Hiram Bingham announces discovery of Machu Picchu.

1924
Exiled Victor Raúl Haya de la Torre founds Alianza Popular Revolucionaria Americana (APRA).

1931
Haya de la Torre is allowed back to Peru to contest elections, but is defeated. Numerous *apristas* are killed in the subsequent uprising.

1941–2
Border war with Ecuador ends in victory for Peru, cementing its control over the Upper Amazon.

1948
Military coup brings General Manuel Odría to power.

1963–8
President Fernando Belaúnde initiates modest land reform, but is swept from power in another military coup.

1968
General Juan Velasco introduces land reforms and nationalization. Quechua is recognized as the second language.

1970
Massive earthquake strikes northern Peru, killing 75,000–80,000 people.

1972
Second major El Niño event of the 20th century.

1975
Centrist policies follow a palace coup by General Francisco Morales Bermúdez, but economic woes pile up.

1980
Belaúnde returns to power in democratic elections. Terrorist organization Sendero Luminoso (Shining Path) becomes a serious threat.

1983
Third major El Niño event causes disastrous flooding.

1985
APRA takes power for the first time, under youngest-ever president Alán García. His policies cause hyperinflation,

Disgraced former President Alberto Fujimori.

President Pedro Pablo Kuczynski.

shortages, and chaos, while nationwide terrorist violence spirals out of control.

1990
Unknown Alberto Fujimori defeats novelist Mario Vargas Llosa to win presidency.

1992
Fujimori suspends Congress and Constitution and introduces tough economic and anti-terrorist measures. Sendero Luminoso leader Abimael Guzmán is captured.

1995
Border clashes lead to major military conflict with Ecuador, ending in ceasefire. Fujimori is re-elected.

1996–7
Members of armed Tupac Amaru hostage-taking group killed after four-month siege at Japanese ambassador's residence. All but one of 72 hostages survive.

1998
Peace treaty with Ecuador leads to final settlement of border dispute.

2000
Fujimori wins third term amidst widespread charges of vote-rigging. Leaked videos of high-level bribery trigger mass protests. Fujimori flees to Japan and faxes his resignation.

2001
Outsider politician Alejandro Toledo takes office as first elected indigenous president of Peru. His term is marred by strikes, protests, and the rise of ultra-nationalist opposition politics, but also sees high prices for Peru's export commodities, and vigorous economic growth.

2006
Alán García achieves political resurrection, promising economic stability; he narrowly wins a second term.

2007
Ex-president Fujimori is extradited from Chile. Sentenced in Lima, he receives six years in prison for abuse of power. In August an 8.0-magnitude earthquake hits the coastal region of Ica, killing more than 500 people.

2009
Fast economic growth brings only limited benefits to the poor. Protests in Bagua province lead to around 50 deaths.

Earthquake damage in Pisco.

2011
Leftwing nationalist Ollanta Humala wins the presidency but leaves market-friendly economic policy intact.

2012
Pacific Alliance trade bloc, made up of Chile, Peru, Colombia and Mexico, is founded.

2014
The UN court in The Hague defines the maritime boundary between Peru and Chile, ending a long dispute.

2015
480th anniversary of Lima's foundation. The city hosts the annual IMF and World Bank meetings.

2016
Pedro Pablo Kuczynski (PPK) becomes the new president after defeating Keiko Fujimori, daughter of jailed former-President Alberto Fujimori. Emergency state declared in half the country following the outbreak of Zika virus.

2017
Floods – prompted by El Niño – kill 100 in northeast Peru and leave tens of thousands homeless.

The ancient walls of Chan Chan, near Trujillo.

LOST EMPIRES: PERU BEFORE THE INCAS

More than a millennium before the Incas ruled Peru there were societies creating adobe cities, woven garments, and exquisite objects of gold and silver.

Civilization in the Andes has long been equated with the Incas. Almost every account of Peru by 16th-century Spanish chroniclers told of fabled Inca wealth, and lauded their achievements in architecture and engineering, inevitably comparing them to the feats of the Romans. However, archeologists working on the Peruvian coast and highlands have since shown that the origins of Peruvian civilization reach back more than four millennia, some 4,000 years before the Incas emerged from their highland realm to forge Tahuantinsuyu, their enormous empire of the four quarters of the world (see page 41).

Not until the mid-19th century did early scientific observers begin to suspect the true antiquity of Peruvian civilization. No one imagined at the time that civilization in the New World could be almost as ancient as that of the Old. Data emerging from Peru, however, shows that the earliest monumental architecture is roughly contemporary with the pyramids of Egypt and pre-dates the large-scale constructions of the Olmec in Mesoamerica by more than 1,000 years.

THE BEGINNINGS OF CIVILIZATION

The first traces of human settlement in Peru have been found along the coast, where some 41 river valleys, running off the western slope of the Andes, slice through the desert, creating fertile oases interspersed by arid expanses of sand. In the years 3000–1800 BC, a time known to archeologists as the Cotton Preceramic, small communities thrived along the coast, harvesting the rich Pacific Ocean for its bounty. On river floodplains they cultivated cotton and gourds and hunted for deer. In the *lomas*, lush belts of fog vegetation located a few miles inland, they gathered wild plants. Before the introduction of

A restored mural at Sechín.

true weaving, they created twined and looped textiles of cotton and sedge, some decorated with intricate designs that attest to technological and esthetic skills.

Toward the end of the Cotton Preceramic, larger settlements emerged, such as that of Paraíso just north of Lima. Over 100,000 tonnes of quarried stone were used here to build monumental platforms. At Aspero in the Supe Valley, 145km (90 miles) north of Lima, the largest mound, comprising rubble and stone blocks, is 10 meters (33ft) high and measures 30 by 40 meters (98 by 130ft) at its base. Both of these centers were surrounded by sprawling residential areas containing burial grounds and thick midden, or waste, deposits.

THE INITIAL PERIOD

Sometime around 1800 BC, at the beginning of what is known as the Initial Period, these fishing communities began to move inland. Although the majority of sites documented from this time average only 20km (12 miles) from the coast, they were far enough up-valley to tap the rivers and construct irrigation canals, substantially increasing the ancient Peruvians' subsistence base. Evidence from the middens indicates that in addition to cotton and gourds they grew squash, peppers, lima and kidney beans, peanuts, and avocados, and

and white. The temple facade has been reconstructed at Lima's Museo de la Nación.

Facing Moxeke lies Huaca, or Mound A – once almost 6 meters (20ft) high and 135 meters by 135 meters (450ft by 450ft) wide. Here, access to storage areas was controlled by wooden doorways, and the images of two fanged felines guard one of two entrances.

These architectural monuments, with U-shaped platforms and sunken circular courtyards, have been documented from sites just south of Lima to the Moche or Trujillo valley, 595km (370 miles)

Wall carvings at Sechín depicting decapitation.

supplemented their diet with marine products. Maize, which would become an Andean staple, was introduced later, possibly from Mesoamerica.

Two further revolutionary inventions belong to this period: the introduction of pottery and of simple weaving techniques.

In the Casma Valley, 275km (170 miles) north of Lima, large Initial Period settlements flourished at sites such as Moxeke-Pampa de las Llamas. Located 18km (11 miles) inland, the complex once covered an area of 2.5 sq km (1 sq mile), dominated by two mounds. The 27-meter (90ft) high pyramid of Moxeke, excavated in the early 20th century, is decorated with awesome adobe friezes of snarling felines and human attendants, which are painted red, blue,

north of Lima. Near Trujillo stands the Huaca de los Reyes, which also contained elaborate adobe friezes of felines, once painted red, yellow, and cream, long faded by the desert sun. The arms of the U-shaped temple point upriver, toward the Andes and the source of water, a constant preoccupation on the rainless coast.

The Initial Period also saw the construction of sites such as Sechín, which is in the Casma Valley too, and was first excavated in the 1930s by the first indigenous archeologist, Julio C. Tello. Here, carved on stone monoliths surrounding an adobe temple, a macabre procession of victorious warriors and their dismembered victims commemorates a battle – although who the victors or the vanquished were is still uncertain.

SIERRA CULTURES

The emergence of complex societies on the coast was paralleled by developments in the highlands, where archeologists have documented the rise of ceremonial architecture at sites such as Huaricoto in the Callejón de Huaylas. Unfortunately, preservation of organic matter is not as good in the highlands as it is on the arid coast, so the archeological record for this area is not as complete.

Nonetheless, excavations have unearthed ceremonial structures with fire-pits, where offerings were burned. Llamas had already been domesticated by this time, serving both as beasts of burden and as an important food source. Llama caravans carried highland produce – potatoes and other Andean tubers and grains – to the coast, where they were exchanged for goods from the warm coastal valleys: dried fish and shellfish, seaweed, salt, cotton, peppers, and coca leaves, to supplement the heavy inland diet. The guinea pig *(cuy)*, an Andean delicacy, was probably also domesticated about this time.

THE EARLY HORIZON PERIOD

In the highlands, construction began around 800 BC at the ceremonial center of Chavín de Huantar, near Huaraz (see page 191). One of the most famous sites of ancient Peru, Chavín was believed until recently to have been the inspiration for the similar art style that spread throughout much of coastal and highland Peru during the period (approximately 800–300 BC) often referred to as the Chavín Horizon.

However, research since the mid-1970s has shown that Initial Period developments on the coast (including U-shaped temples, circular sunken courtyards, stirrup-spout ceramics, and an elaborate iconography featuring fanged felines and snarling gods) merely culminated at Chavín.

Perhaps because the culture was based midway between the coast and the jungle, Chavín iconography even incorporated jungle fauna into its elaborate system. The Tello Obelisk, on view at Lima's Museo de la Nación, features a fierce caiman.

The spread of the Chavín cult brought with it innovations in textiles and metallurgy, and coastal sites contemporary with the Chavín temple were perhaps branch shrines of a powerful Chavín oracle. Painted cotton textiles found at Karwa, near the Bay of Paracas, about 170km (105 miles) south of Lima, for example, depict

deities reminiscent of those carved on stone slabs at Chavín de Huantar.

The weavings found buried with mummy bundles at Paracas and dated to about 300 BC are perhaps the finest ever produced in ancient Peru. Because of the hundreds of mummy bundles buried in stone-lined pits, this is sometimes known as the Necropolis Phase. Evidence for a far-flung trade network is also visible at Paracas: obsidian from the highland region of Huancavelica; cameloid fiber, probably alpaca, also from the highlands; and feathers of tropical birds used to adorn fans,

Chimú textile.

⊘ A TEXTILE AGE

By the beginning of the Common Era, virtually every textile technique to be invented was already in use in Peru. The first Europeans met natives using weaving techniques to make roofs, bridges, armor, slingshots, accounting devices, and of course cloth, woven from cotton, llama, alpaca, and – as the highest privilege – the finest vicuña wool. Soldiers were paid in cloth, and the coded symbols in the tunics of the nobility displayed a rich store of social and cultural information. Woven fabrics were also exchanged for other products or offered as presents to the conquered people.

which probably came from the jungle. Traces of the use of cameloid fiber in north-coast weavings, again probably alpaca, also appear at this time.

Metalworking techniques, such as soldering and repoussé, and gold-silver alloys were first used by ancient Peruvians on the north coast during the Early Horizon Period. The Moche were to add to the metalworking repertoire a few centuries later.

THE NAZCA AND MOCHE CULTURES

The decline of Chavín influence led to the emergence of regional cultures in river valleys on the coast and in highland valleys during a time known as the Early Intermediate Period, which lasted until about AD 600. In the Nazca Valley, weavers and potters followed the Paracas tradition, but instead of producing painted and incised pottery, they began to make ceramics decorated with a variety of vividly colored mineral pigments, some showing scenes of domestic life.

On an arid plain north of modern-day Nazca, the Nazca people etched giant images by brushing away surface soil and stones to reveal the lighter-colored soil beneath. Images of birds,

The Huaca del Sol.

⊘ QUEEN OF THE DESERT

Maria Reiche, the German mathematician who dedicated her life to studying the Nazca lines, initially went to Peru in the 1930s, where she worked as a translator for Paul Kosok, an irrigation expert who first spotted the lines from the air. She took measurements and made charts, and, having concluded that the lines were part of an astronomical calendar, wrote *Mystery on the Desert*. Reiche was awarded the Order of the Sun – the country's highest honor. She died in 1998. Her tomb can be found in a small garden adjacent to Casa Museo Maria Reiche, a museum that documents her life and studies.

some measuring 60 meters (200ft) across, predominate, but they also drew killer whales, a monkey (90 meters/300ft across), and a spider (45 meters/150ft long). All these creatures feature on Nazca ceramics. The straight lines and trapezoids appeared a few hundred years later.

There are numerous theories about why the lines were drawn. Maria Reiche, who spent much of her life studying the phenomenon, believed they formed part of an astronomical calendar; Erich von Däniken attributes them to visitors from outer space – a theory given no credence by archeologists. More recent theories suggest that the geoglyphs were paths linking sacred sites or a surface map of underground aquifers, or that they were linked to mountain worship and fertility. Indeed, many of the animal images can be tied to Andean fertility concepts, and some of the lines point to the mountains in the distance, the source of valuable water.

The ancient Nazca lived in settlements dispersed around the Nazca drainage area. They worshiped at the ceremonial center of Cahuachi, downriver from the modern city of Nazca.

On Peru's north coast, the Moche people flourished in the Moche or Trujillo Valley, known in ancient times as Chimor. From their early capital at the Huacas del Sol y de la Luna (Temples of the Sun and the Moon) south of Trujillo, the Moche held sway over 400km (250 miles) of desert coast. The Temple of the Sun, one of the most imposing adobe structures ever built in the New World, was composed of over 100 million mudbricks.

The Moche built irrigation canals, aqueducts, and field systems that stretched for miles, connecting neighboring valleys, and cultivated maize, beans, squash, peanuts, and peppers. In their *totora* reed boats they fished and hunted for sea lions, and captured deer along the rivers. They kept domesticated dogs and traded for luxury goods such as turquoise from present-day Argentina and lapis lazuli from present-day Chile, which they crafted into jewelry, and exotic seashells from north of Guayaquil. They also practiced human sacrifices, a proof of which is the altar discovered in 2012 at the top of Campana Hill near Trujillo.

Famed for their ceramics, Moche potters created realistic portrait heads and fine line drawings of gruesome sacrificial ceremonies. The most imaginative and skilled metalsmiths in ancient Peru, they perfected an electrochemical-plating technique that gilded copper objects.

THE LORD OF SIPÁN

The discovery in 1987 of the tomb of a Moche lord at Sipán, near modern Chiclayo some 800km (500 miles) north of Lima, has provided much new data on the ancient Moche, including evidence that most valleys under Moche influence had their own powerful regional governors. The lord had been buried with hundreds of pieces of funerary pottery, as befitted his status, but also with an astonishing amount of gold and silver. In 2010 archeologists discovered another funeral chamber at Sipán with remains of an entire family who most probably belonged to the local elite.

Sometime in the period AD 650–700 the Moche Kingdom came to an end. It is thought that the El Niño phenomenon – when the warm waters flowing from the equator replace the cold waters of the Humboldt Current – could have produced torrential rains and destroyed irrigation canals, causing widespread famine.

THE MIDDLE HORIZON PERIOD

With the fall of Moche in the north and the decline of Nazca to the south, a powerful southern highland kingdom exerted its archi-

A gold artifact found in the tomb of the Lord of Sipán.

tectural and artistic influence over large areas of Peru between AD 600 and 1000, wiping out the styles of the conquered peoples in the process. The capital of this empire was Wari (or Huari), a large urban center near the modern city of Ayacucho. Archeologists have excavated Wari military sites at Piquillacta near Cusco, at Cajamarquilla near Lima, and at Marca Huamachuco, in the highlands to the east of Trujillo. In 2013 a team of archeologists discovered a 1,200-year-old imperial tomb at El Castillo de Huarmey, a coastal mausoleum north of Lima. More than a thousand artifacts including silver and gold jewelry, bronze axes and gold tools were unearthed, along with the bodies of three Wari queens and 60 other individuals.

The Wari style is strongly reminiscent of the ceramics and sculpture from the Bolivian Altiplano site of Tiahuanaco, which flourished between 200 BC and AD 1200. Situated at the southern end of Lake Titicaca at 3,856 meters (12,725ft) above sea level, Tiahuanaco was the highest urban settlement in the New World. Its people employed an ingenious cultivation system that archeologists estimate could have sustained a city of 40,000 people.

Tiahuanaco farmers cultivated potatoes, *oca*, and *olluco* (Andean tubers), as well as quinoa

Chiclayo. Here a team of archeologists have used radar techniques to assist in excavating a number of tombs. These elaborate burial sites have yielded fascinating evidence of the Sicán culture.

The burial chamber of one important male was surrounded by numerous female skeletons, thought to be weavers, who may well have been sacrificial victims. The remains of a richly decorated expanse of cloth were also unearthed. Scores of gold, silver, and copper masks and vessels were discovered, including an exquisite gold-alloy mask with emerald eyes, which sug-

The adobe city of Chan Chan.

and *cañiwa* (grains) on raised fields known as *camellones* in Spanish, formed by digging lake-fed canals and heaping up the resulting soil to construct raised fields about 10 meters (33ft) wide. During the day the sun heated the water in the canals, which radiated its warmth at night to protect the crops from frost. Recent experiments have shown that crops grown in this way may have produced harvests seven times greater than the average yield.

THE SICÁN DISCOVERIES

With the decline of Wari influence, regional cultures again flourished in the coastal valleys. In the north the Lambayeque or Sicán culture appears to have been centered some 50km (30 miles) north of

gest that the site was an important metalworking center. The size of the complex also suggests that it was the capital of what must have been an extremely wealthy and powerful culture. However, the complex appears to have been abandoned in about AD 1100. The remnants of the population moved a few miles south to Túcume, where they constructed 26 flat-topped adobe pyramids and many smaller structures. Túcume was conquered by the Chimú a few centuries later, and subsequently used by the Incas.

THE CHIMÚ CULTURE

It was probably around 1300, during the period known to archeologists as the Late Intermediate (c.1000–1470), that construction began at

The Chimú inherited the rule over Peru's Pacific Coast from the Moche, ruling for close to 500 years as far south as Arequipa until their defeat by the Incas.

Chan Chan (near Trujillo), the Chimú capital near the ancient Moche site of the Temples of the Sun and the Moon. It seems that Chan Chan was then continuously occupied by the Chimú dynasty until it fell to the powerful Inca armies of Tupac Yupanqui in about 1464.

Rising to prominence in the north while the Incas gained power in the south, the Chimú realm stretched 965km (600 miles) along the coast, from the Chillon Valley in the south to Tumbes in the north. Spanish chroniclers of the 17th century recorded a Chimú myth of the arrival on a lithe raft of the dynasty's legendary founder, Tacaynamo. Details of his life are largely mythical, with a sole mention by an anonymous 17th-century Spanish chronicler. The legend spoke of 10 Chimú kings, who ruled for about 140 years, which gives the early 14th-century date for the founding of Chan Chan.

There are nine rectangular compounds at Chan Chan, the largest adobe city in the world, each corresponding to a Chimú monarch. Each compound served as an administrative center as well as a palace, a royal storehouse, and, on the king's death, his mausoleum. The succeeding monarch then built a new one, and the deceased ruler's compound was maintained by his family and loyal retainers.

Around the royal compounds, in small, crowded dwellings, lived a population of about 50,000, chiefly weavers, potters, and metalsmiths, who supplied the royal storehouses. Today the sprawling mudbrick capital of Chan Chan is a bewildering labyrinth of ruined adobe walls, some 7.5 meters (25ft) high and stretching for 60 meters (200ft). At its height in 1450 the city covered 23 sq km (9 sq miles). The eighth compound, or Tschudi Complex, has been partially restored and gives some idea of what the capital must have been like. Remains of adobe friezes showing patterns of waves, fish, seabirds, and fishing nets, all vital to the survival of these coastal people, can still be seen adorning some of the walls.

THE CHACHAPOYAS CULTURE

Contemporary with the Chimú was the Chachapoyas culture (AD 800–1470). It flourished in the northern highlands before the Incas ended its independence. Their conqueror, Tupac Yupanqui, resettled communities of its half a million people, also dubbed the "Cloud Warriors," further south. Angered by their treatment at the hands of the Incas, the Chachapoyas sided with the invading Spaniards a few decades later. The remains of Kuélap, a huge stone city rivaling other major sites in the Americas, stands

Artifacts from the tomb of Lord Sipán.

at 3,000 meters (9,850ft) on a ridge above the River Utcubamba, as the main testimony to their grand architectural skill. Kuélap's vast size indicates it may have been used to protect large numbers of people during sieges. Chimú and Moche ceramics, however, are of higher quality. Another major site, Gran Sapososa, was uncovered in the 1990s. The Chachapoyas buried their dead in vertical sarcophagi or mausoleums chiseled into cliffsides. Circular houses and major fortifications are among the standout features of their architecture. The Chachapoyas, however, died out after the Spanish conquest, decimated by measles and smallpox, leaving them one of the most enigmatic major ancient Peruvian cultures.

The Inca citadel of Machu Picchu.

THE INCAS

The Peruvian empire of the Children of the Sun was short-lived but brilliant. It spread rapidly from the central highlands, bringing order, material abundance, and a sophisticated culture.

Peru's pre-Hispanic history is a long one, filled with the marvels of ancient civilizations that fed multitudes by irrigating deserts, wove textiles so fine they cannot be reproduced even today, and built adobe cities that have survived millennia of earthquakes. Some left behind traces that have allowed archeologists and scholars to reconstruct pieces of their societies. Others may always remain nameless and obscure. However, no group is as well known, or as astounding, as the Incas – the magnificent culture dominating much of the continent when the Spanish conquistadors arrived.

The Inca nation – the Children of the Sun – started as a small culture based in the central highlands. Like the Chimú, Chancay, Ica, and other groups, they exerted local autonomy over large population centers and had distinct styles of textiles and pottery. But in the early 1400s, under the reign of Pachacutec, the Incas began one of the greatest and most rapid expansions that has ever been recorded.

Inca terracing is still in use today.

> The royal mummy, housed in the panaca, was attended to as royalty after the death of the ruler as during his lifetime. It received daily offerings of food and drink, and at certain festivals it was paraded around Cusco.

In little more than 50 years, Inca domination was extended as far north as modern Colombia and south into present-day Chile and Argentina. Groups that resisted were summarily vanquished and relocated as punishment. Others, through peaceful negotiations, joined the kingdom with little loss of regional control provided that they were prepared to worship Inti, the sun, as their supreme god, and paid homage to the Inca leaders.

As each regional culture fell, Inca teachers, weavers, builders, and metallurgists studied the conquered people's textile techniques, architecture, gold-working, irrigation, pottery, and healing methods. As a result, they quickly accumulated massive amounts of information more advanced than their own.

By the time the Spanish arrived, Cusco, the Inca capital, was a magnificent urban gem; irrigated deserts and terraced mountainsides were producing bountiful crops, storehouses of food had eliminated hunger, and Inca military might had become legendary.

Although the accuracy of Spanish chronicles are suspect, and the Incas themselves left no written records, scholars, anthropologists, and archeologists have managed to piece together fragments of a magnificent world.

A STRICT WORLD ORDER

Inca society was clearly hierarchical and highly structured, but not necessarily tyrannical or repressive. Everyone had a place and a part to play. Food and resources were stored and distributed so that all were fed and clothed. There was

The quipu was used to record numbers and possibly words.

little private property, and most everything was communally organized. A majority likely accepted their role without feeling exploited, though resentment remained among conquered peoples.

The Inca polity was a pyramidal system of government, with the ruling Inca (as the emperor was called) and his *coya*, or queen, at the apex. Under him stood the nobility, the "Capac Incas," supposedly the true descendants of Manco Capac, the founding Inca, and belonging to some 10 or 12 *panacas*, or royal houses. Each emperor founded a *panaca* when he came to power, so the current ruler's was the only one headed by a living man. The other *panacas* centered their lives and cults around the mummified remains of a former Inca. The city of Cusco was filled with the huge palaces

built by Inca rulers to house their personal retinue, their descendants, born to their many wives and concubines, and, finally, their own mummy.

The *panacas* of Cusco coexisted with a similar number of *ayllus* – large kinship groups – of lesser nobility, the so-called "Incas-by-privilege," who were early inhabitants of the Cusco region, pre-dating the Incas. They held lands, had ritual and economic functions, and many other aspects of life in common. The *panacas* and noble *ayllus* belonged to two separate divisions, Upper and Lower Cusco, whose relationship was both competitive and complementary.

Below these two groups stood the regional nobility, who were not Incas at all, but held aristocratic privileges along with intricate blood relationships and with reciprocal obligations to the ruling caste. Everyone in the empire was bonded to the whole by such connections, except for one large, amorphous group, the *yanacona*, who were a domestic class serving the *panacas*. They received no formal benefits and, although they could reach a high status, their loyalty was usually negotiable. Many of them defected to the Spaniards after the Inca Atahualpa's capture in 1532.

THE PRIVILEGES OF POWER

The nobility reserved many privileges for themselves, granting them selectively to outsiders. Polygamy was common, but exclusively aristocratic. Likewise, chewing coca leaves and wearing vicuña wool were privileges of the ruling caste. Noble males wore huge, ornate gold plugs in their pierced ears. Their beautifully woven tunics carried heraldic symbols called *tokapu*. All citizens wore the clothes and hairstyles befitting their station and ethnic group. The streets of Cusco were colorful, for hundreds of groups were represented in the city, each with its own distinctive costume.

Scores of local languages existed, but the lingua franca of the empire was Quechua, a language spoken today from northern Ecuador to northern Chile. Its origins are obscure, but the Incas are believed to have acquired it from some other group. The nobles also used a private language, possibly a "high" chivalric dialect with elements of both Quechua and the Aymara language of the Lake Titicaca region.

The lords were fond of hunting, and a royal hunt was a spectacular affair. Animals were not slaughtered indiscriminately, but culled. Young females of most species were released for future reproduction. The myth of power within the Inca state held that the emperor was a divine being unlike ordinary mortals, descended from the sun via his founding ancestor, Manco Capac. He gave voice to the desires and intentions of this deity.

The sun may have become the supreme Inca deity after the rise of the ninth emperor, Pachacutec; before that, the supreme deity was Viracocha, an almighty creator also worshiped by other cultures. Inca religion was not confined to the sun and Viracocha. Cusco's great temple, the Qoricancha, or Court of Gold, contained shrines to the moon, lightning, the Pleiades, Venus, and the rainbow. There were also shrines to scores of local deities – idols or sacred relics brought to Cusco by innumerable regional peoples. The Incas did not attempt to erase local religions, but included their gods in an ever-expanding pantheon.

Beside local and celestial deities there were the *apus* – the spirits of great mountains – and the *huacas* – stones, caves, grottoes, springs, and waterfalls, believed to contain spirit powers. More than 300 *huacas* existed around Cusco, many of them housing the mummies of lesser nobles, and all of them connected by imagined lines that radiated from Qoricancha like the spokes of a wheel. This system of sacred geography, the *ceque* system, was closely linked to the ritualistic and economic life of Cusco. The *panacas* and *ayllus* had care of individual *huacas* and groups of *ceque* lines.

HEART OF THE FOUR QUARTERS

Young Inca nobles were educated by *amautas*, scholars who transmitted cultural knowledge often in the form of mnemonic songs and verses. Music and poetry were respected arts among the nobility, as was painting. An immense "national archive" or "gallery" outside Cusco, called Poquen Cancha, was probably destroyed during Pizarro's conquest.

The Inca calendar featured an array of important festivals, which marked stages of life and the agricultural calendar. The summer and winter solstices were the greatest celebrations, held with numerous sub-festivals. The *Capac Raymi* summer solstice, for example, also featured the coming-of-age celebrations for the new crop of young nobles. The males underwent trials, including ritual battles, and a death-defying

race. Another great ceremony was *Sitwa*, in September, when foreigners had to leave Cusco, and the Incas engaged in a ritual of purification, casting out sickness and bad spirits.

Cusco itself was a holy city as well as the administrative capital of the empire. It was the centre of Tahuantinsuyu – the formal name of the Inca Empire, meaning the four quarters of the world. The great royal roads to the four *suyus* began at the main square. Here all things came together, and soil from every province was ritually mingled with that of Cusco.

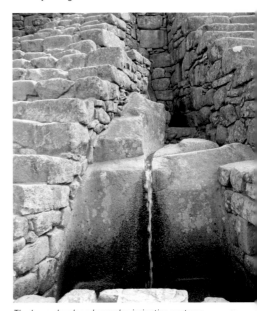

The Incas developed complex irrigation systems.

⊘ CHOSEN WOMEN

A special place in Inca high society was occupied by the *acllas*. The Spanish drew a simplistic parallel between them and the Roman Vestal Virgins, labeling them Virgins of the Sun. Some may have been virgin devotees of certain deities, but chastity was not a major preoccupation of the Incas. The *acllas* were selected for their talents and beauty, and many were concubines of the Inca. Others served the main temple, producing weavings for the sacrificial fires of the Qoricancha. It is also likely that some belonged to a caste of astronomer-priestesses associated with the cult of the moon.

Everyone from the highest to the lowest was involved to some degree in working the land. Even the emperor ritually tilled the soil with a golden foot-plow, to inaugurate the new planting season.

The four *suyus* corresponded to the cardinal points. The northern quarter was the Chinchay-suyu – northern Peru and modern Ecuador. The south was the Collasuyu – Lake Titicaca, mod-

An example of Inca stonework at Machu Picchu.

ern Bolivia, and Chile. The Antisuyu was the Amazon forest to the east. The Kuntisuyu was the region west of Cusco, much of it also rugged country, but including the south and central Peruvian coast.

A RURAL EMPIRE

The Tahuantinsuyu was not significantly urbanized. There was the great complex of Chimú on the north coast and, of course, Cusco. And there were a few large administrative centers along the spine of the Andes, housing a mainly transient population, which mustered and distributed the resources of entire regions. But most of the population lived in small rural communities scattered across the land.

The complex organization of the Inca state rested on a foundation of efficient agriculture. It is notable that virtually any Inca ruin, no matter what its original function, is surrounded and penetrated by agricultural terraces and irrigation channels. Fields of corn stood in the very heart of Cusco.

Corn was the prestige crop. The great irrigated terracing systems whose ruins we see today were mainly devoted to its cultivation. Other Inca staples were potatoes and some other indigenous Andean root crops, plus beans, quinoa – a species of the beet family – and the related amaranth. The huge altitude range of the tropical Andes allowed the Incas to enjoy a great variety of foods, but it also required them to develop many localized crop strains for particular microclimates. This they did, with typical thoroughness, at several experimental agriculture centers whose ruins survive today, such as Moray in the Sacred Valley.

The Incas' great food surpluses enabled them to divert labor to a variety of enterprises. They created a vast road network – so expertly laid that much of it still exists – and built astonishing structures of stone, so finely worked and of blocks so large that they required staggering amounts of time and effort. The Incas employed thousands of artisans to produce works of gold and silver, pottery, and fine textiles. They also raised great armies, able to march thousands of miles without carrying provisions, so extensive was their network of storehouses.

The system that made these works possible was called *mita*, or *minga* at the *ayllu* level. It was a kind of community tax, paid in labor. Every community sent some of its able-bodied young men and women for a limited period into the service of the state.

The period varied according to the hardship of the work – mines, for example, were a tough assignment, and accordingly brief. Working in a state pottery was easier, and correspondingly longer. Some communities – such as the famous one which rebuilt the Apurímac suspension bridge, Q'eshwachaca, each year – rendered their *mita* in a specific task. One *ayllu* provided the emperor with inspectors of roads, another with inspectors of bridges, and one supplied the state with spies.

The life of a transient *mita* worker was rewarded by institutional generosity and punctuated by public festivals of spectacular drunkenness. Peasants who were otherwise tied to their villages for life mingled with groups from exotic locations worlds away, and caught a glimpse of the dazzling world of the Inca nobility. It was probably the most exciting time of their lives. Later the Spanish took over this institution and turned it into near slavery in their *encomienda* system.

BINDING THE ANDES TO CUSCO

About every 10km (6 miles) along the great skein of roads that knitted the empire together stood a *tambo*, a kind of lodge, with storage facilities for goods in transit and communal quarters for large groups of people. Closer together were little huts that served as relay stations for the *chasquis*, the relay message-runners, who could allegedly cover the 2,400km (1,500 miles) between Quito in Ecuador and Cusco in 10 days.

Every major bridge and *tambo* had its *quipu-camayoc*, an individual who recorded everything that moved along the road. Their instrument was the *quipu*, a strand of cord attached to color-coded strings, each carrying a series of knots tied so as to indicate a digital value. The *quipucamayocs* were the accountants of the empire. *Quipus* may also have served as a means of sending messages, with certain types of knot being assigned a syllable value, so that a row of knots formed a word.

Crimes of property were rare; stealing was regarded as an aberration and dealt with ruthlessly when it occurred. Offenders suffered loss of privileges, with public humiliation and perhaps physical punishment. Serious or repeated crimes were punished by death, the victim being thrown off a cliff or imprisoned with poisonous snakes and dangerous animals.

A combination of techniques sustained the growth of the Inca Empire. Military conquest played a part, but so did skillful diplomacy; some of the most important territories may have been allied confederates rather than subordinate domains. The glue holding the empire together was the practice of reciprocity: ritual generosity and favors to local rulers on a huge scale, in exchange for loyalty, labors, and military levies, women for the Inca nobility, products specific to the region, and so on. The emperor maintained fabulous stores of goods to meet his ritual obligations and create new alliances.

THE PATH TO POWER

The Incas were perhaps not imperialist, in our sense of the word, at the outset. There was an ancient Andean tradition of cultural influences, spreading out by means of trade and pilgrimage from important religious centers such as Chavín, and later Tiahuanaco. It is likely that Cusco started in this way, too; later the Incas extended their sway in southern Peru by means of reciprocal agreements and blood alliances.

Then, in 1438 came the pivotal war of survival against the Chancas, a powerful group

Wooden hand-painted vase.

⊘ DIVIDE AND RULE

Another Inca institution, less benign than the *mita*, was the *mitmaq*. Loyal Quechuas were sent to distant, newly incorporated provinces in order to pacify and "Inca-ize" the region. Recalcitrant subjects displaced by the incoming group were then moved into the Inca heartland, where they were surrounded by loyal Quechuas, and either indoctrinated into believing that the ways of the empire were not so bad after all, or else too isolated from fellow malcontents to cause trouble. It was a system that cannot have been popular, but it was a lot less harsh than those employed by many empire builders.

from the north. The historical existence of the Chancas has never been confirmed by archeology, but the Inca version was that the man who took the title Pachacutec – "transformer of the world" – defeated the invading Chancas at the gates of Cusco. Subsequently he transformed Inca culture, and launched the expansion which would be continued by his son, Tupac Yupanqui, and grandson, Huayna Capac. As the Incas extended farther from their center, they confronted groups with ideas and identities increasingly different

An engraving of a rope suspension bridge.

⊘ BROTHERS AT WAR

While the marriage of Huayna Capac and his sister Coya Cusirimay remained childless, he fathered numerous offspring, including Atahualpa and his older half-brother, Huascar. With the line of succession unclear after the death of firstborn heir Ninan Cuyochi in 1527, a civil war broke out between them on Huayna Capac's death as they sought to assert control from their respective centers of power, Cusco and Quito. The fighting lasted five years and left major cities in ruins and the empire severely weakened. Atahualpa eventually emerged victorious, shortly before the arrival of the Spanish conquerors.

from their own. Thus, continued expansion increasingly required the use of force.

When the Incas used military force they used it sparingly. Many opponents surrendered without a fight when they saw the size of the army sent against them. The Incas still preferred to cut off an enemy's water supply, or starve him into submission, rather than confront him directly in battle.

War and warriorhood were an important part of Andean life from early times, yet they surely cannot have been of paramount value to the Incas. If they had, then military tactics and technology would have been at their peak, whereas in fact their weapons and methods of warfare were still extremely primitive – far inferior to their attainments in administration, architecture, agriculture, and engineering – and had not evolved since the earliest times of Andean culture. They fought with clubs, stones, and all-wooden spears. Even the bow and arrow, though known to them, were not widely used in battle. The gulf between their fighting capacity and that of the steely Spanish conquistadors was tragically wide.

Many groups the Incas had conquered, such as the Huanca from Peru's central highlands, resented Inca domination. They had to be held in place by threat of force, and later they happily deserted to fight with the Spanish.

In the years just before the Spanish invasion, Pachacutec's grandson, Huayna Capac, was far from his homeland, fighting in the mountains along the present northern frontier of Ecuador. Quito, the base from which the campaigns were launched, had become a de facto second capital, and a northern aristocracy had formed. On the death of Huayna Capac the two groups fell into violent conflict, resulting in civil war between half-brothers Huascar and Atahualpa.

ARTISTS IN STONE

Like other peoples of the New World, the Incas had not discovered how to smelt iron ore, but their use of other metals was quite sophisticated. They had mastered many techniques for working gold and silver, and created bronze alloys of varying types for different uses.

None of these metals was much use for working stone, which was one of the glories of the Inca civilization. Modern research shows that the finely fitted stones were primarily cut and shaped using hammer-stones of harder rock. This process was laborious, but not as slow as we might imagine. The Incas' vast manpower and their reverence for stone enabled them to persevere through the many years it took to complete such astounding structures as Machu Picchu and Sacsayhuamán.

The mystery of how the Incas moved and fitted enormous stones has been patiently investigated by the US architect Vincent Lee. He has demonstrated a possible method, within the

however, inherit the distaff spindle for spinning thread, which has been used in the Andes for thousands of years.

The absence of a clearly recognizable form of writing is harder to explain. The *tokapu* textile symbols and the *quipus* were the closest they came. Quechua is full of ambiguities, puns, and multiple meanings, relying heavily on context for its true sense. It is the language style of an oral culture, but whether this is the cause or the effect of having no written language is impossible to say.

Inca ruins at Pisac in the Sacred Valley.

technical capabilities of the Incas, by maneuvering stones onto massive log sleds, which were then levered along wooden rails. Fitting might have been by trial and error, although Lee believes a plumb line and pantograph device were used to project the profile of a finished stone onto an uncut block.

Despite their wondrous skills, the Incas never devised the wheel, nor a form of writing except for the *quipus* (see page 43). Andean terrain is extremely steep, and the Incas' only draft animal was the small, lightly built llama, unable to pull a load exceeding 45kg (100lb). So the absence of a wheel is understandable. Thus, lacking the first reason to devise a wheel, the Incas never discovered its other uses. They did,

Another invention the Incas lacked was the arch. To span great gaps they built sturdy suspension bridges. In buildings they used the trapezoidal aperture. This shape – tapering upwards, with a stone or wooden lintel across the top – will take a fair amount of weight from above. All four walls of almost every Inca building also leaned slightly inward, making them very stable. This technique, combined with the brilliantly interlocking joins of their stonework, made their buildings almost earthquake-proof – a useful feature in Peru. While the Incas lacked certain things we take for granted, they nonetheless created a sophisticated civilization, whose echoes still reverberate throughout the Andes.

The conquistadors set sail for the New World.

THE CONQUEST

Lust for gold, fueled by rumors of glittering temples and fabulous treasures, made the Spanish conquest of Peru one of the bloodiest episodes in the history of empire.

It was in 1532 that a motley collection of Spanish conquistadors first appeared on the fringes of the Inca Empire, the largest and most powerful empire that South America had ever known. In the months to come, these 62 horsemen and 106 foot soldiers commanded by a professional soldier named Francisco Pizarro would march to the heart of Peru and brutally seize control of the Inca throne. Within a decade, a glittering Andean world would be firmly in the grip of the Spaniards, its glories stripped and its people virtually enslaved.

Few historical events have been as dramatic or cruel as the conquest of Peru. Although only a handful in number, the invading Spaniards had on their side an astonishing streak of good luck, complete technological superiority, and a lack of principle that would have made Machiavelli shudder. Apparently experiencing no emotions other than greed and fear, they were repeatedly able to trick their way into the confidence of the Inca rulers and nobility, only to betray them. By the time the Incas realized the ruthlessness of their foes, it was too late.

Francisco Pizarro, the Spanish leader.

THE INVASION OF AMERICA

Cautiously marching into Peru's coastal desert, Pizarro and his men were in the front ranks of Spain's explosion into the New World. It had been only four decades earlier, in 1492, that Christopher Columbus had landed in the West Indies – the same year that Castile drove the last Moors from Spanish soil. With no foe inside its boundaries and a need to bolster national pride and replenish the royal coffers, Spain soon directed the violent energies of its soldiers across the Atlantic. In 1519, Hernán Cortés, with 500 men and 16 horses, conquered the fabulously wealthy Aztec Empire in Mexico. Panama

⊘ MUTUAL DISTRUST

One contemporary chronicler recorded the Spaniards' surprise at the sight of Atahualpa's army in the valley outside Cajamarca: "Nothing like this had been seen in the Indies up to then. It filled all us Spaniards with fear and confusion. But it was not appropriate to show any fear, far less to turn back. For had they sensed any weakness in us, the very Indians we were bringing with us would have killed us." One can only speculate about how the Incas felt on seeing the Spanish soldiers for the first time, clad in armor and mounted on strange, unknown beasts with "golden shoes" upon their four feet.

was settled, and conquistadors were soon looking toward the newly found Pacific Ocean as a route to even further riches.

Although the existence of Peru was still no more than a rumor at that time, it was only seven years later that two already relatively wealthy soldiers from Spain's barren Extremadura region, Francisco Pizarro and Diego de Almagro, led two expeditions down the west coast of South America before stumbling on the city of Tumbes and gathering information about the Inca Empire. Intoxicated by the prospect of

Atahualpa is carried on his throne to meet Pizarro.

conquering another Mexico, Pizarro went back to Spain, where he gained permission from the Spanish Crown to undertake the conquest. He recruited a band of adventurers from his hometown, Trujillo, before setting sail again.

By the time Pizarro returned to Tumbes in 1532 with his 168 men, it was in ruins. In a stroke of fortune that would determine the fate of Peru, the Spaniards had found the Inca Empire in an unparalleled crisis, weakened by a bitter civil war. Several years earlier, a virulent disease – probably smallpox, spreading like wildfire among the Indians from European settlements in the Caribbean – had struck down the supreme Inca, Huayna Capac, together with his son and designated heir. Two other sons who survived

the epidemic, the half-brothers Huascar, who was based in the capital city of Cusco, and Atahualpa, the commander of the imperial armies in Quito, fought a bitter war for the succession. The civil war ended with Atahualpa victorious, but the empire was rocked and badly weakened by the struggle (see page 44).

When Pizarro landed, Atahualpa had only just become the undisputed Inca. He was heading in triumph south from Quito to the capital when news arrived that a group of tall, bearded men had entered his lands. Atahualpa was camped not far from the Spaniards' marching route, and on hearing the news the Inca decided that he would meet the strangers himself.

INTO THE ANDES

Pizarro and his force turned away from the barren coast to climb the rough road into the Andes. Although exhausted by the thin, high-altitude air, the conquistadors marveled at the first signs of the Inca civilization: steep valleys were lined with rich terraces of maize, shepherds stood by with flocks of ungainly llamas, and powerful stone fortresses overlooked the Spaniards' path. But the Inca warriors and their subjects watched the advancing strangers impassively: Atahualpa had given orders that they should not be hindered.

Finally Pizarro arrived at Cajamarca. Stretching into the valley beyond were the tents of the Inca's army and entourage. Pizarro entered the near-deserted town and sent his brother Hernando with a group of horsemen to meet Atahualpa. The Inca received the envoys with all the pomp and splendor of his magnificent court. When permitted to speak, the Spaniards used a translator to convey that Pizarro "loved [the Inca] dearly" and wished to meet him. Atahualpa agreed to a meeting in Cajamarca the following day.

Only that night did the Spaniards fully appreciate what they had got themselves into. Pizarro had no definite plan, and the conquistadors heatedly debated what should be done. They were several days' march into an obviously huge empire. Outside, the campfires of the Incan army lit up the surrounding hillsides "like a brilliantly star-studded sky." They were terrified, but the lust for gold was even stronger than fear.

> The Incas were mystified by the conquistadors' lust for gold. Manco Inca, who came to the throne in 1533, observed "Even if all the snow in the Andes turned to gold, still they would not be satisfied."

THE CAPTURE OF THE INCA

Next morning, November 16, the Spaniards prepared an ambush. Hidden in Cajamarca's main square, the soldiers waited tensely all morning without any sign of movement in Atahualpa's camp. Many began to suspect that their treacherous plan had been detected and they would all be slaughtered outright. It was not until nearly sundown, after Pizarro had once again sent envoys to promise that "no harm or insult would come to him," that the Inca decided to pay his visit.

Atahualpa and his nobles arrived in full ceremonial regalia. "All the Indians wore large gold and silver discs like crowns on their heads," one observer wrote. Atahualpa himself wore a collar of heavy emeralds and was borne on a silver litter by 80 blue-clad nobles. Surrounding him were "five or six thousand" men, either unarmed or carrying clubs and slings. But Atahualpa found no Spaniards in the square, and called out impatiently: "Where are they?"

Friar Vicente de Valverde emerged from the darkness with a translator and a copy of the Bible. What happens next is confused by the chroniclers, but has been pieced together by John Hemming in his classic *Conquest of the Incas*. It appears that Valverde began to explain his role as a priest. Atahualpa asked to look at the Bible, never having seen a book. "He leafed through [the Bible], admiring its form and layout. But after examining it he threw it angrily down amongst his men, his face a deep crimson." This "sacrilege" was all that the Spaniards needed to justify their actions. Valverde began screaming: "Come out! Come out, Christians! Come at these enemy dogs who reject the things of God!"

Pizarro gave his signal. Cannons blasted and the Spaniards piled into the plaza with their battle cry of "Santiago!" Cavalry crashed into the horrified Indian ranks and began a wholesale slaughter: the natives "were so filled with fear that they climbed on top of one another – to such an extent that they formed mounds and suffocated one another."

Retreat had been blocked, and none of the entourage escaped alive. Pizarro himself hacked a path straight for the Inca and grabbed his arm. He suffered the only wound to befall the Spanish troops, inflicted by one of his own men who went to stab the Inca. Pizarro deflected the blow, cutting his hand. Atahualpa was rushed away from the carnage and locked, ironically enough, in the Temple of the Sun.

Atahualpa asks Pizarro if the Spaniards eat gold.

⊘ A TRUE LEADER

While awaiting the arrival of the promised treasure, the Spaniards became impressed by their royal prisoner. One of Pizarro's men later wrote that "Atahualpa was a man of 30 years of age, of good appearance and manner, although somewhat thickset... He spoke with much gravity, as a great ruler." The Inca possessed an incisive intellect, grasped Spanish customs quickly, and learned the secrets of writing and the rules of chess. During the time he remained a prisoner, Atahualpa's servants and wives maintained the royal rituals, bringing the Inca his cloaks of vampire-bat skin and burning everything that he touched or wore.

THE ROYAL PRISONER

The Spanish could hardly believe their luck in capturing Atahualpa. The Inca Empire, already divided by the civil war, was now without its absolute leader. On the instructions of the Spaniards, Atahualpa issued orders from captivity, and his stunned people could only obey.

The conquistadors took whatever they wanted from the surrounding camp. Inca soldiers looked on as Hernando de Soto demanded men as porters, women as slaves, llamas for food – and, naturally, as much gold, silver, and jewelry as his squadron could carry. Atahualpa, seeing that the Spaniards were interested above all in precious metal, assumed that they must either eat it or use it as a medical remedy (as depicted in drawings by the 16th-century indigenous chronicler Huamán Poma de Ayala). Atahualpa offered a ransom for his freedom: a room of 88 cu meters (3,100 cu ft) in size would be filled once over with gold and twice with silver.

The Spaniards were amazed at the offer, and Pizarro hastened to agree – summoning a sec-

Atahualpa begs for mercy from Pizarro.

⊘ GOLD FEVER

The Spaniards waiting in Cajamarca for Atahualpa's treasure heard endless rumors of Cusco's magnificence. Cusco's holiest site, the Qoricancha, was covered in gold sheets and its Sun Temple sported a golden disk studded with jewels. A nearby field was filled with plants and animals crafted in precious metals. Atahualpa, anxious to regain his freedom, urged Pizarro to send men to loot this imperial treasure. Three illiterate soldiers were dispatched, and they stripped the Qoricancha with their own hands. Thus no educated Spaniard ever saw it in its glory, and the memory of its full splendor was lost for ever.

retary to record the details as a formal pledge and give a stamp of legality to the deal. In return, Pizarro promised to restore Atahualpa to Quito. It was a blatant lie, but one that served the conquistadors' purpose brilliantly: the whole Inca Empire was mobilized to supply them with booty. Llama trains from Quito to Lake Titicaca were soon starting out, loaded down with precious statues, jugs, and dishes.

ABUSE AND MURDER

Meanwhile, a small group of Spaniards went to Jauja, where Atahualpa's greatest general, Chalcuchima, was stationed. Trustingly, the general agreed to accompany the Spaniards back to Cajamarca, thus giving Pizarro the only other man who might have led a coordinated resistance to his invasion. Having treated the general well until his arrival at Cajamarca, they then tortured him to obtain more information about gold, and set about burning him at the stake. He was released "with his legs and arms burned and his tendons shriveled."

Atahualpa now realized that he had made a grave mistake in cooperating with the invaders, and that they had no intention of releasing him or leaving his empire. In mid-April 1533, Pizarro's partner, Diego de Almagro, arrived

that the Inca could no longer be counted on to support Spanish rule. The council fast decided that he should die.

Pizarro's secretary coldly recorded the sordid proceedings. The Inca was "brought out of his prison... and was tied to a stake. The friar [Valverde] was, in the meantime, consoling and instructing him through an interpreter in the articles of our Christian faith... The Inca was moved by these arguments and requested baptism... His exhortations did him much good. For although he had been sentenced to be burned

The death of Atahualpa.

from Panama, with 150 Spanish reinforcements, before leaving again for Spain with news of the conquest and booty for Holy Roman Emperor Charles V. The influx of treasure into Cajamarca turned it into an undisciplined boomtown and made the Spaniards bolder. But rumors began that Inca forces were massing to rescue their leader.

Many Spaniards became convinced that they were in danger so long as Atahualpa remained alive. Others saw the value of the Inca as a prisoner, and argued that it would be difficult to justify an execution. Chroniclers record that a captured native claimed to have seen an Inca army marching on Cajamarca. Pizarro panicked and called an emergency council. It was obvious

alive, he was in fact garroted by a piece of rope that was tied around his neck."

News of the execution horrified Atahualpa's supporters, especially when it was learned that there was no Inca column advancing on the city. When news arrived in Europe, educated opinion was equally appalled. Even Holy Roman Emperor Charles V was upset about the execution, protesting that it offended the divine right of kings upon which his own rule – and that of all contemporary monarchs – was based. But by then the Spanish Crown's share of booty was arriving from Peru, and such scruples could be overlooked. The priceless art and sculpture of the great Inca Empire went straight to the smelters of Seville.

ONWARD INTO THE HEARTLAND

In August 1533, the Spaniards marched on Cusco. It seems an audacious project, but it is important to realize that a large part of the Inca Empire's population, especially around the southern Sierra, welcomed the news of Atahualpa's death. To those who had backed his brother Huascar in the civil war, Atahualpa was a usurper and his troops from Quito an enemy occupying force. It should also be remembered that the invaders were not dealing with a united people, but with a collection of disparate groups,

The Spaniards' steel armor was almost impenetrable to the natives' bronze hand-axes, clubs, and maces. And Pizarro's men were some of the most experienced fighters Europe had to offer. Again and again the invaders would use their technological advantage to press home victories against apparently overwhelming odds.

Pizarro founded Jauja as the new Peruvian capital and pressed on. What followed was a desperate race to cross the several rope bridges spanning the Andean gorges before the Quitans could destroy them. On one occasion the Indians

The Plaza des Armas in modern-day Cusco.

some of which were happy to be part of the Inca Empire, while others still resented the Inca yoke and were willing to fight on the side of the Spaniards. Realizing this, Pizarro was now ready to pose as the liberator of the Andes.

At Jauja, a contingent of Atahualpa's army tried to make a stand. The Spanish cavalry charged and routed them immediately. This first armed clash of the conquest revealed a pattern that would be repeated: the native foot soldiers were no match for the mounted and well-armored Spaniards. Horses gave the conquistadors mobility and allowed them to strike downward on their opponents' heads and shoulders, while the strange animals also created fear and confusion amongst the Incas.

attempted an ambush and managed to kill several Spaniards in hand-to-hand battle. Pizarro decided that the captured general Chalcuchima had planned the attack and ordered him to be burned alive. But the attack had been to no avail: there was a final pitched battle in the pass before Cusco, and the Quitans' morale broke. They slipped away from the Urubamba Valley under cover of night and left the Inca capital to the invaders.

DIVIDING UP THE SPOILS

Pizarro and his men marched unopposed into the nerve-center of the Inca world, the "navel of the universe," Cusco. "The city is the greatest and finest ever seen in this country or anywhere

The Spaniards' behavior was a source of amazement to the Incas. Not only were the all-powerful conquerors falling out among themselves, they had shown themselves capable of stealing from one another.

in the Indies," Pizarro wrote back to Charles V. "We can assure Your Majesty that it is so beautiful and has such fine buildings that it would be remarkable even in Spain." But the invaders barely had time to marvel at the precise Inca masonry and the channels of running water in every street before installing themselves in the Inca palaces and starting on the serious business of pillaging the city.

Pizarro realized that his small force would not survive a true popular uprising, and so attempted to keep the looting of Cusco relatively orderly – at least until reinforcements arrived. He offered his men tracts of land and the right to the unpaid labor of the local population. This attempt to induce the Spaniards to become settlers, and to produce rather than destroy, would later become institutionalized in Latin America as the *encomienda* system. After "founding" the city in the name of the Spanish king, Pizarro rode back to the barren coast of Peru and created his colonial capital, facing the sea: modern-day Lima, where his statue stood until it was finally removed in 2004.

Pizarro had also accepted the offer of the 20-year-old Manco, another of Huayna Capac's sons, to become the new Inca. Manco wanted the Spaniards to restore him to his father's crown, and the conquistadors were happy to have him as a puppet leader in the southern Sierra. He was installed in Cusco while two groups of Spaniards headed toward Quito to take on the retreating imperial army that remained loyal to Atahualpa's memory.

THE REALITY OF CONQUEST

Under Manco Inca's nominal rule, Cusco seemed tranquil enough. But it wasn't long before the puppet ruler began to see the Spanish "liberators" in their true colors. Their greed and brutality grew in proportion with their confidence; they were obviously in Peru to stay.

Manco was distressed to see the Inca world crumbling before his eyes. The natives of Cusco refused to obey him, while many of his subject tribes began to assert their independence. The swelling ranks of Spaniards began forcing the locals into pressgangs, extorting gold from nobles, and raping Inca women. They harassed Manco Inca for treasure, captured his wife, and pillaged his property.

Manco could tolerate no more and announced his intention to rebel. Vast numbers of native soldiers were mobilized, and Manco slipped

The Inca rebellion.

away from Cusco into the mountains. It was 1536, and the great rebellion had begun.

INCAS ON THE OFFENSIVE

Manco's troops quickly took Sacsayhuamán, the great fortress overlooking Cusco whose massive stone blocks still awe visitors today. Chroniclers record that the Inca force was about 100,000 strong against the Spaniards' 80 cavalry and 110 foot soldiers, commanded by Francisco Pizarro's brother Hernando. Their defenses were bolstered by large contingents of native forces, but the outlook for the Spaniards was grim: Cusco was surrounded and, for all they knew, they might have been the last Spanish outpost in Peru.

The Inca attack finally began with slingshot stones, made red-hot in campfires, hailing down onto Cusco's thatched roofs, which immediately set them alight. But black slaves extinguished the flames on the roof of the building where the main body of Spaniards were sheltering. Even so, Manco Inca's forces captured the majority of the city. In retaliation the Spaniards decided on a desperate plan: to counterattack the strategic fortress of Sacsayhuamán.

Another of the Pizarro brothers, Juan, led 50 horsemen in a charge straight at the native

had their heads and feet cut off. Indian prisoners were impaled or had their hands chopped off in Cusco's main square.

The rebellion was more successful in other parts of the empire. Francisco Pizarro organized several relief expeditions from Lima, but the Incas had learned to use geography against the Spanish. One group of soldiers was caught in a narrow gorge by a hail of rocks; most were killed, the remainder captured. Another force was trapped, and their heads sent to Manco Inca. Now the victorious natives marched on Lima.

The ruins of Sacsayhuamán, Cusco.

lines. Despite their overwhelmingly superior numbers, the Incas still did not have a weapon that could seriously injure the Spanish cavalry. Although Juan Pizarro was killed, the conquistadors forced their way to a safe position on the hill opposite Sacsayhuamán. They prepared a night attack using medieval European siege tactics, and took the outer terrace of the fortress.

THE SPANISH HOLD ON

The capture of Sacsayhuamán was the key to Cusco's defense. Although the city remained surrounded for another three months, the Incas found it impossible to take. Fighting continued with extraordinary cruelty. Captured Spaniards

The attack on the town came from three sides, but in the flat coastal plains the Spanish cavalry proved invincible. A determined charge routed the main native force, and the commanding general was cut down in his tracks.

Meanwhile the Spaniards went on the offensive in Cusco, with an attack on Manco in the nearby terraced fortress of Ollantaytambo. Manco cunningly diverted the nearby river to flood the approaches, incapacitating the deadly Spanish cavalry. The rebel Inca was seen riding a captured horse along the heights, directing his troops with a lance, as rainforest archers and warriors wielding captured Spanish weapons claimed the lives of several Spaniards. The conquistadors beat a hasty retreat and the siege dragged on – but the tide had turned.

RECONQUERING PERU

Spanish governors from other parts of the Americas were quick to come to Pizarro's aid. Reinforcements soon arrived from Mexico and Nicaragua, while Diego de Almagro returned with troops from a failed expedition to Chile. When Almagro relieved Cusco in April 1537, Manco Inca decided that his cause was lost and retreated with his forces into the remote Vilcabamba Valley. The Spaniards chased him as far as Vitcos, but became distracted by looting. The Inca escaped under cover of darkness, carried in the arms of 20 fast runners. The Spaniards would have time to regret their greed: deep inside the subtropical valley, behind an almost impenetrable series of narrow gorges and suspension bridges, Manco created an Inca court-in-exile that would survive in various forms for another 35 years.

By now there was a new twist to the complicated politics of the conquest: Almagro and Francisco Pizarro, the original partners in the invasion, had never reached agreement on how the empire should be divided between them, so the plotting between the two former allies plunged Peru into civil war.

No sooner had Manco Inca fled than the three surviving Pizarro brothers united against Almagro, pitting Spaniard against Spaniard on Andean battlefields. Eventually, in 1538, the Pizarrist faction defeated Almagro outside Cusco, and the general was garroted.

VICTORY AND REVENGE

At 63 years of age, Francisco Pizarro was at the peak of his bloodstained career. Although no longer active on the battlefield, he was undisputed governor of a Peru that, notwithstanding the occasional harassment by Manco Inca of Spanish travelers from his jungle hideaway, was firmly under Spanish control. He possessed fabulous wealth and had been made a marquis by the grateful Spanish Crown. But on June 26, 1541, Pizarro's past caught up with him: he was surprised in his Lima palace by a group of supporters of his murdered partner, Diego de Almagro. He was able to kill one of his attackers before being hacked to death. His corpse was thrown into a secret grave.

Pizarro's ally, Bishop Vicente de Valverde, the priest who had first attempted to convert Atahualpa, tried to escape to Panama. But the ship was wrecked off the island of Puná where he was killed by natives, possibly because he tried to Christianize them – or extract their gold.

The deaths of Pizarro and Valverde seem a fitting end to the first stage of the conquest. But the era that was beginning would be no less brutal. Now that most of the easily appropriated Inca treasures had been seized and distributed, the Spanish began to exploit the popula-

Engraving of Diego de Almagro.

tion mercilessly. The conquistadors who had received land and the right to native labor under the *encomienda* system became the elite of the new colony. They extorted tribute in the form of grain, livestock, and labor, and forced the native peoples into a brutal form of feudalism.

In 1542 a new viceroy arrived from Spain to impose order. Fearing for their own interests, some Spaniards mustered behind Gonzalo Pizarro (Francisco Pizarro's half-brother), who marched into Lima in 1544 and was declared governor of Peru. But unrest continued, and two years later the viceroy was killed in battle against Gonzalo's troops. When this news reached Spain, Pedro de la Gasca was sent to rule the troublesome colony. Gonzalo initially held his own but in 1548, deserted by his own men, he was forced to surrender, and was put to death, another victim of the greed and disorder that characterized the conquest.

THE LAST INCAS

While this infighting was going on, Manco Inca had maintained his court in Vitcos, teaching his troops Spanish military techniques in order to wage a guerrilla war. Manco's fatal mistake was to spare a group of pro-Almagro Spaniards who had fled to Vilcabamba. The refugees

Tupac Amaru.

grew bored with exile and, believing they would be pardoned by the Pizarrist faction if they murdered the Inca, they fell on their host and stabbed him. They paid with their lives for their treachery, but the Inca leader was irreplaceable; with his death, any real resistance to the Spanish virtually collapsed.

As the Spaniards consolidated their rule, Manco Inca's son Titu Cusi maintained the Vilcabamba court. The Spanish understood that, as long as any legitimate royal figure stayed free, there would always be some faint hope for Indian freedom. Long negotiations were aimed at drawing the Inca out to live in Cusco, but to no avail. Then, in 1569, two Augustinian friars entered the secret Inca nation and attempted to convert the Inca to Christianity.

In 1570, Friar Diego Ortiz became a close companion to Titu Cusi, and when Titu became ill, Friar Diego Ortiz prepared a healing potion which he hoped would save him. Unfortunately, the Inca died as soon as he drank it. His horrified troops, believing their leader had been poisoned, immediately killed Friar Diego Ortiz. The other friar was dragged along the ground for three days by a rope driven through a hole behind his jaw, before being dispatched by a blow to the skull from a mace.

This "martyrdom" gave the Spanish a pretext to invade Vilcabamba yet again. This time the conquistadors gathered an irresistible force. The new Inca, Tupac Amaru, put up a spirited defense against the invading column, but the Spaniards captured first Vitcos and then Vilcabamba.

Tupac Amaru tried to escape into the thick Amazon jungle, but his progress was slowed down by his wife, who was on the verge of giving birth, and a local chief betrayed the party's movements. Finally, a pursuing team of Spaniards spotted a campfire in the rainforest and pounced on the Inca, capturing him and bringing him back to Cusco with a golden chain around his neck.

With all resistance ended, and no leader to rally dissident spirits, the Spaniards were left in total control of the vast empire. But there was no time to rest on their laurels: they were already beginning to discover that governing the country was going to be just as difficult a task as subduing it had been.

⊘ DEATH OF AN EMPEROR

Viceroy Francisco de Toledo, fifth viceroy of Peru, was possessed with a determination to destroy the Inca royal lineage, along with its prestige. He had rebel generals tried and hanged and, ignoring all appeals for clemency (a number of clerics begged him to be lenient), had the last emperor, Tupac Amaru, swiftly converted to Christianity, tried for the deaths of various Spaniards in Vilcabamba, and sentenced to beheading in Cusco's main square. In September 1572, 40 years after Pizarro's capture of Atahualpa in Cajamarca, the wailing of thousands of conquered natives announced the death of the last Inca.

🔍 LOOKING FOR THE PAST

The birth of archeology in the 19th century brought explorers to Peru in search of "lost cities" such as Vilcabamba, to which the last Incas had retreated.

Gene Savoy, Hiram Bingham, Thor Heyerdahl, and Maria Reiche are just a few of the foreign explorers who have been drawn to Peru. One of the first archeologists to explore Peru was Bingham, who visited many important ruins, in 1911 discovering Machu Picchu, which he declared was Vilcabamba. He also found the Inca ruins at Espíritu Pampa, but dismissed them as unimportant.

In 1963 another American, Gene Savoy, who described himself as "a non-professional archeological explorer" and who had already made important discoveries of pre-Inca civilizations in the northern coastal valleys, turned his sights on the southern jungles, intent on disproving the widely held belief that Machu Picchu was the lost city.

Basing his work on his interpretations of the texts of the same Spanish chroniclers as used earlier by Bingham, Savoy took a closer look at Espíritu Pampa. It is a large site containing at least 60 buildings and some 300 houses, but unspectacular and overgrown with rainforest vegetation. Some buildings had been roofed with Spanish-style terracotta tiles, proving that they were constructed after the Spanish conquest. This evidence, coupled with location and topographical details, clinched the identification of Espíritu Pampa as the site of Vilcabamba the Old.

Savoy made two more expeditions to the area, uncovering more Inca sites and remains of roads, then switched his attentions farther north in search of the ancient cities of the Chachapoyas, a pre-Inca tribe that ruled much of the northern Peruvian Andes (c.AD 1100–1400). At Gran Pajatén on the fringes of the empire, he credited himself with discovering a vast complex with large circular structures, decorated with stone reliefs depicting carved animal and human heads, suggesting that the site had ceremonial as well as defensive functions.

Other researchers, however, dispute that Savoy was the first to discover the fragile site.

In the late 1960s Savoy explored many other known ruins in the Chachapoyas area, including Kuélap, an impressively defended fortress, and publicized, for the first time, the existence of remains at Monte Peruvia (Purunllacta). He estimated that this site, 155 sq km (60 sq miles) in extent and spread across more than 30 hilltops linked by roadways, was one of the great cities of the Chachapoyas culture eventually conquered by Inca Tupac Yupanqui.

Gene Savoy in the 1960s.

In 1969 Savoy changed direction again. Fascinated by the legend about the founder of the Chimú culture who arrived by sea, he hoped to prove that early Peruvians traded across the Pacific. To this end, he constructed a *totora* boat and sailed up the South American coast to Panama. Savoy died in 2009.

The Chachapoyas region was the scene of another major discovery in 1997, when superbly preserved cliff-face tombs filled with Inca and Chachapoyan mummies were found at Laguna de los Cóndores, near Leimebamba. In 2013 archeologists discovered what is thought to be a children's cemetery near San Jeronimo. It contained 35 painted clay sarcophagi, each about 70 centimeters (28ins) tall.

16th-century map of Peru.

FROM COLONY TO REPUBLIC

From early colonial mismanagement, through the battles for independence, to 20th-century coups, Peru has known little stability on its path to becoming a modern state.

The chaotic years of early colonial administration were to change with the arrival in 1569 of Francisco de Toledo, Peru's fifth viceroy. A brutal but efficient ruler, Toledo consolidated Spain's command over the former Inca Empire. After finally crushing the rebel bastion of Vilcabamba and dealing with a revolt by dissatisfied conquistadors, he set about ordering every aspect of colonial life.

SPAIN'S IRON FIST

The effects of Toledo's decrees were to alter the face of the Andes for ever. One of his most drastic measures was the establishment of *reducciones*, the forced resettlement of indigenous people into Spanish-style towns complete with a central plaza, church, town hall, and prison – the symbols of Spanish authority. *Reducciones* facilitated the collection of tribute from the Indians and their conversion to Christianity.

The new viceroy also formalized the *encomienda* system, whereby Indians provided labor and tribute to an *encomendero*, their Spanish landlord. The *encomienda* system ensured a life of luxury for the landowners. Contemporary records show that one group of tributaries in Conchucos were obliged to provide their *encomendero* annually with 2,500 pesos of gold, the harvest of more than 1,500 hectares (3,700 acres) in wheat, maize, barley, and potatoes, 30 sheep, 12kg (26lb) of candle wax, 25 donkeyloads of salt, and 45 pairs of grouse, as well as give their master 20 eggs every Friday.

The premise of the *encomienda* was completely alien to the Andean way of life, which was a system based on reciprocity and redistribution. In addition, the large tracts of land that formed the *encomiendas* ignored the Andean concept of

An ornate colonial altar.

verticality, whereby an ethnic group living near, say, Lake Titicaca, had access to land and produce – cotton, fish, and hot peppers – from the warm coastal valleys. Under the colonial order, distribution of goods went in only one direction: from tribute payer to local ethnic lord (*curaca*), and thence to *encomendero*.

Because *encomenderos* rarely traveled outside the towns where they lived, it was usually the *curacas* who collected the tribute. Terrorized by the Spanish, they in turn terrorized their own people into fulfilling their tribute obligations. They soon learned Spanish and borrowed the trappings of colonial nobility, dressing in Spanish-style clothing, carrying firearms, and riding on horseback.

SQUEEZING PERU DRY

The Spanish colonial economy was initially based on coercion and plunder. The treasures of Cusco had already been distributed, but there were others. In the north-coast city of Trujillo, named after Pizarro's birthplace in Spain, the Spanish Crown granted licenses for the pillage of the ancient *huacas* (temples).

Once the Spanish had exhausted tombs to plunder, they turned to mines, a quest that led to the discovery in 1545 of Potosí. Today a bleak tin-mining city in the Bolivian highlands, 4,070

on the task involved. In return, the transient workers had received hospitality from the local community as well as a look at the world outside their own village. Under the Spanish version of the system, Indian workers were force-marched hundreds of miles to Potosí, where two out of every three died as a result of the appalling working conditions, since miners were forced to remain below ground for six-day stretches.

Even more horrific were the mercury mines in Huancavelica – one of which, Santa Barbara, soon became known as the "mine of death." Thousands

The horrendous conditions in the Potosí mines.

meters (13,350ft) above sea level, in its heyday in the 17th-century Potosí was the richest and largest city in the world, with a population near 200,000. Potosí's silver filled the coffers of the Spanish Crown with the necessary cash to finance battles across Europe. The town's coat of arms read: "I am rich Potosí, treasure of the world and envy of Kings."

But the discovery of Potosí brought with it renewed hardship for the indigenous peoples. In 1574 Toledo legalized the *mita*, the traditional Inca system of enforced labor on a rotational basis. It was another example of an Andean institution twisted to suit Spanish needs; under the Incas the system had involved young people working in the service of the state for a limited period, depending

of people from neighboring provinces died in the mines, asphyxiated by lethal fumes of cinnabar (sulphide of mercury), arsenic, and mercury.

The traditional chewing of coca leaves had initially been condemned by the Catholic Church until it was realized that the Andean peoples could not survive the brutal mining *mita* without it. The leaf was soon touted by the Spanish as a cure-all to ward off hunger, thirst, and fatigue. The trade was organized and controlled: thousands of local highlanders, unadapted to life in the torrid jungle, died working the coca fields. Llama caravans carried coca leaves from Cusco, the center of production, to Potosí, 1,000km (620 miles) away. The Church also reaped the benefits of the lucrative trade,

> By the early 1700s, the colonial system was firmly established throughout the Andes. At its height, the viceroyalty of Peru was 15 times the size of Spain, and for two centuries ruled from Panama to Argentina.

collecting a tithe on each full basket. Although some authorities tried to limit the production of coca, too many fortunes were made from the trade. "There are those in Spain who became rich from this coca, buying it up and reselling it and trading it in the markets of the Indians," wrote Spanish chronicler and soldier Pedro Cieza de León in the 1540s.

Francisco de Toledo also initiated the *mita de obrajes* (textile workshops). Working under harsh factory conditions, workers were forced to weave for their Spanish masters, producing cloth for local consumption and export. Toledo tried to limit the wealth of the *encomenderos* by ensuring that their land reverted to the Crown after a couple of generations, to be replaced with *corregimientos*. But this system had few advantages for the native peoples, as the *corregidores* (or co-regents) were also charged with collecting tribute and providing workers for the *obraje* and mining *mitas*.

CHRISTIANS ON THE MARCH

The early 1600s saw a far-flung campaign against idolatry, spurred on by a revival of native religion in 1565. The renewed religious zeal of the Catholic Church led to a push to stamp out native beliefs once and for all. At the same time, this crusade gave rise to valuable dictionaries and accounts that are still being studied by historians today. Priests visited outlying provinces, collecting information on cults and sometimes torturing villagers to reveal the whereabouts of idols and *huacas*.

In many ways, the Catholic campaign served to entrench native faiths; rather than taking over, Christianity formed a veneer over traditional cults and beliefs, many of which still exist today. This syncretism, in which traditional beliefs dominate, led to the replacement of Andean pilgrimage centers and festivals by superficially Catholic ones.

Under the prevailing system of mercantilism, which promoted exports and restricted imports and goods produced for local consumption, the elite grew rich, while the mass of people remained impoverished. Spain decreed that all trade from South America should pass through Lima, ensuring a massive influx of taxes. Lima, the opulent "City of Kings," was crammed with magnificent churches and mansions.

In Spain, meanwhile, the end of the War of the Spanish Succession (1700–13) saw the Habsburg dynasty replaced by the Bourbons, who reigned

The San Francisco monastery library in Lima.

until Napoleon occupied Madrid in 1808. Efforts by Bourbon monarchs to improve the colonial economy and stem corruption were to little avail but disaffected Creole subjects.

INDIGENOUS UPRISING

During the 18th century, exploitation of the indigenous population sparked off various rebellions, from Quito in present-day Ecuador to La Paz (capital city of today's Bolivia). The most serious of these was the uprising instigated by José Gabriel Condorcanqui, also known as Tupac Amaru II, as he claimed to be descended from the renegade Inca emperor killed in 1572 (see page 56). Born in Tinta, south of Cusco, Tupac Amaru II studied in Cusco at a school for Indians of noble birth. It was not his intention to rid Peru of the Spanish yoke; rather, he fought against the tyranny of the *corregidores*, the miserable conditions at the haciendas, mines, *obrajes*, and coca plantations, and the subsequent malnutrition and disease. Increasingly, he lobbied for indigenous rights, demanding that the mine *mita* be lifted and the power of the *corregidores* limited.

In 1780 he had Tinta's hated *corregidor*, Antonio Arriaga, taken prisoner and hanged in the public square. It was the start of a public revolt that spread throughout the Peruvian highlands.

Spanish reinforcements were sent from Lima to quell the uprising. At a decisive battle in Checacupe, in 1781, the Spaniards dispersed Tupac Amaru II's men and captured the rebel leader and his wife. Tupac Amaru II, like his ancestor before him, was executed in Cusco's public square, and forced to witness the execution of his family before he was drawn and quartered. As a result of the rebellion, the viceroy Teodoro de Croix (1784–90) began to institute long-overdue reforms. He set up a special *audiencia*, or royal court, in Cusco to deal with indigenous legal claims. Meanwhile

16th-century illustration of Spanish vessels in the harbour at Lima.

⊘ THE PROGRESSIVE PRIEST

Fascinated by natural history and colonial life, the bishop of Trujillo, Martínez de Compañón, and his team of artists produced drawings covering antiquities, flora and fauna, customs, music, and the costumes of northern Peru. The 18th-century cleric is considered by many to be the grandfather of Peruvian archeology: he collected some 600 pre-Columbian artifacts for shipment to the Spanish king, who founded a "Cabinet of Natural History and Antiquities" in Madrid. He also left a valuable linguistic testimony – a list of 43 terms in seven indigenous languages spoken in his diocese, translated into Spanish and Quechua.

in Spain, Charles III, who had come to the throne in 1759, ordered that commerce be opened up, allowing ports other than Lima to conduct trade. He banned the *repartimiento*, the forced sale of inferior goods to native peoples at inflated prices, and ended the *corregimiento* system. He also divided the viceroyalty into seven intendancies under royal rule, paving the way for the regionalism that would break South America into its present patchwork of republics.

Not all the Spanish government and clergy exploited the indigenous population. One clergyman, Don Baltasar Jaime Martínez de Compañón y Bujanda, stands out. Appointed bishop of Trujillo in 1779, he spent his years traveling around a vast diocese covering the northern third of Peru. In a letter to Charles III dated 1786 he described the "wretchedness" he encountered everywhere.

THE PUSH FOR INDEPENDENCE

On the eve of Napoleon's march on the Iberian peninsula, Spain's hold on its colonies was already waning. Despite the best endeavors of the authorities, news of the French Revolution (begun in 1788), as well as the United States' War of Independence from Britain (1775–83), had filtered through to the colonies – at least to

Tupac Amaru II.

the criollos (American-born Peruvians of European descent) – and inspired hopes for self-determination. When Napoleon forced Charles IV to abdicate in 1808, and then placed his own brother Joseph on the Spanish throne, there were rebellions in many parts of South America. Declarations of independence in Upper Peru (now Bolivia) and Quito (Ecuador) in 1809 were followed by uprisings in the Peruvian cities of Huánuco and Cusco. But freedom from Spain was not so easily won: royalist troops regained control in many parts of the continent, and bloody wars were waged for the next 15 years.

There were many Peruvians who supported the colonial system, since Lima was still its wealthy administrative capital. Peru became

According to the legend, the colors of Peru's republican flag were inspired by the red and white feathers of the flamingos General José de San Martín saw upon landing at Paracas.

the strongest bastion of pro-Spanish feeling, and other newly independent countries could not feel secure until it, too, was liberated.

After Argentinian General José de San Martín's successful invasion of Chile in 1819, a rebel navy commanded by the British admiral Lord Thomas Cochrane sailed from the Chilean port of Valparaíso and landed in Paracas, on Peru's south coast. The following year the armada attacked Lima, dispersing royalist troops, who fled to the central and southern highlands. Meanwhile, the northern cities of Trujillo, Lambayeque, Piura, and Cajamarca declared their independence. General San Martín entered Lima in 1821, proclaiming independence for all Peru on July 28.

His first move was to abolish the tribute system, the mining *mita*, and the *corregimiento*, reforms which had been attempted earlier by Charles III. He even went so far as to ban the term "Indian" and proclaimed the descendants of the Incas to be citizens of Peru.

But Peru was not prepared for self-rule. San Martín opted for a new monarchy to replace Spanish rule and searched for a European prince to rule the former colony. In the subsequent tumultuous months, the monarchical plan was scuttled following the election of a parliament. The seven viceregal intendancies became departments headed by prefects, modeled on the French system of government.

FREEDOM AND CHAOS

In 1822 San Martín sailed to Guayaquil (Ecuador), where he met Venezuelan statesman Simón de Bolívar, El Libertador. A far-sighted political thinker influenced by the ideas of the Enlightenment, Bolívar had liberated his home country, and wanted San Martín's help to establish Gran Colombia, comprising Venezuela, Colombia, and Ecuador (which lasted only from 1823 to 1830).

San Martín needed troops to root out the last Spanish royalist forces in the Andes and offered

Peru's leadership to Bolívar. During his brief presidency (1824–6) Bolívar advocated republicanism. He commanded troops at the Battle of Junín in 1824, but it was not until the Battle of Ayacucho later that year that rebels headed by Venezuelan General José de Sucre crushed the royalist troops.

Bolívar's departure for Colombia in 1826 created a power vacuum, and the congress elected José de la Mar as president. San Martín's promises to abolish the tribute system, *mita*, servitude, and to recognize Quechua as an official language, were never followed through. The wars of independence had left the country ravaged, crops unattended, and food scarce. Instead of indigenous peoples being granted equal status as citizens of a republican Peru, an all-out assault on indigenous landholdings began.

Between 1826 and 1865, 35 presidents, many of them military officers, governed Peru. Chaos reigned. Charles Darwin, who visited the capital during his journey of scientific discovery in the 1830s, recalled: "Lima, the City of Kings, must formerly have been a splendid town." But he found it in a "wretched state of decay; the

Crossing a canyon in La Oroya, c.1908.

Simón de Bolívar, El Libertador.

⊘ RICH PICKINGS

By 1830 a new resource had replaced minerals as the country's main export: guano. The piles of bird droppings deposited on Peru's offshore islands were much sought after in Europe as fertilizer and fetched enormous prices. The first guano contract was negotiated with a British company in 1840. Indigenous people worked in appalling conditions at the guano stations, where ammonia fumes shriveled the skin and often caused blindness. By 1849, Peru's economy was almost entirely in the hands of two foreign firms, one based in London, the other in Paris, with exclusive guano marketing rights.

streets are nearly unpaved, and heaps of filth are piled up in all directions, where the black *gallinazos* (vultures) pick up bits of carrion."

ECONOMIC BOOM

Despite the political chaos of the early republican years, the economy grew, with large cotton and sugar estates developing on the coast. In 1849 Peru began to import Chinese labor to work the fields. In 1865 Spain, hoping to regain a foothold in its former colony, occupied the Chincha guano islands. A year later President Mariano Prado declared war on Spain and, after the Spanish navy bombarded the port of Callao, Peru decided to revamp its fleet, buying arms in Europe. Using the guano concession as a guarantee for the vast sum of 20 million pesos, Peru acquired the *Huascar* and *Independencia* warships from Britain.

The guano boom also initiated an era of railroad construction in the 1870s. A US railroad entrepreneur, Henry Meiggs, won the bid for the Callao–La Oroya line, an engineering feat of tunnels and bridges that began at sea level and rose over 5,000 meters (16,400ft) to the mining town of La Oroya. In 1877, unable to pay its British creditors, the Peruvian state became bankrupt. Worse was to come.

million tonnes of guano. The Peruvian Corporation was set up in 1890 to manage their interests.

By 1900, US interests were beginning to replace the British in controlling the Peruvian economy. Following the Spanish-American War over Cuba in 1898, US expansionists had begun to show an interest in Latin America. Many businessmen, seeing their domestic market as saturated, were looking for new outlets.

US investors set up the Cerro de Pasco Mining Company, which soon controlled all the mines in the central Sierra. In 1922 a smelter at La Oroya

General José de San Martín proclaims Peru's independence.

WAR BREAKS OUT

In 1879 Chile declared war on Peru and Bolivia over a dispute concerning sodium nitrate and borax deposits in the province of Tarapacá. The War of the Pacific (1879–83) found the armed forces of Peru and Bolivia woefully unprepared. Following naval victories, Chilean troops occupied southern Peru and then captured Lima, cutting off the capital from the hinterland. Following the peace treaty of 1883, Peru ceded its southernmost territories to Chile.

The war brought economic hardship. The tribute system was reinstated and a salt tax levied. In 1886, British bond-holders began negotiations: Peru's debt was canceled in exchange for a 66-year control of the major railroads and 2

⊘ RUBBER BARONS

The Peruvian rubber boom lasted from 1880 to 1912. The existence of latex in the rubber trees of the Amazon was common knowledge, but it was only after Charles Goodyear discovered the process of vulcanization, which kept rubber firm in high temperatures, that its commercial possibilities were realized. The city of Iquitos enjoyed a short-lived glory as the rubber capital of the world and its population swelled from less than 700 in 1866 to over 9,000 in 1903. The rubber barons lived in luxury until an Englishman smuggled the seeds to Asia (via Kew Gardens in England) and the monopoly came to an abrupt end.

began belching fumes of arsenic, lead, and zinc into the atmosphere, ravaging its surroundings, and fishmeal began to be exported from Peru's abundant anchovy plants.

Workers in the mines, coastal factories, and urban sweatshops began to form unions. But it was on the north coast, where laborers on the sugar haciendas began to organize, that a new class-consciousness found political expression. In 1924, while exiled in Mexico, a popular activist named Victor Raúl Haya de la Torre formed the Alianza Popular Revolucionaria Americana

General Juan Velasco.

(APRA), with a loose platform based on anti-imperialism and nationalization that attracted middle-class voters who felt neglected by the oligarchical rule. Haya de la Torre was allowed back to contest the 1931 elections, but was defeated in what *apristas* denounced as a fraud. Party members rebelled in Trujillo, killing 60 military officers. In reprisal, the military executed over 1,000 *apristas* in the ruins of Chan Chan.

URBAN DRIFT

For the next 50 years, APRA was kept out of power as Peru oscillated between Conservative and military regimes. Manufacturing industry developed, and thousands of *campesinos* (subsistence farmers) flocked into Lima. Pressure for land reform

and some redistribution of wealth grew. The first government of Fernando Belaúnde (1963–8), who promised some cautious progressive measures, was a failure, and, after widespread disgust at tax concessions given to the International Petroleum Company (a subsidiary of Standard Oil of New Jersey), yet another coup occurred. Belaúnde was marched out of the Presidential Palace in his pyjamas, and into exile. But General Juan Velasco, who headed the new junta, was not a typical military ruler, and went on to champion many of the radical APRA reforms.

Velasco's measures were drastic. They included sweeping agrarian reform, expropriating vast landholdings, and turning family-run estates into cooperatives. Petrol, mining, and fishing industries were nationalized at a stroke. Food for the urban population was subsidized by the state. And, in a profound symbolic gesture, Peru was recognized as a bilingual country, with Quechua as the second language.

A BLOODLESS COUP

Well intentioned Velasco's measures may have been, but they were not backed by sound economic planning. The newly nationalized industries were badly managed and lacked the necessary finance, and the country was already slipping into economic chaos well before the 1973 international oil crisis. The military split into factions, and in 1975, Francisco Morales Bermúdez, heading an alliance of Conservative and reformist officers, staged a bloodless coup against Velasco, who died soon afterwards.

The new military government again proved incapable of running the country. Debt soared, and inflation ran out of control. A wave of industrial unrest culminated in a general strike in 1977, which marked a turning point. A constituent assembly was elected, and its president, Haya de la Torre, lifted the last barrier to adult suffrage, giving 2 million illiterate adults the right to vote.

Peru returned to civilian rule in 1980, when President Belaúnde was elected to a second period in office. Ironically, this also marked the emergence of the Sendero Luminoso (Shining Path) guerrilla group, when its members burned ballot boxes in Ayacucho. The following decade was marked by the single-minded violence of this group and the state's response to it.

THE COVERED ONES

Friction between Peru's Spanish-born residents and its upper-class mestizos did more than spark the independence revolution. It gave Lima its most scandalous fashion.

Spanish women in 18th-century Lima enticed men in traditional fashion, showing off their tiny waists and wafting elaborate fans. Not to be outdone, the *mestizas* created an alluring look of their own by covering their faces with Arab veils – except for one eye which peeked out. They were known as the *tapadas* or "covered ones."

Although veiled, the *tapadas* were far from modest. Their skirts were hiked shamelessly up to show feet tinier than those of their Spanish rivals, and necklines were lowered, while the fairer-skinned Spaniards remained covered under Lima's strong sun, this being long before the European craze for finding a suntan attractive.

When the European women squeezed their middles even more, the thicker-waisted *mestizas* scrimped on the fabric encircling their ample hips. As a result, skirts in the 1700s became so tight that their wearers could take only the tiniest of steps. But one part of the costume remained constant throughout these changes: the veil hiding all but one eye, with which a great deal could be said.

The *tapadas* spent their afternoons strolling, and the "consequences" of their tantalizing fashion ranged from playful flirting to sinful trysts. Ironically, it was said that some of them even caught out their own husbands. So scandalous was the behavior the costume permitted that the archbishop attempted to condemn it, but the *tapadas* refused to serve their husbands, attend their families, or carry out church duties while the sanction was in effect.

Conspiracy was endemic in the early 19th century, and many *tapadas* used their afternoon walks to pass messages to organizers of the revolution, thus playing an important part in forming the nation. The site for this romantic and political intrigue was the Paseo de Aguas – a walkway of reflecting pools and gardens built for a woman who inspired one of South America's most famous romances.

By stealing a viceroy's heart, *mestiza* Micaela Villegas placed herself firmly in history and legend. Count Manuel Amat y Juniet built her Lima's finest house, bought her a gold and silver coach and, although in his sixties when they met, fathered her only child.

Villegas was known as "La Perrichola," Amat's mispronunciation of *perra chola*, literally "half-breed

The women who covered their faces were known as tapadas.

bitch," an epithet he threw at her during a heated argument. Despite the harshness of this name, Amat adored the actress, who had first caught his eye on a Lima stage. Their love inspired Jacques Offenbach's 1868 opera *La Périchole*.

But the Perrichola story has a sad ending. Inconsolable when her aged lover was ordered back to Spain (where, in his eighties, he married one of his nieces), La Perrichola vowed that she would never love again. She gave her considerable wealth to the poor, and entered a convent.

A Cristal beer factory now stands on the site of the opulent mansion, but the Paseo de Aguas survives in the Rímac district, behind the Presidential Palace and next to the Convento de los Descalzos, which boasts a collection of colonial paintings.

The police presence in Lima's Plaza Mayor.

DEMOCRACY, CRISES, AND RESURGENCE

Peru has become a democracy, the battle against
terrorism has been won, and inflation is under control,
but the rural–urban divide has still to be bridged.

Peruvian politics appeared to have turned full
circle when Fernando Belaúnde Terry was
elected president for a second time in 1980.
But he returned to a country that had changed
a great deal after 12 years of military regimes,
with a high level of popular frustration and the
beginnings of violent armed opposition aimed at
toppling an unfair state.

Belaúnde brought with him a free-market-
oriented economic team that hastily undid some
of the Velasco legacy (see page 66) by returning some state companies to private control, and
trying to increase competition and lower tariffs.
They also turned their back on the experiment
to kick-start a Peruvian industrial base, focus-
ing instead on capitalizing on the country's rich
natural resources.

External forces did much to disrupt their efforts.
From 1982 raw material export prices slumped,
while in 1983 a powerful El Niño current triggered
flooding and natural disasters that devastated
fishing and agriculture. Meanwhile, Belaúnde,
known for his high rhetoric, continued to build
roads into the jungle and colonize eastern Peru,
thus ensuring that public spending remained high.
The Latin American debt crisis also undercut the
economy, causing credit lines to dry up, leaving
Peru faced with the choice of defaulting or stran-
gling any hopes of economic advance.

As popular discontent grew, the Belaúnde
government became increasingly repressive,
responding to strikes and protest marches with
tear gas and riot police. The government badly
misjudged the Sendero Luminoso (Shining Path)
terrorists in the Andes, ignoring early signs of
activity, then allowing counterinsurgency forces
to use indiscriminate violence against the indigenous population.

Fernando Belaúnde Terry.

*Tens of thousands of people are thought to have
died in the "years of violence" under the Belaúnde
government. Most lived in the highland regions of
Ayacucho or neighboring provinces.*

HOPES DASHED

The first-ever Peruvian president from the
ranks of the mass Alianza Popular Revolucionaria Americana (APRA) Party, the youthful Alán
García, represented the country's hopes for
unity and economic relief. García retreated from
the previous government's ties with the IMF. In
July 1985 he dropped a bombshell on the foreign

In the last years of García's presidency inflation soared at around 40 percent a month, people's savings were wiped out, and food shortages ensued. Shock austerity measures left many with no option but the soup kitchens.

banks, announcing that Peru would limit its foreign debt payments to 10 percent of its export earnings, with the result that international

reputation as a man of the masses suffered as he appeared incapable of reining in the tactics of the military, who were determined to put down insurgency in the Andes. Thousands continued to be killed or "disappeared" by brutal attacks from rebels and the military. In Lima, the massacre of hundreds of rioting *senderistas* at two top-security prisons in July 1986 further undermined García's human rights record. There was a growing sense of anarchy as a third of the country came under emergency rule.

Alán García's first election victory.

Abimael Guzmán, leader of Sendero Luminoso.

bankers and lending agencies refused to offer any more credit to Peru.

The policy fanned domestic consumption and started a two-year spurt of growth. Yet this ran out of steam as foreign reserves tumbled and credit lines dried up. Inflation romped ahead and the value of wages slumped. The disastrous García administration ended its days amid allegations of widespread extortion and corruption.

JOCKEYING FOR POWER

García also failed to find a way of containing the threat from Sendero Luminoso and the smaller pro-Cuban Movimiento Revolucionario Tupac Amaru (MRTA), with the former moving its attention from the Andes to the capital. His

One of García's legacies was popular disgust with all traditional parties. That disillusion turned into a tidal wave of support for a former agricultural university rector, Alberto Fujimori, in the 1990 elections. At first, no one took any notice of the engineer of Japanese descent campaigning in shantytowns on the back of a tractor, but Fujimori began creeping up the opinion polls.

The front-runner, well-known novelist Mario Vargas Llosa, made the crucial mistake of accepting an alliance with the old rightist parties, including Belaúnde's AP (Popular Action Party), which sparked voters' concerns that he was a Trojan horse for the same old political elite. Rejecting the *blanquitos* (white elite), people turned to a candidate they related to more easily: Fujimori. The little-known candidate of the Cambio 90 Party romped to victory against Vargas Llosa. The novelist left shortly afterwards and took up Spanish nationality, further alienating himself from his home country.

THE RULE OF FUJIMORI

No one made a bigger impact on the Peru of the 1990s than Alberto Fujimori. He seized power with both hands and ruled with an instinctive sense of the popular mood, which he at first expertly manipulated. He began by breaking

leader, Abimael Guzmán, whose status was near-mythical, dealt a fatal blow to the rebel organization. Shown to the press in a huge circus-size cage, dressed in a striped prison suit, Guzmán was seen to be just an aging man. Although Sendero remained active for a while, the capture of Guzmán and other top members destroyed its organization.

Fujimori's autocratic style at first found an echo in a society that had been on the brink of chaos. Backed by army tanks, his decision in April 1992 to dissolve parliament and sack top judges met with majority support. He claimed

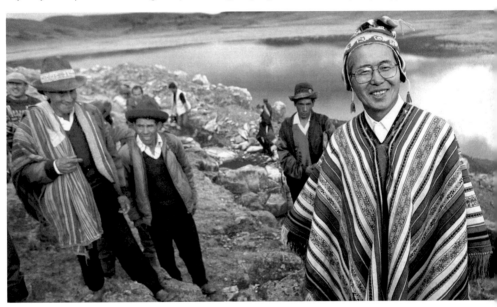

Alberto Fujimori with farmers in Ayacucho.

electoral promises and adopting the economic shock programs championed by the defeated Vargas Llosa. The economic measures he introduced began with price rises and currency devaluation, which hit Peruvians hard. He combined these with a radical program of privatization, cutting tariffs, and simplifying taxes.

The Fujimori administration set its sights on returning to the international financial community, in order to win IMF approval. Gradually the economy appeared to recover, but the sale of state enterprises led to thousands of job losses, and workers' wage rates declined in real terms.

The main achievement of Fujimori's first term (1990–5) was not an economic one. In September 1992, the capture of the Sendero Luminoso

⊘ WAR IN THE NORTH

In January 1995 an old wound reopened when Peruvian and Ecuadorean troops clashed in a disputed area of the remote rainforest frontier. Fighting upslope in dense jungle against well-defended and concealed Ecuadorean positions, Peru took heavier casualties, losing scores of soldiers. Exact losses have never been independently confirmed. Fujimori acquired some domestic prestige by standing firm, and the bitter fighting ended in an uneasy brokered ceasefire. But the seriousness of the conflict led both sides to modify their previously intransigent positions, and in 1998 a border treaty finally settled the 160-year dispute.

he needed to bypass a corrupt parliament and judiciary. Further radical measures followed, with the decision to try alleged terrorists in "faceless" military courts, where the judge's identity was kept secret, and the repentance law that encouraged rebels to turn themselves in and receive pardon or lower sentences if they denounced others. In practice, that measure led to hundreds of innocent people being jailed for years on the say-so of others.

Yet Fujimori weathered criticisms, and the election of a constituent assembly in 1993 persuaded the US government to lift a suspension on aid. The economy began to expand, and by 1993 Peru's growth rate was among the highest in the world.

LA CANTUTA MURDERS

The darker side of Fujimori's authoritarian regime was seen in the killings of La Cantuta. A death squad of intelligence agents murdered nine students and a professor from the university and buried their bodies in sand dunes outside Lima. Several agents were tried and sentenced, but the Amnesty Law, passed in 1995, gave immunity to

A demonstrator holds a photo of former Peruvian spy chief Vladimiro Montesinos at a protest in Lima in 2000.

⊘ THE DARK LORD

During the Fujimori years, Vladimiro Montesinos presided over the national intelligence services as the embodiment of unchecked power, menace, and corruption. No fiction could improve on his sinister, infinitely complicated résumé: ex-army officer, cashiered for forging his commanding officer's signature; a law degree earned while doing time in a military prison; onetime CIA agent; drug- and arms-trafficker, death-squad overseer – above all, master of political chicanery.

His debut in national politics was to cause to "disappear" the court files on a case charging presidential candidate Alberto Fujimori with fraudulent property deals. Thereafter, it seems, he also ensured the "disappearance"

of the records in Japan that would have proved Fujimori was born there, invalidating his constitutional right to be president of Peru. After Fujimori won the presidency in 1990, Montesinos acquired extraordinary power as the president's right-hand man, while amassing a huge illegal fortune. In hundreds of private meetings he cajoled and bribed public officials, legislators, journalists, judges, and generals. And secretly, he videotaped them all.

After Fujimori's rigged election for a third term in 2000, some of the "Vladivideos" were smuggled out and shown on national TV, unleashing an uncontrollable scandal. Montesinos was first to fall. He is now in a maximum-security prison which, ironically, he himself had built.

members of security forces who had taken part in human rights abuses since 1980, and freed those convicted of the killings.

By the end of his first term, Fujimori was credited with almost removing the twin evils of the 1980s: inflation and terrorism. In gratitude, Peruvians not only voted him back in with a 64 percent majority in 1995, but also gave his Cambio 90–Nueva Mayoría alliance a majority in Congress.

Fujimori's resounding victory in what independent observers termed a generally fair and free election meant he recovered international political legitimacy. Yet hopes that he would relegate army and intelligence services to less important roles proved unfounded. The unofficial head of the intelligence services, Vladimiro Montesinos, became increasingly powerful.

JOB SHORTAGES

Equally, the privatization program that the Fujimori government embarked on began to falter in his second term. Public discontent with the cost of privatized services like electricity seemed to have sparked indecision on the part of policy-makers. In 1998, with Peru in the third year of an IMF program, the fund's team was expressing praise for the meeting of macroeconomic goals, and growth in 1997 had been a healthy 7.4 percent.

Yet most Peruvians were perplexed that the figures were not reflected in an improvement in their standard of living. "If the economy is doing so well, why am I doing so badly?" was the front-cover headline of the weekly magazine *Caretas*, echoing the popular sentiment, with the main complaint being the shortage of properly paid jobs.

THE SIEGE

Fujimori's second term faced its greatest crisis at the end of 1996, when a group of masked and well-armed rebels of the Movimiento Revolucionario Tupac Amaru (MRTA) blasted their way into a reception at the Japanese ambassador's residence in Lima and took hundreds of guests hostage. Dignitaries of many nationalities were among the captives, and the 126-day hostage crisis put massive international pressure on Fujimori's government.

The siege came at a time when most Lima residents believed that terrorist attacks were a thing of the past. For the MRTA, an organization that grew out of far-left groups in the early 1980s, the siege was a last-ditch attempt to save

the movement, whose support had dwindled to around 100 armed rebels, and to push for the release of hundreds of members then in prison.

During the standoff that ensued through the hot Lima summer, groups of hostages were released from the besieged residence, until there remained a core group of 72, including Foreign Minister Francisco Tudela and Fujimori's brother, Pedro.

While the International Red Cross mediated, and talks to discuss the rebels' demands began, Fujimori took a gamble. Miners were drafted in to dig

Soldiers help hostages escape from the Japanese ambassador's residence in 1997.

a warren of tunnels under the residence, and on April 22, 1997, a commando unit blasted its way in and rescued the hostages. One hostage, two commandos, and all 14 rebels were killed – according to some reports, after they had surrendered. Fujimori claimed credit for the successful rescue operation, and his popularity ratings soared. But this could not halt popular discontent, especially when Fujimori pushed for a third term in office in the 2000 elections. When he was declared the victor over his closest rival, Alejandro Toledo, there were claims of widespread fraud, and thousands protested during his inauguration in Lima.

Even so, Fujimori might have held onto power had it not been for the "Vladivideos." The secretly

> *The Truth and Reconciliation Commission's report concluded that 69,000 people had died as a result of attacks by Sendero Luminoso and other extremist groups, the majority innocent peasants.*

filmed tapes incriminated both Montesinos and scores of public figures, and when they began to appear on television the scandal overwhelmed the Fujimori government.

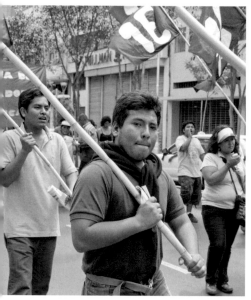

A May Day demonstration in Lima.

Fujimori and Montesinos fled the country. Fujimori went to Japan, country of his parents' birth, and faxed his resignation as president. The Peruvian Congress stripped him of his office for "moral incapacity." The former President was later sentenced to 25 years in prison for corruption and authorizing death squad killings.

After spending several months in hiding in Venezuela, Montesinos was caught and returned to Peru to stand trial. He has been convicted on corruption, abuse of power, and arms-trafficking charges, on top of the forced disappearance and murder of two students and a teacher in 1993. He is now serving multiple long-term sentences.

A caretaker government under the veteran politician Valentín Paniagua took over. It had three main tasks: to organize fresh elections, to guarantee continuity in economic affairs, and to investigate the corruption of the Fujimori regime and the human rights abuses committed in the struggle against the armed opposition groups since 1980.

TRUTH AND RECONCILIATION

In 2001, the government set up the Truth and Reconciliation Commission to look into the "years of violence" between 1980 and 2000, establish responsibilities, and also pave the way for reparations.

The Paniagua administration also established an independent electoral commission, which organized fresh presidential and congressional elections for April 2001.

Center-left economist Alejandro Toledo, the indigenous shoeshine boy who went on to graduate from Stanford and Harvard, took office soon after. Despite his reforms aimed at reducing poverty and restoring faith in the country's corrupt institutions, his presidency was marked by strikes and scandals. In the mountain town of Andahuaylas, an insurrection led by Antauro Humala, brother and ally of the ultra-nationalist politician Ollanta Humala, claimed five lives and rocked the government.

Nevertheless, in 2006 Toledo presided over orderly elections and handed over a buoyant economy to the new president, a resurgent Alán García.

UNANSWERED SOCIAL QUESTIONS

García struggled to fulfill pledges of improved government services, especially in health and education. He left intact most of Toledo's economic policies, including a free-trade agreement with the US. Blistering growth averaging more than 7 percent annually during his term helped lift many Peruvians into the middle class, bringing poverty down from 45 percent in 2006 to around 30 percent by 2011. Yet many who still fail to enjoy prosperity feel disgruntled. Poverty and social unrest persist in the Andes and Amazon.

Aside from the social problems, García again faced corruption allegations, and had to replace part of his cabinet in response to a bribery scandal at oil company Perupetro. The successors had to resign in the wake of the June 2009 violence in Bagua on the Upper Amazon, when dozens of people were killed in protests against mining and oil development.

Hoping for political resurgence, ex-president Fujimori forsook his comfortable Japanese exile and surfaced in Chile in a doomed bid for political resurrection. Extradited to Peru in 2007, he was sentenced to a lengthy stint in prison (his longest sentence is 25 years), in a proof of justice helpful for the maturing of the democratic state. He remains popular, however, among Lima's poor, who helped his daughter Keiko come close to winning the 2011 elections. The victory, however, fell to Humala, who shifted his platform to a more centrist position, and was careful not to rock the economic boat during his term.

Despite promises to diversify the economy, Humala pinned his hopes for sustained growth on mining, giving his consent to build several new copper mines. However, plans for a new gold mine, known as Conga, in the Cajamarca region had to be shelved following protests from local communities. 2013 saw country-wide protests and strikes as civil servants and university lecturers opposed new laws introducing annual performance assessments.

In view of failed attempts to tackle rising crime rates and social inequality, support for Humala swiftly started to evaporate, dwindling to 25 percent in early 2014. His reputation was also badly tarnished by the Óscar López Meneses affair. In 2012, this former political operative of Vladimiro Montesinos was given a four-year suspended prison sentence for corruption, illegal possession of arms and interception of telephone calls. A year later it was revealed that he had also been given round-the-clock police protection at his home. As a result, an interior minister, three police generals, and two colonels were forced to resign. Amid claims by the opposition that close associates of the president himself were involved in the scandal, a special congressional commission was set up to investigate the case.

Humala had greater success on the international scene, deepening co-operation within the Pacific Alliance – a new dynamic free trade bloc including Chile, Mexico, Colombia, and Peru. He also oversaw the end of a long border dispute with Chile. In January 2014, the International Court of Justice in The Hague awarded more than half of a disputed 38,000-sq-km (14,670-sq-mile) stretch of ocean to Peru while letting Chile retain the bulk of the valuable coastal fishing grounds within the area.

In 2016 Humala was succeeded by former World Bank economist Pedro Pablo Kuczynski, popularly known as PPK, who won a runoff election by a whisker, coming a mere 0.2 percent ahead of Fujimori's daughter – Keiko. PKK called for a "social revolution" to reduce inequalities among Peruvians, as well as between provinces and big cities. He also promised 24-hour access to potable water for all Peruvians by 2021 (as of 2017 around 4 million Peruvians still lack access to safe water).

However, water access is not the only problem haunting modern Peru – so are seasonal floods

President Pedro Pablo Kuczynski with Bolivia's Foreign Minister.

brought by the unpredictable El Niño phenomenon. In March 2017, record rains triggered massive floods and landslides that left 100 people dead, damaged more than 200,000 homes, and collapsed 260 bridges; almost 3,000 kilometers (1865 miles) of road were also damaged, while Lima's water supply was temporarily affected by the floods. President Kuczynski had to announce a state of emergency in about half of the country, and warned that the reconstruction process may cost up to US$9 billion.

Despite facing some serious and pressing challenges, Peru remains one of the world's most diverse, fascinating, and beautiful destinations.

A CHANGING SOCIETY

Almost 500 years of foreign settlement and interracial mixing have produced a complex blend of indigenous Peruvian, European, and African cultures.

Since pre-Columbian times, Peruvians have been divided by geography. There are three main geographical regions: the arid *costa* (coastal strip); the Andean Sierra or highlands; and, to the east of the mountains, the Amazon basin. Almost half of Peruvians live in the coastal region, some 10 million of them in the capital, Lima. It is a city of extremes, with the richest and most Europeanized Peruvians living not far from the poorest shantytowns, where mestizo migrants from the provinces have come in search of work or to escape the violence that has marked Peru in recent years.

From the arid deserts of the coast, the Andean Sierra rises up to more than 6,000 meters (19,700ft) above sea level. For the modern nation state, this mountain mass poses major problems for development and integration into a single society. The huge natural barrier severely limits the penetration of motorized transport and telecommunications, while frequent earthquakes and landslides further complicate the already arduous terrain. The result is dramatic regional diversity, and considerable inequalities in services and living standards. Health, education, and law-enforcement programs are unevenly distributed across Peru. About a third of the country has few conventional medical services: people rely on the *curanderos* and *shamans* – healers who use a variety of natural and spiritual remedies.

MANY WORLDS

Over the past 470 years or so, there has been a long process of inter-cultural mixing, creating the mestizo – a mixture of indigenous and European heritage. Today the majority of Peruvians fall into this category, and it is possible to become mestizo by choice as well as by birth. Anyone assuming Western dress in the rural

City life.

highlands is usually referred to as mestizo or sometimes *cholo*. Peruvian social divisions are culturally, as much as racially, defined.

There are two large ethno-linguistic groups in the Andes: the larger of the two speaks Quechua, the language of the Inca empire; the smaller group speaks Aymara and lives around Lake Titicaca and in neighboring Bolivia. The Quechua language is far from uniform, and someone speaking the dialect of Huancayo might not be fully understood by a Quechua-speaker from Cusco.

Beyond these broad distinctions, other complexities arise. There are "white" ethnic groups, like the Morochucos of Pampa Cangallo (Ayacucho) who have light-colored eyes and hair, speak

Quechua, and see themselves as *campesinos* (subsistence farmers). The *misti*, the dominant social class in the Andes, speak Quechua and share other cultural traits, but enjoy access to education and some of the luxuries of modern life. To the east, the Andes mountains fall away to the River Amazon system. The *selva alta* (higher slopes) were colonized by *campesinos* only in the second half of the 20th century. Some of the valleys here are where most of Peru's coca crops are grown. The lower foothills of the Andes gradually give way to the vast Amazon river system and its *selva baja* (low-lying jungle). It is here that more than 50 ethno-linguistic indigenous groups (some 5 percent of Peru's population) live, although their lands are increasingly being encroached upon by settlers.

Until the trade was banned in the 19th century, landowners brought in black Africans to serve as slaves on their haciendas and frequently used them to repress the local Indians. Black influence on the music and dance of Peru has been extensive and has also made an impact on the country's cuisine. Today, Afro-Peruvians are prominent in sport, but noticeably absent in political life, and still suffer discrimination.

The first Chinese indentured laborers were brought to Peru in the late 19th century and put to work in the notorious guano mines. The survivors settled on the mainland, where they helped build the railways, worked on cotton and sugar plantations, and set up small stores and restaurants. Japanese immigrants followed a similar trajectory in the 20th century, forming the backbone of the small-business class, and later producing a controversial president, Alberto Fujimori.

Lima has a strong Anglo community, while in the high jungle, around Oxapampa, there are descendants of German and Austrian immigrants, mainly coffee growers, who still retain firm links with their countries of origin.

THE URBAN-RURAL DIVIDE

Peruvian culture is sharply divided between indigenous and colonial societies, between the mountains and the city. There are elite white criollos, most of whom live in Lima, who trace their bloodlines back to the Spanish conquest of 1536. They are joined by incomers from Italy, Spain, and other European countries. A surprising number of politicians have Arabic surnames, as there was an influx of Palestinian refugees to Peru after 1948. The *criollos* and other "gringos" enjoy the cultural legacy of colonialism, and their eyes are firmly fixed on Europe and North America.

US brand culture, from designer trainers to Disneyland, has become an integral part of their children's upbringing, and shopping trips to Miami for clothes and consumer goodies are quite common. Most of these products can now be found in the mega shopping centers of Lima, but they still cost a lot more. A visitor

Women play an important role in rural communities.

☉ QUECHUA

It is thought that Quechua probably originated somewhere in the central highlands, later becoming the common language of Andean traders. When the Incas adopted it, Quechua acquired new power and status as the lingua franca of the empire. With an estimated 8 million speakers today, it has official language status and is the most widely spoken indigenous language of the Americas. Yet, despite this, Quechua is endangered. For those migrating from rural communities to the cities, Quechua becomes a social handicap, while millions of children nationwide receive Spanish education, and parents cease to teach them Quechua.

from Europe or the USA will feel a comfortable familiarity in Lima's cafés, department stores, and supermarkets.

> The highlands comprise a quarter of Peru's territory, but are home to half the population. Social anthropologist John Murra aptly described the Andes as an archipelago, a series of island-like pockets of isolated communities.

Rural communities now also aspire to ownership of televisions and jeans, but this comes into conflict with their traditional values. Heirs to awe-inspiring pre-Columbian cultures, the people of the Andes are maintaining the traditional practices of their ancestors in a rapidly changing world. Their livelihood continues to be based on family-owned fields, or *chacras*, which are farmed by hand or with the help of draft animals.

The social organization of communities in the Andes differs greatly from that of Europeanized *criollo* culture. Work, marriage, and landownership are centered on a complex extended family organization – called the *ayllu* in Quechua – which dates back at least to Inca times. One of the main functions of *ayllus* is to organize reciprocal work exchanges. These often take the form of group projects like roof raising or potato harvesting, which are usually made more festive and enjoyable by communal meals and plentiful supplies of *chicha* (homemade corn beer).

The Quechua- and Aymara-speaking peoples of Peru inhabit some 5,000 peasant communities located throughout the Andean Sierra. These communities are based on an agricultural economy, but families frequently supplement their incomes with labor-intensive cottage industries in which they produce the distinctive handicrafts found on the tourist trail, in addition to foodstuffs such as bread, cheese, and honey.

A large majority of highland people live a marginal and impoverished existence. Fiercely loyal to their ancestral heritage, the poor of the Andes are nonetheless eager to share in the benefits of a modern lifestyle, which include educational opportunities, electricity, sewage systems, and clean water.

GROWTH OF A MONSTER

Many Andean communities suffered greatly during the 20th century, and between the 1960s and the 1980s Lima seemed like a promised land to the rural poor. Thousands of migrants from as far afield as Ayaviri, Bambamarca, and Huaraz gradually filled the city with a huge Andean population. Added to endemic poverty in the highlands, there were various other reasons for the influx: President Velasco's agrarian reform in the early 1970s was unsuccessful, as the *campesinos* did not know how best to work the land

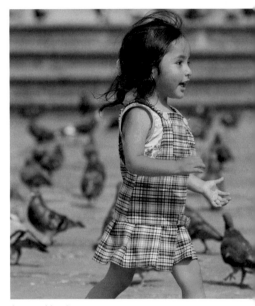

A young Limeña.

they were allotted, while in the 1980s and early 1990s Sendero Luminoso guerrillas terrorized the rural poor, the very people in whose interests they claimed to be fighting.

Urban authorities were unable to satisfy the basic needs of these migrants, and thus the multitude of *pueblos jóvenes*, or shantytowns, surrounding Lima came into being, as there simply was no place within the city for all these people to go.

With the end of rural violence, migration to the capital has slowed. But Lima still receives a huge proportion of Peru's resources and services, and has the greatest population mix of the entire country, with groups from the interior often concentrated in their own neighborhoods.

Many people in recent years have returned to their villages, with help from a state repopulation program. But when the state aid runs out, some trickle back to the cities before they can reap a harvest, and their children, used to a degree of urban living, find it difficult to settle in the inhospitable *puna*. It is unlikely that the trend to move to the cities will be reversed.

MIDDLE-CLASS PERU

The most difficult social area to define is that of the middle classes. Until the 1960s, it was the

but, as recent history has demonstrated, the middle class is vulnerable because it depends for its lifestyle on a disposable income.

IMPROVEMENTS IN EDUCATION

The latter half of the 20th century saw a dramatic rise in the number of people receiving an education. *Campesinos* and their recently migrated cousins in the cities sacrificed a great deal to get an education so that they could gain access to status and income. Schooling represents a great lifestyle change for rural people,

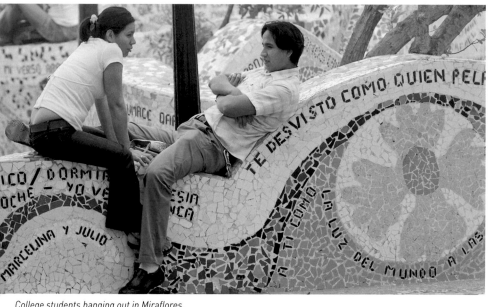
College students hanging out in Miraflores.

poor cousin of the oligarchy, providing clerks, merchants, and civil servants. Once modernization started in earnest in the 1970s, the middle class came into its own, both in Lima and in provincial cities. This was due to the diversification of the economy and to the expansion of the Peruvian state, both as a purveyor of public services and as an employer.

However, middle-class prosperity was short-lived, as these were the very same people who suffered most under García in the 1980s, when hyperinflation wiped out their savings and reduced the buying power of their salaries. Many professionals, teachers among them, were forced to eke out a hand-to-mouth existence. Their situation is somewhat better now,

as children traditionally work on the farms and tend the livestock.

It also represents a new expense, as the communities themselves often fund the schools. In the Río Tambo area dedicated young teachers are working in one-room schools in remote rainforest villages, largely funded by local communities. These added expenses, together with the loss of child labor on the farms, obviously complicate rural education programs. Although successive governments kept building of new schools a priority, about 10 percent of children in Peru still fail to complete basic education.

But progress is being made, and in many villages the sharpest students are sent to the cities to finish their schooling, as their parents

> *Thousands of poor Andean communities have built one-room schools with dirt floors, benches, and painted blackboards. The communities bore the cost of constructing the schools, and they also pay the wages of the teachers.*

realize that learning to read and write can lead to full citizenship.

HAPHAZARD DEVELOPMENT

Westerners often take for granted the progress achieved in the 20th century. In Peru, material progress has caused many problems in a poor, mainly rural society. It is only in the past 30 years that many remote regions have come into contact with the outside world, with new roads built, electrification, and the modernization of agriculture.

The state is still regarded with suspicion and fear by many rural Peruvians, who cling to their traditional social structures and practices. The idea of democratic rule is recent – it was only in the 1980 elections that some 2 million Peruvians who could not read or write were given the vote.

Even the Roman Catholic Church, a pillar of the old order, has changed tremendously in recent decades, with consequences for Peru's predominantly Catholic population. Since the late 1960s, there has been increasing tension between the conservative Catholic Church hierarchy and the so-called "liberation theologists" who argue that the Church must fight to reduce poverty and injustice in this world. They have encouraged Masses in Quechua, Aymara, and other languages, and helped lead social protest movements. But today the counter-revolution championed by leaders calling for the Church to focus on its spiritual message has been largely won, with archbishop Juan Luis Cipriani of Lima and many other Peruvian bishops now belonging to the ultra-conservative Opus Dei movement. In recent years there has also been a big increase in evangelical sects, particularly among the groups newly arrived in the cities from the country areas.

A WOMAN'S PLACE

The shake-up of Peruvian society that came with the terror of the Sendero Luminoso years

in the 1980s brought a sud... role of women. Although... Andean Peru women had righ... on a more equal footing tha... era, that standing had gradually been eroded in a society best described as *machista*, where women generally took traditional wife-and-mother roles. In many ways, the 1980s marked a shift. In the Andes, and later in the Amazon, the disruption of normal life by Sendero Luminoso attacks and migrations often left the women in charge of reorganizing life; some 78

Peru, a country of contrasts.

⊘ KEEPERS OF THE INCA FLAME

Q'eros, a remote, mountainous area of southeastern Peru, caused a minor stir in the 1950s when anthropologists discovered that its people maintained traditions and beliefs almost untainted by European influence. The Q'eros people claimed to be descendants of Incas who had fled from the Spanish invasion and thus preserved their way of life and customs. These people still cling to their remote homeland, marry among themselves, and maintain a powerful mystique. Their music and dress are distinct from other Quechua-speakers, and their traditional shamans are frequently called upon by both city dwellers and tourists to perform healing rituals.

...nt of migrant families had a woman head ...household at one point. In Lima shantytowns, where economic chaos left many impoverished, it was women who were the backbone of daily life, holding the family together with the *vaso de leche* (glass of milk) breakfast clubs and the ubiquitous *clubes de madres* (mothers' clubs). The community soup kitchens the women organized were vital to feed their families, and the work of organization brought forward many female community leaders at a time when other popular organizations like trade unions and local political parties were falling apart because of rebel and military threats.

Divorce is not uncommon, but can be hard to obtain. Many married men openly take lovers, and in this predominantly *machista* society this is accepted without much fuss. In many rural communities the attitude toward women is still extremely traditional: in societies like that of the Ashaninka in the central Amazon jungle, men still take two or more wives. Women do most of the work in the fields, while men restrict themselves to hunt-

Many religious customs are a fusion of ancient and Christian beliefs.

⊘ MOUNTAIN EXPORTS

Alarmed by the widening economic gulf between highlands and coast, the Peruvian government signed a free-trade treaty with the US in 2007 with the aim of encouraging the cultivation of non-traditional export crops such as blueberries and quinoa, a protein-rich grain hailed as "superfood" by Western lifestyle and culinary gurus. Peru is the largest global exporter of quinoa, banking nearly US$143 million in 2015 alone from its exports. There has been some debate in recent years over whether the Western desire for quinoa is threatening food security in the region or in fact improving Peruvian farmers' lives.

ing and fishing. Alán García's 2011 claim that illiteracy, which affects women much more than men, was eradicated has been met with widespread scepticism.

In urban Peru, women are starting to shake off the restrictions of the *machista* society, with students going to university now almost equally split between the genders, and women starting to have a presence in professional ranks as judges, academics, and bankers. In public life, women now occupy ministerial posts.

The wide-reaching family-planning program given priority by Fujimori in the early 1990s has meant a decline in births, with population growth now down to around 1.2 percent a year. That same program came in for some serious criticism, including allegations that many thousands of poor uneducated women were being sterilized without sufficient information or aftercare. Large numbers of them died as a result – an indication of the disregard for the wellbeing of rural peasant women. A lack of health services in many parts of Peru means that maternal mortality is still high, with 68 maternal deaths for every 100,000 births. Life in Peru still revolves largely around the family. For economic reasons young people usually live with their families until they marry, and many continue to do so afterwards.

A hotel worker; many Peruvians have more than one job to make ends meet.

LAW AND ORDER

Terrorism has been almost eradicated, apart from a few incidents in the remote Andes. Although there are reports of assaults and muggings in the larger cities, pickpocketing or bag-snatching is the most commonly encountered crime.

The power of the military was greatly diminished following revelations of its involvement in the corrupt Fujimori regime. The Toledo government subsequently made efforts to cut the military budget and began a reform of the police and the judicial system. However, bribery still occurs frequently.

As a sign of Peruvians' renewed confidence after the fear of the 1990s, there have been many street protests against government measures. Most of these have been quickly brought under control by the police, although there was terrible violence during demonstrations in the northern town of Bagua in 2009. Since 2011, more than 53 people have been killed in social conflicts in Peru, mostly related to the mining industry.

THE BLACK ECONOMY

One striking feature of contemporary society is the massive scale of the informal or underground economy, in which more than 50 percent of the nation's population are involved. However, the *ambulantes* (street vendors) who once crammed the streets of Lima have been swept away, and many of the vendors have now been reorganized in markets and given tax ID numbers.

The informal sector is epitomized by the so-called *combi* culture, a result of large-scale government lay-offs that led to an explosion of independent *combi* (minibus) and taxi drivers attempting to replace jobs lost in the state sector. Cars and *combis* would be bought with severance pay and launched into direct competition with existing transport services.

Such examples are common, and are not confined to the poorest sectors. As full-time jobs and careers have become scarce, more and more middle-class and professional Peruvians also work at two or three jobs in order to survive. Everyone is looking for a *chamba* – a way to stay afloat in an uncertain world.

⊘ BLACK MARKET INNOVATIONS

Now that most of the *ambulantes* have been moved off the streets of Lima, those remaining tend to be the more desperate and most needy people, wandering the city streets with bags of chewing gum, sunglasses, hairclips, or trinkets. Among the more inventive people working in the informal economy are those who set up stalls outside the prisons and hire out the long skirts and low-heeled shoes that female visitors are required to wear; and those who wait at traffic lights, not to clean your windshield as you might expect, but to waft a herb called *ruda* over your car, to bring you good luck in exchange for a small sum of money.

A woman leading her livestock.

DAILY LIFE IN THE ANDES

Traditional hospitality and hard work remain the norm in Andean villages, where the traditions of life – from marriage and community work to cooking and clothing – still defy globalization.

The route to most villages in the Peruvian Andes is a narrow, graded-earth road, baked concrete-solid under the fierce sun of the dry season, and awash with torrents of rain, slick with mud, narrowed or closed by rockslides, during the rains. The villages reached by these roads are mostly inhabited by Quechua-speaking descendants of groups once ruled by the Incas. These resilient people have adapted, whenever it was inevitable or advantageous, to the alien Spanish culture forced on them, creating a distinctive version of the ardent Catholicism of their conquerors, and incorporating introduced crops and livestock into their agrarian repertoire.

Spanish peasant costumes of the 16th century were adopted, and in derivative forms are still worn to this day. The fundamental outline of highland rural life today more resembles that of a medieval European village than the lifestyles of the Information Age.

Houses are typically made of adobe bricks or stone, with packed-earth floors and thatch roofs, and an occasional flash of corrugated steel indicating some source of cash income. The open rafters inside are blackened from years of cooking over an open hearth or clay oven in the corner.

Communities often consist of farmhouses scattered about the mountainside, whose center is a soccer field, and perhaps a schoolhouse and chapel. The landscape is stitched with precarious stone walls, built more for removing rocks from the soil than for setting boundaries.

Larger Andean villages often reveal a markedly different plan. These were the *reducciones*, forced settlements created by the Spanish in the 1570s, as they swept scattered communities into organized towns, the better to control, tax, and

Alpacas are bred throughout the highlands for their wool.

evangelize the native population. The orderly grid-pattern streets, with main squares fronting a church, town hall, and police station, are often crumbling and semi-abandoned, as many inhabitants have drifted back to their native communities.

HIGH-ALTITUDE LIVING

The essence of rural life is the ruling fact of altitude and the necessity of having access to lands from the high *puna*, where animals graze, through lower slopes where beans and potatoes are grown, on down to warmer valleys where maize and vegetables thrive, and often even lower, into the tropical regions of avocado, fruits, and coca. The need to control these different ecological zones has been a driving force in everything from inter-village rivalry to trans-Andean trade and the rise of empires.

Fundamental to traditional village life is the *ayllu* – the extended kinship group, of which there might be several in one village – and the social glue of *ayni*, a reciprocal work obligation whereby everyone gathers to help build someone's house, say. *Minka* (also written *minga* or *minca*) is community work such as cleaning irrigation channels, whereby everyone benefits.

In the midst of all this, some families have more or better land, and others are worse off.

Taking pigs to market.

Though actual wealth is rare, and most farming is for subsistence, the better-off can sell some of their livestock or produce in the markets and perhaps buy a battery-operated radio or CD player. Electrification has now reached many rural areas which barely had candles as late as the 1980s, along with clean water from communal taps and a growing variety of processed foods and factory-made goods.

As families increase, land often becomes too scarce to support the numbers living off it, and younger people migrate seasonally or permanently to the cities, in search of paid work. Urban life usually begins with the discarding of traditional clothes, the Quechua language, and Andean values. City life can be harsher than the highland village, and the typical migrant starts out selling candy on street corners.

AGRICULTURAL CYCLE

The highland agricultural cycle begins in August and September, when the Andean winter – a succession of warm, cloudless days and clear, frigid nights – begins to draw to a close. The crops are generally planted from low altitude to high altitude, and harvested in reverse order. Summer, the growing season, is also the rainy season. During these months the fields are hoed and weeded, and the earth of the fallow fields is turned in preparation for the coming year's crops, often under most unpleasant conditions such as rain, hail, and mud. The potatoes are harvested in May, after the rains.

When the potato harvest is over, the task of preparing part of the bounty for long-term storage begins. The *papas* are spread out on the ground and allowed to freeze during the winter night. Next day, as they thaw beneath the Andean sun, the farmers trample on them, squeezing out as much moisture as possible. This process is repeated until the potatoes are completely dry. The dark little nuggets, *chuño*, have an earthy flavor when cooked and can be stored for years.

Later the grains and beans are cut and allowed to dry for threshing, and lastly the maize is harvested. After the harvest has been threshed and stored, the community turns to the dry-season activities of weaving, pottery-making, building, and repairing the damage done by the rains.

⊘ THE CONTROVERSIAL LEAF

Long before 19th-century chemist Friedrich Gaedcke isolated the "active principle" in the coca leaf – cocaine – ancient Peruvians were chomping on wads of leaves, while busily creating sophisticated civilizations. Modern scientists have discovered beneficial substances, such as vitamins, in the leaf. They have also documented its ability to stabilize heart-rate and blood-sugar levels, and alleviate the symptoms of altitude sickness. Coca chewing persists in Andean society to this day, infusing village life with decorous exchanges of leaves. The leaves are also used in medicinal applications and as sacramental offerings.

From their ancestors, the Quechua have inherited tireless devotion to a ritual calendar bound to the annual cycle of life. Every village celebrates

The fermented corn beer called chicha plays a vital role in Andean life. It is both a mildly alcoholic social lubricant and a nutritious component of the daily diet. The beige-colored sour liquid is more like soup than beer in appearance.

the fields, continued under the roof of one set of parents, and has often produced at least one child. The formal wedding is often undertaken on the occasion when the couple is fulfilling an important religious *cargo*, when it is deemed auspicious to get married in church. Every family of some status – that is, with a broad circle of members as well as associates that can be called on for support – must ascend a hierarchy of *cargos* in a generation, thus establishing its prestige and authority in the community.

An Andean cemetery.

a series of Catholic saints' days, each of which seems to have absorbed some aspect of the old pre-Christian festivities. After the celebration of Mass come ritual drinking and feasting, and often the attendance of masked dancers in elaborate costumes with bands playing raucous music. Libations are preceded by careful "feeding" of the earth with ritual drops of liquor and, in a back room away from the eyes of the priests, village shamans make symbolic offerings to the earth and the mountain deities. The fiestas are organized by a rotating series of sponsors known as *carguyocs*, whose contribution denotes their status in the social organization of the village.

Marriage is seen as just one step in a long period of mutual relationship that began in

⊙ PAYING THE EARTH

The persistence of Andean religion is most evident in the ceremony known as *pago a la tierra*, or "payment to the earth." Every significant event in an Andean village is preceded by a ritual offering to Pacha Mama (Mother Earth), which is carried out by a trained specialist.

A package containing tiny wrappers of llama fat, sugar, candy, and dozens more items, is laid out in combination with multiple *k'intus* – clusters of three coca leaves, and huayruro seeds. These offerings are accompanied by prayers and invocations, then sprinkled with wine and alcohol, burned, and buried in a special place.

Matsés woman.

PEOPLES OF THE AMAZON

Over the centuries Amazon peoples have faced many threats to their way of life, from bounty hunters and missionaries to oil companies and globalization. Miraculously, however, "uncontacted" tribes still exist.

The indigenous peoples of the Amazon have long played a part in Peruvian history. According to Inca oral history, hordes of native Amazonians, known as Antis, were said to have climbed over the Andes and sacked the Inca capital of Cusco several times. The Inca fortress of Pisac is thought to have been an outpost protecting the capital from attack by jungle tribes to the east.

When the Incas and the Antis were not warring, trade was carried out between them, the former trading cloths, manufactured goods, and bronze axes in return for gold, feathers, tropical fruits, woods, animal skins, and medicinal plants.

> The Incas referred to the eastern quarter of their 4,500km (2,800 mile) long empire as Antisuyo, and to the tribes who inhabited its jungles as the Antis – from which the name Andes may derive.

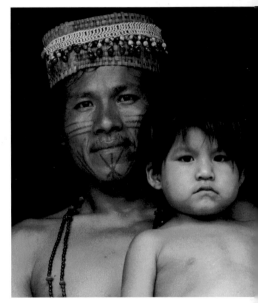

Jivaro father and son.

THE LURE OF GOLD

After the collapse of the Inca Empire, the Spaniards concentrated on mining wealth from the Andes and from coastal areas, and generally left the indigenous people alone. The few expeditions mounted into the jungle generally met with disaster. In some cases, such as among the Shuar people – called *jívaros*, or headhunters, by the Spanish in northern Peru – the Spaniards did establish towns and attempt to tax the Indians increasing quantities of gold. In 1599, however, the Shuar staged a massive revolt, burning and sacking the cities and slaughtering thousands. They then captured the Spanish governor, who was on a tax-collecting mission.

"They stripped him naked, tied his hands and feet and while some amused themselves with him, delivering a thousand castigations and jests, the others set up a large forge in the courtyard, where they melted the gold. When it was ready in the crucibles, they opened his mouth with a bone, saying that they wanted to see if for once he had enough gold. They poured it little by little, and then forced it down with another bone; and bursting his bowels with the torture, all raised a clamor and laughter," wrote one colonial chronicler.

Such victories were few for the indigenous peoples, however. As elsewhere, their greatest nemesis was not so much Spanish military force as the introduction of European diseases: their immune systems were totally unprepared for European pathogens. In the Inca Empire there are thought to have been about 7 million *indígenas* at the time of the Spanish conquest, but 50 years later there were fewer than 2 million. The same pattern was repeated in the jungle, beginning in the zone of greatest contact – the Amazon and its major tributaries – and gradually working its way into deeper parts of the forest.

Slave-raiding, started by Portuguese and mixed-blood Bandeirantes in the 16th century, gradually worked its way further into the Upper Amazon and Peru. Within 100 years of Francisco de Orellana's first descent, the "teeming Indians"

Asháninka women cooking food over an open fire.

⊘ FIRST CONTACT

The first of the conquistadors to get close to Peru's Amazonian tribes was Francisco de Orellana, who was part of Gonzalo Pizarro's expedition that left Quito in 1540 in search of El Dorado. He later recalled: "We saw coming up the river a great many canoes, all equipped for fighting, gaily colored, and the men with their shields on, which are made out of the shell-like skins of lizards and the hides of manatees and of tapirs... they were coming on with a great yell, playing on many drums and wooden trumpets, threatening us as if they were going to devour us." Orellana survived and even learned enough words to talk to the native Amazonians.

who had once thronged the Amazon's banks were nowhere to be seen. Tribes that hadn't been captured or wiped out by disease simply retreated further upstream into the interior of the jungle.

The biggest incursion into Peru's Amazon, however, didn't occur until the rubber boom in the late 19th century. Almost overnight, the most isolated jungle rivers and streams were overrun by rubber tappers who carried the latest Winchester carbines (rifles). Rubber trees were few and far between – hence rubber-tapping demanded intensive labor. Entire villages were sacked to capture indigenous people as slaves. In the case of especially hostile tribes, *correrías*, or armed raids, were carried out, in which villages were surrounded and their inhabitants slaughtered by the employees of the great rubber barons. Whole areas of the Amazon were thus wiped clear of native populations in a matter of decades. But in 1912 the rubber market began to collapse and, almost overnight, the rubber tappers withdrew. The remaining tribes were left alone except for occasional visits by missionaries.

THE BULLDOZERS ARRIVE

In the 1960s, Peru's government became concerned about the numbers of peasants moving from the Sierra to the coastal cities, yet was unwilling to enact the land reforms which might have kept them in their villages. It preferred to encourage these people to move into the vast, unsettled Amazon that makes up two-thirds of the country to help control the frontier. A north–south highway was partially bulldozed through the jungle to encourage settlement, and soon impoverished Peruvians began to pour in. New communities, some of them organized by religious sects anxious to make new converts, were established.

The systematic extraction of hardwood trees – mahogany, cedar, and caoba – repeated the pattern of the rubber boom, as day laborers bankrolled by wealthy patrons moved into the virgin forest looking for quickly extractable wealth. Gradually, one by one, isolated tribes were contacted by missionaries, woodworkers, or oil-drillers. At the start of the 20th century there were perhaps 40 uncontacted tribes in the Peruvian Amazon, and there are now estimated to be 15 such tribes left, two on the northern border with Ecuador, and the remainder in the southeastern rainforest. Today most of Peru's

200,000 native Amazon peoples exist in varying stages of acculturation.

INDIGENOUS CULTURES

In the 16th century there was considerable discussion in Europe as to whether the native peoples of the New World were "the sons of Adam and Eve," and hence deserving of the rights of real human beings. Finally, in 1512 a Papal Bull decreed that Amazonian Indians did, indeed, possess souls.

Alexander von Humboldt (1769–1859) was the most famous of the early scientists to make exploratory trips into the Amazon; and eventually anthropologists began living among different tribes and recording a bewildering variety of cultures.

The Amazon jungle is characterized as having extremely poor soils, and game animals which, while diverse, are few and far between. As a result, Amazon villages on the terra firma – the immense areas of land between the large rivers – are typically tiny (25 to 100 people), mobile, and widely spaced due to the jungle's low bioproductivity and the rapid exhaustion of the soil. In addition, these tribes almost universally practiced contraception techniques or infanticide in order to keep their populations down. The Shuar penchant for head-shrinking was simply a variation on warfare patterns widely practiced throughout the Amazon.

But tribes on the *varzea* – the more limited floodplain areas where the soil is renewed annually – did not fight among themselves, and instead had permanent villages running into thousands of inhabitants. Although battles were sometimes fought with the terra firma tribes in order to take slaves for work in *varzea* fields, population control did not exist. The necessity for carefully monitoring seasonal planting patterns and river fluctuations gave rise to an infrastructure which eventually came to include complex systems of rules and food storage. And although the *varzea* tribes were the first to be hit by European contact and disease, Orellana's men, back in the mid-16th century, reported many living in towns with temples and roads leading off into the interior.

As a result of their similar habitats, the Amazon tribes had other features in common. Almost invariably, they viewed their forest and the animals in it as sacred and imbued with spirits. Most Peruvian tribes took hallucinogenic

drugs such as *ayahuasca (Banisteriopsis caapi)*, the "vine of death" or "vine of the spirits," which allowed them to see and interact with the powerful spiritual world. The forest was their provider, their mother, and not to be abused.

Even today, most scientists concede that no one understands the jungle better than the remaining tribes. For thousands of years they have lived there harmoniously, and while they do not possess our own far more powerful technology, they have a unique understanding of, and reverence for, this most complex habitat on earth.

Yanomani people partake of a traditional drink made from manioc.

> *Different indigenous groups have gradually realized that only if they put aside historical enmities and organize themselves can their rights be defended or secured.*

A PEOPLE LEFT IN LIMBO

Currently there are some 200,000 indigenous people in the Peruvian Amazon, who are divided into 53 different ethnic groups, speaking languages from 12 different linguistic families. Some groups, such as the Toyeri in southeastern Peru, were said to number several thousand at the turn of the 20th century but are composed of only a couple of individuals today. Others, such as the Machiguenga and Campa, living in the jungles north and east of Machu Picchu, number tens of thousands.

Unlike Brazil, which has a governmental entity (FUNAI) to regulate indigenous affairs, Amazonian tribes in Peru have little governmental support. Legislation allowing indigenous communities to possess land was finally passed only in 1974. In the last two decades over 30 native organizations have sprung up to defend their rights. Some progress has been made in recent years, however. In 2015,

Traditional Yagua ceremony.

the first autonomous indigenous government was created in the Santiago River basin. The Wampis government now controls more than 1.3 million hectares of Amazonian rainforest.

Despite increasing organization, Peru's Amazon peoples continue to exist in a social and legal limbo. At best they are seen as a hindrance to a government whose goal is to "develop" the Amazon. The native peoples' limited territorial rights have not been helped by the government's threat to sell off state land that it considers "uncultivated." As a result, over two thirds of the Peruvian Amazon is divided up into oil and gas concessions. Indigenous groups have been encouraged to reject their own culture and become, in effect, rootless Peruvian citizens. Because of the Peruvian

government's lack of interest in its people's history, foreign missionary groups have taken on the job of contacting and integrating Peru's Amazonian tribes into the national culture.

A US Protestant missionary group, the Summer Institute of Linguistics (SIL), has worked with dozens of tribes over the past 50 years, giving their languages a written form into which they hope to translate the Bible. Although SIL has nursed a number of tribes through contact-induced epidemics, it has been widely criticized for contributing to the destruction of cultural identities, and it now has a much lower profile.

Some cultures seem to withstand or assimilate acculturation better than others. The Shipibo people living along the River Ucayali have, despite long historical contact, maintained much of their traditional culture. They operate their own cooperative store (Maroti Shobo), where they sell and export their exceptionally high-quality weavings and pottery, decorated with striking geometric designs, using traditional materials and methods. The Asháninka ethnic group living east of Cusco suffered brutally in the war with Sendero Luminoso and the MRTA, but succeeded in having the Parque Nacional Otishi established to help protect their way of life. Other tribes, however, have less resistance to change and have lost their cultures within a very few generations.

CONTEMPORARY PROBLEMS

The greatest new pressure on indigenous groups comes from oil and gas exploration and mining. Reserves in the northern jungles, which have been exploited for over three decades, are declining, and the Peruvian government has begun auctioning off new prospecting blocks along the eastern flanks of the Andes, including the Upper Amazon basin.

In Madre de Dios during the 1990s, a consortium headed by Mobil Oil attracted strong international criticism for entering the remote Las Piedras region, home to uncontacted native groups.

At that time Mobil also explored the Candamo Valley, one of the most biodiverse areas known on earth, finding significant, but at that time uneconomic, natural gas deposits. Mobil abandoned the concession, and the area was incorporated into the new Bahuaja-Sonene National Park. In 2007 the government attempted to remove this vital section from the park and lease it for drilling. National and international protests forestalled the initiative, but uncontrolled influx of miners has devastated formerly pristine areas of the Tambopata area.

To the west of the Parque Nacional del Manu, where uncontacted Machiguenga and Yaminahua groups live, lies the enormous Camisea natural gas deposit. The pipelines that run to Lima and Paracas on the Peruvian coast have been plagued by accidents since the gas began to be exploited in 2004, and the gas (LNG) is being exported by sea to countries including Mexico and Spain.

potential. Due to one of their discoveries, huge quantities of *uña de gato* (cat's claw), known to alleviate some symptoms of cancer and Aids, have been harvested in an uncontrolled manner and sold to outsiders.

On a more positive note, the land-titling program for indigenous communities proceeds apace, especially in central and northern Peru, with several million hectares titled in recent years. Change is inevitable, but it must be handled carefully, and in partnership with the indigenous peoples so as to protect their culture.

Commercial logging poses a grave threat to the Peruvian Amazon and its people.

In the north the Achuar, closely related to the Shuar, have maintained their reputation as fiercely independent and refused to allow oil workers into their territory. Despite government threats and new laws stating that indigenous lands no longer belong to them by right, the impasse remains.

One notable success for local people was the exclusion of oil companies from the Pacaya-Samiria protected area. Native representative groups are having to learn fast how to deal with multinationals and persuade them to respect their lands and offer fair compensation.

Biological prospecting is another threat: several large pharmaceutical companies have visited the region to assess its biological

⊘ NO CONTACT

According to Survival International, there are an estimated 15 uncontacted indigenous groups in remote regions of the Peruvian Amazon. They are so rarely seen that the government agency overseeing petroleum resources has suggested that they were invented by conservationists to block oil exploration. However, in 2007 members of one such group were spotted and photographed from an aircraft in the Río de las Piedras region, while another group was "discovered" in 2015. Contact with outsiders is potentially fatal for these people with no immunity to contagious diseases. And, although legally protected, their homelands are threatened by illegal loggers and oil and gas exploration.

Handicrafts stall in the Colca Valley.

HOW CRAFTS HAVE ADAPTED

Many of Peru's crafts have pre-Columbian origins, yet have incorporated new designs and contemporary motifs.

Long before the Incas, Peru was a land of craftspeople. Fine weaving found in the funeral bundles at Paracas, gold pieces worked by the Chimú people in northern Peru, and startlingly realistic Moche ceramics pay testimony to a people for whom work done with the hands was always important. In the Inca Empire, specially chosen women dedicated their lives to such tasks as weaving delicate capes from the feathers of exotic birds. Metallurgy was also a high-status occupation long before the Spaniards arrived in the New World.

Artisan stores in Lima stock a variety of handmade items of the highest quality, from every geographical region of Peru. Arrangements can be made for shipping, and prices are quite attractive.

Alpaca woman hand-weaving alpaca fiber.

Fortunately, these artistic traditions were not obliterated by the European conquest, and today there are few places in Peru where handicrafts – some little changed from those of centuries ago, others modified for the tourist market – cannot be found.

ANCIENT ARTIFACTS

Handicrafts played multiple roles in indigenous cultures that had no written language. Moche ceremonial cups were not simply for drinking: they told stories – depicting everything from festivities to daily events. Through these finely detailed ceramics archeologists have identified diseases afflicting the Moche people, discovered that pre-Columbian

societies punished thieves by amputating their hands (then fitted the reformed criminals with prosthetic limbs), and determined that they practiced rudimentary birth control. Likewise, the patterns on clothes woven in the highlands have unraveled some of the secrets of how the Aymara people lived.

The designs used in some clothes depicted the status of the wearer; other garments were used only for special celebrations, and still others had woven into them motifs that were important to the community. (Nowadays the designs include airplanes and other modern inventions.) After the Spanish conquest, handicrafts began to fuse the old and new ways, as Indian woodcarvers whittled statues of the

Virgin Mary dressed like a *campesina*, or angels with Indian faces.

Some handicrafts are found all over the country, but in different colors and designs, such as the popular wall-hangings displayed in outdoor markets. Other items come from only one community or region. The decorative gilt-edged mirrors sold in Peru generally originate in Cajamarca; authentic ceramic Pucara bulls are crafted in Pupuja, near Puno; real Yagua jewelry comes only from the jungle area near Iquitos; but fine handiwork

leather furniture, grace the store windows. This is also the best place to buy indigenous paintings, jewelry, and traditional gold and silver items.

GOLD AND SILVER

Chile has its lapis lazuli and Colombia its emeralds, but the item most associated with Peru is gold, with silver and copper running close seconds. The 16th-century chronicles of Garcilaso de la Vega tell of the Europeans' first glimpse into the courtyard of Qoricancha, the Temple

An intricately embroidered hat.

Making cotton thread in the traditional way.

from all over the country can be picked up in Lima. Some of the goods on sale, such as the Christmas tree ornaments and *arpilleras* – embroidered and appliquéd scenes – are produced by women's cooperatives in Lima's shantytowns. Visitors can find gold- and silver-rimmed goblets, carved leather bags, woolen goods of all kinds, jungle blowpipes, ceramics carrying both modern and antique designs, and a wealth of jewelry. Bargaining is traditional here, and prices may be comparable with those in Cusco or the jungle.

Lima's Miraflores neighborhood is full of handicraft boutiques. Hand-knitted llama- and alpaca-wool sweaters and ponchos in modern styles, as well as carved wood and

of the Sun, in Cusco. Before them was a life-size scene in blindingly brilliant gold, perfect in detail down to the tiniest butterfly. Worked in gold were llamas, corn stalks, flowers, and birds. What remains in the Lima museums and the Museo Brüning in Lambayeque is but a fraction of the treasure that once existed. Today, gold and silver items, ranging from silver-rimmed crystal glasses to fruit bowls and candelabras, are available from a large number of boutiques in Lima.

The Spanish conquerors also found skilled craftsmen working gold and silver into finely turned jewelry and adornments. This tradition has not been lost, as evidenced by the intricate gold filigree produced in Catacaos outside Piura in the northern desert. These complicated pieces, which try an artist's patience and imagination, dangle from the ears of the townswomen, who claim that gold shines even brighter under the desert sun. These are the big, drooping earrings that women dancing the *marinera* wear. In San Jerónimo, near Huancayo in the central highlands, silver filigree is tooled into peacocks, fighting cocks, and doves.

Jewelry made from out-of-circulation coins is sold in the Plaza San Martín in Lima and around the Plaza de Armas in Cusco. Popular items are earrings, necklaces, and bracelets made from leather, and *sol* coins bearing the image of a llama. Informal jewelry makers also sell jewelry made from chrysocolla (Andean turquoise) and hand-painted ceramic. But Peru's best-quality hand-painted ceramic jewelry is designed by the Association of Artisans of Virgen del Carmen in Pisac, about an hour outside Cusco.

WOVEN TALES

Although much of today's *artesanía* is more practical than illustrative and is geared toward tourists, some items still tell stories. Delicately woven belts sold in the Sunday market at Huancayo carry designs of trains, a tribute to the metal monster that connected that isolated highland city to the rest of the country. The wide belts are worn both for decoration and for support by the women who trudge the highlands with their children on their backs. Colors in the textiles and knitted goods on Taquile, the distinctive weavers' island in Lake Titicaca, can indicate the wearer's marital status or community standing. Some colors are used only on certain holidays.

Everywhere you go on Taquile Island you will see men knitting the distinctive woolen hats which they habitually wear. Legend has it that the rainbow Kuyichi, angered by the Taquile people, took away their color and left them in a world of grays and browns, but the people used their fingers to weave color back into their lives.

Taquile goods can be purchased from the cooperative on the island. Knitted items are available from a number of shops in Cusco, and some of the best bargains (although the quality is hit and miss) come from the women selling their wares in the bazaars in the streets off the main square of that city. Be wary of assurances as to whether the item is made of wool from sheep, llama, or alpaca (usually, they say it is baby alpaca, which local guides cynically refer to as "maybe alpaca"). Stop at some of the upmarket shops and feel the difference between wools from the three animals before starting your shopping.

Woolen cloth that is purported to be antique usually is not, as the damp highland climate

Handmade straw bags.

⊘ FORBIDDEN GOODS

Beware of unscrupulous merchants selling antiques from grave sites, as these are almost certainly fakes; it is illegal to buy or take pre-Columbian antiques out of the country in any case. The same goes for goods made from vicuña. If the item really does contain vicuña fibers, which is unlikely, it may have been made in violation of international law. As for reproductions of colonial and pre-colonial art, make sure you buy them from a reputable dealer and insist on documentation from Peru's National Institute of Culture (INC). Don't even consider buying souvenirs made from the feathers, skins, or shells of rainforest creatures.

does not allow wool to last indefinitely. Many weavers now use dark colors and ancient designs to give the impression that the textile has been around for centuries, but such cloth is no more antique than are the rustic-looking dolls that some unscrupulous sellers claim have come from ancient graves.

Knitted and woven goods are definitely the purchases most popular with visitors. Highland markets – including the big Sunday market in Pisac outside Cusco – abound with alpaca sweaters, llama rugs, small woolen

Decorative hair clip.

bags called *chuspas* that are used to carry coca for chewing, blankets, and cotton cloth. In Cajamarca, women in layered skirts called *polleras* walk down the streets with drop spindles dangling from their fingers.

The quality of woven items ranges from those made with crude wools still embedded with flecks of thistle to the fine yarns and modern designs found in Lima's boutiques. Brilliant dyes made from seeds, herbs, and vegetables are often used to produce the typical vivid colors. Cloth may come from the Andean highlands, particularly Cusco, Puno, and Cajamarca, or from the jungle where the Conibo and Shipibo peoples weave cotton with designs incorporating serpents and Christian crosses.

Crafts from the Amazon region can be obtained in the Lima suburb of Miraflores at the Antisuyo store.

BASKETWARE

From frigid Puno to the hot desert near Chiclayo, Peru is proud of its basket weavers. On Lake Titicaca, *totora* reed baskets and miniature boat souvenirs are produced by the indigenous people, who live in reed huts on reed islands. In the port of Huanchaco, on Peru's northern coast, the fishing boats themselves are woven from reed; tourists can purchase miniature versions. This coastal region is also known for its finely woven straw hats, similar to panamas, and known as *jipijapas*. These mostly Ecuadorian hats, and white cotton ponchos, make up the traditional dress of the northern cowboys, or *chalanes*.

RELIGIOUS SCENES

A very different kind of handicraft are the colorful *retablos*, originally made in Ayacucho, which derive from the small portable shrines brought to Peru by the conquistadors. Usually smaller nowadays, and tucked into decorated wooden boxes or the hollow of a reed, these depict busy scenes that may be solemn or comical in mood, depending on the artist's inclination. The subject matter used always to be religious, and often still is – Nativity scenes are the most common – but even the scenes showing religious processions may be turned into rollicking fiestas, overflowing with figures made of wood, plaster, papier mâché, or clay, which may include a snoozing drunk, disruptive children, and wayward animals, or even artisans making hats or weaving cloth.

Superb *retablos* fashioned of hollow gourds are still a specialty in Ayacucho, as well as the traditional wooden ones, some tiny, some as much as 1 meter (3ft) high. Wooden *retablos* may be found in most outdoor markets, but the most delicate ones – carved from the white and gray Huamanga stone some call Peru's marble – are found only in boutiques and cooperatives such as Artesanías del Perú. Actually a type of soapstone, Huamanga is carved into anything from matchbook-sized Nativity scenes to oversized chess sets – with figures of Incas and llamas replacing kings and knights. Incidentally, much of what appears to be marble in Peru's churches is actually Huamanga stone.

POTTERY CULTURE

As far back as 1500 BC, the ancient civilizations of Peru produced fine pottery in many different styles.

The first major center of pottery production was the Chavín culture in the central Andean region from around 1000 to 300 BC. The pots they produced are often in the shape of images of the jaguar god and other mythical animals. Others show that the Chavín potters were masters in the use of subtle colors, producing geometric patterns in reds and browns. It was this group which had already begun to make the typical "stirrup-spout" pottery, where handles from twin vessels rise to form a central spout.

From a similar period on the south coast come the wares produced by the Paracas culture. Here geometric designs predominate, and the colors used, including blue, green yellow and white, are much more vivid, with patterns made from incisions into the fired clay. Other pots show a wide range of fruits, vegetables, and plants of use to humans, suggesting they were symbolic food for the dead.

But the most astounding Peruvian pottery comes from the Moche people, who thrived on the northern coast from AD 100 to 700. Moche pottery is extraordinarily realistic, especially in the pots known as "portrait-head effigies," which display individual characteristics, emotions, and even diseases, as well as scenes from their mythology.

The most popular Moche pottery takes realism to even greater lengths in its *huacos eróticos* (erotic vessels) showing every permutation of the sexual act. The Museo Larco in Lima has a particularly good collection (see page 157). So realistic are these pots that they are also used by anthropologists to study the sexual behavior of the ancient Peruvians, and they are thought to be ceremonial rather than pornographic in intent. The Moche were also the first group in Peru to mass-produce their pottery thanks to the use of molds. Moche potters used a special molding technique to make stirrup spout bottles, handle bottles, whistling bottles, jars, and many other forms.

A very different style of pottery was produced to the south by the Nazca people. They were master potters, producing highly colored vessels with stylized geometric forms. Farther inland, the harsh mountain conditions often meant that pottery traditions were not so developed. But the Huari people near Lake Titicaca produced some pots with remarkably realistic portraits and highly skilled ceremonial ware.

The Chimú people (AD 1000–1470) learned the secret of making black pottery by reducing the oxygen during firing. These were often burnished before firing to give them a characteristic silver

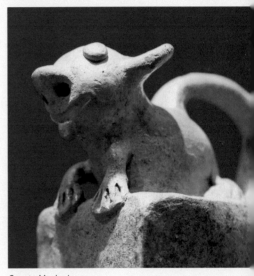

Ornate Moche jug.

sheen. Entirely abstract and strikingly modern are the black-and-white ceramics currently being produced in northern Peru's Piura, available now in many handicraft markets in Lima.

Inca pottery was minimally sculpted and tended to employ repetitive geometric patterns with few naturalistic motifs. As with many things in their empire, utility was the most important factor, so their most typical pottery is the large water containers or *aryballos* that could be strapped onto people's backs. The arrival of the Spaniards meant that much of this pottery was smashed, particularly anything considered idolatrous, and the old traditions and culture were lost. But for the tourist, some of the colonial wares are also very beautiful pieces, to be appreciated in their own right.

Dancers at the Virgin de la Candelaria festival in Puno.

MUSIC AND DANCE

The harps and pipes of the Andes are joined in a musical melting pot by African rhythms on the coast and salsa in the cities.

Whether we are aware of it or not, many of us became acquainted with Andean music through the late 1960s recording called *El Cóndor Pasa*, released by Paul Simon and Art Garfunkel, accompanied by a group called Los Incas. Its English lyrics were new, but the melody, with its haunting native tonalities, was written in 1913 by the Peruvian folk composer Daniel Alomías Robles. Los Incas, who later called themselves Urubamba, were in the vanguard of a movement to preserve the indigenous music of the Andes, to present it proudly to the world beyond the borders of its native countries. Now this music is played by *conjuntos folklóricos* in settings – dimly lit restaurants and European theaters – which would be inconceivable to the indigenous peoples for whom it is simply a part of daily life.

The music can also be heard on the street corners, played by native musicians who depend on their talents – sometimes extraordinary – and other people's appreciation of them to gain a meager living. It can also be heard, far from the nightlife of the cities, in villages, where a less well-rehearsed group of musicians may accompany the private celebration of a wedding or a public dance performance during a festival, or where a lone shepherd might play a melancholy song to keep himself company on the mountainside.

ANCIENT TRADITION

The instruments, the forms of the songs, and the lyrics have constituted a linked tradition of oral poetry in a culture that until recently had no written language. Its roots lie deep in Peru's pre-Columbian history. In the ruins and ancient graveyards on the Peruvian coast you can still find small broken clay panpipes and whistle-like flutes which produce pentatonic or diatonic

A marching band in Trujillo.

☉ SORROWFUL LAMENT

The 16th-century chronicler Felipe Huamán Poma de Ayala offered the words of a song which he called a *huanca*: "You were a lie and an illusion, like everything which is reflected in the waters... Perhaps, if God approves, we shall one day meet and be together for ever. Remembering your smiling eyes, I feel faint; remembering your playful eyes, I am near death...". Huamán Poma's example of the *yaravi* genre which merges Incan and Spanish musical tradition reveals the same universal themes of love, loss, and loneliness. The term *yaravi* (or *haravi*) comes from Quechua and means "poem," usually a sad one.

scales, and sometimes other exotic scales that defy Western musical notation. They have been tossed aside by *huaqueros* (grave robbers) in search of the fine textiles and pottery buried in the tombs. The Incas inherited an astonishing variety of wind instruments, including flutes and panpipes of all types and sizes. Inca musicians also played conch-shell trumpets, and drums made from the skin of the Andean puma.

Quenas are notched end-blown flutes with a fingering style similar to that of a recorder. *Quenas* were often made of llama bone, but are now

of a quick, smooth-flowing melody, never missing a beat.

HISPANIC INFLUENCE

To this ensemble the Spanish introduced strings, which native musicians readily adopted, inventing new, uniquely Andean instruments such as the *charango* (a small mandolin, scarcely the size of a violin, the body made from the shell of an armadillo), and the Andean harp with its great, boat-like, half-conical sounding-box. The instruments melded together perfectly; an ensemble

Drummers at a festival in Puno.

usually carved of wood. They produce a pentatonic scale which, to ears trained to a Western musical tradition, has a distinctly melancholy tone to it. *Quenas* vary in size and pitch, so that each has its own reedy voice.

The panpipes, called *antaras* or *zampoñas*, also vary in size, and there may be one set of four or five pipes, or three or four joined sets of eight or ten pipes, each of a different octave, to be played by a single musician with astonishing dexterity. *Antaras* or *zampoñas* are played by blowing across the end of the pipes, a technique which gives a breathy sound which may be as high-pitched as a bird call or almost as deep as a bassoon. They are often played in complex duets, with musicians alternating single notes

> *Music accompanies most aspects of life in the Peruvian highlands, from mundane activities to solemn rituals and jubilant celebrations. Quechua people say that all new clothing is "for dancing."*

of *quenas* and *zampoñas* weaves a rich tapestry of windy pentatonic harmony, and into this fabric are woven, like golden threads, the bright, quick sound of the *charango* – which may be strummed or plucked – and the voice of the harp.

The Andean harp has 36 strings spanning five octaves of the diatonic scale, though it is usually played in a pentatonic mode. Its deep sounding-box gives it a full, rich sound and a powerful bass voice, so that a bass line is usually played by the left hand while a melody or harmony is plucked by the right. Percussion is provided by a simple, deep-voiced frame drum – a *tambor* or a *bombo* – played with a stick with a soft, hide-covered head, or by an even simpler instrument called the *caja*, which, as its name implies, is a wooden box with a sound hole for reverberation, upon which the player sits to thump out a rhythm with the hands.

These, essentially, are the instruments which are played today – joined occasionally by a violin or accordion – though the drums now are more likely to be covered with goat than puma skin, and the eerie, wind-like call of the conch-shell trumpet may be heard only in the most traditional highland villages. There is also an element of improvisation – the composition of a village group may depend on who is available at the time.

The effect is magical, utterly characteristic of the Andes, evocative of high, windy passes, of the breeze blowing through the reeds of Lake Titicaca, of the dwarfing immensity of the mountains on a clear, bright winter day.

The indigenous chronicler Felipe Huamán Poma de Ayala, in his massive descriptive history of life under both Inca and Spanish rule (*Nueva Crónica y Buen Gobierno*, written between 1576 and 1615), listed the names of a number of song forms, which are the ancestors of contemporary Andean music: the *yaravi*, the *taqui*, the *llamaya*, the *pachaca harahuayo*, the *aimarana*, the *huanca*, the *cachiva*, and the *huauco*.

Many of these he attributed to particular characters or activities – a shepherd's song (the *llamaya*), a song for victory in war, or for a successful harvest, or to accompany work in the fields. Of these names only the *yaravi* (or *haravi*) seems to have survived in common usage, but the lineage of contemporary Andean music and perhaps the very songs named by Huamán Poma can be traced back to the 17th century, and probably to pre-Columbian origins.

POPULAR REVIVAL

Music never stands still, however. The traditional music, which has survived in relatively pristine form among native musicians, and in the past few decades enjoyed a renaissance as folklore, has also evolved a parallel, popular form. Today

this is not only performed in the *chicherías* or *cantinas* frequented by both urban and rural Quechua speakers, but is also recorded in sound studios on records and CDs, and played on the radio. The recording artists, like pop musicians and vocalists everywhere, become household names, and their careers are followed attentively, especially by the young. They come into fashion, then disappear, like groups anywhere in the world.

The primary form of popular music that has evolved from those traditional forms is the *wayno* (or *huayno* in its Spanish spelling, and pronounced

Playing the quena (flute).

"wino" in both), which constitutes a rich complex of poetry, music, and dance. The *wayno* is a rural music, a bit like bluegrass, and each region has developed its own characteristic variation. It is fundamentally dance music and is typically played in 2/4 time with an insistent, infectious rhythm; the dance is usually performed by couples, their hands joined, with much stamping of the feet to cries of "*Más fuerza! Más fuerza!*" ("Harder! Harder!").

But the *wayno* is also a literary form, representing a tradition of oral poetry that goes back at least to the time of the Incas. The *wayno* is essentially a love song, but a melancholy and melodramatic one: a song of love found and lost or rejected, a song of rivalry and abandonment, and of separation and wandering in strange lands far from home. The modern *wayno* is clearly a direct descendant of the songs of Huamán Poma's day.

Melodramatic as they may be, however, anthologies of lyrics disclose a sophistication of poetic form and poetic voice, ranging from tragic to ironic to comic, which is remarkable in a completely oral tradition. *Waynos* to this day are learned and preserved within a social context, transmitted informally and usually anonymously, from musician to musician, in the setting of private celebrations or great religious festivals in every village of the Peruvian Sierra.

The *wayno* will certainly continue to evolve; today an urbanized form of this fundamentally rural music is developing, in which the traditional naturalistic motifs are being replaced by abstract, more universal terms. But, in the light of its long history, it seems safe to guess that this music will survive for nearly as long as the Andes themselves.

MÚSICA CRIOLLA

Peruvian music cannot be fully understood without looking at the contributions made by

Dancers in Trujillo's Plaza de Armas.

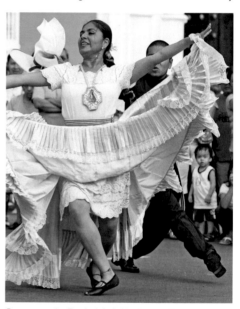

Dancers at the Festival de la Marinera in Trujillo.

⊘ MUSIC ABOVE AND UNDERGROUND

Born in the 1960s, out of Colombian *cumbia* via Peruvian Amazonia, laced with infusions of melancholy Andean scales and lyrics, and named after an immortal home-brewed beer, *chicha* is Peru's most popular modern musical style. Twangy, wailing, intensely electronic, with a loping, danceable rhythm, you will probably hear it on the radio during your first taxi ride in Peru.

In its 1990s incarnation, as *tecnocumbia*, it became indelibly identified with the Fujimori decade, but it retains its traditional ties to both Andean and Amazonian Peru, with the most popular of the ephemeral bands in this genre emerging from Iquitos

and Pucallpa in the Amazon basin, and Tarapoto in San Martín province.

Chicha is strongly associated with the new urban migrant population, rudely known as *cholos*; it is never played at middle- or upper-class parties, which usually feature imported rock, salsa, and Latin pop. Salsa's infectious rhythms, which originated in the Carribean, are now heard in *salsatecas* throughout the continent and beyond. The vibrant live rock scene in Lima is underground and classless, including bands like Los Mojarras, Cementerio Club, Leusemia, Libido, Dolores Delirio, the moody rebel Daniel F., and the Quechua-language Uchpa.

the country's black population. The first black people to arrive in the Americas came on Christopher Columbus's first voyage, in 1492. They were brought to the New World as servants of the conquistadors and at first enjoyed a measure of liberty. But by the end of the 16th century, shiploads of blacks were being brought in from various regions of Africa as slave labor.

In Peru – where slavery was not as pervasive as it was in some other parts of Latin America – Africans were brought in to raise the crops of cotton, sugar cane, and grapes grown on the central coast. They were concentrated mainly in places like Lima, Chincha, and Cañete, where there are still significant black populations today.

Their masters, not content with working them for punishingly long hours in the fields, made their slaves entertain them at parties and other social occasions, by playing instruments or dancing. Because the slaves came from different parts of Africa, their music thus became a mixture of these different regional forms, gradually blended with Andean and Spanish rhythms, to emerge as *música criolla*.

Slavery in Peru lasted until President Ramón Castilla abolished ownership of humans on December 3, 1854. But although they were legally free, blacks were still marginalized. They lived in what were known as *palenques* (an Antillan name which means "an inaccessible place"): isolated villages which became focuses of resistance to the abuse that their people still suffered. Although geographically isolated, the *palenques* were linked to the city markets, establishing interaction between the outcasts and society.

This interaction helped the Afro-Andean population to develop a musical culture. Their music was a way of expressing resistance, and asserting themselves where they were otherwise dominated and suppressed. Music was also the practice of an art and, just as importantly, a way of having fun. The *panalivio*, or "bread relief," was a musical form with a lamenting tone, in the vein of the black music of the southern United States, which reflected the social conditions under which the blacks of the time lived, and which ended in an upbeat tempo. From this music arose other rhythmical variations such as the *festejo* and the *resbalosa*.

DANCE VARIETY

Dance, naturally, grew up alongside Afro-Peruvian music. The *zamacueca* stands out as the unmistakable precursor of the stately and elegant *marinera*, which has become the national dance, with *limeña* and *norteña* versions. In and around Trujillo, you may well stumble across one of the frequent *marinera* dance competitions. The Festival de la Marinera in January is the biggest one.

Varieties of black music and *zapateo* (a form of rhythmic tapping) can often be seen and

Peruvian singer and former Minister of Culture Susana Baca.

heard in various parts of Lima and in Chincha, where it is especially popular. (Chincha's Fiesta Negra in February is a good time to hear all kinds of Afro-Peruvian music.) The guitar, the *cajón* or *caja*, sometimes a donkey's jawbone, and other instruments combine to create rhythms that accompany the *zamacueca* and the *festejo*.

Another typical dance is *El Alcatraz*, in which dancers bearing lit candles attempt to inflame their partners. A *conjunto* called Perú Negro is one of the most popular dance groups in the country, while black singers such as Susana Baca and Eva Ayllón have gained numerous fans since the 1990s.

📷 FESTIVALS AND FUSION

Peru's festivals are a fusion of Catholic, Inca, and even older agricultural rites, celebrated with high spirits and a fitting sense of drama.

In any Andean community at any time of the year, you may stumble on a village fiesta. These local events are colorful occasions, always accompanied by music, dance, vivid dress, and large quantities of food and *chicha*. Coastal festivals can also be lively, especially in Chincha, where the black population stages the Fiesta Negra in February with Afro-Peruvian music and dance.

Major festivals, like the Fiestas Patrias in late July, commemorating Peru's Independence, are celebrated nationwide. Others are specific to one location, like Lima's celebration of El Señor de los Milagros, which sees thousands of people following a procession headed by a black figure of Christ on the Cross.

One of the reasons Peru's festivals are so exciting is that they blend the rites of the Catholic Church with those which go back much farther – to Inca times or the veneration of Pacha Mama, Mother Earth. A good example of this is the Inti Raymi celebration in Cusco. The Festival of the Sun had been a huge event under the Incas, and Catholic leaders, realizing it could not be stamped out, nudged it to June 24, the day of John the Baptist, and everyone was happy.

Pre-Lent Carnival, which was grafted onto pagan celebrations in Europe, is widely celebrated, very noisily, with lots of water-hurling. La Virgen de la Candelaria (Candlemas), in February, is another event where Catholic and pre-Columbian rites mingle, particularly in Puno, where the *diablada*, a devil dance involving grotesque masks, is the main event.

The Virgen de la Candelaria festival is known for its grotesque masks and dancing devils.

During the Virgen de la Candelaria festival, local people dance in honor of Mamacha Candelaria, the patron saint of Puno.

During the festival of Inti Raymi in Cusco, the Inca Sapa is carried on a golden throne from Qoricancha to the fortress of Sacsayhuamán.

A statue of Christ decorated with red petals is carried through Cusco.

Lord of the earthquakes

Celebrated on the Monday of Holy Week, this is a major event in Cusco. Our Lord of the Earthquakes (Nuestro Señor de los Temblores), the image of Christ on the Cross which hangs in the cathedral, is credited with saving the city from destruction during a major earthquake in 1650. The statue is carried through the streets on an ornate silver litter. Red flower petals, symbolizing the blood of Christ, are scattered in its path and thousands of *cusqueños* join the procession, along with civic leaders, priests, nuns, and military representatives.

When a severe earthquake rocked the city in 1950, the image was set up in the Plaza de Armas, while townspeople begged the Lord to stop the tremors. Like many other festivals, this is a mixture of superstition, genuine religious feeling, and enjoyment of ritual for its own sake, and it is a splendid occasion.

Each May thousands of people make the pilgrimage to Quoyllur Riti, a sacred glacier in the Cordillera Vilcanota. Pilgrims leave miniature models of things they desire in the hope that the Lord of the Snow Star will help them realize their dreams.

A festival dancer wearing brightly colored shawls and a traditional multi-layered skirt known as a pollera.

Clams fresh from the Pacific.

FUSION OF FLAVORS

From the fish-based cuisine of the coast to the substantial, spicy dishes of the highlands and the fruits of the jungle, Peruvian cooking offers plenty of tempting tastes.

Peru's different geographical regions, its varied climates, and its mixture of peoples combine to provide a cuisine that is among the most extensive and interesting in South America. This food appears not only on dining tables but is also immortalized in pre-Hispanic pottery, which sometimes takes surprisingly realistic forms of fruits and vegetables, in the centuries-old weavings found in many of the burial grounds that have been excavated, and in wall paintings.

> *Fish is traditionally believed to have rejuvenating powers, and aguadito – a thick rice and fish soup – was traditionally served to all-night revelers after the three-day wedding celebrations once common along the coast.*

FRUITS OF THE SEA

The best dishes in Lima and other coastal cities are based on the abundant seafood available. The collision of the Humboldt and other currents means the Peruvian sea is full of the plankton that larger fish eat, providing fishermen and cooks with a great variety to choose from.

The most typically Peruvian dish is *ceviche*, a plate of raw white fish in a spicy marinade of lemon juice, onion, and hot peppers. Each restaurant has its own marinade recipe, and when the fish is freshly caught, *ceviche* can be delicious. It is healthier to avoid buying the cheaper versions sold in the street, however. *Ceviche* is traditionally served with corn and sweet potato, and there are many variations on the basic formula, often with the addition of shellfish in *ceviche mixto*.

Delicious fruits are grown in the Peruvian selva (jungle).

Among the best shellfish are *camarones* (shrimp), *calamares* (squid), and *choros* (mussels), all prepared in a number of ways. Any dish listed as *a lo macho* means it comes with a shellfish sauce.

Another cold fish recipe is *escabeche de pescado*, cold fried fish in a sauce of onions, hot peppers, and garlic, adorned with olives and hard-boiled eggs. The king of fresh sea fish is the *corvina* or white sea bass, together with another excellent white fish, the *chita,* and the *lenguado* or sole. These are usually served *a la plancha* (grilled) or with any number of sauces.

In Cusco and other towns of the highlands, *trucha* or rainbow trout is very plentiful, as they are farmed in many rivers and lakes. Less common but more distinctive is *pejerrey* or king-fish, served steamed with potatoes and yucca.

In the jungle region, the main ingredient of many dishes is fish from the Amazon and its tributaries. The most succulent is the huge but overfished *paiche*, with its abundant soft white flesh. Broiled or grilled, it may be accompanied by *palmito* (strips of soft palm heart that look like ribbons of pasta), yucca, and fried bananas; or wrapped in banana leaves and then baked on coals to make a dish known as *patarashca*. Other fish worth trying in the jungle region are the *zúngaro* and even the *piranha*, which despite its vicious reputation is soft and tender on the plate.

As well as the seafood, the cities and towns of the coastal desert region offer hearty dishes with chicken, duck, or goat. A favorite on the northern coast is *seco de cabrito* (roasted kid goat), often cooked with fermented *chicha* and served with beans and rice. A similar recipe is used to cook lamb, which becomes *seco de cordero*. A popular way of serving chicken is *ají de gallina*, a rich concoction of creamed chicken and a touch of hot peppers, served on boiled potatoes.

In Lima, especially during the gray winter months, the *Limeños* often prepare a thick vegetable stew called *sancochado* served with meat. Another hearty meal common in the capital is *cau cau*, tripe cooked with beans and potatoes, served with rice.

SPICY PEPPERS

Hot peppers are grown all over the country and are used to add spice to everything from fish to stews. On the north coast, where fish is a big part of the diet, sauces of hot peppers and onions are heaped on top of the main dish or offered as accompaniment in small side bowls. In the Amazon, where the food tends to be less spicy, people dip jungle vegetables and yucca into fiery pepper sauces.

But it is in the highland region where *picante* (as the hot, spicy taste of peppers is known) reaches an art form. The degree of spiciness

A demonstration of Peruvian cooking.

⊙ PERU'S STAR CHEF

Although he didn't start Peru's *novoandina* movement, no chef epitomizes the country's culinary rise more than Gastón Acurio. In Lima, where he was born in 1967, Acurio practically enjoys rock star status, and according to the *Financial Times*, the restaurant empire he has launched is worth some US$60 million.

Acurio's father, a politician from Belaúnde's Acción Popular Party, had wanted his son to become a lawyer. While studying in Madrid, however, Acurio snuck off to become a chef, later pursuing that passion at Le Cordon Bleu in Paris. In 1994 and back home in Lima, he opened his first restaurant, Astrid y Gastón, with his wife, German pastry chef Astrid Gutsche. Hands-on hard work, a talent for his country's myriad dishes, and exposure to television helped him expand the restaurant to branches elsewhere in Latin America, the US, and Spain, winning local acclaim in the process. His franchise currently comprises more than 30 restaurants in eleven countries. In Peru, Acurio's creativity appears unstoppable. Besides his flagship restaurant, he has gone into fast food with Pasquale Hermanos, Sino-Peruvian with Madam Tusan, T'anta bistro food, *cevicherías* with La Mar, steakhouses with Panchita, and regional Peruvian cuisine with Chicha. In 2016 Astrid y Gastón was ranked 30th in the S. Pelligrino World's 50 Best Restaurants list.

depends on the type of *ají* or chili pepper used. These can vary from the moderately sharp taste that novices can tolerate to the screamingly hot *rocoto* peppers whose fire-engine red is not only decorative but a warning signal. Tourists beware: as in Mexico, locals love to confuse newcomers with the strength of the *picante*, which can destroy your tastebuds for the rest of the day.

It is thought that early farmers in Peru grew about five species of hot peppers, which were transported over the years to Central

---

The Paracas area is known for its fresh seafood, used in dishes such as chupe de camarones, a thick shrimp stew, and tacu tacu, an invigorating mix of different shellfish with rice and beans.

America, the Caribbean, and Mexico. Christopher Columbus, who was searching for the black pepper of the eastern isles when he came upon hot chilies in the Caribbean, may be responsible for their English name. "There is much *axí*, which is their pepper, and it is stronger than pepper, and the people won't eat without it for they find it very wholesome," he wrote in his journal in 1493. The hot peppers he brought back were an immediate success in Spain and the rest of Europe.

Restaurants in Arequipa vie with each other to serve their version of *rocoto relleno* (stuffed peppers), which are delicious with fresh local cheese. However, tourists unaccustomed to hot spices should beware: eating too much *picante* can cause a kind of diarrhea known as *jaloproctitis*; this is why Peruvians do not serve it to small children, nursing mothers, or the infirm.

A WORLD STAPLE

The small subsistence farms of the Peruvian highlands are home to a vegetable now found all over the world: the humble *papa* or potato. There are more than 3,000 mostly uniquely Peruvian varieties, including the yellow *limeña*, the small purple potato, and the dried *chuño*, which is frozen in the harsh climate around Puno and Lake Titicaca. These potatoes can be stored for up to four years. In some areas around the lake,

the Aymara still ritually stuff potatoes with coca leaves and bury them as a tribute to the earth mother, Pacha Mama, in the hope of a bountiful next harvest. "Only" a few dozen varieties, however, are regularly consumed.

Potatoes are an essential part of most of the filling one-pot dishes common in highland cuisine. A famous dish named after them is *papas a la huancaína*, a creamy concoction of potatoes, peppers, and boiled eggs. Or they can be served with a peanut sauce in *papa ocopa*, or simply stuffed with meat, onions, boiled eggs, and rai-

Hot peppers and bags of salsa picante.

sins for *papa rellena*. They also take their place in *estofado* (a stew of chicken, corn, carrots, and tomatoes), as well as the ever-present *lomo saltado* (strips of beef with onions, tomatoes, and fried potatoes). The *papa amarilla* (yellow potato) is considered the best.

Peru's highland soil also produces other tubers that form part of the national cuisine. There is the *olluco* vegetable, which can range in colour from red to orange, and has a taste like new potatoes. It is often shredded and served with dried llama meat or *charqui* (beef jerky) in a stew. In a few places you may find *oca* or *arracacha* served instead of the usual potato. The sweet potato or *camote* is also plentiful and full of taste.

RITUAL FOOD

Corn was introduced to Peru from Central America many hundreds of years ago. It was the most sacred food for many of its peoples before the Spanish invasion, and is found in nearly as many colors and varieties as the potato. The fermented corn drink *chicha* is made into a cloudy and extremely strong beer that is ceremoniously poured onto the ground during planting and harvest festivals, and then drunk in enormous quantities. Purple corn is converted into a refreshing non-alcoholic drink

Mixing a pisco sour.

known as *chicha morada*, and turned into the purple dessert called *mazamorra morada*.

Corn is cooked and presented in many ways. *Choclo*, boiled large-grained ears of corn, are sold on every street corner, usually with slices of cheese and *picante* sauce. Corn kernels are also part of stews such as *chicharrón con mote*, with pork and tomatoes. Fried corn kernels called *cancha* are a common snack, served before meals, or to nibble with beer or *pisco*.

Before the arrival of the Spaniards, the different highland civilizations in Peru cultivated many other grains. Some of them, including the purple-flowered *kiwicha* and the golden quinoa – both kinds of amaranth – were

banned by the Vatican on religious grounds, and disappeared from the Peruvian diet for several centuries. They are now being rediscovered as healthier variants to the potato, and are being used once more in breads, cookies, soups, and salads.

Nineteenth-century Chinese immigrants brought their cooking style to Peru, and it is now embedded in the Peruvian gastronomic repertoire. Even the ubiquitous *lomo saltado* is derived from a Chinese dish. Chinese restaurants are known as *chifas*, and they are found all over the country. Many *chifa* menus list their offerings in Chinese, but *arroz chaufa*, sautéed rice with chopped meats and vegetables, and *wantan cam lu*, a sweet, sour pork-based dish, are reliable choices.

JUNGLE FARE

Beyond the plentiful fish of the Amazon and other tropical rivers, the jungle area offers many other culinary delights. There is *peccary* or wild boar, and other game, but visitors should seek advice to ensure they aren't contributing to overhunting. There are *juanes* – a *tamal* stuffed with chicken and rice – and turtle soup. In the Amazon, bananas replace potatoes as the staple, with many different kinds for frying, boiling, or eating fresh. The other staple is yucca, which accompanies most meals, and is also fermented to make a strong alcoholic drink called *masato*.

ACQUIRED TASTES

There are two dishes served throughout Peru which are very popular, although visitors are often taken aback when offered them. Many street corners and restaurants offer *anticuchos* – skewers of meat which were originally grilled cattle and pig hearts, but can now include even pieces of fish and vegetables. If you are invited to a Peruvian barbecue, this is more than likely what you will be served. Around Cusco, a choice delicacy is the *cuy* or guinea pig. This is often presented deep-fried like Southern chicken, and the taste is somewhere between chicken and rabbit.

SWEET TEETH

Peruvians love to finish a meal with a sweet dessert. Often this will be something that is part of the culinary tradition brought over from Spain. Favorites include *manjar blanco,* a kind of fudge made from boiled milk and sugar; *cocadas* (coconut macaroons); or the typically Spanish *churros,* pastry dough similar to donuts fried and eaten with honey or chocolate. *Manjar blanco* and meringue, along with a dash of Port and a sprinkling of cinnamon, go into Peru's most famous dessert, *suspiro limeño* ("Lima sigh").

During the October celebrations honoring the Lord of Miracles (El Señor de los Milagros) another Spanish delicacy, *turrones,* are sold everywhere. In the summer months, cones of crushed ice *(paletas)* flavored with fruit syrups (and optionally topped with condensed milk) are sold on street corners – but be careful with them, as the water used to make the ice may upset travelers' stomachs.

Other common sweets include *yuquitas,* deep-fried yucca-dough balls rolled in sugar; *picarones,* donuts coated in honey; and *tejas,* a sweet biscuit filled with *manjar blanco.* One of the oldest traditional desserts is the crunchy cookie known as *revolución caliente,* which dates from the independence era in the early 19th century. Street sellers call out: *"Revolución caliente, música para los dientes"* ("Hot revolution, music for the teeth").

As well as these sweet concoctions, Peru has a wonderful variety of fruit, served fresh or as juices *(jugos).* Passion fruit or *maracuyá* is perhaps best as a juice, but the jungle region also provides mangoes, papaya, and other tropical fruit. *Lúcuma,* a small brown fruit found only in Peru and Chile, has a strong, nutty, exotic taste, and is used in ice creams and sorbets. Another delicate tropical fruit is the *chirimoya,* or custard apple, while the highlands supply *tuna,* the fruit of the prickly pear cactus, which can be eaten alone or as part of a salad.

THIRST-QUENCHERS

As with other Latin American countries, it was the Spanish missionaries who first established vineyards in Peru. But until recently the Peruvian wine industry has not been as developed as those of Argentina and Chile, and only a few of the vineyards around Ica – the Tacama, Tabernero, and Ocucaje labels for example – are of any note. Most of the grapes are used instead for making *pisco,* which in turn is the basic ingredient for the Peruvian national drink, *pisco sour.* This cocktail is a mixture of *pisco,* egg whites, lemon juice, and sugar, plus a few drops of bitters. The result seems innocuous, but can be explosive. So important is *pisco* to national identity that in 1988 the Peruvian government declared it to be part of the "cultural heritage of the nation."

Mate de coca, tea made from coca leaves, is served throughout the highland region as

Novoandina food, as personified by superchef Gastón Acurio.

an antidote to altitude sickness. (Note that *mate de coca* is illegal in the US.) *Manzanilla* or camomile tea is also a popular way to finish a meal. Coffee usually comes as a concentrated liquid known as *esencia,* which is then diluted with boiling water. Peru grows high-quality coffee; the best is from Chanchamayo, and one of the best brands is Café Britt.

Carbonated drinks are called *gaseosas,* and the extremely popular local one is known as *Inca Kola.* There are many lager-type beers *(cerveza),* including brands such as Pilsen, Cristal, Arequipeña, and Cusqueña – the last generally considered by connoisseurs to be the best in Peru.

ANDEAN ADVENTURES

Peru offers superb opportunities for outdoor activities, such as trekking, mountaineering, horseback riding, and river rafting, with organized excursions to suit a range of abilities, time frames, and budgets.

Few places in the world allow you to drive by car in one day across almost rainless deserts near sea level, climb 5,000 meters (16,500ft) to frigid regions of permanent snow, and then descend again to hot and dense tropical rainforests. But this is Peru.

In an area about the size of Britain, France, and Spain combined, Peru contains 84 of the world's 101 known ecological life zones. With so much geographical, cultural, and biological diversity, and with wild rivers, a huge coastline, and much of the mountain landscape being open, unfenced, and crisscrossed with trails, the range of possible adventure experiences is almost limitless.

Trekking is the nation's first and foremost adventure activity, the headline hike being the incomparable Inca Trail to Machu Picchu, but with dozens of other popular routes scattered across the country and winding their way across the high passes and astounding scenery of the tropical Andes. Major areas for trekking are the Cusco region and the Cordillera Blanca, with Arequipa and the Colca Canyon, Chachapoyas, and mountain areas closer to Lima also growing in popularity.

Rafting and kayaking are well-established and exciting options on some of the dramatic Amazon tributaries, such as the Apurímac and the Tambopata, or on some of the Pacific watershed rivers, such as the deep Cotahuasi Canyon, or the easier waters of the Río Cañete near Lima.

Mountain biking has mushroomed in popularity in recent years, especially in the Cusco region, while horseback riding, paragliding, and mountaineering all have their devotees and favorite areas. Certain spots on the coast have some of the world's finest waves, worshiped by congregations of devoted surfers.

Hiking among the snowy peaks of the Cordillera Blanca.

Two main climate patterns reign in Peru: the coastal cycle and the mountain/rainforest cycle. The southern-hemisphere winter brings low cloud and drizzle to Lima and the central coast from about April through November, when the ocean is cold with stiff winds most of the way to the border with Ecuador. December brings warmer weather and sunshine, and city dwellers take to the beaches. In the mountains, winter (May to October) is dry and sunny, and this is the season for most adventure activities. November and December bring on the highland rains, which grow intense from January through March. Some trekking on the better-maintained trails is possible during these months, but stay away from the remoter areas, or be prepared for highway washouts, mud-clogged trails, and major delays. The rainforest is always hot, but with much less rain in the winter months.

TREKKING

Adventurers should be very aware of altitude as a potential cause of suffering, disappointment, and occasionally serious problems. Andean trekking routes often cross high passes ranging from 4,000 to 5,000 meters (13,200 to 16,500ft). Before you set out, know what altitudes you will be facing, and above all, take time to acclimatize

All popular trekking routes are served by villagers offering mules, horses, or portering services. Horses are forbidden on the Inca Trail, however, where all groups use porters.

the problem. Any appearance of these symptoms should be treated as an emergency, and the victim must be taken to a significantly lower altitude immediately.

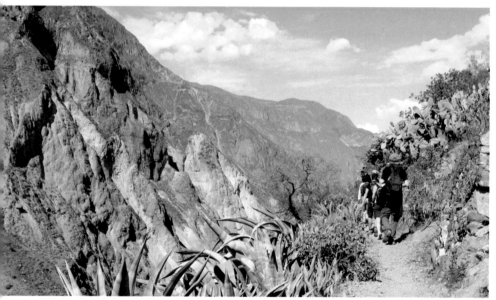

Trekkers in the Colca Canyon.

and exercise gently at high-altitude locations such as Cusco or Huaraz before beginning any strenuous activity.

The condition that trekkers often suffer, Acute Mountain Sickness, known locally as *soroche*, features headaches, nausea, insomnia, and shortness of breath. At higher altitudes this can sometimes turn into pulmonary edema or cerebral edema, when fluid collects in the lungs or brain respectively. Both of these are dangerous and potentially fatal conditions. Symptoms are a dry, persistent cough, excessive fatigue, cyanosis (purple lips and fingernails), mental confusion, incoherence, and lack of coordination. Group members should look out for these signs in others, since the victim is usually unaware of

No skill is required for trekking, but some degree of fitness is recommended. Hat, sunblock, sunglasses, raingear, flashlight, extra batteries, insect repellent, layers of both lightweight and warm clothing, a good pair of walking shoes or boots, and a good sleeping bag are essential items to take with you. Need for a tent, multi-fuel or camping gas stove (wood fires are both impractical and unecological), and a first-aid kit, depends on whether or not you decide to sign up with one of the numerous agencies offering trekking services. These vary a lot in price and quality of service. As a rule of thumb, if time is your constraint, sign up with an outfitter; if money, go independent, although this is not an option on the Inca Trail.

Most essential trekking equipment can be bought or rented in Cusco or Huaraz, but not elsewhere. When hiring equipment be sure to assemble, check, and test every item thoroughly before setting out. In Cusco brand-name lightweight trail boots can be purchased at Molinopampa, a sort of smuggler's supermarket near the airport.

Trekking food can be bought in the large towns and cities, but is not readily available on trails, so carry all you need for your trek. Packet soups, pasta, and noodles can be purchased in

However, the overwhelming numbers of hikers on these ancient paths have forced the authorities to restrict access, raise costs, and impose strict regulations. Today, would-be trekkers must reserve months ahead and sign up with a licensed operator. Though only the fortunate few can do the Inca Trail these days, the new limits have had one fortunate side effect: hikers are spreading out into undeveloped and unrestricted areas, and discovering scores of less well known but wonderful treks.

A mule train crosses a mountain pass on the Salcantay route.

stores and markets, along with dried fruits and grains. Most common spices are also available.

All drinking water should be sterilized with purification tablets, iodine solution, or a filtering pump. Powdered flavorings to disguise the unpleasant taste of treated water are available in stores.

THE INCA TRAIL

The **Inca Trail** to Machu Picchu was for years *the* hike to do in Peru. Nothing else can compare with the startling variety of scenery, Inca ruins, and ecological zones, packed into three or four days of exquisite hiking. There is also a popular short one-day version of the trail that feeds in from the railroad near Machu Picchu.

THE CUSCO REGION

The **Ausangate Loop** is a well-known high-altitude classic of dramatic mountain scenery and cultural encounters with traditional Quechua alpaca and llama herders, making a full circle around Ausangate (6,380 meters/20,930ft), the highest mountain in southern Peru. Beginning and ending with glorious open-air hot springs, no campsite is much below 4,000 meters (13,200ft), and two of the passes are at around 5,000 meters (16,500ft). Huge glacial moraines, raw cliffs and slopes in multicolored mineral shades, and lakes in intensely varied blues, make this an unforgettable five-day journey. The road from Cusco to the trailhead at Tinqui is part of the Trans-Oceanic highway to Brazil and takes only about four hours.

The back-door route to Machu Picchu, from **Salcantay to Santa Teresa**, was promoted by local guides when Inca Trail permits grew scarce. It has some of the glory of the Inca Trail, and crosses a higher, more spectacular mountain pass between Humantay and Salcantay (6,270 meters/20,570ft), two of the highest peaks in the Cordillera Vilcabamba. Starting at Soraypampa after a three-hour drive from Cusco, you cross the high pass on the first day of this

A section of the Salcantay route to Machu Picchu.

three- or four-day trek, and the rest is downhill, descending from frigid wasteland through grasslands, dwarf forest, and tropical cloud forest down through the Santa Teresa Valley. From here there are road and rail links to the town of Aguas Calientes, near Machu Picchu. A variant adds an extra day over an Inca highway through the ruins of Patallacta, with spectacular views eastward to Machu Picchu.

Both the Ausangate region and the Salcantay route now offer the option of lodge-to-lodge hiking – the latter a rather high-end private service, the Ausangate a mid-level cooperative effort involving local communities.

Choquequirao is a spectacular five-day round-trip journey to an Inca site that rivals Machu Picchu for its setting. The journey begins with a scenic five-hour drive west from Cusco across the Apurímac River to the trailhead at the canyon-rim town of Cachora, with optional visits (which add time) to fascinating Inca sites at Limatambo and Sayhuite along the way. A nearly 1,800-meter (6,000ft) descent into the hot semi-desert floor of the Apurímac Canyon is followed by a 1,500-meter (5,000ft) ascent to the cloud-forest site of Choquequirao. Thought to have been a royal estate of the emperor Topa Inca, who ruled from 1471 to 1493, this is a sprawling, well-preserved site, with superb, massive terracing features, including a set of terraces inlayed with 22 large llama figures in white stone. Terrain is very steep, and a measure of fitness is called for. In 2017, plans were announced to construct a cable car, which will whisk tourists to the site in 15 minutes.

It is possible to continue this hike northward into the Vilcabamba region, over the Minas Victoria pass, then either east over Puerto Yanama (4,700 meters/15,400ft) to Machu Picchu or north following imposing Inca stone highways over the Choquetacarpo pass (4,600 meters/15,080ft) to Huancacalle and the ruins of Vitcos: about 10–12 days in total, in either case. If trekking only to Choquequirao, using pack-horses, you must retrace your steps to Cachora. Brave souls carrying their own backpack or using porters can take the steep route out via San Ignacio and Huanipaca.

North of Cusco, beyond the Urubamba Valley, lies a broad region of mountains known as the **Lares region**, where traditional Quechua people herd their llamas and alpacas. At the eastern end lies Lares, locally famous for its superb hot springs, and to the west lies Ollantaytambo, jumping-off spot for Machu Picchu. Several hiking routes cross the mountains northward into this area from the Sacred Valley, or one can drive to Lares and trek westward to Ollantaytambo.

For those who prefer short overnight treks or camp-free day hiking, there are several short hikes around Cusco, including the route from Tauca, near Chinchero, to the stunning and little-visited Inca site of Huchuy Cusco, which overlooks the Sacred Valley at Lamay. It can be done in one rather long day (with a very early start), or with an overnight camp at the ruins. Possible day hikes around Cusco include climbs of nearby mountains Mama Simona, Huanacauri, Senca, and Picol.

THE CORDILLERA BLANCA

Eight hours north of Lima by bus, the city of **Huaraz** is the starting point for an array of spectacular treks among Peru's highest mountains. The Cordillera Blanca is home to the country's highest peak, **Huascarán** (6,760 meters/22,200ft) and 30 other summits above 6,000 meters (19,700ft), and a maze of trails climbing between them from two parallel north–south valleys, the Callejón de Huaylas and the more remote Callejón de Conchucos to the east. Routes range from day hikes out of Huaraz to lengthy two-week circuits encompass-

along with an array of discos, *peñas*, and bars for winding down after strenuous trekking.

THE CORDILLERA HUAYHUASH

This stunning, more remote region of high peaks is reached from Huaraz via **Chiquián**, a small town at the north end of the range. For serious and fit trekkers only, a 12-day circuit of the entire range, with at least one very high pass every day, starts here. Still steep, but much shorter at four days, is the round-trip from Chiquián to Jahuacocha, a lake with stunning views of the highest peak, Yerupajá

A climber on the Alpamayo ice face in the Cordillera Blanca.

ing most of the Cordillera. The most famous route is the five-day **Llanganuco–Santa Cruz** trek, but many other scenic hikes carry less traffic. At least one short acclimatization hike out of Huaraz – such as the **Laguna Churup** trail – is advisable, since most of the Cordillera Blanca trails cross passes of at least 4,400 meters (14,430ft).

Huaraz is also the jumping-off point for the less scenic, but popular and relatively easy **Olleros–Chavín** route, which ends at the ancient ruins of Chavín de Huantar. In Huaraz, the Casa de Guías can provide the latest information on trails and mountain conditions, along with names of porters and mule-wranglers. The main street of Luzuriaga sports dozens of trekking outfitters and equipment rental stores,

⊘ RESPONSIBLE ADVENTURES

It's hard to know, until after a trip, how well a company treats its staff and the environment, but one thing is clear: both will suffer if visitors haggle excessively. Make sure your company is packing out garbage and not burying or dumping it en route, and not contaminating water supplies. Avoid disposable plastic water bottles – boil or purify water instead. See that your outfitter treats its crew properly, providing them with proper food, shelter, and medical attention, and not overloading porters. When trekking independently with hired crew, remember that those concerns are your responsibility.

(6,634 meters/21,760ft). **Cajatambo** at the south end of the Cordillera is a possible exit point to Lima for a shorter circuit, and also provides access for excellent shorter hikes in the vicinity.

AROUND AREQUIPA

Although not a famous trekking area, the capital of the south offers hiking out of **Cabanaconde** at the western end of the Colca Canyon, down into one of the world's two deepest canyons, Colca or Cotahuasi. It's also possible to ascend the summit of Misti, the enormous active volcano that looms over the city of Arequipa. But be warned – although technically easy, this three-day climb peaks at 5,820 meters (19,000ft). Arequipa is too low for acclimatization, so it's essential to spend time in Cusco, Puno, or the Colca area immediately before this ascent.

NORTHERN SIERRA

More isolated and less known than Peru's major trekking areas, this region of mountainous cloud forest filled with hilltop ruins and cliff tombs also offers many superb routes, accessed from

The annual Megavalanche mountain-bike race outside Cusco.

⊘ SURF'S UP

Modern surfing in Peru can be traced back to 1942 when Carlos Dogny founded Waikiki, the first surf club in Lima. A boost for the sport came in 1965 when the ASP World Championship was won by a Peruvian, Carlos Pomar, for the first time. World-class waves batter Peru's arid coastline, generating three distinct surf clusters.

Far north: Máncora offers lively beachlife and steady waves, while rocky Cabo Blanco features a radical but intermittent left-hand barrel.

Around Trujillo: west and north of Trujillo, long left-point breaks rise at Huanchaco, Chicama, and Pacasmayo, while these last two (uncrowded,

despite their renown) both claim the world's longest rideable wave (up to 2.2km/1.5 miles).

Around Lima: Punta Hermosa, the cradle of Peruvian surfdom, has 17 major spots for everyone from beginners to champions, less than an hour south of Lima. In Lima itself, surf's up just minutes from downtown Miraflores, with everyone rushing to nearby Herradura when big swells fatten its mighty pointbreak.

Winter is prime time for surf, summer for weather, but all seasons have good surf. Most water is cold year-round, but the far north is warm. Off the beach, consider the dunes for sandboarding.

the towns of **Chachapoyas** and **Leimebamba**, northwest of Cajamarca.

MOUNTAIN BIKING

The sport has taken off in recent years, with the Megavalanche downhill marathon near Cusco really putting Peru on the mountain-biking map. Cusco is the major center, with lots more options out of Huaraz, Arequipa, and even Lima. Stupendous scenery, wide open country, a multitude of trails, and from Cusco, major day-long downhill runs, constitute the attractions.

From walk-ups to extreme, technical climbs, the Cordillera Huayhuash region offers stellar climbing, but the altitude makes acclimatization a major consideration.

Rentals and tours are available in all cities. Check bikes carefully, and make sure the fee includes gloves, a good helmet, and a repair kit. Tours should always provide a support vehicle.

Surfers preparing to catch some Pacific Ocean waves.

A classic one-day outing near Cusco is the Maras–Moray plateau route, which is both easy and scenically dramatic. Great downhills include the aforementioned Málaga pass, whose western slope route can be planned to end with a hike into Machu Picchu from Santa Teresa. A staggering descent from frigid grassland at Tres Cruces into the steamy eastern rainforest can run one or two days, and another one-day downhill run from the Lares pass near Calca follows an Inca road.

Huaraz has spectacular tours from one to three or four days, into the heart of the Cordillera Blanca. Arequipa is a good jump-off point for biking in the Colca and Cotahuasi canyons, and shorter day runs around the city. Lima also has access to big downhill runs from the mountains to the beach.

MOUNTAIN CLIMBING

The Peruvian Andes have some famous climbing areas, first and foremost the Cordillera Blanca, out of Huaraz, with some 30 summits above 6,000 meters (19,680ft), among them Peru's highest mountain, **Huascarán** (6,760 meters/22,200ft). A popular acclimatization warm-up climb is the **Nevado Pisco** (5,800 meters/19,000ft). This has a steep yet rapid ascent, offering spectacular views from the saddle, and there is a mountain refuge at the base of the mountain. The Cordillera Blanca is the only area in Peru with a system of mountain refuges, accredited guides, and mountain rescue services.

The Arequipa region has both walk-ups and harder peaks, and Cusco has some hard technical climbs with longer approaches. These areas have little support for mountaineers, although there are one or two companies in each city that provide guiding and equipment services.

HORSEBACK RIDING

One of the draws for horse lovers is the Peruvian *paso* horse, a local breed that has been developed for its unique gait, and is famously comfortable to ride. Traditionally they are more adapted to coastal conditions, but today some companies offer *paso* treks in the mountains, while other outfits prefer the sure-footed mountain horses.

Around Cusco a variety of horse treks set off from the Sacred Valley into and across the spectacular Cordillera Urubamba, along with easier one-day journeys on the nearby Maras plateau. For a fun outing near Cusco itself, horses can be rented behind the Inca site of Sacsayhuamán, just outside the city. But be sensitive: some (not all) outfits mistreat their horses, and if the animals are thin, displaying saddle sores, and in visibly poor condition, do not encourage these

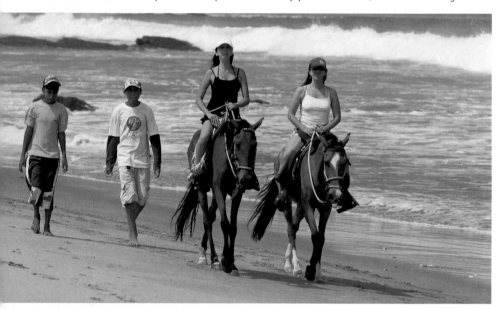

Horseback riding along the beach at Máncora in northern Peru.

⊙ TOUCHING THE VOID

In 1985 British climbers Simon Yates and Joe Simpson were descending from the summit of Huayhuash peak Siulá Grande (6330 meters/20,800ft) when Simpson slipped and broke his leg. Yates's attempt to lower him to safety ended with a crippled Simpson dangling over an abyss. Unable to move, Yates finally cut the rope. Simpson survived the fall, and crawled out alone to their base camp. Yates was heavily criticised by climbing veterans for cutting the rope, but Simpson always insisted he would have done the same had the roles been reversed. His book about the experience, *Touching the Void*, became an award-winning film.

practices by renting them. The Cordillera Blanca also has good horseback-riding options, as does the popular Colca Canyon near Arequipa.

PARAGLIDING

In Lima, steady coastal winds rising off the cliffs fronting Miraflores offer some paragliding excitement in reliable conditions. Cliffside outfits will take you on a tandem high above the beach, soaring past the balconies of shiny high-rise hotels and apartment blocks.

Paragliding in the mountains is more problematic, due to unpredictable air currents, but intrepid souls who ride paragliders above the Sacred Valley near Cusco are rewarded with stunning views of mountains, remote villages, and Inca ruins.

RUNNING THE ANDES

Virtually all rafting in Peru offers stunning and varied scenery. Colossal rivers run off the Andes, not least the Amazon, which is called the Apurímac at these latitudes.

With its five biggest rivers running for more than 7,000km (4,350 miles) and over a dozen others each exceeding 600km (373 miles) in length, Peru offers unmatched rafting experiences all year long.

Just hours from Cusco by road, the four-day Apurímac run through a deep and spectacular canyon is one of the most exciting short rafting trips anywhere. Class Four-plus rapids generate the full adrenaline experience, along with stretches of dreamy floating where wildlife such as torrent ducks, foxes, otters, condors, and even mountain lions may be seen.

Rafting experience is not essential, but travel with a reputable company that takes time for training and safety sessions, and therefore beware of cheaper three-day trips. The highland weather timetable applies to most trips, which are run mainly from May through October.

The Urubamba Valley, close enough to Cusco for day-rafting excursions, has lost its luster due to water pollution from the mushrooming city of Cusco. However, upstream of Cusco the river is still clean, and here the Chuquiqawana to Cusipata section makes a boisterous and scenic full-day trip, runnable most of the year.

Also starting from Cusco, the remote upper Tambopata River affords a world-class cloud-forest rafting adventure, a week-long ride down a mighty Amazon tributary, with frequent wildlife sightings. As the river flattens out, other highlights kick in: a clay-lick teeming with macaws and parrots, and remote rainforest lodges offering last nights of comfort before Puerto Maldonado, and a flight back to Cusco.

Arequipa features a fun and easy rafting trip, the half-day Río Chili run. At the other extreme, the Cotahuasi claims to be the planet's deepest canyon, and connoisseurs rate this run among the world's top ten. The trip begins with hiking down Inca trails, and lasts for six stunning days, with camping in

seldom-visited Inca ruins. The nearby Colca Canyon is only for hard-core rafters, but its lower section, known as the Río Majes, has some easy rafting, with the nearby petroglyphs of Toro Muerto adding interest to a day's outing.

Near Lima, the Río Cañete can be run during the summer months from December to April. It's short and easy rafting, usually occurring in warm, sunny weather, out of the resort town of Lunahuaná.

A whitewater-rafting excursion.

Further north, out of Huaraz, the Río Santa, running along the Callejón de Huaylas, has good, moderate rafting with stupendous views.

River running can be dangerous. Regulation is scant, so anyone can set up a company; meanwhile, hard-bargaining budget travelers drive down prices, compromising safety. The cheapest deal, with the shortest time on the river, means overworked, underpaid guides; a tendency to run, instead of walk around, dodgy rapids; no safety kayak; spiffy-looking life-vests, sporting new outer fabric but worn core material lacking buoyancy; beat-up helmets, etc. So choose carefully, inspect equipment, and ask for the guide's Swiftwater Rescue Technician credential, and Wilderness First Aid certificate.

Vicuñas in the Reserva Nacional Salinas y Aguada Blanca.

WILDLIFE OF THE SIERRA

From cameloids and condors to wooly monkeys and spectacled bears, the Peruvian Andes and the cloud forest are home to an amazing variety of wildlife.

Condors, guanacos, and pumas are only some of the animals of the Andes, many of which have been worshiped by native peoples through the ages. In Inca times all Andean wildlife enjoyed a form of protection, and although periodic hunts occurred, these were few, and the privilege of the ruling class. After the Spanish conquest and the breakdown of the Inca infrastructure, wild animals were hunted indiscriminately and consequently suffered a population decline that was further advanced by the cutting of high Andean woodlands, which give essential cover to many animals.

Today, the persecution of wild animals continues, in some cases because of damage caused by animals to crops, in most cases because of misconceptions. The careful observer, however, can still find a wide variety of Peruvian fauna while traveling in the Andes.

ENDANGERED SPECIES

The most conspicuous mammals encountered by a visitor to the Peruvian Andes are the cameloids. There are two wild cameloids in the country: the vicuña and the guanaco, from which llamas and alpacas were domesticated many centuries ago.

The vicuña, reputed to have the finest wool of any animal, has been brought back from the verge of extinction through concerted conservation efforts. Special areas have been established for the species, such as the Pampas Galeras reserve in south-central Peru. They are now to be found in quite large numbers in many areas, but are still considered vulnerable. In Inca times, vicuña wool was obtained by running the animal to the ground, picking its fleece by hand and then releasing it. This not only assured a

Guanaco crossing.

⊘ PRECIOUS FIBERS

Vicuña is the finest, warmest, softest – and consequently the most expensive – wool in the world, costing up to US$3,000 per yard. This is partly because the animals are so rare, and partly because each one produces only a very small amount of wool. Vicuñas cannot be shorn annually, but only about every third year. Hence they are a protected species, and their wool is not commercially produced.

The far more numerous alpaca can only be shorn on alternate years, but the wool yield is much greater, softer than that of the sheep, and much finer than that of the llama.

regular supply of wool each year but also maintained population levels.

The modern-day illegal hunter resorts to firearms, the primary cause of the vicuña's demise. Prosecution is rare, however, since the people who possess guns are often influential and therefore above the law.

The other wild cameloid, the guanaco, reaches its northernmost limit in the highlands of central Peru, and from here extends down the Andean chain to the southern tip of South America – Tierra del Fuego. In Peru the guanaco is most

Whatever the exact relationships, the domesticated cameloids are to be found throughout the Peruvian highlands.

The only natural enemy of the cameloids is the puma or mountain lion. This large, tawny cat was much revered by the Incas as a symbol of power and elegance.

Unfortunately, after the conquest, Andean people lost the conservationist outlook of the Incas, and the puma has suffered dramatically as a result of indiscriminate hunting. The puma's habit of picking off an unwary llama

Mountain vizcacha.

likely to be seen in the departments of Tacna, Moquegua, Arequipa, and Puno, and is to be found in isolated rocky ravines with bunch grass. Guanacos are wild relatives of the llama and alpaca, but they are instantly distinguishable from their domesticated cousins by their bright tawny coloration, similar to that of the vicuña, but more reddish, albeit with grey facial fur.

The precise relationship between the domestic llamas and alpacas and the wild guanacos and vicuñas is not entirely clear. All possible crosses of the four cameloids have been accomplished, and the offspring of all crosses are fertile. Most taxonomists now agree that the domestic llamas and alpacas are a product of the cross-breeding of guanacos and vicuñas.

has not endeared it to the local people, and these days it is possible only to catch a fleeting glimpse of this magnificent cat as it crosses remote Andean valleys or stalks its prey.

RARE CATS

Two smaller members of the cat family are also to be found in the high Andes. Both species are shy, and little is known of their status and habits. The pampas cat (*Felis colocolo*) is typically an animal of the intermontane Andean valleys, although it does occur close to the coast in northern Peru and in the cloud forest of the eastern slopes of the Andes.

The Andean cat (*Felis jacobita*) is rarer still, and in Peru is limited to the southern highlands.

This is a high-altitude species, mostly nocturnal, and seems to prey on rodents. Tracks of this species can be seen at the snow line nearly 5,000 meters (16,000ft) above sea level, but for the short-term visitor to the Andes an encounter with any of the Peruvian wild cats is a very rare event indeed.

WOODLAND CREATURES

More conspicuous, and more frequently seen by backpackers in the highlands, are the two species of deer. Both species were once more com-

see. The *taruka* is a species in danger of extinction and is found at extremely high altitudes. Its presence is governed by the availability of cover, mostly small isolated patches of woodland. This type of woodland is disappearing at an alarming rate, as it is a primary source of fuel at high altitudes. Consequently, the barrel-chested, short-legged *taruka* is on the decline. If encountered, it is easily distinguished from the white-tailed deer by its two-pronged antlers (the white-tailed deer has one prong only). It is still possible to find this species on the Inca Trail to Machu Picchu.

The elusive Andean huemul.

mon than they are now, and the principal causes of their demise are hunting and the cutting of the high Andean woodlands that provide essential cover. The white-tailed deer is still relatively abundant in more remote areas where hunting pressure is low, since this species shows a remarkable adaptability to various habitat types. It occurs from the coastal plain (in zones of sufficient vegetation) to 4,000 meters (13,000ft) above sea level, and then into the cloud forest of the eastern slopes of the Andes, down almost to the Amazon basin at 600 meters (2,000ft). It is quite common for a hiker in the Andes to encounter this animal.

Its much rarer relative, the Andean huemul (or *taruka* as it is known in Peru), is harder to

Among carnivores, the Andean fox is ubiquitous in all parts of the Andean region, and can be found at all altitudes up to 4,500 meters (14,800ft). This species of fox is larger and longer-legged than its North American and European counterparts, and commonly investigates any empty cans or leftover food outside tents. The Andean fox is everywhere regarded as a dangerous stock killer, especially of sheep, because it may occasionally pick off lambs. It remains common despite the indiscriminate hunting it suffers as a result. The stomachs of these animals often contain quantities of vicuña wool, but it is not known whether it is a predator of this species or only a carrion eater.

Easiest of all to see while hiking through the highlands of Peru are the rodents. While walking along stream banks or dry-stone walls, the observant hiker will notice a large number of small rodents, ranging from the typical house-mouse type familiar to all of us, to mice with a striking color combination of chocolate-brown and white. It is not that there are a greater number of mice-like creatures in the Andes, but simply that, because of very low temperatures at night, most Andean rodents are diurnal. They are also the principal food source of a variety of predators, including the Andean weasel (*Mustela frenata*), a vicious mustelid that will tackle prey twice its size. The abundance of diurnal rodents also accounts for the high density of birds of prey, such as the red-backed and puna hawks, the cinereous harrier, the black-chested buzzard-eagle, and the aplomado falcon.

The guinea pig, or *cuy* as it is known in Peru, is domesticated extensively in the Andes, and wild ones are also fairly common along stony banks and dry-stone walls, where they live in

The unpopular Andean fox.

⊘ THE SPECTACLED BEAR

The spectacled bear, the only bear species found in South America, is a good example of the conflict between conservation and, for the poor, self-preservation. Although an important animal in Andean folklore, the bear has a very poor reputation among small farmers due to its habit of raiding maize crops at the edge of hill forests. Unfortunately for the bear, its fat is much sought-after and its body parts have medicinal uses. Moreover, extensive logging and farming has led to the destruction of its habitat. None of this bodes well for the survival of the bear, which is at dangerously low population levels. The Spectacled Bear Conservation Society is working hard to protect those remaining.

colonies. Any Quechua household will have its colony of guinea pigs living in the kitchen area, as the animal is regarded as a delicacy.

The last two conspicuous animals of the Andes are the hog-nosed skunk and the mountain vizcacha. The former, which may be familiar to visitors from North America, is mostly nocturnal and can often be picked up in car headlights. The latter is a sociable burrower commonly found in rock screes and boulder fields. Very well camouflaged, it often betrays its presence with a high-pitched whistle. Looking like a cross between a chinchilla and a hare, the mountain vizcacha (the prey of large carnivores) can be seen sunning itself on boulders in the early morning and late afternoon. They can often be seen in the ruins of Machu Picchu.

THE CLOUD FOREST

On the eastern slope of the Andes the environment is dominated by humid, temperate forest. Where left undisturbed by humans, the forest continues from 3,600 meters (11,800ft) down to the tropical rainforest of the Amazon basin. The type of forest above 2,500 meters (8,200ft) is commonly known as "cloud forest," a name derived from the fact that for most of the year the trees are shrouded in mist. Indeed, most of the moisture needed by the forest is captured from the enveloping clouds. The cloud forest grades into high grassland at about 3,400 meters (11,200ft) and harbors many exotic animals. The spectacled bear is perhaps the most impressive animal of the zone, with a total body length of up to 183 cm (6ft). This animal is a true omnivore, eating a wide variety of foods such as fruits and berries, large insects, succulent plants, and, at high elevations, the lush hearts of terrestrial bromeliads. The spectacled bear will also eat small mammals and rodents when given the opportunity.

Other shy inhabitants of the cloud forest include two species of small deer. The larger of the two is the dwarf brocket deer. About half the size of the white-tailed deer, it is found to a height of 3,300 meters (10,800ft) in the departments of Puno and Cusco. The other is the pudu, the size of a small dog, difficult to see and mostly nocturnal. It is relentlessly hunted with guns and dogs and must be considered vulnerable at present. Occupying the same habitat as the pudu is the wooly monkey, found in small family groups where hunting pressure is low. It can be spotted in cloud forest beyond Paucartambo in the department of Cusco.

DIVERSITY OF BIRDLIFE

Southeast Peru has a greater diversity of birdlife than any other area on the planet. The majority of the species occur in the cloud forests and lowland rainforests of the eastern Andean slopes, but a wide variety can be seen right up to the snow line.

The bird that first comes to mind when one is writing of the Andean peaks is the Andean condor. This huge member of the vulture family is a carrion feeder, but is not averse to starting its meal a little prematurely. The condor is not a hunter and is incapable of grasping or carrying prey, having feet not unlike those of

---

The Andean condor is the largest flying bird in the world, with a wing span of up to 3 meters (10ft). It covers huge distances in search of the carrion on which it feeds.

An Andean condor soaring above the Colca Canyon.

a chicken (sensational reports of condors carrying off unattended babies must therefore be dismissed). The sight of a condor sailing effortlessly against the backdrop of ice-capped Andean peaks will not be forgotten quickly.

The condor is still a familiar sight throughout the high country, but far more commonly seen are the smaller songbirds such as sierra finches, cinclodes, miners, and seedsnipes. At the limit of the cloud forest, the number of species increases, and the birds are more brightly colored. Anyone taking a stroll here in the morning will see mixed-species flocks of colorful mountain-tanagers and flycatchers, as well as various species of hummingbird, flitting between the moss-festooned branches.

Plaza Mayor, Lima.

View from Amantaní island.

INTRODUCTION

A detailed guide to the entire country, with principal sights clearly cross-referenced by number to the maps.

Palacio Torre Tagle.

Mapping out an itinerary for Peru might seem a daunting prospect. The country is three times as large as California, and many times more varied, with the Andean mountain range and Amazon jungle creating imposing barriers to travel. Yet journeys that were all but impossible 50 years ago are now everyday events. Peru's major cities are linked by air, while long-distance buses and trucks connect towns and villages. These days, the threat from Sendero Luminoso (Shining Path) guerrillas has almost disappeared, and most areas are regarded as safe.

Most travelers to Peru begin their journeys in Lima. As the former center of Spanish South America, it retains some fine colonial architecture, and treasures from all over the country can be found in its impressive museums. The Panamericana highway runs the length of the coast: to the north it leads to the ancient Chimú site at Chan Chan and relaxed coastal cities like Trujillo, and to the south, it takes you to Nazca, whose plains are etched with gigantic drawings made by a mysterious pre-Inca culture.

A 40-minute flight from Lima takes travelers straight into the heart of the Andes, to the Inca capital, Cusco. Apart from its own attractions, Cusco serves as a base to visit the Urubamba Valley and the most famous site on the continent: Machu Pic-

Máncora.

chu. The southern city of Arequipa is one of Peru's most elegant colonial cities, set in the shadow of the snowcapped Volcán Misti, and renowned for its intellectual life. From Cusco and Arequipa, many travelers fly or take the popular railway journey to Puno, by the shores of Lake Titicaca. The world's highest navigable lake is populated by fascinating indigenous communities, who still ply its waters in *totora* reed canoes.

Increasing numbers of travelers are visiting an area that takes up over half of Peru's landmass: the Amazon basin. The northern city of Iquitos is the place from which to begin an Amazon adventure, while in the south there is the Parque Nacional del Manu, one of the purest sections of rainforest in South America.

Peru

0 ___ 100 km
0 ___ 100 miles

SAN MARTIN
DE PORRAS

Av. Peru

Materiales

República

Av. Benavides

BRENA

Av. República de Venezuela

EBLO
BRE

Museo
arco

Jose le
uia y Melendez

Mercado
Artesanal

la Marina

Av. Brasil

Perez Aranibar

Orfelinato
z Aranibar

ya Mar Bella

LUM
(Lugar de la Memoria)

Playa los Delfines

Playa la Pampilla

Playa Makah

Playa Costa Verde

Playa Redondo

Playa la Estrella

Playa las Piedritas

Playa las Cascadas

Playa Barranquito

Playa Barranco

Playa los Yuyos

Playa Sombrillas

Playa Agua Dulce

Playa Pescador

Salto del Fraile

U Playa la Herradura

Monasterio
de los Descalzos

Cerro
San Cristóbal
▲ 409

G RÍMAC

Jirón Cajamarca

Santuario de
Santa Rosa

F

Palacio de
Gobierno

Pl.
Mayor

Plaza
de Acho
Museo Taurino

La
Merced

Catedral de
San Juan Evangelista

Ancash

SANTA ANITA

EL AGUSTINO

Cerro El Agustino
▲ 482

N Museo
de Arte Italiano

Pl. Grau

O Museo de Arte
de Lima

Museo Metropolittano
de Lima

Estadio Nacional

Fuente
Mágica

LA VITORIA

Av. Jaime Bauzate y Meza

Unanue

I. Católica

Gamarra

Av. Pablo
Patron

Av. Nicolás Arriola

Nicolás
Arriola

Av. Industrial

Q Museo Nacional de
Arqueologia, Antropología
e Historia

Museo
Javier Prado

LINCE

PARQUE UNIÓN
PANAMERICANA

SAN LUIS

Museo de
la Nación

P

M

Javier
Prado

LA MOLINA

Jockey
Plaza

Hipódromo
de Monterrico

SAN ISIDRO

Museo
Enrique Poli

Huaca Pucllana

Museo
Amano

MIRAFLORES

PARQUE
KENNEDY

SAN BORJA

SURQUILLO

Primavera

Monte
Reyes

S Museo
de Oro

SANTIAGO
DE SURCO

Los
Cañitos

Museo de Arte
Contemporáneo
MAC

W BARRANCO

MATE
Museo Mario Testino

Museo
Pedro de
Osma

Jorge
Chávez

Atocongo

San
Juan

Aeropuerto
Las Palmas

V CHORRILLOS

SAN JUAN
DE
MIRAFLORES

LIMA

Major urban renewal schemes have given Lima back some of its former splendor. But it remains a sprawling city with many different faces, from the old colonial heart to modern Miraflores.

Herman Melville (the 19th-century American author of *Moby Dick*) called **Lima** "the saddest city on earth." Many visitors have agreed with him, while some residents have been even less complimentary – "Lima the horrible" was how writer Sebastián Salazar Bondy described his native city in the 1960s. But tourists who take such descriptions at face value risk missing out on a rapidly changing city of rare fascination.

Lima has both decaying colonial splendor and the teeming vitality of an oriental bazaar; melancholy, cloudy winters and warm, breezy summers; impoverished urban sprawl and quiet, elegant corners among ancient buildings where the night air is scented with jasmine.

THE CITY OF KINGS

Lima was founded by the Spanish conquistador Francisco Pizarro on January 18, 1535. The foundation was planned for January 6 – Epiphany, or the Day of the Kings – and despite the delay the capital was still known as La Ciudad de los Reyes or "The City of Kings." Pizarro traced a grid of 13 streets by nine to form 117 city blocks on the site of an existing indigenous settlement beside the southern bank of the Río Rímac (from which the name Lima was derived). But he had no great army of workers: the city's first inhabitants numbered fewer than 100.

Pizarro had originally made his capital at Jauja, in the Andes. The rapid switch was determined by a strategic need to be close to his ships – his only lifeline in a rebellious, still largely unconquered country. The Rímac Valley provides the best line of communication through the Andean peaks to the interior of central Peru, while the rivers Chillón and Lurín also reach the sea within the present-day boundaries of the city, making the site one of the best watered in the coastal desert. Several *huacas*, or funeral mounds,

Main Attractions

Plaza Mayor
Catedral
Palacio de Gobierno
Monasterio de San
  Francisco
Palacio Torre Tagle
Museo de la Nación
Avenida Petit Thouars
Huaca Pucllana

Maps on pages
142, 162

Clowning around in Plaza San Martín.

⊙ Fact

If you are wondering why some street names include the word "Jirón," they are the major thoroughfares, made up of several blocks. Each individual block may have a different name.

The austere interior of the cathedral.

along with other pre-Columbian ruins, survive in greater Lima as testimony that the area was populated centuries before the conquest. The most important pre-Inca religious site in coastal Peru was nearby at Pachacámac.

The only drawback was the future city's microclimate. Because of a meteorological phenomenon known as thermal inversion, Lima is often draped in a damp blanket of low cloud – the *garúa* – from May through October, although the summer months can be agreeable. And though the visitor, seeing exuberant gardens of yellow amancaes or purple bougainvillea (the product of careful irrigation), may often forget the fact, rainfall rarely amounts to more than a few nights of drizzle – insufficient to wash the desert dust from the facades of buildings that require frequent repainting.

CAPITAL OF THE NEW WORLD

For two centuries after its foundation, Lima was the political, commercial, and ecclesiastical capital of Spanish South America, and the seat of the Inquisition as well as of the viceroys. But its beginnings were modest, and gave little clue to its later splendor. The mestizo chronicler Garcilaso de la Vega described it as having "very broad and very straight streets, so that from any of its crossroads the countryside can be seen in all four directions," adding that the houses were roofed with reeds rather than tiles.

But by the early 17th century, Lima's population had risen to about 25,000, the majority of whom were indigenous people working as servants or artisans, and African slaves. In the 1680s a protective wall with 12 gateways was built around the city, because of fears of raids by English privateers. The most powerful earthquake, in 1746, destroyed much of the city, and the palaces, churches, mansions, and monasteries we see today were subsequently rebuilt and expanded. Across the Río Rímac, pleasure gardens for the aristocracy were carefully laid out. Despite being frequently damaged by earthquakes, the city was rich as well as powerful.

⊙ CURBSIDE GOURMET

Lima is at the heart of Peru's world-class cuisine scene, most famously serving up innovative *novoandina* food and *chifa* (Chinese-Peruvian). But as one of South America's biggest cities, Lima offers food from around the globe and many different traditions to taste. It's ubiquitous, and a source of inspiration for the crop of new chefs that has enabled Peru to stake its claim to fame firmly as the home of one of the world's great cuisines. Two Limean restaurants, Central and Maido, made it into the top 10 of the World's Best Restaurants list for 2016.

Many a restaurant has emerged from a lowly cart selling *anticuchos* or corn on the cob. Travelers from overseas – bar those whose hardy stomach can take almost anything – might find some of the street food a bit of a challenge though, as there are some health risks involved for constitutions unaccustomed to the germs of a teeming tropical-latitude metropolis. Conversely, chic restaurants, while safer, will likely remove visitors from contact with the most obvious experts when it comes to local cuisine – the Peruvians themselves. Head therefore to the Surquillo No. 1 market, at Paseo de la República expressway and Narciso de Colina. Renovated in 2010, the market has its own restaurant section, perfect for sampling the best of Peru at low prices. Many of the star chefs of Miraflores themselves buy their ingredients here.

Lima's gradual decline from pre-eminence began in the late 18th century, as new viceroyalties were created in Bogotá and Buenos Aires, and the city's monopoly on trade between Europe and South America was broken. As would be expected of a royalist city, independence from Spain was initiated from outside. Expeditionary forces, first from Argentina under General José de San Martín and then from Colombia under Venezuelan Simón de Bolívar, "The Liberator," occupied the city. Installed as republican Peru's first president in the suburb of Magdalena, even the austere Bolívar was affected by Lima's sybaritic elegance. It was at a ball in the city that he met and fell in love with Manuela Sáenz, the Ecuadorian wife of a British doctor, who was to become his lifelong companion. Bolívar's presidency lasted only from 1824 to 1826, and when he left for Colombia a period of political instability and economic chaos ensued.

BURSTING ITS BOUNDARIES

After a turbulent period, the city's development resumed in the mid-19th century. The first railway in South America opened between Lima and its port of Callao in 1851, followed swiftly by further lines to connect the city with the growing coastal villages of Miraflores and Chorrillos. The city walls were demolished in the 1870s, although fragments can still be seen beside the railway line in the Barrios Altos, as the city grew beyond its Spanish limits. But setbacks followed, as Lima was occupied and partially sacked by Chilean troops in 1881 during the disastrous War of the Pacific, and Lima's number of residents fell back below 100,000. It was only in the early 20th century that the city resumed a process of change and growth that has lasted to the present day, the product of both massive migration from the Andean hinterland and the exit of the upper classes as Peru moved falteringly toward democracy. The outline of the modern city dates from the beginning of this period. Industry began to spread westward along the Callao railway, and up the central highway to Vitarte in the east.

Statue of General José de San Martín in Plaza San Martín.

Living on the edge: Lima seen from Barranco.

Inside Lima's cathedral there is a gallery of religious art that can be visited free of charge.

The building of Paseo Colón and Avenida Nicolás de Piérola or La Colmena (begun in 1898), and of Plaza San Martín (1921), created new arteries and a new central focus to the south of Pizarro's Plaza de Armas, which was revamped in 1997 and renamed the Plaza Mayor. The rising urban upper middle class moved away from the crowded center to the spacious south, toward Miraflores and the new district of San Isidro, laid out as a leafy garden suburb. Working-class suburbs sprang up over the river in Rímac, in El Agustino to the east, and in La Victoria to the southeast. By 1931, Lima's population had reached 280,000, having doubled in little more than two decades.

In the years since then, two trends have given Lima its present urban structure. Infill development of middle-class suburbs has completed a triangle enclosing the area between the city center, Callao, and Chorrillos. Outside this triangle, Andean migrants made their homes in sprawling, self-built shantytowns stretching north, south, and northeast, occupying the vacant desert

Plaza Mayor.

sands in the shadow of the Andean foothills. The shantytowns now contain half the city's population of nearly 11 million and decades of hard work have turned some into pleasant districts.

But the migrants and their children have changed the character of the city irrevocably. Many of them came to Lima during the 1980s, when the violence of the Sendero Luminoso terrorists and the military, of which *campesinos* (subsistence farmers) were often the innocent victims, made rural life intolerable. As the wealthy departed, the city swelled with rural migrants and the old downtown area fell into decay. Businesses and hotels took flight, re-establishing themselves in better-run districts like San Isidro, Miraflores, and La Molina.

Successive mayors have since imposed a clean-up campaign which moved the street vendors – *ambulantes* – from the historic center. This was accompanied by a certain amount of strife, but has proved successful. Many of the vendors are now operating in organized markets, achieving commercial success.

PLAZA MAYOR

A major program of urban renewal is in progress in the historic center of the city. Under the auspices of Unesco it has been declared part of "the Cultural Heritage of Mankind," and there have been spectacular changes in both architectural restoration and street cleanliness and security. Some streets (namely Jirón Ica, Ucayali, Ancash and Carabaya) have been converted into pedestrian zones. The usual starting point for exploring Lima is **Plaza Mayor** Ⓐ (formerly Plaza de Armas). Stand in the middle of this handsome square, by the 17th-century bronze fountain, and you are at the city's historic heart. Look out for the Angel of Fame on the fountain: it's a copy of the original, which, it is said, flew away in 1900. Most of the buildings are 18th-century reconstructions, but the spirit of the conquistadors permeates the square.

The eastern side of the square is dominated by the **Catedral de San Juan Evangelista** Ⓑ (Mon–Fri 9am–5pm, Sat 10am–1pm, Sun 1–5pm) on a site chosen by Francisco Pizarro, but reconstructed several times after earthquakes. The present building was begun in the 18th century, after the almost complete devastation of the previous one in the 1746 earthquake. Much of the exterior has been painted in yellow-ochre, as part of a successful policy to brighten up dusty facades with colors used in the colonial period.

Inside, the cathedral is large and unusually austere for a Baroque church, following extensive late 19th-century restorations. Notable are the 17th-century wooden choir stalls. To the right of the entrance is a small side-chapel dedicated to Pizarro, where his skeleton lies in a sealed wooden coffin. Found in 1977 during excavations in the cathedral crypt and put on display in 1985, to mark Lima's 450th anniversary, it replaced the remains of an anonymous conquistador, long mistakenly thought to have been Pizarro. The cathedral also houses the **Museo Religioso de la Catedral de Lima** (Museum of Religious Art; same hours; charge) featuring sculptures, paintings, chalices, and chasubles owned by the Cathedral as well as private collections.

⊘ Eat

There are a lot of good places to eat pizza in Lima. Try El Italiano (www.pizzeriaelitaliano.com) at Jirón E. Leon García 376 in La Victoria or Spizza at Av. Dos de Mayo 455 in Miraflores (www.spizza.pe).

Changing of the Guard at the Presidential Palace.

The Central Post Office building, which now houses Serpost, is regarded as a national monument.

Next door to the cathedral is the **Palacio del Arzobispo** (Archbishop's Palace; Mon–Sat 9am–5pm), rebuilt in the 1920s with an impressive wooden balcony. Opposite stands the **Municipalidad de Lima** (City Hall; tel: 01-632 1300; guided tours by appointment), built in the 1940s after fire destroyed its predecessor. The pleasant interior includes a fine library (Mon–Fri). Next to it on the square is the headquarters of the **Club de la Unión**, a lunchtime haunt of politicians and professionals. Between them at the mouth of Pasaje Santa Rosa is a monument, in the form of a large chunk of rough-hewn stone, to Taulichusco El Viejo, the last *cacique* (chief) of pre-conquest Lima, which was unveiled in 1985 as a belated antidote to the ghost of Pizarro.

On the north side of the plaza is the **Palacio de Gobierno** Ⓒ (Government Palace; to arrange a tour of the palace reserve at least 48 hours in advance via tel: 01-311 3908). It is built on the site of Pizarro's palace, where he was assassinated in 1541 – the first Latin American coup d'état. The present building was completed in 1938, and suffers from the

Colonial buildings just off the Plaza Mayor.

taste for grandiose French Baroque that afflicted dictatorial leaders of the time. Much of the ground plan at the rear of the building remains the same as in Pizarro's day. Every day at noon you can catch the Changing of the Guard, performed in the front courtyard by goose-stepping troops from the Húsares de Junín regiment, dressed in the red-and-blue ceremonial uniforms and ornamental helmets of the independence period. Opposite the palace stands the **Casa de Aliaga** (tel: 01 427-7736; daily 9.30am–5pm by appointment; http://casadealiaga.com). Dating back to 1535, it is said to be the oldest house in the Americas. Its first owner was Captain Jerónimo de Aliaga y Ramírez, Francisco Pizarro's trusted ally. Now it boasts a beautiful collection of Peruvian art and artifacts, including Aliaga's sword.

In a small side square, between the palace and the Municipalidad, stands an equestrian statue of the ubiquitous Pizarro, somewhat disregarded these days. Behind him, the building topped with antennae houses an office of Peru's National Intelligence Service. Nearby stands the restored building of the former Central Post Office, or Correo Central, with the Museo Postal y Filatélico del Perú (Philatelist Museum; Mon–Sat 8.30am–1pm and 2–7pm, Sun 8.30am–1pm). The building also houses the **Casa de la Gastronomía Peruana** (Gastronomy House; Tue–Sun 9am–5pm), offering an interesting insight into the 500-year old history of Peruvian cuisine.

Farther up toward the river are a couple of splendid old hat shops. This is where the booming contraband market of **Polvos Azules** used to be, but the street vendors and shop-owners have been moved to the old industrial area just outside the center. Thieves abound here and in the city center generally, and visitors should take great care of their valuables. Until you become accustomed to the city, you would also be best advised not to wander alone in the center by night.

Doubling back into Plaza Mayor again, on a charming street corner (the intersection of Jirón Carabaya and Jirón Junín) you will find **La Casa del Oidor**. Dating from the early 18th century, it has the wooden balconies in the form of enclosed galleries projecting from the first floor that were colonial Lima's most graceful feature. Farther up Carabaya, past several shoe shops, is the **Desamparados Station**, a neoclassical building dating from 1908. This is the terminal for the spectacular journey to Huancayo, along one of the highest rail tracks in the world, via Ticlio, which reaches 4,800 meters (16,000ft) above sea level (see page 203). Nowadays, it also happens to be the house of Peruvian literature, with temporary art exhibits, a library, and frequent readings (Tue–Sun 10am–7pm; www.casadelaliteratura.gob.pe).

With the removal of the street vendors, a new promenade, the Paseo Chabuca Granda, has been created behind the Presidential Palace on the southern bank of the Río Rímac. Many Limeños (the people of Lima) like to stroll here at the weekends. If you turn right at Jirón Ancash 209, the **Museo de Sitio Bodega y Quadra** (Tue–Sun 9am–5pm; free) is an interesting museum which sheds light on colonial society and life in republican times.

MONASTERIO DE SAN FRANCISCO

If you continue along Jirón Ancash, you will come to the **Monasterio de San Francisco D**, the jewel of colonial Lima. Even if you are not a fan of colonial churches, don't miss this one. The outside is attractively painted in colonial yellow, but it is the interior that is most fascinating; much of it is decorated in the geometrical *Mudéjar* (Andalusian Moorish) style. Established soon after the foundation of Lima, it has suffered earthquake damage over the years, but has been sensitively restored in the original style. Its outstanding features include the 17th-century library,

with 25,000 leather-bound volumes and 6,000 parchments dating from the 15th to the 18th century. The cupola has a superb *Mudéjar* carved wooden ceiling of Panamanian cedar, dating from 1625. In a gallery above the nave of the church are 130 choir stalls and 71 panels with carvings of Franciscan saints, made of the same wood. Restoration work has exposed (under eight layers of paint) 17th-century murals in the cloister and adjacent chambers (www.museocatacumbas.com, daily 9am–8.15pm; guided tours).

The monastery's collection of religious art includes paintings from the workshops of Rubens and Francisco de Zurbarán and, in the refectory, a *Last Supper* painted in 1697 by a Flemish Jesuit priest. San Francisco has probably survived more recent earthquakes because of the solid base provided by its catacombs, which were used as Lima's cemetery until 1810. A network of underground chambers, which are open to the public, contain hundreds of skulls and bones, stored in racks according to type. A secret passage

Eat

For mouthwatering homemade ice cream, head to Heladería Speciale, Jirón. Libertad 1231 in Magdalena, or to 4D (http://4d.pe/web/locales/) at Angamos Oeste 408, in Miraflores.

Feeding the birds outside the San Francisco monastery.

One of the catacombs in the Monasterio de San Francisco.

The opulent Palacio Torre Tagle.

(now bricked up) led from here to the Government Palace.

There are many other colonial churches in the center. To reach the **Iglesia de Santo Domingo** (daily 8.30am–5.30pm), retrace your steps along Ancash to the corner of Jirón Camana. The church, which has a pleasant cloister with tiling from Seville, contains the tomb of San Martín de Porres, a black saint who lived and died in Lima and is venerated throughout Latin America. There is also an urn here that holds the ashes of Santa Rosa de Lima, the patron saint of the New World and the Philippines, as well as the city of Lima. The adjacent convent houses a museum and a library with some 25,000 books. To reach the **Santuario de Santa Rosa** continue along Conde de Superunda and turn right on Avenida Tacna. The sanctuary, a modest hut built in the 16th century on the site of the saint's birthplace and now set in a pleasant garden, contains relics of Santa Rosa (Mon–Sat 9am–1pm and 3–6pm, Sun 9am–1pm).

As you walked along Conde de Superunda, between Santo Domingo and the Santuario, you may have noticed that this is one of several streets in the center with good colonial balconies. Since the city council's "Adopt a Balcony" campaign, many balconies – previously in a sad state of decay – have been restored by private investors. The **Casa de Osambela** (Jirón Conde de Superunda 298; tel: 01-427 7987; Mon–Fri 9am–12.45pm, 2–4.45pm; free) is open to the public and well worth visiting. A late 18th-century mansion with an ornamental cupola, beautifully restored in the 1980s, it houses a small art gallery.

ACROSS THE RIVER

At this point, make a small detour. You could cross the Puente Santa Rosa here or, better, return to the little bridge behind the Palacio de Gobierno, the **Puente de Piedra** (Stone Bridge), built over four round arches in 1610 (its mortar reputedly bound with thousands of egg whites for strength), which leads over the river to **Rímac** , once the playground of the aristocracy and now a lively working-class district.

Turn right and you will come to **Plaza de Acho**, the oldest bullring in the Americas. The **Museo Taurino** (Mon–Sat 9am–4.30pm; tel: 01-481 1467) has a collection of bullfighting memorabilia and, notably, some Goya engravings. There is a panoramic view of the city from Cerro San Cristóbal. Organized tours visit the Rímac district and this hill several times a day. Buses leave from the main plaza, and the tour includes a visit to the bullfighting museum.

At the foot of the hill is the **Alameda de los Descalzos**, laid out in 1610 as a pleasure garden with statues and wrought-iron railings. It leads to the restored **Monasterio de los Descalzos** (Monastery of the Barefoot Friars; Wed–Mon 9.30am–1pm, 2pm–5.30pm), worth a visit for its collection of colonial paintings. To the right is the **Paseo de Aguas**, another beautifully renovated pleasure garden created in the 18th century by Viceroy Amat for his famous mistress, La Perrichola.

CHURCHES AND MIRACLES

On the south side of the River Rímac, on the corner of Avenida Tacna and Jirón Huancavelica, stands the Baroque **Santuario y Monasterio de las Nazarenas** Ⓗ. It houses the image of El Señor de los Milagros (The Lord of Miracles), the black Christ painted by a freed African slave that has become the most important focus of popular religious feeling in Lima. The miracle was that the wall on which the painting appeared was the only part of a 17th-century shantytown to survive an earthquake. In October the image is borne around the city center for several days (October 18, 19, and 28) by teams of men wearing the purple robes of the brotherhood of El Señor de los Milagros. Hundreds of thousands of people turn out to accompany the image. The church can be visited (daily 6am–noon, 6–8.30pm; free), but the convent is a closed Order.

Leaving Las Nazarenas, go to the next corner and turn left down Avenida Emancipación and then left again on Jirón de la Unión, which brings you to the **Iglesia de la Merced** Ⓘ. This church, which, like most in Lima, suffered severe earthquake damage and was rebuilt in the late 18th century, is built on the site of the first Catholic Mass celebrated in the city, in 1534 (7am–1pm, 4–8pm; free).

Leaving La Merced, go down Jirón Miro Quesada, then turn left on Jirón Azángaro and you will reach the **Iglesia de San Pedro** (daily 8.30am–1pm and 2–4pm; free), another Baroque church with *Mudéjar* influences, which was consecrated in 1638.

COLONIAL MANSIONS

The city center contains several fine examples of secular colonial architecture. Outstanding is one on Jirón

One of the ornate balcony grilles of Palacio Torre Tagle.

The open-air Pasaje de la Casa de Correos by the Central Post Office.

Making traditional ham sandwiches at Bar Cordano, a Lima institution.

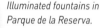

Illuminated fountains in Parque de la Reserva.

Ucayali, close to San Pedro: the **Palacio Torre Tagle** ❶ (Jirón Ucayali 363; tel: 01-311 2400; visits only Sat 9am–4pm; free) was completed in 1735 and gives a good idea of the opulence of Lima in its colonial prime. It now houses the Foreign Ministry, but you can have a peer into the courtyard, from where you can see the finely carved wooden balconies. Opposite Torre Tagle, in another colonial mansion, is **L'Eau Vive Restaurant** ❷, run by French-speaking nuns. Customers are encouraged to join them in singing the Ave Maria at 3pm and 9pm.

From here, make a slight detour to the **Museo de la Inquisición y del Congreso** ❸ (Museum of the Inquisition and Congress; temporarily closed for renovation), on Jirón Junín. This is the building where generations of alleged heretics were tortured and tried. You can visit the main hall (with a fine 18th-century wooden ceiling) and the sinister, underground dungeons and torture chambers. The stocks are original, and there are mock-ups of other torture techniques. Between here and the river is a huge daily market, and an archway proclaiming that this is Lima's **Chinatown**.

REPUBLICAN LIMA

South of the Plaza Mayor, the largest square is the **Plaza San Martín**, a hub of the city center. If you approach the square from Plaza Mayor, you should take the pedestrianized **Jirón de la Unión**, once Lima's most elegant shopping street. As recently as the 1940s it was considered scandalous for women to stroll along Jirón de la Unión without wearing a hat.

The colonnaded Plaza San Martín, restored and repainted and brightly lit, is an important gathering place for political meetings. In the center is an equestrian statue of General José de San Martín, Peru's Argentinian independence hero. On its west side is the **Gran Hotel Bolívar** ❹, built in the 1920s. The hotel retains much of its former atmosphere. A Palm Court trio serenades people drinking afternoon tea and its giant *pisco* sours (called *catedrales*) remain

⦿ FUENTE MÁGICA

One of Lima's favorite attractions is the **Circuito Mágico del Agua** in the Parque de La Reserva (park Tue–Sun 3–10.30pm), situated to the south of the Estadio Nacional. Thirteen spectacular fountains make an incredible display of music, water, and light. Visit at dusk and you'll see them come to life in a kaleidoscope of spotlit colors. There's a tunnel of water which you can walk through (and stay relatively dry), and a fountain in which you can attempt to dodge the timed water spouts (and end up soaking wet).

The **Fuente Mágica** spouts 80 meters (260ft) into the air, reaching its climax with an orchestral crescendo that you can watch from a classical folly nearby.

justly famous. The Bolívar is the perfect place to stop and rest during a city tour; the decor and ambience make the high price of the drinks worthwhile.

Next to the Bolívar is **Jirón Ocoña**, the center of Lima's street foreign exchange market, where money-changers buy or sell dollars round the clock. Across La Colmena from the Bolívar is the **Club Nacional**. Though it is no longer the watering-hole of Peru's once all-powerful oligarchy, it has taken on a new lease of life with the revamping of the city center. The clients are now a blend of old-money families and prominent members of the business community.

TOURING THE MUSEUMS

Lima has a wealth of museums, some of them displaying the best of the pre-Columbian treasures unearthed from sites around the country. It is a very large city and the museums are scattered around it, but transport is not hard to find. The Tourist Office will be able to help you find the best routes between places of interest. Taxis are inexpensive and there is no shortage of them. They come in all shapes and sizes, some smart, some very dilapidated, and they don't have meters; take local advice and fix a price in advance.

Leaving Plaza San Martín, head south down Unión (which becomes Belén) to the Paseo de la República and the **Museo de Arte Italiano** (www.museos.cultura.pe/museos/museo-de-arte-italiano; Tue–Sun 10am–5pm). There is a good selection of Italian and other European paintings from the early 20th century, and the neoclassical building itself is worth seeing for its fine mosaics.

On the other side of Avenida 9 de Diciembre (usually called Paseo de Colón) is the **Museo de Arte de Lima** (MALI; http://www.mali.pe/; Tue–Fri and Sun 10am–7pm, Sat until 5pm), containing an extensive collection of Peruvian art from the conquest to the present day. The museum is also an important center for music, cinema, and theater performances. At the

⊘ **Kids**

Lima's zoo (http://leyendas. gob.pe/; daily 9am–5pm) is located in the Parque de las Leyendas in Pueblo Libre. It is split into the three geographical regions of Peru – the coast, mountains, and jungle – and also has a children's playground.

Views from the Larcomar complex.

⚲ OASIS OF HOPE

There's a side of Lima very different from the affluent streets of Miraflores. Like many of Lima's barrios, Villa El Salvador started as a squatter camp and evolved into an officially recognized suburb.

Villa El Salvador is more than just another shanty-town formed by aspiring Andean migrants. Tucked behind sand dunes not far from the Inca shrine of Pachacamac, about 30km (20 miles) south of Lima, it was founded in 1971 by an initial wave of 10,000 migrants who had fled from the mountain areas around Huaraz in the wake of an earthquake. Today it is home to around 350,000 people, and is a proto-type of self-determination by Peru's marginalized Andean majority.

The settlement's success has brought international recognition. It has been nominated for the Nobel Peace Prize, won Spain's prestigious Prince of Asturias award for social achievement, and been designated by the United Nations as a Messenger of Peace. Its key factor is the Andean tradition of community organization centered on the family unit.

Each block of houses, or *manzana*, comprises 24 families; 16 blocks make up a residential group, and 22 of these form a sector. Health centers, communal

Child street vendors in Villa El Salvador.

kitchens, and sports grounds bond the groups together. Education is prioritized, and illiteracy in Villa El Salvador is minimal, unlike in other similar shanty-towns. Most of the houses are built of adobe bricks or concrete, and have drainage, mains water, and electricity. The community is crisscrossed by roads and dotted generously with shady poplar, eucalyptus, pomegranate, and banana trees.

Clever irrigation, worthy of the residents' Inca forebears, has converted hundreds of hectares of sandy desert into arable land, using the community's own treated sewage. Fruit and cotton are cultivated in the fields, as are corn and fodder crops for the thousands of privately and communally owned cattle whose milk and cheese are sold locally.

Villa El Salvador's first martyr was Edilberto Ramos, who was killed resisting police attempts to expel the original settlers. It was his death that forced the government to hand over the land. But the powerful sense of local identity, forged by such bravery and collective action in combating poverty, was shaken by terrorist infiltration during the early 1990s.

In 1992, popular community leader and deputy mayor María Elena Moyano was shot dead in front of her children by Sendero Luminoso guerrillas. Later that same year the mayor of Villa El Salvador was wounded in a terrorist attack after criticizing Moyano's killers. These deaths helped to strengthen the sense of community in Villa El Salvador, and to reinforce local political development.

The town's libraries, community radio station, and written bulletins demonstrate the determination to communicate, and the belief that education genuinely brings self-advancement and change. The industrial park, created in 1987, provides much-needed local employment and exports products to many parts of the world. The district is also where the Panamerican Village is being constructed for the 9,000 athletes who will take part in the Panamerican Games in 2019.

The community continues to flourish despite enormous problems of malnutrition and continuing under-employment. It is an oasis that has tapped a spring of hope from beneath the desert floor. While there are no official tours to Villa El Salvador, it's often possible to arrange a visit through your hotel. If you do go, be respectful (and careful) with your camera.

other end of a very pleasant public park is the **Museo Metropolitano de Lima** (Tue–Sun 10am–5pm), presenting the history and the future of the Peruvian capital through a range of media, including 4D exhibits.

From the museum, take the Avenida 28 de Julio, then turn right down Avenida Aviación to the San Luis district. Here, on Avenida Javier Prado Este in San Borja, you will find the **Museo de la Nación** ❶ (National Museum; Tue–Sun 9am–5pm), which has a wonderful collection of artifacts from the Chavín culture – among other things an ingenious replica of a Chavín stela, woven articles found at Paracas, and ceramics from Nazca, making it one of the best museums in the city.

The next stop on the museum tour is the **Museo Nacional de Arqueología, Antropología e Historia** ❷ (National Museum of Archeology, Anthropology, and History; http://mnaahp.cultura.pe/; Mon–Sat 8.45am–5pm, Sun until 4pm), located on (another) Plaza Bolívar in the suburb of Pueblo Libre. Although some of the collections have been moved to the Museo de la Nación, it is still one of the most interesting museums in the country, with a superb collection of pottery and textiles from all the main cultures of ancient Peru. It is well laid out, in chronological order, and the curators have resisted the temptation to swamp visitors with too many displays.

Close by on Avenida Bolívar is the **Museo Larco** ❸ (www.museolarco.org; daily 9am–10pm), which has a vast collection of pre-Columbian ceramics, gold and silver objects, and some interesting textiles. A small annex holds a fascinating collection of erotic pottery from the Moche period. Few of the displays are labeled, but they are impressive for their fine quality.

In 1998 it was discovered that a large proportion of the artifacts at the **Museo de Oro** ❹ (Gold Museum; Av. Alonso de Molina 1100; www.museoroperu.com.

pe; daily 10.30am–6pm) were modern replicas. However, the museum also has a collection of genuine textiles, weapons, stone carvings, and ceramics on display.

THE MODERN CAPITAL

Two main arteries, the Avenida Arequipa and the Paseo de la República expressway, link the city center with the business district of **San Isidro**, where you might take a look at another museum: a very special private collection called the **Enrico Poli** (Lord Cochrane 466; daily 11am–7pm; tel: (511)-422 2437 or (511)-654-4351, call one or two days before for an appointment). It's well worth a stop to see the School of Cusco paintings and silver and gold work from colonial and pre-Columbian times. Not far from there, overlooking the ocean, is the **Lugar de la Memoria** (LUM; Museum of Memory; Bajada San Martin 151; http://lum.cultura.pe/; Tue–Sun 10am–6pm; free), built to commemorate the victims of domestic armed conflict. Permanent and temporary exhibitions explore the

> **⊙ Tip**
>
> One of the best ways to see Lima's beaches and to get a perspective on the city from above is to take a paraglider flight. There are tandem flights for beginners, and one-day and multi-day courses. Contact Aeroxtreme, Av. Tripoli 345, Dpto 503, Miraflores, tel: (511)-242 5125, www.aeroxtreme.com.

Selling handicrafts in Miraflores.

Shoeshine in Miraflores.

terrorism and violence that rocked Peru between 1980 and 2000, exploring the facts, how the Peruvian population was affected, and the process that led to its end. LUM aims to provide a space for healing and reflection.

These two long avenues lead to **Miraflores ①**, the main area for restaurants, cafés, nightlife, and some shopping. Avenida Larco used to be the main shopping area, but in recent years new commercial centers like Centro Comercial Larcomar (www.larcomar.com), Plaza San Miguel (www.plazasanmiguel.com.pe), and Jockey Plaza Shopping Mall (http://jockeyplaza.com.pe) have become the places for those born to shop. A good selection of handicrafts is sold at hundreds of shops and stalls on **Avenida Petit Thouars** in Miraflores. Be sure to do some (respectful) bargaining, as prices here are higher than elsewhere in Peru.

Miraflores is really a place for the here and now, but there is one museum worth a look, the **Museo Amano** (Retiro 160, 11th block of Av. Angamos; tel: 51 1 441 2909; www.museoamano.org;

Path down to the sea.

Tue–Sun 10am–5pm, Mon upon previous appointment). The museum displays a beautiful collection of textiles, mostly from the Chancay culture.

Close to Avenida Arequipa is the massive pre-Inca adobe pyramid site called the **Huaca Pucllana**. This has been restored, and there are frequent guided tours (Wed–Mon 9am–5pm; www.huacapucllanamiraflores.pe). There is also a small museum, and an excellent bar and restaurant (www.resthuacapucllana.com/es/).

At the top end of Larco is the **Parque Kennedy**, where artists sell paintings at the weekend. Here, next to the Cinerama El Pacifico cinema, is the Café Haiti (www.haitimiraflores.pe), a prime spot for people-watching. Walking down Diagonal, you will find export-quality coffee in the trendy Café Café (www.cafecafe.com.pe) or La Lucha (www.lalucha.com.pe), and a little farther on, a pedestrianized side street crammed with pizzerias with open-air tables. Continue down the Diagonal and you reach the cliffs overlooking the Pacific, laid out with gardens – a lovely place to watch the sunset. A cobbled road Bajada Balta leads down a gully to the sweep of beaches called the **Costa Verde**. This beautiful part of town is safer than it used to be, although it is not advisable to walk here alone or after dark. The resorts to the south of the city are better for swimming.

Nonetheless, the Costa Verde is an attractive place, for the coast road sweeps on round (with fine views of the city) to the isolated beach of **La Herradura ⓤ**, a popular spot to eat ceviche while watching the Pacific breakers. Closer to Miraflores are two well-known fish restaurants (with international prices): the Costa Verde on the beach, and the traditional Rosa Náutica (www.larosanautica.com), built on a pier surrounded by the ocean.

From Playa la Herradura, the road doubles back through a tunnel, leading to **Chorrillos ⓥ**, a mixed area socially speaking, high on the sandy cliffs. Down on the beach is a fishing wharf, where small boats can be hired.

The road now loops back toward Miraflores and takes you to **Barranco 🅦**, a beautiful district of colonial and 19th-century housing, much of which has been restored. This romantic neighborhood is home to many bohemians, writers, and artists, and is celebrated in Peruvian waltzes. It has become the center of the city's nightlife, with a score or more of *peñas* (folk clubs) and bars where music of all kinds is played. La Noche (Pasaje Sanchez Carrion 199; www.lanoche.com.pe) is a popular place for a beer, and recommended for a night out in Barranco. For a more traditional evening, go to Juanito's (Av. Grau 270), a charming traditional bar on the plaza and a popular haunt of generations of *barranquiños*.

Opposite the attractive main square is the wooden **Puente de Los Suspiros** or Bridge of Sighs, a traditional meeting place for lovers, set among gardens overlooking the Pacific. Cross the bridge, follow the path by the church, and you'll find several small bars where *anticuchos* (cured and marinated beef-heart kebabs) are served. From the bars right at the end you have a good view of the Costa Verde. On Saturday evenings you can sample *anticuchos* the traditional way, from the stalls that are set up outside the church. For a touch of culture, visit the **Museo Pedro de Osma**, a private museum containing colonial art (Pedro de Osma 421; http://museopedrodeosma.org; Tue–Sun 10am–6pm) or the **Museo de Mario Testino** (MATE; www.mate.pe; Pedro de Osma 409; Tue–Sat 10am–7pm, Sun till 6pm), presenting the work of the Peruvian high fashion photographer Mario Testino. The **Museo de Arte Contemporáneo** (Av. Almirate Miguel Grau 1511; www.maclima.pe; Tue–Sun 10am–6pm) houses a collection of works by Latin-American artists such as José Luis Cuevas, Fernando Botero, Jorge Eduardo Eielson, and Rafael Hastings.

THE PACIFIC PORT

Now joined to the capital, the port of **Callao ❌** was originally a settlement apart, some 15km (9 miles) west of the city. Efforts are being made to revive tourism in the area including the construction of a Costanera highway linking Callao with San Miguel. The port has several points of interest, such as The **La Punta** area. There the Rana Verde (Green Frog; Parque Gálvez; tel: 51 1 429 5279) is open to visitors at lunchtime. You need to obtain permission to enter the docks, but from the neighboring wharf launches take passengers for trips round the bay. Nearby is the 18th-century **Real Felipe Fort** (www.realfelipe.com/MuseosMilitares/MuseoRFelipe.html), the last royalist redoubt in Peru, captured by Bolívar's forces in 1826 after a year-long siege. It now contains a military museum – the **Museo del Ejército** (daily 9am–4pm).

Taking a siesta in the gardens in Barranco.

The pre-Inca Huaca Pucllana.

THE NORTH COAST

The colonial city of Trujillo, a wealth of archeological digs, and Peru's best beaches are some of the highlights along the north coast – with a witchcraft market thrown in for good measure.

Undeservedly, the north coast of Peru is not visited as much as the area farther south, but it has much to offer, including a wealth of archeological sites near the colonial city of Trujillo, as well as beach holidays. Regular buses ply the Panamericana north from Lima to the border with Ecuador. Ancient sites in the desert are worth breaking the trip north for. **Caral ❷**, 185km (115 miles) due north of the capital, rose up around 2600 BC to become what is now considered the oldest civilization in the Americas. Three thousand people lived on the now arid, isolated 66-hectare (163-acre) site that was then irrigated from the Supe River and close to the ocean. Six pyramids amid a series of other buildings, notably a circular amphitheater, have been dug up so far. Archeologists have found that the ancient civilization of fishermen and shell collectors built large buildings by carrying the construction materials in woven, reed *shicra* sacks, piling them up to form walls just like modern-day sandbags are used to counter flooding. These sacks were flexible enough to allow the structures to withstand earthquakes.

The history of the Caral civilisation is well documented at the **Museo Communitario de Supe** (daily 9am–5pm; www.zonacaral.gob.pe) near the Plaza de Armas in Supe, where more than 300 artifacts from Caral are on display.

Trujillo's town hall.

Further north, **Sechín ❸** is an archeological site decorated with extraordinary wall carvings showing bellicose warriors and their hapless, dismembered victims. The first excavation work here was done in the 1930s by the eminent Peruvian archeologist Julio Tello. The site is still under excavation, but much of it can be seen, and there is an informative museum on the site (daily 9am–5pm). The site is believed to date to the end of the Initial Period (c.1000 BC), but nothing is known about the people who built it. You can get to Sechín by taking

Main Attractions

Caral
Sechín
Colonial Trujillo
Huacas del Sol y de la
  Luna
Chan Chan
Huaca del Dragón
Huanchaco
Mercado de Brujos
Museo Tumbas Reales de
  Sipán
Máncora

Maps on pages
162, 164

PACIFIC

OCEAN

North Coast

0   50 km

0   50 miles

one of the frequent buses from Lima (about 350km/220 miles) to the small town of Casma, from where you can get a taxi or a *colectivo* to the ruins.

COLONIAL-STYLE TRUJILLO

The next stop along the coast is at **Trujillo ④**, Peru's most important northern city (and the third-largest in the country, with a population of a little over 1 million). Charming, formal, and simple, this is the perfect spot from which to explore Peru's gentle but fiercely patriotic north. Founded in 1535 and named after Francisco Pizarro's birthplace in Spain, Trujillo was the resting place for Spaniards journeying between Lima and Quito. It soon merited the title "Lordliest City," and its well-preserved colonial homes with intricate wooden, Andalusian-style balconies and window grills pay testimony to an elegant past.

Although European ways were firmly planted here, *trujillanos* eschewed blind loyalty to the Spanish Crown. In December 1820, it became the first Peruvian city to proclaim its independence from Spain, and liberator Simón de Bolívar, moving down the coast from Ecuador, set the seat of his revolutionary government here. From Trujillo he prepared his campaigns for the decisive battles of Junín, Pichincha, and Ayacucho. At the last battle, on the plain bearing the same name, soldiers under Mariscal José de Sucre turned back the royalist troops once and for all.

A century later, political fervor coursed through Trujillo when the city gave birth to the progressive political party APRA, the American Popular Revolutionary Alliance. But the ideas of its founder, Victor Raúl Haya de la Torre, were too radical for the government of the day; the party was outlawed and forced to operate in secret. Government repression and torture of *apristas* (as APRA party members are called) culminated in 1932 in the brutal "Trujillo Massacre." After a rebellious crowd of party followers attacked an army post and killed the officers in charge, 1,000 people were executed by military firing squads among the adobe walls of Chan Chan.

Another of Trujillo's militant *apristas*, the writer Ciro Alegría, was exiled to Chile, where he published part one of the trilogy, based on his childhood and *campesino* (subsistence farmer's) life, that would make him one of the continent's most acclaimed authors. He won literary attention with *La Serpiente de Oro (The Serpent of Gold)*, but is best-known for *El Mundo Es Ancho y Ajeno (The World is Wide and Alien)*.

AROUND THE PLAZA DE ARMAS

These tumultuous days of exile and bloodshed seem distant now in Trujillo, where formality and colonial charm hang in the air. The best way to see this city is on foot, and the best place to start is the huge **Plaza de Armas** (also known as the Plaza Mayor), at the center of which is a statue of a running winged figure – Liberty, whose face closely resembles Simón Bolívar's – holding a torch. This landmark stands on disproportionately short legs, designed to appease officials who feared the monument would end up taller than the cathedral facing it.

The plaza is dominated by the **Catedral Santa María** Ⓑ (Mon–Fri 7am–noon, 4–9pm, Sat 8am–1pm, Sun for Mass only), dating from the mid-17th century. The cathedral once had elaborate metal adornments and railings, like many of the colonial houses, but they were melted down for armaments during the War of Independence. Its Museo Catedralicio (Cathedral Museum) is worth a visit (Mon–Fri 9am–1pm, 4pm–7pm, Sat 9am–1pm) for its Baroque paintings and liturgical instruments.

The **Hotel Libertador Trujillo** Ⓒ (www.libertador.com.pe), housed in a beautiful colonial-style building, stands on the northwest corner of the square. Even if you are not staying in the hotel (it's about the most expensive in Trujillo), try to have breakfast or lunch in its small-windowed dining room

looking out onto the plaza. From this vantage point one can see the comings and goings of the city's elderly men who stake out shady benches to read their morning newspapers, the young mothers carrying their market baskets with toddlers in tow, or uniformed schoolgirls huddled together sharing secrets.

Two blocks from the square, on Jirón Independencia, is the colonial **Iglesia San Francisco** Ⓓ (daily Mon–Sat 7–9am, 4–8pm, Sun for Mass only). Almost opposite stands the attractive **Casa de los Leones** Ⓔ (Mon–Fri 9am–1pm, 2–6pm, Sat 9am–1pm), also known as the Casa Ganoza Chopitea, which houses a small art gallery as well as an office of the Policía de Turismo. It got its name from the statues of lions that guard the front door. Most of Trujillo's mansions have been elegantly restored by national banks or other private enterprises, and are well worth visiting if you can get inside. If not, you must be content with the view from outside of the detailed window grilles and intricately carved wooden balconies. The window grilles are purely decorative; over the centuries their

The Statue of Liberty in Trujillo's Plaza de Armas.

Trujillo's Plaza de Armas.

The once exclusive Club Central is now home to a ceramics museum.

simple designs became increasingly elaborate as the colonial *trujillanos* tried to outdo one another. The balconies, on the other hand, had a practical purpose: they allowed upper-class women to look down onto the street, but prevented interested menfolk from looking in.

Half a block onward, on the corner with Jr. Junín, is the Museo del Juguete (Toy Museum; Wed–Sat and Mon 10am–6pm, Sun until 1pm), with its bohemian café downstairs, a good spot for a break. Santa Clara, a 19th-century church, is on the other side of the street. From Junín, turn right again on Jirón Pizarro, to see the **Palacio Iturregui** **F** (Mon–Sat 8–10.30am), a neoclassical building where Trujillo's unilateral independence from Spain was declared in 1820. It is now the home of the rather smart Club Central, which runs a small ceramics museum. Rather oddly, it is not this building but another one nearby that is called **La Casa de la Emancipación** **G** (House of the Emancipation; Mon–Fri 9am–1pm and 4–7pm, Sat 9am–1pm). This mansion is typical of those constructed in

the 16th and 17th centuries, and is one of the few containing its original furniture. Like many of Peru's most elegant colonial mansions, this is now the property of a bank, the Banco Continental, and the staff are happy to show visitors where earthquakes and remodeling over the centuries have changed the building's original lines. Back towards the Plaza de Armas you will find the **Iglesia de La Merced** **H**, where a small crowd of visitors can often be found peering upward at the intricately carved dome. The next stop, on the corner of Orbegoso and Bolívar, is the **Casona Orbegoso** **I** (Mon–Sat 9am–5pm; free), a stately colonial mansion impressive for its grand exterior. Almost opposite is the Iglesia de San Agustín, the oldest church in the city. Back on the Plaza de Armas is the elegant colonial **Casa de Urquiaga** **J**, which belongs to the Banco de la Nación (Mon–Fri 9.30am–3.30pm; free).

A couple of blocks away from the Plaza de Armas, on Jirón Junín, lies the **Museo de Arqueología** **K**, run by the National University of Trujillo (Mon–Sat

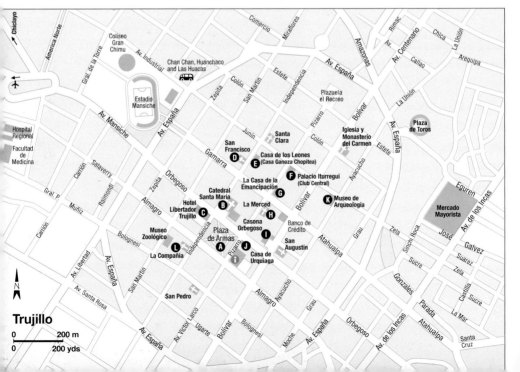

Trujillo

0   200 m
0   200 yds

9am–1pm and 3–7pm, Sun 9am–4pm). Among the artifacts here are fine pieces of Moche and Chimú pottery and copies of some of the wall paintings found at the Huaca de la Luna (see page 166). Follow Ayacucho and turn right into Almagro and after three blocks you'll come to **La Compañía ⓛ**, another notable colonial church, which is now used as an auditorium by the University of Trujillo. Close to the church is the Museo Zoológico (Mon–Fri 9am–6pm), but the stuffed exhibits are not very exciting.

TRUJILLO'S DANCING HORSES

Trujillanos are proud of their *caballos de paso*, a fine breed of horses with a tripping gait that has made them known worldwide. Another legacy of the conquest, since there were no horses on the continent before the arrival of the Spaniards, these horses have been immortalized in Peruvian waltzes. In particular, composer Chabuca Granda, for whom a monument is erected in the bohemian neighborhood of Barranco in Lima, wrote of the *chalanes* or riders in their *jipijapa* sombreros upon their honey-colored mounts. These riders still compete in their own form of the *marinera* dance, smoothly guiding their horses through the steps. The best of these trotters are bred in and around Trujillo, and buyers from around the world congregate to see them shown at the annual Spring Festival – *Festival de la Primavera*. Don't forget, though, that Peru's spring is the northern hemisphere's fall, and this festival takes place in September.

The *Festival de la Marinera* is celebrated in the last week of January, when dancers from all over the country compete for the title of *Campeones de la Marinera*. It's a spectacular show, and the whole town has a party atmosphere, particularly during the finals on the last weekend. The *marinera* is a graceful dance rooted in African and Spanish rhythms; some say its steps mimic the strutting of a rooster courting a hen. Women in ruffled lace skirts seductively flit toward white-garbed men in ponchos before quickly pulling away. The men attempt to win back their attention, tossing up hats and catching them in mid-fall.

Colonial opulence in La Casa de la Emancipación.

Palacio Iturregui.

Replica tumis, knives that were used in human sacrifice by the Moche people, on sale at the Huaca de la Luna site.

Murals at the Huaca de la Luna.

NEARBY TEMPLES

About 10km (6 miles) southeast of Trujillo lie the **Huacas del Sol y de la Luna** ❺ (Temples of the Sun and the Moon). You can get there by minibus or taxi from Trujillo, or go with a guide on an organized tour. These two pyramidal temples were built by the Moche people (100 BC–AD 850) over several generations. The Huaca del Sol (arguably the largest pre-Columbian building in the Americas) is still being excavated, as is the smaller Huaca de la Luna; years of archeological work have begun to unveil a series of temples superimposed on one another to form a pyramid covered in beautiful, brightly colored murals (www.huacasdemoche.pe; daily 9am–4pm). In 2017, three new tombs with remains of members of the Moche elite – along with valuable vases – were excavated west of the Huaca de la Luna.

CHAN CHAN

To the northwest of Trujillo (take one of the frequent minibuses or *colectivos* from Trujillo) are the ruins of **Chan Chan** ❻ (daily 9am–4pm), possibly the world's largest adobe city. Laid out over 20 sq km (7.5 sq miles) just 600 meters/yards from the ocean, its seven citadels are enclosed by a massive adobe wall. Chan Chan was the capital of the Chimú Empire and was once home to some 100,000 people. Its citizens fished and farmed, worshiped the moon, and had no written records – leaving it to archeologists to unravel their secrets. An echoing silence surrounds visitors to this ancient city, whose walls bear carvings of sea otters, fish, seabirds, fishing nets, and moons. To learn more about Chan Chan's history, visit its small museum (Mon–Fri 9am–4.30pm).

Aided by sophisticated aqueduct and irrigation systems, the Chimú turned the arid wasteland around them into fertile fields of grain, fruits, and vegetables supporting a population that may have reached 35,000. When conquered by the Incas, the Chimú were not forced to change their ways – except for the addition of the sun to their collection of gods. Rather, Inca teachers were sent to study their farming and irrigation systems and Chimú goldsmiths were sent to Cusco. It wasn't until the Incas, under Tupac Yupanqui, sabotaged the aqueducts after repeated attempts to invade Chan Chan that the fearless Chimú left the protection of the city – and were conquered.

An entrance ticket to Chan Chan also allows visitors to see the **Huaca del Dragón** – also known as the Huaca Arco Iris (the Rainbow Temple) – with its beautifully restored wall carvings, and the ruins of **Huaca La Esmeralda** nearby. Licensed guides can be hired at the ticket office. Tourists are advised to begin their visit in the morning and avoid going alone; the tourism police at Chan Chan frequently go home in mid-afternoon, and there have been a number of thefts at the site. Visitors should also avoid vendors hawking what they claim is antique pottery. Most pieces are fakes, and genuine items can be confiscated and the holder fined or jailed for trying to take them out of Peru.

Archeology enthusiasts should also visit the **Huaca el Brujo** (www.elbrujo.pe; daily 9am–5pm) site 60km (40 miles) north of Trujillo in the Chicama Valley and worth a visit for its colorful Moche reliefs. However, its main attraction is the famous Lady of Cao, a Moche queen whose tomb was discovered in 2005. Along with the remains of the powerful queen of the Chicama kingdom, the tomb contained 60 objects of pure or part gold and nearly 50 objects of pure or part silver. The contents of the tomb and queen's mummy can be seen at the on-site **Museo de Cao** (hours as above).

SUGAR AND SURF

Before you set off north, another short trip (about 15km/10 miles) from Trujillo is to the seaside village of **Huanchaco,** which has been improved by the restoration of its Baroque church and by landscaping. Today Huanchaco is a popular destination for surfers and beach lovers, although it still retains a village air. Sunbronzed fishermen head out each morning with their nets tucked into *caballitos de totora*, literally "little horses" woven

from *totora* reed, just as they have for many centuries. The design of these peapod-shaped boats is not very different from that of the craft used by pre-Inca people, and the *caballitos* contrast startlingly with the brightly colored surfboards that now share the Pacific waves.

Some 40km (25 miles) north of Trujillo (there are buses) are vestiges of one of the sources of Trujillo's past wealth: sugar. Owing to its gentle climate, the Chicama Valley region produces most of Peru's sugar crop, an important product in a country where three spoonfuls go into every cup of coffee and all children seem to be born with a sweet tooth. Land reform, begun in the late 1960s, turned most of the great haciendas into cooperatives, but the opulence of the past is still evident. The most impressive are Casa Grande and Hacienda Cartavio, now large-scale agro-industrial projects; the latter is where the sugar is used to make Cartavio rum.

MAGIC AND MOCHE FINDS

The next stop north is the busy port of **Chiclayo ❼**, some 200km (125 miles)

A brightly colored fishing boat at Santa Rosa.

Huanchaco village and its one-man horse-shaped rafts.

⊘ LITTLE REED HORSES

Huanchaco's *caballitos de totora* are one-man reed rafts with high prows that resemble the head of a horse. The design of the craft dates back at least to the Moche civilization that first ruled this coast some 2,000 years ago. Huanchaco's 40 or so fishermen paddle out to sea each day to set nets for scale fish, and traps for crab and octopus. At midday they surf back in with their catch for the restaurants of Huanchaco and markets of Trujillo. The rafts, made of bundled reeds, remain tough and buoyant for about three months. To build a new *caballito*, cut, dried, and bundled reeds are lashed tightly together, which takes the most experienced less than an hour. Each fisherman has two rafts – one for fishing in the morning and one for the afternoon so that they don't get saturated with water.

WITCH DOCTOR AND WELLNESS

There is a fascination with Peru's ancient cultures which includes an appreciation for current religion and tradition, most commonly associated with the mother earth, but also for mystical healing.

Although a mostly Catholic society, Peruvians have remained fascinated by their native spirituality, be it Amazonian or Andean. Tribute to the *Pacha Mama*, the mother earth – or more exactly, "mother world," the fertility goddess – is kept alive in much of the Andean world by raising a toast to her or spilling a small tribute to the ground, known as *challa*.

SHAMANISM AND AYAHUASCA

There is also a growing interest on the part of travelers in participating in traditional, religiously

At the Mercado de Brujos.

oriented healing ceremonies, be it the syncretic *santería* in Brazil and the Caribbean or pre-Hispanic rites in Peru and other Andean countries. Much of this is centered around experiences with the hallucinogenic extract from the Ayahuasca vine (see page 211), used by **shamans** – also known as *brujos*, or witch doctors – to cure ills and predict the future of their patients. According to the shamans, these ceremonies must take place at night, as the impact of the drug would be potentially overwhelming in daytime. The use of Ayahuasca in Peru, along with the San Pedro cactus, is common and legal, and traditional shamanism is condoned and to some extent even advertised by the state; but caution must be exercised. Being spat at might not be everyone's idea of a good time, and there are more serious issues of health and personal safety to consider – don't accept just anyone claiming to be a shaman. There are no shaman academies, *brujos* becoming accepted in their communities or neighborhood by experience alone.

However, some reputable tour companies do offer competent and safe introductions to the mystical aspect of Peru's religions, along with the necessary guidance and respect on both sides. Among them are Etnika's Tours (www.etnikas.com; tel: 0051-984 109 74) in Cusco, offering modern retreat centers in the Sacred Valley; Peru Traces (www.perutraces.com; tel: (511) 242-9408), with mysticism-oriented tours near Lima, Cusco, and in the Amazon. Other well-known hotspots of shamanic healing are the Túcume pyramids near Lambayaque, supplied by Chiclayo's witch doctor market, as well as Pucallpa and Wanamey (www.wanamey.org), on the fringes of the Amazon.

MYSTIC ENERGY

Esoteric publications also maintain that Peru has numerous areas where cosmic energy is particularly concentrated, the most famous of these areas being Machu Picchu and Lake Titicaca, but with sites such as Tipón in the Sacred Valley and Chavín de Huanta also included. Closest to Lima are the beautiful rock formations of Marcahuasi, a worthwhile visit even without their mystic connotations.

up the Panamericana – there are regular bus services as well as frequent flights from Lima. This bustling city is a major commercial hub for northern Peru, and is a lively and friendly spot with few pretensions. Unfortunately, the city is now mostly modern, but for some isolated remnants of colonialism in the winding streets.

One unmissable sight within the city is the extensive **Mercado de Brujos** (Witchcraft Market; Mon–Fri 7am–8pm, Sat 7am–2pm), also known as the Mercado Modelo, one of the most comprehensive in South America. Here is an overwhelming choice of herbal medicines, potions, charms, and San Pedro cacti, from which a hallucinogenic drug is extracted and used by *curanderos* (healers) in traditional shamanic healing rituals.

A short distance away is the coastal resort of **La Pimentel**, with a good sandy beach – an excellent place to try the local specialty of *pescado seco*, a kind of rayfish known as *la guitarra*, which can often be found hanging out to dry in the sun in Chiclayo's market. Just south of Pimentel is **Santa Rosa**, where beautiful fishing boats can be seen drawn up on the beach.

Chiclayo is, of course, the starting point for visits to two of the continent's most exciting archeological digs. The greatest attention has been lavished on the Moche burial area at **Sipán** ⑧ (Tue–Sun 9am–5pm; guided tours available), about 30km (18 miles) south of the city. Here, Peru's best-documented grave, known as the tomb of El Señor de Sipán, was uncovered in the late 1980s, originally by *huaqueros* (grave robbers), before the excavation was taken over by Dr Walter Alva. The site is well worth visiting, but to see the stunning gold, silver, and ceramic artifacts taken from it (when they're not touring the world's museums) you must visit the Museo Tumbas Reales de Sipán (Sipán Royal Tombs Museum; Tue–Sun 9am–5pm), in Lambayeque,

about 17km (10 miles) from Chiclayo. Near the square, the **Museo Brüning** (www.museotumbasrealessipan.pe; daily 9am–5pm) also exhibits excellent Moche gold artifacts, including the remarkable gold and silver treasure of the Sacerdotisa de Chornancap (The Chornancap Priestess), the first female ruler of the Moche culture.

From Lambayeque you can go on to the huge site at **Túcume**, with its numerous pyramids, while nearby in Ferrañave, the fine **Museo Sicán** (Tue–Sun 9am–5pm) houses objects from the Batán Grande site not far away.

Travel north from Chiclayo through the great coastal desert, sometimes turned green by the heavy rains induced by El Niño. **Piura** ⑨ is a hot commercial city best known for its folk dance, the *tondero*, a more rustic version of Trujillo's *marinera*, and the black magic still practiced by the descendants of slaves. The *tondero* is a lively barefoot Afro-Peruvian dance accompanied by strong rhythmic music and sashaying dancers in multicolored outfits. Many Peruvian

⊙ **Fact**

Piura is famous for its cuisine, notably its sharp flavors and elaborate preparations. The best dishes include seco de chavelo (mashed plantains with fried pork), majado de yucca con chicharrón (mashed manioc with fried pork), chifles (fried plantain), and natilla (molasses made from goats' milk and sugar cane).

Visitors at the adobe city of Chan Chan.

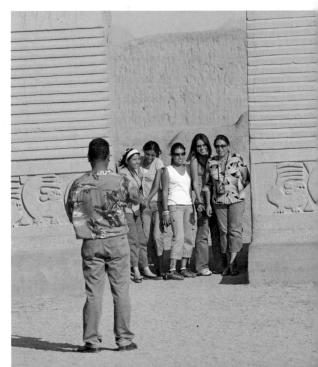

visitors come to see more than the dancers. There are Lima business executives who travel here annually to consult the area's *brujos* – witch doctors and folk healers who use herbs and potions to cure patients.

Piura has a proud history, beginning with its foundation by the Spanish in 1532 – three years before Lima – and continuing through the War of the Pacific with Chile (1879–83). That war's most famous Peruvian hero was Admiral Miguel Grau, and his home on Jirón Tacna across from the Centro Cívico has been converted into a museum, the **Casa Museo Gran Almirante Miguel Grau** (hours vary; donations welcome). Of interest there is the scale model of the British-built *Huascar*, the largest Peruvian warship in that conflict.

HEMINGWAY HAUNT

North of Piura, on the way to the Ecuadorian border, lies **Talara**, a desert oasis and petroleum-producing center. Closer still to the northern border are some of the best and most fashionable beaches in Peru: **Máncora**, **Punta Sal**,

Fishermen in Punta Sal.

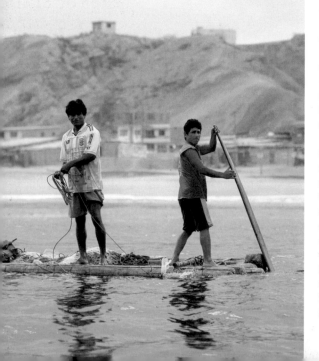

and **Las Pocitas**. **Cabo Blanco** (south of Máncora) is a popular spot for marlin fishing, once frequented by Ernest Hemingway. Peru's north coast also has some of the world's most spectacular waves, and Máncora is frequently the site of international surfing competitions.

Talara is as unattractive as any oil town, and travelers are recommended to seek accommodations in the abovementioned beach resorts. Camping is permitted at Cabo Blanco and other nearby beaches. South of Talara are the **Brea Tarpits**, where the Spanish boiled tar to caulk their ships.

FRONTIER TOWN

About 140km (85 miles) north of Talara is **Tumbes** , a frontier town with a military post and immigration offices, although it is about 30km (18 miles) from the Ecuadorian border. Although there has been an ongoing effort to give this city a facelift, there continues to be a problem with theft – particularly affecting tourists – often occurring near the bus offices or at the colorful outdoor market. A few miles outside the city, at the actual border, called **Aguas Verdes** on the Peruvian side, travelers are barraged by unscrupulous money-changers, porters, and over-friendly individuals with dubious motives. Police corruption is notorious here, although new customs facilities have improved services. Macará is an easier place to enter Ecuador.

Tumbes is also within spitting distance of the few Peruvian beaches that offer white sand and warm water for swimming year-round. **Caleta La Cruz**, which has an attractive fishing fleet, can be reached by taxi, in *colectivos*, or by combis heading north from Máncora, as can **Zorritos**, a larger fishing village with a couple of hotels. **Puerto Pizarro** has intriguing mangrove swamps around the village with some interesting birdlife, and boat tours can be arranged with fishermen in the port.

Fishermen carry a statue of San Pedro, saint of fishermen, during the San Pedro y San Pablo festival in June.

📷 BURIED TREASURES

Excavations of grave sites in Peru have revealed fascinating evidence of rich and varied cultures that flourished long before the Incas.

The architectural remains of the Inca Empire are so awe-inspiring that it is easy to forget that a number of earlier civilizations flourished in Peru. They left no written records, so much of the information that has been gleaned about them comes from grave sites.

The best known are at Sipán and Sicán, both in northern Peru. Originally unearthed by grave robbers in 1987, the tomb of the Lord of Sipán, believed to be a ruler of the Moche Period (c.AD 100–700), yielded unimaginable riches: gold masks, turquoise and lapis lazuli jewelry, copper headdresses, ceramic pots, and domestic implements, and provided archeologists with vital information about the Moche way of life.

At Sicán similar riches were discovered, including golden death masks, a copper crown, and a beaded cloak. The Sicán era spanned the 9th and 10th centuries, the period between the Moche and the Chimú. At both sites, there is evidence of what appears to be human sacrifice: at Sicán the bodies of young women were buried with that of their lord, and at Sipán servants or soldiers accompanied their master to the grave. The Sicán museum is at Ferreñafe, north of Chiclayo.

In the southern desert, at the Paracas Necropolis (c.1st century AD), excavations in the 1920s yielded hundreds of mummified bundles, wrapped in intricately embroidered cloth. Examples of these textiles can be seen in the Museo de la Nación in Lima. At the Chauchilla Cemetery, farther south, remains of the Nazca culture (c.AD 200–800) were discovered in the early 1900s. Designs on the pottery buried with the dead gave important clues about their daily lives.

A gold representation of a Moche deity found at the tomb of the Lord of Sipán. Like most of the important Sipán finds, this artifact has now been placed in the Museo Brüning in Lambayeque.

An archeologist painstakingly excavates a skeleton buried with copper artifacts at the Sipán site.

A golden mask from the Tomb of the Lord of Sipán, its opulence denoting the status and importance of the wearer during his earthly life.

Macabre remains at the Cementerios de Chauchilla.

Disturbing the dead

The smuggling of antiquities is a multimillion-dollar international trade, so it's little wonder that ancient grave sites have attracted looters. Around the Cemetery of Chauchilla, near Nazca, the desert is strewn with bones and skulls unearthed by *huaqueros* (grave robbers), stripped of valuables, and left to bleach in the sun. Priceless treasures have been lifted illegally from burial sites all over the country and sold to collectors.

It was the *huaqueros'* discovery of the Sipán tomb in the late 1980s that provoked a clampdown. Initiated by Dr Walter Alva, curator of the Museo Brüning in Lambayeque, a government-backed program now targets looters, rewards informers, and uses educational campaigns in an attempt to end the lucrative trade. At a local level, it is having a measure of success. Aerial surveillance is vital to the program due to the large number of sites. Archeologists board air-force flights over the Lambayeque Valley to chart mounds that may conceal ancient complexes and sites where human destruction is obvious.

The skeleton of the Lord of Sipán was adorned with gold ornaments, including pieces to cover the eyes, ears, and face. On his feet were a pair of copper slippers that would have been used for ceremonial occasions. The bodies of servants and soldiers were buried in the tomb, along with jewelry, utensils, and ceramic pots to make him comfortable in the afterlife.

Exquisite gold and turquoise jewelry, such as this earring, were part of the treasure trove at the Sipán site.

The irrigation ditch at Cumbemayo.

NORTHERN SIERRA

Journeys in the highlands are long and the roads are poor; but the rewards are colonial towns, breathtaking scenery, and some spectacular ruins.

Across the dusty desert into the Andean highlands lies **Cajamarca** ❶. Now dotted with cattle herds and dairy farms where Peru's best cheese is made, this was one of the largest cities in the Inca Empire and marks the site where the Inca people and the Spaniards had their first – and crucial – showdown. It was in Cajamarca that the Inca Atahualpa was taken prisoner and later executed.

Pizarro had sent envoys to the Inca, camped in the valley with his huge army, telling him that "he loved him dearly," and wished to meet him in Cajamarca. But Atahualpa walked into an ambush: in the Plaza de Armas the heavily armed Spaniards massacred thousands of Inca subjects who were futilely trying to protect their leader. Despite the Spaniards' numerical disadvantage, their audacity in kidnapping the Inca threw an already divided empire into confusion.

A demand went out across the Inca Empire to assemble an outrageous ransom for Atahualpa's release. Leading llamas laden down by riches, groups of people from as far away as Cusco began the journey to Cajamarca, filling the "Ransom Room" with some of the Incas' most valuable treasures – which the Spanish promptly melted down into bullion. The Ransom Room is still there; a red line on one wall shows where the tall and powerful Atahualpa

allegedly drew a mark, agreeing to have his subjects fill the room to that line twice with silver and once with gold. But once the majority of the ransom had been collected, the conquistadors, afraid that the Inca would serve as a focal point for rebellion as long as he remained alive, had him garroted after he had been baptized with Pizarro's own name – Francisco.

COMING TO CAJAMARCA

Cajamarca can be reached by daily flights from Lima, by bus from Trujillo,

Main Attractions

Iglesia San Francisco
El Cuarto del Rescate
Complejo Belén
Cerro Apolonia
Baños del Inca
Ventanillas de Otuzco
Gocta Falls
Kuélap ruins

Map on page 176

Twin sisters at a festival in Cajamarca.

which takes about nine hours, or Chiclayo (about seven hours), or on a better, faster road that turns off the Panamericana near Pacasmayo (about five hours).

The hub of this slow-paced city of some 225,000 inhabitants, built on the banks of the Río San Lucas, is the Plaza de Armas, the spot where Atahualpa was executed. It is still sometimes said that the pink grain on a stone slab, where the Inca was allegedly killed, is the indelible mark of his blood. The massive Inca palaces that stood here are gone, and the plaza is now ringed by colonial buildings, the Cathedral, and the lovely San Francisco church.

The center of the square is graced by an imposing stone fountain, frequented every evening by locals stopping for a chat with friends, and all day long by birds dipping down for a drink.

The Baroque **Catedral Santa Catalina** (Jirón Cruz de la Piedra; Mon afternoon, Tue–Fri 8am–11am, 4–6pm, Sat morning, Sun during masses), founded in 1665, is the most noteworthy building on the plaza. Its carved wooden altars are covered in gold leaf,

and its facade of intricately carved volcanic rock is impressive.

On the opposite side of the plaza is the **Iglesia San Francisco** (Church of San Francisco; daily 7am–noon, 4–8pm), older and more ornate than the cathedral, and home to the **Museo de Arte Religioso** (Museum of Religious Art; Mon–Sat 9am–5pm), which is filled with colonial-era paintings and statues, often portraying violent and bloody subjects. A guided tour of the museum, which is a veritable storehouse of silver candelabra, gold altar vessels, jeweled vestments, and portraits of saints, includes entrance to the church's eerie catacombs – precursor to the present city cemetery.

Situated next door to the cathedral stands the Hotel Costa del Sol, a four-star lodging house with rooms furnished with heavy wooden antiques. There are a number of reasonable places to stay in Cajamarca, located in and around the Plaza de Armas, and a handful of inexpensive restaurants. One of them is the family-run Restaurante Salas, described by one *cajamarquino*

Cajamarca's Plaza de Armas.

(the name by which the city's citizens are known) as the "city's nerve center." Here locals catch up on the news and gossip while downing the city's best, and most economical, home cooking: anything from crisp salads and thick *chupe verde* (potato and vegetable soup) to hearty beef ribs and spicy *cuy* (guinea pig) stew. No meal is complete without *panqueque con manjar blanco*, a sweet, rich dessert consisting of a thick crêpe bathed in condensed milk fudge. Hung on the restaurant's walls are paintings by local artist Andrés Zevallos, one of the founding fathers of Cajamarca's longstanding community of poets, writers, painters, and musicians. Most notable of these was Mario Urteaga, the first Peruvian artist to have his work in the permanent collection at New York's Museum of Modern Art, and a person so much loved in his hometown that the procession at his funeral in 1957 lasted into the night. Urteaga's oils depict *campesinos* (subsistence farmers), simple yet human, and the Cajamarca countryside was his studio. Contemporary local photographer Victor Campos Ríos meanwhile captures the beauty of the country and its people in photographs and documentaries.

A KING'S RANSOM

A few blocks from the main plaza, on Avenida Amalia Puga, is El Cuarto del Rescate (The Ransom Room; Tue–Wed 9am–1pm and 3–8pm, Thu–Sat 9am–8pm, Sun 9am–1pm; entrance fee also gives admission to the Complejo Belén and the Museo Etnográfico de Arqueología, see page 179). This is the sole surviving Inca structure in the city, and there is some debate about whether it was where Atahualpa was imprisoned, or where the treasure collected from across the empire was stored. As *rescate* means both "ransom" and "rescue" in Spanish, it could be either; whichever it was, it forges a very real link with a past that sometimes seems almost mythical.

Also close to the plaza, on Apurímac, is the Teatro Municipal, now known as the Teatro Cajamarca, rescued by this culture-loving city after being used first as a movie theater and then as a storehouse for industrial cleaners. Built by a wealthy German merchant, the theater has an impressive stamped metal ceiling, and its seating almost exactly duplicates that in the original plans. Ticket prices are kept low to entice students and less affluent *cajamarquinos*, but unfortunately performances are not staged on a regular basis.

THE COMPLEJO BELÉN

Heading east along Junín from the theater, you will come to the Complejo Belén (Tue–Sat 9am–1pm and 3–6pm, Sun 9am–1pm), housing the Institute of Culture, Cajamarca's most picturesque chapel, a museum, and an art gallery. The 17th-century Belén church is undoubtedly the city's loveliest, with elaborately carved stone and woodwork, and brightly colored statues and side altars. The small white carved dove suspended over the pulpit represents the

Fact

Cajamarca enjoys many festivals. The pre-Lent carnival is a riotous celebration, lasting for four days, which includes music, processions, masks, and the inevitable water fights.

Hat seller, Cajamarca.

HUALLAGA, VALLEY OF COCA

The battle against the cultivation of coca for cocaine has made the fertile Huallaga Valley something of a no man's land, though the ubiquitous coca leaf is innocent enough.

In *la ceja de la selva* (the eyebrow of the jungle), where the mountain flanks meet the Amazon basin, lies the broad tropical valley of the Río Huallaga. Maize and rice are grown on a large scale in the fertile valley, but it is known for another product – coca.

In the Andean highlands of both Peru and Bolivia, coca has been a part of the traditional culture for more than 4,000 years. The leaves are to be found for sale in any mountain market. Ask at a café for mate de coca and you will get a cup of coca-leaf tea, a drink that is the best prevention and treatment of the symptoms of *soroche* – altitude sickness.

Coca gives energy, and dulls the senses against cold, hunger, and exhaustion. The biggest consumers have always been miners, who use up to half a kilo a day each, but it is used at many other times. Before giving birth, a woman chews the leaves to hasten labor and ease the pain. When a young man wants to marry a girl, he offers coca to her father. And when

Brewing mate de coca (coca-leaf tea).

somebody dies, *mate de coca* is drunk at the wake and a small pile of leaves placed in the coffin.

Coca was first cultivated in the Andes around 2000 BC. Centuries later the Incas turned its production into a monopoly, as a means of controlling subject populations. Its use was restricted to royalty, priests, doctors, and the message runners, known to travel vast distances on the energy gained from chewing the leaves. The Incas had relaxed their monopoly by the time the Spanish arrived, but the Catholic Church tried to ban the leaf, denouncing it as "the delusion of the devil." However, the Church changed its tune, and established a monopoly of its own, when it discovered that the Indians needed the leaf in order to survive the brutal conditions they faced in the mines and plantations.

Back in Europe and the United States, coca was almost unheard of until the mid-1800s, when a Corsican chemist, Angelo Mariani, marketed a wine made from the leaf that became immensely popular. This Vin Mariani inspired American soft-drink companies to produce other coca-based drinks, such as Coca-Cola. At the same time, cocaine was being developed, and was quickly taken up by such luminaries as Sigmund Freud, who called it a "magical substance."

In the 1970s, the drug became more popular, particularly in the United States. Much of the crop grown in the Andes is crushed by foot in chemicals, turned into a gummy paste and flown to Colombia or smuggled to Ecuador. After being refined into powder there, the cocaine is then smuggled to consumers now anywhere in the world.

Cocaine has brought violence to the Huallaga Valley, in the shape of a complex conflict between the Peruvian drug squad – backed by US Drug Enforcement agents – and Colombian cocaine traffickers, left-wing guerrillas, and the coca farmers themselves. More than 40 light aircraft used by drug-traffickers to smuggle paste were shot down over Peruvian airspace until a plane carrying missionaries was hit by accident.

Although the Huallaga Valley is an area of great natural beauty, and around the fringes there are places, such as Tingo María, that can be visited safely, only the most foolhardy tourist will venture into the heart of the valley.

Holy Spirit and allegedly gives those who stand under it the power of eloquence. The chapel's cupola and altar depict the three levels of life: on the ground level are the common people, in an intermediary area the saints and priests, and on the top level – heaven – God and the Virgin Mary, represented by the sky-blue dome of the cupola. Many visitors are fooled by the brilliantly painted details on the upper walls and ceiling of the church; these saints and cherubs are not made of painted wood or plaster, but are intricately carved stone. More carving is found on the massive wooden doors in the church, most of them solid pieces of Nicaraguan cedar.

Connected to the church is the Pinacoteca, a gallery of local artists' work in what was once the kitchen of a hospital for men. Off the Pinacoteca is the former hospital ward, a room with alcoves along its side walls. The alcoves were the patients' "bedrooms," and the images of saints originally painted above them corresponded to their illnesses. The sickest were bedded closest to the altar, conveniently located near the door to the cemetery. An example of an alcove with blankets and its painted saint can be seen across the street at the **Museo Etnográfico y de Arqueología** (Ethnographic and Archeological Museum; Tue–Sun 8.30am–1pm and 2.30–6pm), which was once a maternity hospital. The only difference between the two hospitals was that from the tops of the women's alcoves dangled long scarves, which the patients pulled to help them when giving birth.

The museum has an interesting collection of ceramics from indigenous cultures that dominated this region of Peru, various samples of local handicrafts, and costumes used during the annual carnival celebrations – the most raucous in the country. Across the street at the Instituto Nacional de Cultura, Spanish-language books and the area's best postcards are on sale. The Institute has details of ongoing archeological digs that can be visited from October to May, before the highland's rainy season begins. Excavations include the Huacaloma and Kuntur Wasi digs sponsored by the University of Tokyo.

⊙ **Tip**

If you enjoy adventurous travel, try to get to the Parque Nacional Cordillera Azul, an isolated park which protects mega-diverse cloud forest on the border of San Martín and Loreto provinces. The area is home to the Cacataibo-Camano people and an amazing variety of wildlife. Talk to agencies in Tarapoto or Moyobamba about organizing a trip.

The Complejo Belén.

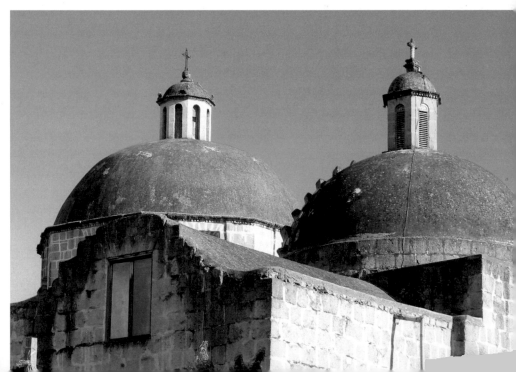

CAJAMARCA BY NIGHT

There's not a lot to do in Cajamarca after sunset. The town rolls up its sidewalks early, as befits a farming community where work begins at sunrise. But nocturnal souls can listen, and dance, to boisterous local music at the Peña Usha Usha (Amalia Puga 320), Los Frailones (Jr. Alfonso la Torre 300), or join the camaraderie near the UNC university campus. Here local people meet to sing, drink, and play their music, ranging from boleros to the huaynos of the Andean highlands; however, the food isn't always as good as the music.

SCALING THE HEIGHTS

For the physically fit, the best way to delight in Cajamarca's charms is from above. That means climbing steep Cerro Apolonia (daily 8am–6pm). Stone steps take climbers as far as a little chapel – a miniature version of Nôtre-Dame Cathedral, about halfway up the hillside – and the rest of the journey is on a curvy road bordered by cacti, flowers, and benches for the fatigued.

Cerro Apolonia.

Near the top is the Silla del Inca (the Inca's Chair), a rock cut into the shape of a throne where, it is said, the Inca Atahualpa sat and looked out over the valley. A bronze statue of the Inca, and parking for those who arrive by taxi or car, top the hill.

The view is of green, rain-fed fields, red-tiled roofs, and whitewashed houses. At night, the Cajamarca skies – which in daytime may switch in minutes from brilliant blue to stormy gray – are usually clear and star-studded. Early risers are in for a special treat: sunrises in these highlands are beautiful, and the show is a long one. It can take the sun up to 45 minutes to switch from a silhouetting blue-black to a brilliant red-orange before lightening to a hazy yellow.

An equally spectacular view of the city can be found at **Hacienda San Vicente** (Jirón Revolución; tel: 076-362 644), the most intriguing hotel in town. A charming country inn perched on a steep rocky hill at the edge of Cajamarca, this lodge was constructed using Inca techniques, with a few modern twists. The walls are made of packed earth painted with ocher and vegetable dyes. Skylights give illumination, fireplaces heat common areas after nightfall, and guest rooms are decorated with local handicrafts. San Vicente was built on the site where a colonial estate house once stood; its original chapel remains next door, and on San Vicente's day local farmers still take up their musical instruments and bouquets of flowers and parade to the tiny church.

ANCIENT INCA SPA

If you look out from the Cerro Apolonia by day, you may see a white mist hovering over the edge of the city. This is the steam rising from the **Baños del Inca** (Mon–Fri 24 hours), reputedly the Incas' favorite bathing spot. A sign over a huge stone tub at the bubbling mineral springs claims that it was here that Atahualpa bathed with his family. The springs are so hot at their source that local people use them to boil eggs. Whether or not they are curative, as the locals believe, they merit a visit – you can get a bus or a *colectivo* (a taxi which takes a number of different people) from the center of town. The city has channeled the water from the springs into a lukewarm Olympic-sized outdoor pool, and built rustic cabañas where families or groups of friends can splash privately, and modern "tourist baths" where one or two people can soak in tiled hot tubs. There is a charge for the use of these facilities.

At the springs, several tourist hostels have sprung up, all of them with bathtubs or swimming pools fed by the springs. The best-known is the **Laguna Seca**, a pleasant, converted colonial-style hacienda (farm estate; https://lagunaseca.com.pe/), which has a pool, a pungent sauna where eucalyptus is steamed on hot coals, a weightlifting room, and – a thing you don't find every day – a small bullfighting ring and a cockfighting arena, as well as "Baños del Inca" water running into the deep bathtubs of every room.

CERAMIC TRADITIONS

Cajamarca and its environs are good places for buying ceramics. The Complejo Belén artisan shop and others near the Plaza de Armas are filled with pottery, as well as good-quality knitted sweaters, baskets, leather goods, and the gilt-framed mirrors popular in this northern region. But the most fascinating – and least expensive – spot to buy ceramics is a few kilometers to the south of the city at the village of Aylambo, where there is a series of ecologically balanced workshops. Sewage at the workshops is processed into natural gas, which is used to generate heat and light, and, rather than buying expensive fuel and imported heat-resistant bricks, the students who learn their skills at the workshops collect kindling from the hillside and make their own heat-tolerating kiln tiles – in much the same way as their ancestors did.

Products here range from plates bearing traditional Indian motifs to teapots with modern glazes – designed and concocted by the students – and the proceeds from pottery sales go to the people who work in the studios. Aylambo artisans, who range in age from children to the elderly, are not charged a fee to learn the crafts, but economic necessity would force them to leave the workshop and find paid jobs if study stipends were not available. The long-term goal of the project is to inspire a series of environmentally sound workshops providing jobs, reclaiming ancient pottery designs, preventing further deforestation of the hills, and keeping *cajamarquinos* living in the countryside.

BEYOND THE CITY

There are many possible excursions outside Cajamarca, all of which are best organized through a travel

⊙ MAGNIFICENT RUINS

The ruins of Kuélap rival Machu Picchu in their magnificence. This extensive citadel was the principal administrative center of the Chachapoyas civilization (AD 200–1475), and its jungle-covered ruins were rediscovered in 1843 by Juan Crisóstomo Nieto, a judge from Chachapoyas. The center is thought to have been a sanctuary for a powerful elite who administered agricultural production and religious practices.

This enormous complex extends on a north–south orientated platform for more than 600 meters (1,900ft), with stone walls measuring up to 19 meters (62ft) in height. Despite its grand dimensions, the city only has three narrow entrances, which served to control entry to the site and strengthen its defenses. Inside the complex are 335 circular buildings, some near complete, adorned with geometrical friezes. There's also an ingenious system for channeling rainwater. A guide can be arranged in Chachapoyas, which is two hours from the site by road, and you're unlikely to have to share the ruins with other visitors. In 2017, a cable car came into operation, allowing visitors to access Kuélap fortress from Tingo Nuevo in just 20 minutes. The 4km (2.5-mile) ride offers unrivalled views over the surrounding area.

agency, which can arrange transportation to the isolated area; there are several agencies in Cajamarca that provide these services. From here it is possible to visit the puzzling Ventanillas de Otuzco (about 8km/5 miles from town; daily 9am–6pm), the cliffside "windows" that served as ancient Indian burial grounds. Anthropologists and archeologists still have not unraveled the mystery of how the pre-Inca people were able to open the burial holes on the sides of sheer cliffs, but they have counted the openings to get an idea of the population – and importance – of the area before the conquistadors' arrival.

Equally astonishing is the site of Cumbemayo (daily 9am–5pm), about 24km (15 miles) west from Cajamarca, a valley cut by an Inca irrigation ditch of carved rock. The sophistication and precision of the ditch's angles – hewn by stone tools – leave modern-day hydraulic engineers marveling. Sharp turns in the ditch prevent the water from rushing too fast, as do imperceptible inclines. In the same valley are Los Frailones (The Friars), huge rocks that have eroded into the shape of hooded monks – sparking a number of local legends – as well as some primitive petroglyphs and caves once used as places of worship.

Those who start their countryside ramblings early may have time to reach the dairy farm called Hacienda La Colpa before cow-calling time. Every day, just before 2pm, the cows at this cooperative are called by name – to the delight of the crowd that gathers to watch. The animals respond by sauntering up to the milking areas bearing their names. Colpa is an example of the many cooperative dairies outside Cajamarca, famous for its butter, cheese, and *manjar blanco*. A hostel offers travelers a pastoral spot to spend the night, although most people, after admiring the nearby pretty village of Llacanora, head back to Cajamarca.

TOWARD THE AMAZON

There is a rough but scenic route from Cajamarca to **Chachapoyas** ❷, heart of the pre-Inca culture of the same

The Baños del Inca.

name. The good paved cross-Andean highway from Chiclayo provides easier access and is recommended during the rainy season. Both routes have fabulous mountain scenery. Flights from Lima to Chachapoyas are rare, but growing tourism has led to plans to expand services.

Chachapoyas alone, although pleasant, would not be worth the long journey, but the spectacular surrounding area, including many hilltop ruins, make it a trip worth taking. The effort needed to reach the **Gocta** waterfall, at 771 meters (2,530ft) the third-highest in the world, is also a worthwhile one. First measured in 2006, the cloud forest fall is particularly attractive during the October–April rainy season.

The Chachapoyas, who were roughly the contemporaries of the Chimú (c.800–1470), left extraordinary remains, including vast fortifications as these "Cloud Warriors" defended their independence from the Huari and, later, the Incas. The most stunning of the hilltop sites is **Kuélap** ❸, a great pre-Inca walled city perched high above the Río Utcubamba. The location and the ruins are nothing short of spectacular, and it is likely the biggest site of its kind in South America. Access to Kuélap has become easy, and the site sees nowhere near as many visitors as those of the Sacred Valley. Minibuses leave in the morning for the village of Tingo, from where a road goes to within 15 minutes' walk of the ruins. It is also possible to hike there on little-used Inca trails. Discoveries are still being made here. In 1997, 219 mummies were uncovered in a cliff tomb up by a lake near Leimebamba. They are now protected in a good museum at Leimebamba (Tue–Sun 8am–4pm), along with textiles and ceramics. At nearby Revash, Chachapoyas mausoleums cling from the cliffs like miniature villages. Vilaya Tours (tel: 51 941 708 798; www.vilaya tours.com) offer visits to these areas, or ask a local guide to accompany you. Archeological and environmental foundation Camayoc (http://camayoc peru.com) has further information on trips and resources.

Kuélap ruins.

The Alpamayo ice face.

CALLEJÓN DE HUAYLAS

Spectacular scenery and the challenge of climbing Huascarán, Peru's highest summit, are among the attractions of this remote area.

Stretching for 160km (255 miles) and ranging in altitude from a mere 1,800 meters (5,900ft) to 4,080 meters (13,380ft), the valley known as the **Callejón de Huaylas** rates as one of the finest areas in all of South America for its superb mountain vistas and a wealth of opportunities for outdoor pursuits. Many dedicated enthusiasts arrive prepared for sports ranging from trekking and climbing to (more rarely) snowboarding, paraskiing, and skiing, while others are content to spend their days relaxing in a spectacular mountain setting and exploring the villages that sprawl along the hillsides.

The Callejón de Huaylas is bordered on the east by the **Cordillera Blanca** (White Mountains) – a mountain range with the greatest number of 6,000-meter (20,000ft) peaks outside the Himalayas – and on the west by the lower range known as the Cordillera Negra (Black Mountains) for their sparseness of vegetation and complete lack of snow. To the north, the valley terminates with the Cañón del Pato, a narrow gorge of a canyon with sheer rock walls, steep precipices, and a dirt road winding its way through numerous crudely constructed tunnels down toward the coast. There are daily bus services from Chimbote to Huaraz – go by day for the exciting views. The hair-raising narrow road has been widened,

Trekking in the Cordillera Blanca.

and is now known as the Carretera de Huallanca, which is good news for those approaching Huaraz from the north. The 40km (25-mile) wide Callejón de Huaylas is renowned not only for its breathtaking scenery but also for Inca and pre-Inca history, unusual flora and fauna, lively markets, and traditional villages.

DISASTER AREA

The Callejón de Huaylas is also well known for a history of natural disasters. Earthquakes and alluvions – the

Main Attractions
The Cordillera Blanca
Huaraz
Parque Nacional
  Huascarán
Chavín de Huantar
Cordillera Huayhuash

Map on page 186

Flowers on the mountain slopes.

Huaraz.

name given to floods of water combined with avalanches and landslides – have caused considerable damage over the past 300 recorded years. The capital city of Huaraz was severely damaged by an alluvion in 1941 when an avalanche caused Laguna Calcacocha to overflow. Much of the central district was destroyed, and nearly 5,000 lives were lost. The most tragic disaster occurred in 1970, when an earthquake measuring 7.7 on the Richter scale devastated the entire region and was responsible for nearly 80,000 deaths.

More than 30,000 people died in Huaraz, and over 80 percent of the city was flattened, but hardest hit was the village of Yungay. The entire town and most of its inhabitants completely disappeared under a massive avalanche of rock and snow when part of the Huascarán massif broke loose and plunged down the valley.

In the aftermath of these catastrophes many of the towns and villages have been almost completely rebuilt, mainly with uninspiring concrete structures. Understandably, the need

to rehouse people was given priority, and little thought was given to preserving an architectural heritage. The colonial charm encountered in other highland areas has been all but lost. Archeological remains are also spread more thinly than in other parts of Peru, with the major exception, however, of Chavín de Huantar. Less traveled sections of the Inca road system remain.

MOUNTAIN RETREAT

The center of most commercial activity and the common destination for visitors to the Callejón de Huaylas is the city of **Huaraz** ❶. There is an airport just outside the town; LC Perú offers three flights per week to/from Huaraz, but there is a luggage restriction (max 15kg), and most people get here by bus, from either Lima or Chimbote – both journeys take about eight hours on a paved road. There are frequent services, and the more expensive buses are quite comfortable. As the capital of the department of Ancash, and with a population of more than 120,000 inhabitants, Huaraz is well

Callejón de Huaylas

equipped to support the demands of tourism and all necessities are readily available. Scores of low-cost hostels offer accommodations of varying kinds, some very basic, others very comfortable, and there are a few higher-priced hotels for those who would like more comfort during their mountain retreat.

Before departing for remote regions, or after a long trek in the mountains, you'll find plenty of activity in the bustling town of Huaraz. Along the main street of Luzuriaga, vendors sell a wide selection of woolen goods, pan flutes, and ceramic replicas of the Chavín temple. Storefront tour companies set out brightly colored billboards promoting day trips to popular tourist sites and advertise an assortment of climbing and trekking gear for hire. Other traditionally dressed highlanders sell regional food specialties from wooden carts. Andean cheeses, rich honey, and *manjar blanco* (a sweet, milky concoction used as a dessert or filling) are a few tasty edibles that are worth trying. A wide range of restaurants cater to international tastes: pizzerias, Chinese food, and hamburgers are found alongside more typical dishes such as *lomo saltado* (strips of beef with potatoes), *pollos a la brasa* (griddled chicken), and *cuy* (roasted guinea pig).

Worth a visit is the **Museo Arqueológico de Ancash** (Avenida Luzuriaga 762; Tue–Sun 9am–5pm), off the **Plaza de Armas**. It has an interesting collection and is considered noteworthy for its display of stone monoliths from the Recuay culture, which date from 400 BC to AD 600. Also on display are mummies, ceramics, and household utensils dating from the same period.

Huaraz nightlife, too, has plenty to offer. There are several cinemas showing recent US films in English with Spanish subtitles, although the sound system frequently leaves something to be desired. *Peñas*, or folklore nightclubs, entertain with traditional Andean musical groups in the early evening, and

switch to disco later on for serious high-altitude dancing. Tambo Taverna and Amadeus Taberna are the most popular and are packed to capacity on weekends and during high season.

The outlying area of Huaraz offers numerous opportunities for day excursions. Footpaths lead to a number of small villages and agricultural areas within walking distance of the city center. Rataquenua, Unchus, Marián, and Pitec are just a few of the pueblos that can be visited in a few hours.

About an hour by local bus south of Huaraz lies the small town of **Catac**, often visited by those keen to see the giant *Puya Raimondi*. This unusual plant is often referred to as a cactus, but is actually the largest member of the bromeliad family. It is a rare species, considered to be one of the oldest in the world, and is found in only a few isolated areas of the Andes. At its base, the *Puya Raimondi* forms a huge rosette of long, spiked, waxy leaves – often reaching a diameter of 2 meters (6ft). As it begins to flower, a process that takes its entire lifespan, which is

⊙ **Tip**

If you're looking for somewhere to go out in Huaraz, try the **Tambo Taverna** at José de la Mar 776, or the Los 13 Buhos at José de la Mar 812 2nd floor. Downstairs is Makondos, yet another nightlife option.

Street stall selling roasted pork.

estimated to approach 100 years, it sends up a phallic spike that can reach a height of 12 meters (39ft).

As the final flowering begins, usually in the month of May, the spike is covered in flowers – as many as 20,000 blooms on a single plant. During this season, if you are incredibly lucky, groups of *Puya Raimondi* may bloom together, creating an unbelievable picture set against the backdrop of the snowy peaks of the Cordillera Blanca.

TREKKING

The Huaraz area is a trekker's paradise. Just above the city is **El Mirador**, a scenic lookout marked by a huge white cross. The route heads uphill east along city streets, which eventually turn into a footpath beside an irrigation canal lined with eucalyptus trees. Fields of wheat ripening in the sun add a serene, pastoral feel. At the top, the highest mountain in Peru, **Huascarán** (6,768 meters/22,200ft) dominates the northern horizon; the lower Vallunaraju (5,680 meters/18,600ft) peeks out over the foothills to the east, and the city of Huaraz sprawls below.

⊙ CLIMBING PERU'S HIGHEST MOUNTAIN

Huascarán is Peru's highest mountain and presents the ultimate challenge for many mountain-mad visitors to Peru. It has two summits: the south one, at 6,768 meters (22,200ft), is a full 113 meters (370ft) higher than its more frequently climbed northern sister.

The climb is not one of Peru's most technical, but it does require a high level of fitness and some high-altitude mountaineering experience.

The ascent begins at the village of Musho, from where donkeys and *arrieros* (muleteers) are hired to transport climbers' gear to the Huascarán base camp above the tree line. The trail then continues up a steep ridge to the moraine camp. From here climbers progress across the glacier to Camp One, at 5,200 meters (17,000ft). Wide crevasses, icy cracks, and massive pillars of tumbled ice are constant reminders that glaciers are anything but static piles of snow.

Next comes the climb to La Garganta (The Throat) at 5,790 meters (19,000ft), a technical test with a 100-meter (300ft), 70-degree ice wall. After a final cold night at La Garganta Camp, comes the summit route, a series of zigzag traverses across the saddle between the two peaks of Huascarán. Finally, Peru's highest summit is in sight.

For advice on hiring a certified guide, contact the Casa de Guías in Huaraz (tel: 51 43-421 811; www.agmp.pe).

Another popular choice is the **Pitec Trail to Laguna Churup**. There is no public transportation to this small village 10km (6 miles) from the center of Huaraz, but often a taxi driver or someone driving a pick-up truck can be found at *el puente* (the bridge) at Huaraz, who will navigate the rough road to **Pitec ②**. Walking is an option – it takes around two hours at a slowish pace – but it's nicer to be fresh at the trailhead and then walk back down to Huaraz afterwards.

The trail begins at the parking lot before the village of Pitec is reached. A well-worn footpath heads north up a ridgeline, and the Churup massif rises just above 5,495 meters (18,000ft) in the distance. At the base of this mountain is the destination of the hike, Laguna Churup, fed by glacial melt-off and surrounded by huge boulders. A picnic lunch and a midday siesta in the warm sun reward the effort of getting here. A leisurely hike back to Huaraz follows a cobbled road through *campesino* (subsistence farmer) homesteads.

ANCIENT REMAINS

About 8km (5 miles) north of Huaraz, and easily reached on foot, is the small pre-Inca ruin of **Willkawain ③** (also called Wilkahuain; Tue–Sun 8am–4.30pm). Little is known about this three-storied structure that stands in the middle of an agricultural valley, but, because of the typical masonry style, it is thought to date from the expansionist period of the Wari-Tiahuanaco culture (AD 200–700). The windowless inner chambers can be explored with a flashlight, or with candles proffered by any one of the hordes of schoolboys who haunt the site and offer their services as guides for a small fee. Most of the rooms within the construction are inaccessible from the debris of centuries, but a few of them have been opened up to reveal a sophisticated ventilation system and skillful stone craftsmanship. Willkawain is a good walk for acclimatization when you first arrive in Huaraz.

Longer excursions to the surrounding country are as simple to arrange as locating the proper rural bus to take you there. A major road stretches the length of the Callejón de Huaylas, running alongside the Río Santa, and local transportation is readily available to a variety of villages situated along the route. It is also very easy to negotiate a minibus tour with one of various agencies in the center of town.

The village of **Monterrey**, just 5km (3 miles) outside Huaraz, is worth a visit for its – quite simple – *baños termales* (hot springs). Two swimming pools of warm water, and private baths of the steaming variety, are extremely inviting, especially after a rigorous trek in the mountains. About 35km (22 miles) farther up the valley is **Chancos**, which claims to have its own Fountain of Youth – more thermal baths with natural saunas and pools of flowing hot water.

Buses frequently leave Huaraz, loaded with an assortment of *campesinos*, their chickens, *cuyes* (guinea pigs), and children, heading for the small village of **Yungay** ❹, which lies north down the valley. This is the village described earlier in this chapter that was completely destroyed by the 1970 earthquake. During the most recent rebuilding of Yungay, the village site was shifted a few kilometers north of its original location in the hope that it would now be out of the way of any future natural disasters. All that remains of the abandoned Yungay, now known as Campo Santo ('cemetery'), is a solitary monument dedicated to those whose lives were lost, and a few battered palm trees that once lined the charming Plaza de Armas.

LLANGANUCO TO SANTA CRUZ

Yungay is the turn-off point for the popular two-hour ride up to the **Lagunas de Llanganuco**. *Camionetas*, small pick-up trucks, wait in the plaza to transport hikers and sightseers up the valley to the dazzling, glacier-fed lakes. It is also one of the starting points for the **Llanganuco to Santa Cruz Loop**. One of the most frequently hiked trails in the region, this five-day route passes under a dozen peaks over 5,800 meters (19,000ft), and panoramic views abound.

Caraz ❺ is the end point of this loop, a pretty town that was fortunate enough to survive several recent earthquakes with relatively little damage. Fields of flowers line the road as you approach, and at the other side of town groves of orange trees sit beneath snowy mountain peaks. There are several small hotels and a few basic restaurants around the Plaza de Armas.

If you choose to start, rather than finish, your trek here, you can get a bus from Huaraz, which is only about 65km (40 miles) away. From Caraz you can take gentle walks in the nearby hills, or visit the stunning turquoise-blue **Lago Parón**, some 30km (18 miles) up a rugged, winding road. It's a magnificent all-day hike, or a relatively inexpensive trip by taxi.

◎ **Tip**

Be well prepared for your trek. In recent years Huaraz has become geared up to the influx of outward-bound visitors and is able to cater for most needs. The Casa de Guías at Parque Ginebra Lote 28 (tel: 51 43-421 811) can supply the names of recommended mountain guides, and a lot of other information.

Ascending Mount Huascarán.

⊘ Tip

Don't forget the usual health precautions when trekking or climbing: altitude sickness can be a problem if you are not acclimatized. Guard against hypothermia by bringing the right clothes and being aware of early symptoms (see page 118).

RESERVE IN THE SIERRA

Much of the Cordillera Blanca above 4,000 meters (13,000ft) and the area around Huascarán mountain fall within the confines of **Parque Nacional Huascarán ❻**. The park is easily visited from Huaraz, and its office, where you can get information before your visit, is located there. Established in 1975, at a time when it marked Peru as a frontrunner in Latin American conservation, the park was made a Unesco biosphere reserve in 1985. Huascarán National Park was formed to protect the indigenous wildlife, archeological sites, geology, and natural beauty of an area threatened by mining and other commercial interests. An entrance fee is charged to help offset the cost of providing park guardians and preserving trails.

Of the more interesting wildlife that you can possibly see, with a little patience and a bit of luck, is the vizcacha, a small, hare-like animal with characteristics similar to the North American marmot; the vicuña, a cameloid cousin to the llama; and (much less frequently) the stealthy puma.

Plaza de Armas, Caraz.

VALLEY LIFE

Throughout the Callejón de Huaylas, a lifestyle dating back centuries continues to thrive. The traditional dress of the villagers has not changed radically in many years. The women, especially, hold on to their heritage, wearing layers of colorful woolen skirts and embroidered blouses which developed during colonial times. In addition, each wears a hat whose style may vary significantly from village to village. The custom of hat-wearing can also be used to indicate marital status, as in the village of Carhuaz. There, a woman wearing a black band round her fedora is a widow, while a rose-colored band is worn by single women, and a white one shows that the wearer is married.

Agriculture, the mainstay of the valley, has also seen little change over the centuries in either methods or crop variety. Double-yoked oxen still drag crude wooden plows through the black, fertile soil. Honey-colored wheat can be seen ripening throughout the valley, and maturing fields of quinoa, a high-altitude grain rich in protein, are easily recognized by the rich colors of burned orange, fiery red, and deep purple that blaze along the hillsides.

Corn – the sacred crop of the Incas and one of the earliest foods, which took man from hunter-gatherer to farmer – is grown in abundance, and is the staple of life along with the ever-present potato. From it, a thick, slightly fermented corn beer called *chicha* is made. *Chicha* is drunk in great quantities in the highlands, especially during festivals. It was originally the royal drink, considered suitable only for consumption by the ruling Inca and his courtiers.

Festivals play a large part in the lifestyle of the indigenous people who inhabit the Callejón de Huaylas. They provide a way to break out of the monotony of day-to-day existence and reaffirm the traditions that give continuity to life in the Andes. Since the Spanish conquest, festivals have assumed a religious veneer and coincide with Catholic feast days, but underneath still lies a strong thread of meaning left behind by ancient cultures. The Catholic Church is well aware of this, but has wisely decided to turn a blind eye.

Every month of the year sees a celebration, or several, in full swing. Some are particular to one village, while others are observed throughout the whole area. The major festivals of San Juan (St John on June 24) and San Pedro and San Pablo (St Peter and St Paul on June 29), celebrated all over the region as in many other parts of the continent, are particularly lively, especially since they fall at the same time as the national day that has been set aside to honor the *campesino* and the ancient Andean celebration of the winter solstice.

On the eve of San Juan, fires are lit throughout the valley, burning the chaff from the harvest and the wild *ichu* grass on the hillsides, and having absolutely nothing to do with John the Baptist. From a high mountain camp, the fires look like starlight brought to earth, and the next day the valley is thick with smoke.

Semana Santa, or Easter Week, is another widely celebrated festival. Many villages have their own special traditions, but the celebrations are always colorful and abundant. Processions of finely adorned religious figures carried on litters, scenes of the Resurrection sculpted in flower petals on the ground, and folkloric bands playing music throughout the village are common events during the festivities of Holy Week.

CHAVÍN DE HUANTAR

Many visitors to the Callejón de Huaylas come not only for the majestic mountains and typical highland life but also to see one of the oldest archeological sites designed by one of the most influential cultures in the Americas.

At the temple complex of **Chavín de Huantar** ❼ (Tue–Sun 9am–5pm) lie the remains of one of the most important pre-Inca cultures. Dating from around 800 to 300 BC, the Chavín culture was typified by a highly developed artistic style and a cult whose influence lasted longer than that of the Roman Empire, and was so widespread that archeologists have termed this formation period "the Chavín Horizon." Some archeologists have come to believe that this culture culminated at Chavín, rather than originating there, but as yet there is no firm evidence either way. The Huaylas culture, which once occupied this valley, was briefly dominated by this more sophisticated civilization.

Archeologists have been able to learn very little about the culture because it left no written records, so much of what is suggested is based on pure supposition. But it is widely accepted that, at the time the Chavín culture was emerging, Peruvian civilization was moving from a hunter-gatherer way of life to a society based on agriculture, which gave people

The giant bromeliad Puya Raimondi.

Grazing livestock, Cordillera Negra.

CORDILLERA HUAYHUASH

Once a place where few outsiders dared to tread, the Cordillera Huayhuash is now considered one of the most scenic trekking areas in Peru.

The high peaks of the Cordillera Huayhuash have long held the fascination of climbers. Joe Simpson's epic retreat from Siula Grande, recounted in the book and film *Touching the Void*, first brought the Huayhuash to international fame. In recent years, while other trails have become overpopulated, this remote region has gained a reputation as the most challenging, and beautiful, trekking destination in Peru.

Until a few years ago, this isolated range to the south of the Callejón de Huaylas was the haunt of bandits, and home to just a handful of rugged mountain men. Sendero Luminoso guerrillas used the area as a base in the 1980s and early 1990s, so until the late 1990s the Huayhuash remained largely undiscovered by Peruvians and foreigners alike, keeping it mysterious and unspoiled: a real zone for adventure.

Though there are several routes through the Huayhuash that allow walkers to see parts of it, the

Trekking in the Cordillera Huayhuash.

best way to visit this magnificent range is to do the full Circuito del Huayhuash, a 12- to 14- day trek of some 170km (102 miles). This route passes over a series of high passes (all well above 4,000 meters/13,300ft), overlooked by awe-inspiring, glacier-shrouded peaks. Trekkers rarely descend below 3,000 meters (9,900ft), making this a taxing high-altitude trek which demands good levels of fitness.

The spine of the Huayhuash is made up of over 20 individual mountains, six of them at over 6,000 meters (19,800ft); Yerupaja, at 6,634 meters (21,836ft), is the second-highest peak in Peru. Slopes of rock and ice extend down into wide grassy valleys with azure-hued glacial lakes. From the mountain paths, the stone-walled, grass-roofed huts of the people who graze their animals here are just visible.

From April to early June the landscape is green and dotted with wild flowers; by July, it has dried to a yellowish hue for the coldest and driest part of the year, when there are nightly freezes and skies as clear as glass. This is the best time for trekking, as daytime temperatures are warm. By September the rains begin, and bitter snowdrifts come to the highest passes and valleys.

Though it was declared a "reserved zone" in 2002, the Huayhuash is not a national park; there is controversial mining on its borders, and even in its remotest spots, this is still a human landscape. Walkers begin and end their treks in the villages of Llamac or Pacllon, and the small village of Huayllapa is visited on most itineraries. People here are extremely poor, though they welcome and benefit from tourism by accompanying walkers as guides and *arrieros* (muleteers), as well as collecting nominal fees at campsites.

Many agencies in Huaraz offer trekking in the Cordillera Huayhuash. Not all have received rave reviews for their services, so check the terms of any contract carefully before you decide on a trek. The Huayhuash is a delicate environment, so try to gauge whether the services you hire will be environmentally responsible and ethical, using *arrieros* from the local area, for example. One highly regarded operation that offers trekking in the Huayhuash is the local tour operator **Huayhuash** (www.huayhuash.com). This organization uses experienced licensed guides and *arrieros with excellent knowledge of the area.*

new-found leisure time to devote to cultural pursuits. The theories that have been put forward about this mysterious culture are mostly based on the study of this 7-hectare (17-acre) site containing a temple, plazas, and a multitude of stone carvings and drawings.

The temple is thought to have been a major ceremonial center, and felines, principally the jaguar, were the most important deities of the cult. It is also believed that the Chavín people were not warlike: their influence on the architecture and sculpture of the northern coast and central highlands appears to have been spread by peaceful means.

VISITING THE TEMPLE

The site is actually located across the mountains in the next valley to the east, near the village of Chavín, but is most accessible from Huaraz. There are regular buses, and the journey takes about three hours. Tours of the site can also be arranged in Huaraz, where there are several agencies. If you go under your own steam you will find guides to show you around, but they may not speak much, if any, English.

What first strikes most visitors upon their arrival at Chavín de Huantar is the quality of the stonework found in the temple walls and the plaza stairways. The dry-stone masonry construction reflects sophistication not expected from a culture that flourished more than 3,000 years ago. Added to this are huge stone slabs with highly stylized carvings of jaguars, eagles, and anacondas; the designs are intricate and fluid.

The temple sits above a large, sunken plaza where it is believed pilgrims came to worship during certain seasons. On one side sits a large granite slab with seven hewn-out indentations that must have served as an altar stone for group rituals. Two 3-meter (10ft) high stone portals overlook the plaza and represent the entry way into the interior of the temple. Finely

etched bird-like figures, one male and one female, face each other across a stairway, symbolically divided into two halves – one painted black and the other white.

Niches set around the outside of the temple walls originally held protruding sculpted stone heads, human in shape but with the snarling grin of a jaguar. Some theories suggest that the eyes were originally inset with crystals, which would reflect the light of the moon and ward off evildoers. Only one of these so-called keystones remains in place; a few have been stolen over the years, and the rest are safely stored within the temple.

The interior of the temple is a subterranean labyrinth of passages and galleries set on at least three levels, which are connected by a series of ramps and stairs. Though there are no windows, a highly engineered ventilation system allows the continuous flow of fresh air throughout – another marvel produced by an ancient civilization. Some of the rooms contain the remains of the sculpted heads and intricately

A mule train in the mountains.

carved slabs that portray a variety of Amazonian and highland animals.

GRANITE GOD

At the heart of the underground complex two narrow passageways cross, and at their junction stands the crowning glory of the Chavín religion – the Lanzón de Chavín. This 4-meter (13ft) high granite monolith is thought to be the principal god-image worshiped by this cult. Its Spanish name comes from the lance or dagger-like shape of the monolith, which appears to be stuck in the ground. A mythological image emerges from the elaborate stone carving, and its demeanor is in keeping with most of the terrifying god-images created by the Chavín people.

The large head of the monolith is square and human-like, yet definite feline characteristics are noted in the grinning mouth, which has a long fang protruding from each corner. The nose has two big holes for nostrils, and an arm and a leg are visible on each side. Round earrings dangle from the creature's ears, and long flowing hair is made up of intricately carved serpents. Carved into the top of the head are thin, grooved channels, and some speculate that animals, or even humans, may have been sacrificed to this god.

Above the god-image there was once an opening in the ceiling, now closed to preserve the figure from exposure to the elements. Here, many believe, a sacrificial rock may have been positioned and, as animals or people were slaughtered, the blood would flow through the opening in the ceiling and run down through the channel in the figure. However, some other archeologists disclaim the sacrificial theory and suggest instead that the Lanzón was merely the dominant figure for worship.

Two other monoliths are considered important in the Chavín cult; both are now housed in the recently reopened **Museo Nacional Chavín de Huantar.** The 1.8-meter (6ft) stone called the *Stela Raimondi* is named after the archeologist Antonio Raimondi (who also gave his name to the *Puya Raimondi* bromeliad described on page 187); he moved the stela to the Museum of Anthropology and Archeology in Lima at the end of the 19th century after it had been used as a table by a *campesino* who had discovered it in 1840. It depicts a monstrous feline anthropomorphic god, with widespread arms, claw-like feet, and a tangle of serpents representing its hair.

The second major piece is the Tello obelisk, which was discovered by archeologist Julio C. Tello. In 2017, it was moved from Lima's Museo de la Nación to the renovated Museo Nacional Chavín de Huantar. This towering, intricately carved piece also depicts feline images, as well as a caiman – a creature not normally associated with highland culture. The significance of this, as of much that we see at the temple, is a mystery, but the experience of a visit is unforgettable.

Northern Platform and Sunken Square Plaza, Chavín de Huantar.

CENTRAL SIERRA

Isolated for years by geography and then terrorism, Ayacucho and the other towns of the Central Sierra are places to enjoy traditional Peru and some spectacular scenery.

Historically, **Ayacucho** and the central highlands have been the link between Lima (and other coastal towns) and Cusco, with the vast eastern jungle region beyond it. It is also here that much of Peru's mineral wealth is to be found, which brought both riches and hardship to the area. In the 1980s, terrorism and emergency military rule made the highland provinces unsafe and unwelcoming, but with the return of peace and the building of a breathtaking highway from Lima, the area is once again welcoming travelers who enjoy its traditional way of life, handicrafts, and often spectacular mountain scenery.

These mountains in central Peru contain caves where, as at Pikimachay, traces have been found of the first known inhabitants dating back to over 15,000 years ago. Ayacucho was also important during the Wari (or Huari) culture, which dominated the region for several hundred years before falling to the Inca in the 14th century. The Incas themselves used it as a communications center, as its valley was on the main route up to what is now Ecuador, and south into Chile. Mining in the area continues, as it has done for centuries, with the giant Cerro de Pasco mine still being one of the world's most important producers of copper. To the north are the imposing peaks of the Cordillera Occidental, and

the mysterious rock formations at Marcahuasi, which attract many visitors.

Much of this area was off-limits for travelers in the 1980s and 1990s, because Ayacucho was the center of activities for Abimael Guzmán and his Sendero Luminoso (Shining Path) guerrilla group. More than half of the 69,000 people killed by the rebel group and in the armed forces' counterinsurgency campaigns came from these provinces, the vast majority of them innocent peasants. This violent period provoked a massive migration to Lima

Main Attractions

Ayacucho Cathedral
Santa Ana
Vilcashuamán
Huancavelica
Lima–Huancayo
  passenger train
Capilla de la Merced,
  Huancayo
Reserva Nacional de Junín

Maps on pages
199, 200

Statue of José Antonio Sucre in Ayacucho.

and other coastal cities, and created a climate of fear and suspicion. The tragic history of what was in fact a civil war is documented at Ayacucho's **Museo de la Memoria** (Jr. Libertad 1229, Mon–Sun 9am–1pm and 3pm–6pm) *para que no se repita* (so that it never happens again).

In recent years, however, with the capture of Guzmán and the virtual disappearance of Shining Path, many people have returned and taken up their traditional pursuits again. The best times to visit are during Easter Week, which is given up entirely to processions and fiestas, or the week at the end of April, when Ayacucho's patron saint is remembered with more riotous celebrations. Another festival well worth attending is the Fiesta de las Cruces in May, when the famous scissor dance is performed, in which a pair of men wielding huge tailors' scissors try to cut each other's trousers.

AYACUCHO'S CHURCHES AND MANSIONS

Ayacucho ❶ was founded by Francisco Pizarro in 1540 as an important

Taxis on the streets of Ayacucho.

communications link between Lima and Cusco. The city was at first called Huamanga, after the local stone similar to alabaster, and is still often, somewhat confusingly, called this by locals. The name was changed in 1824 after Republican forces finally freed Peru of Spanish troops at the nearby battle on the plain of Ayacucho. The impressive archway known as the **Arco de San Francisco de Asis**, or Arco de Triunfo, on the Jirón 28 de Julio in the city center was built in 1924 to commemorate the victory.

Ayacucho's reputation as a city with "a church on every street corner" may be exaggerated, but it does have 33 churches, most of them still in regular use. Perhaps the most impressive is the early Baroque **Catedral ❹**, Nuestra Señora de las Nieves (Our Lady of the Snows; daily 9–noon and 3–6.30pm) on the Plaza Mayor de Huamanga, also known as Plaza de Armas (and previously Plaza Sucre). Begun in 1612, it has superb gilt altars, a silver tabernacle, and a beautifully carved pulpit. It also contains Stations of the Cross paintings brought from Rome. During the famous *Semana Santa* celebrations during Easter Week, this is one of the most visited churches in all Peru. The procession of its statues round the city by different *cofradías* or brotherhoods rivals that of Seville in Spain. The faithful start the week on Palm Sunday with a candle-light procession, when a precious statue of Christ from the cathedral is carried on the back of a white donkey. Each day after this there are more processions, with each statue from the church being revered by its own group of worshipers. At dawn on Easter Sunday, all the bells of the city celebrate Christ's resurrection, the doors of the cathedral are flung open, and 250 men carry the statue of Christ around the square.

Another outstanding church, the Jesuit **Templo de la Compañía ❻** (Mass daily 6.30–7.30am and 10.30am–12.30pm, Sun 11am–1pm), built in 1605, boasts an unusual carved facade of orange-red stone and has a lovely gilded altar. The interior also has richly carved wood and 17th-century religious paintings.

A few blocks away up Jirón 9 de Diciembre stands the Renaissance **church of Santo Domingo** (Mass Mon–Sat 6.30–7.30am, Sun 7–8am). It has an altar richly decorated with gold leaf, but it is this church's role in history that is most significant: bells in its small towers rang out the first peals of Peru's independence following the decisive Battle of Ayacucho. Round the corner on Jirón Callao, the finest carved pulpit of all Ayacucho's churches is to be found in the **Iglesia de San Francisco de Paula** (Mass daily 7am, Sun 9am).

Although Spanish colonial architecture is the pride of Ayacucho, this was an important area for many civilizations prior to the arrival of the Spaniards. Five hundred years before the Incas, the Wari Empire dominated these highlands, and traces of that and other influences are to be found at the **Museo Hipólito Unanue** (Tue–Sun 9am–5pm), part of the **Instituto Nacional de Cultura** on Avenida Independencia. The museum's collection ranges from 1500 BC stone carvings to Wari ceremonial bowls, Chancay textiles, and stone and ceramic Inca pieces.

Ayacucho has several other museums that are worth visiting. **The Museo Joaquín López Antay** in the colonial Casona Chacón (now a bank) on the Plaza Mayor de Huamanga has a good collection of local art, popular objects, and photographs of the city and its surroundings (Tue–Sat 4–8pm). The nearby **Casona Jáuregui** is another exquisitely proportioned 17th-century mansion that holds temporary exhibitions.

The **Museo Mariscal Cáceres** (Mon–Fri 9am–1pm, 3–5pm, Sat 9am–1pm), housed in the elegant 17th-century **Casona Vivanco** on Jirón 28 de Julio, has a fine display of colonial paintings and furnishings. It is named after Andrés Cáceres, a young man from Ayacucho whose rapid military ascent stemmed from his successful organization of *campesinos* (subsistence farmers) to resist the Chilean invaders during Peru's

Street art using flower petals during Ayacucho's Easter celebrations.

Cathedral spire, Ayacucho.

otherwise disastrous performance in the War of the Pacific in the 1880s. Cáceres was rewarded by being made president of Peru in 1886. The *casona* is one of the best preserved of the colonial mansions that are the hallmark of Ayacucho.

Another splendid mansion is the **Casona Boza y Solis** Ⓕ, the seat of the provincial prefecture. Built in 1740, it has a two-story interior courtyard and a wide staircase lined with beautiful imported colored tiles. It also contains the cell where the local heroine of independence, María Parado de Bellido, was held until she was executed by a Spanish firing squad in 1822 (Mon–Fri 8am–1pm and 3–5pm).

ARTS AND CRAFTS

Ayacucho is a center for many traditional handicrafts. A good place to see artisans at work and to purchase their wares is the **Santa Ana** neighborhood behind the Alameda Bolognesi. Many of the houses here still contain family workshops, where several generations make rugs, tapestries, and carpets. Filigree and silver work as well as *retablos* (painted altars) of all shapes and sizes can be bought in Santa Ana and other parts of the city. Another specialty of the city are the etched *mates burilados* (gourds). These often show surprisingly complicated scenes of everyday life or from the Bible, etched onto dried gourds of every dimension. The local Huamanga alabaster is also still worked with great skill into biblical scenes, cribs for Christmas and other, more modern fantasies.

Shopping is also a lively experience at the city's sprawling market, a block south of Jirón San Martín. Here, stalls offer everything from handicrafts and hand-knitted sweaters to rubber boots and hot peppers and other medicinal herbs. Delicious freshly made bread, with cinnamon and aniseed, is sold from cloth-covered baskets, as are herbal drinks known as *emolientes*. You can safely try the bread, but it is perhaps advisable to leave the drinks to the locals: the glasses are not usually properly washed.

But the local drink of *ponche* (punch) is well worth a try. This is a milk-based punch flavored with peanut, sesame, clove, cinnamon, walnuts, and sugar, and spiked with *pisco*. You could accompany this with one of the hearty local dishes such as *puca picante*, a stew made of pieces of pork, potatoes, and toasted peanuts, served with rice and parsley.

BATTLE SITE

In the rolling hills 37km (22 miles) northeast of the city is the village of

Central Sierra

0   50 km
0   50 miles

Quinua. It was on the pampa (plain) 1km (0.6 miles) outside the village that the decisive battle of Ayacucho was fought against the Spanish troops on 9 December 1824. Although outnumbered almost two to one, the Venezuelan general Antonio José de Sucre emerged victorious from the battle, which was the last fought by the Spaniards in Latin America. (Some local guides will even tell you that no battle as such was fought, since the Spanish commander Virrey de la Serna decided to avoid bloodshed and withdrew.) The place of the encounter is marked by a hideous 1970s obelisk some 44 meters (144ft) high, built with Venezuelan oil wealth. Its one redeeming feature is the spectacular scenery to be seen from its viewing platform. The broad plain is a popular place for weekend picnics, and each December the victory is celebrated by an eight-day extravaganza. Dancing and craft exhibitions are central to the celebrations, with the traditional scissor dance to the fore.

The village of Quinua itself is a center for handicrafts, and has been so successful that as many as 6,000 people now live there, most of them producing crafts of one kind or another. Almost all the red-tiled roofs are topped with good-luck symbols: small ceramic churches or pairs of bulls, made originally for festivals coinciding with the branding of cattle. These pieces are also on sale in the village's many stores, together with handmade guitars and sculptures in Huamanga stone.

Several tour companies in Ayacucho organize day trips that include Quinua and the battlefield, and also a visit to **Vilcashuamán ➋**, once an important administrative center for the Inca Empire, and interesting above all for the Spanish constructions built directly on top of Inca architecture. The village is most famous for its *usnu* or ceremonial Inca pyramid, which has been preserved almost intact. Inca remains are also to be found at nearby **Baños Intihuatana** (a 30-minute walk from the highway). Next to a lagoon thought to have been artificially

⊙ **Fact**

Óscar Durand, the last leader of the guerrilla group Sendero Luminoso, was captured near Huancayo in 1999. This marked the end of the group's activities, which had brought death and misery to many.

Memorial commemorating the Battle of Ayacucho.

⊘ Eat

In Huancayo, everyone has to try the fabulous *pachamanca* at least once. This delicious meat stew is cooked in a hole in the ground covered with hot stones.

constructed by the Incas, there are the remains of a palace, baths, a tower, a Temple of the Sun, a sacrificial stone, and a boulder carved with 17 angles.

Another stopover is at the Huari (Wari) ruins about 20km (12 miles) outside Ayacucho on the way to Quinua. These extensive ruins, in a landscape full of tuna cactuses, are thought to be the remains of the Wari culture which flourished here between the 6th and 11th centuries. Archeologists have estimated that up to 50,000 people lived in this settlement, occupying as many as 15 different "neighborhoods." There is a small museum on site, but most of the finds have been taken to the archeological museum in Ayacucho for safekeeping.

As well as the fruit-bearing tuna cactuses, you may find *Puya Raimondi* in these high valleys. The rivers that cut the valleys around Ayacucho also offer good fishing for trout and other native species. No permit is necessary, but there are seasons for different fish – best to ask a local expert.

Street scene, Ayacucho.

NORTH FROM AYACUCHO

Ayacucho's nearest northern neighbors – although it takes several hours to reach them – are the towns of **Huancavelica ❸** and Huancayo. Huancavelica has a lengthy past as one of Peru's main mining towns. Silver was discovered here soon after the Spanish conquest, and through the 17th and 18th centuries it was a great creator of wealth, although many of the indigenous people who worked in the mines suffered from mercury poisoning and died very young. The mines at **Santa Barbara**, some 5km (3 miles) outside the city, can be visited. As in Ayacucho, some of this mining wealth was spent on the city's churches. The red sandstone-fronted **Catedral San Antonio** in the Plaza de Armas in the center of Huancavelica has a fine gilded altar and some Baroque paintings. Nearby, **San Francisco** shows how Spanish Baroque architecture became far more ornate in the 18th century, while the church and convent of **Santo Domingo** includes paintings shipped especially from Rome.

More interesting is the bustling city of **Huancayo** ❹, situated some 400km (250 miles) northwest of Ayacucho. The city's name means "place of stones," and from the remaining monuments it is easy to see why. Its main attractions are the **Capilla de la Merced** (Mon–Sat 8am–noon and 3–6pm), the colonial church where the Peruvian constitution was signed in 1839. The people of Huancayo are also very proud that it was in their city that slavery was abolished in Peru in 1854, and the statue in the main plaza honors Mariscal Ramón Castilla, who pushed the measure through.

There is also an interesting regional museum in the **Museo del Colegio Salesiano** (Mon–Fri 10am–1pm, 3–6pm) in the El Tambo district, while the Cerrito de la Libertad is a hill overlooking the city with panoramic views. A short walk farther on are the remarkable eroded stone towers known as the **Torre Torre**, which also give views over the town.

Huancayo is known throughout Peru for its boisterous festivals. The most famous – as in Ayacucho – is the Fiesta de las Cruces, which is held every May. There is also a Sunday market which brings in artisans from all the surrounding area, and is a good source of bargains.

INTO THE MANTARO VALLEY

Huancayo is also the starting point for journeys to the Mantaro Valley, which has several places well worth a visit. About 8km (5 miles) from Huancayo is the village of **Cochas Chico**, where some of the best local handicrafts can be bargained for. There is also the Convento de Santo Ocopa, founded some 250 years ago as a training place for missionaries who were setting off to evangelize in the vast Amazon regions of Peru. In the convent there is a precious library, with texts dating back to the 15th century. Further north, the **Santuario Warivilca** (8am–5pm) is a fortified ruin from the days of the Wari Empire.

The mountains here form the Cordillera Huaytapallana, which is 17km (11 miles) long and has five peaks

The Cerrito de la Libertad, which overlooks Huancayo.

Train from Lima to Huancayo.

⊘ THE TRAIN TO THE SKIES

The train journey from Lima to Huancayo is one of the most spectacular in the world. The line rises 346km (215 miles) from sea level to a height of 4,800 meters (16,000ft) at the Ticlio pass, and is one of the highest in the world. There are 26 stations, 58 bridges, 69 tunnels and six zig-zag switchbacks through the Andes. Passengers can admire the breath-taking scenery through panoramic windows or from the viewing area at the back of the train which is totally open to the elements. Construction of the railway started in the late 1800s by the US engineer Henry Meiggs, who reportedly told Peruvian government members that he would "place rails there, where the llamas walk." It took over 40 years to complete the line. It is an engineering wonder – but to pay for it, the Peruvian government of the day almost went bankrupt. It was used for transporting copper and zinc from mines in the Andes and farm produce from the valleys.

The train makes the 12-hour journey from Lima and the shorter return trip approximately twice a month, so it is vital to book in advance. Reservations can be made by phone at (51) 01-226 6363 ext. 222 and 235 or via the Ferrocarril Central website (www.ferrocarrilcentral.com.pe). Travelers can also take a cheap daily local train to continue to Huancavelica.

Papa a la huancaína, a specialty of Huancayo.

over 5,000 meters (16,400ft) high, with many important glaciers. The highest of the peaks is the snow-covered Nevado Lasuntaysuyo.

Some 40km (25 miles) from Huancayo is the small town of **Jauja**, best known for being the capital of Spanish Peru before Lima was founded, and for the expression *país de Jauja*, referring to a never-never land of milk and honey. Its narrow streets and blue-painted houses seem to reflect hundreds of years of unhurried existence. Boats can be rented by the hour to coast the azure waters of nearby Laguna de Paca.

THE RESERVA NACIONAL DE JUNÍN

Some 170km (105 miles) north of Huancayo is a favorite destination for keen birdwatchers: the **Reserva Nacional de Junín**. The lakes here abound with aquatic birds and the large Andean species.

Other than that, the northernmost town of any importance in the central highlands is **Huánuco ❺**. Previously part

Templo de los Manos Cruzados, Kotosh.

of the Wari (or Huari) and then the Inca culture, the modern city was founded by Gómez de Alvarado in 1539. It has always been the market center for a mainly agricultural and wooded region, and maintains much of its slow charm today. The central square or Plaza de Armas has a 19th-century sculpture by an Italian designer but, unlike many other Peruvian cities, its cathedral is modern, dating from 1966. Two older churches, though, are the **Iglesia San Cristóbal**, the first built by the Spaniards, which is adorned with fine woodcarvings, and the **Iglesia de San Francisco**, first constructed in 1560 but remodeled in the 18th century in neoclassical style (daily 6–10am and 5–8pm).

This sleepy town comes to life during carnival week, celebrated here in August. In January, it is host to the *danza de los negritos*, when dancers wear black masks to represent the black slaves imported to work in the silver mines, most of whom died.

Five km (3 miles) outside Huánuco stands **Kotosh ❻** and its famous **Templo de las Manos Cruzadas**. As the name suggests, this temple (daily 9am–5pm), which is believed to be from about 2300 to 2000 BC – making it one of the oldest of the Andes – has carvings of crossed hands on the walls. According to some archeologists, this is a sign that the ancient people who lived here had a dual vision of the universe.

On the return trip west nearer to Lima are the amazing, colossal rock formations of **Marcahuasi**. These are a magnet for rock climbers, but have also bred several strange theories that they represent huge human profiles sculpted by a people who inhabited the earth before mankind. The copper-rich stones are reported to have protective properties, and are said to shield visitors from negative energy. A large flat plain in the middle of the formations is the scene each year (28–30 July) of a local festival bringing together music and dance groups from surrounding villages.

View from the forest floor.

THE NORTHERN AMAZON

Travel by riverboat through the Amazon region and discover the huge diversity of flora and fauna – but don't expect to keep to a schedule, for time means little here.

Viewed from the air, Peru's Amazon looks like an endless sea of lumpy green sponges, stretching in all directions to the horizon. It is this thick umbrella of trees – the jungle's equivalent of an enormous housing project – that creates the millions of homes below in which animals and specialized plants live. If you were able to enter the upper canopy slowly from the top you would soon discover that the first layer is virtually a desert. The crowns of the trees are exposed both to the fierce tropical sun and to winds that frequently snap and topple the tallest of them. To reduce evaporation, the leaves at this level are quite small. Many of the epiphytes – plants that live on top of other plants – actually take the form of cacti, to reduce their loss of water.

As you descended through the upper canopy, however, you would immediately begin to enter a different world of reduced light. Protected from direct sun and wind, the leaves are thus larger in size than those above, and the fierce struggle for light has begun. Traveling farther down toward the jungle floor, you would see that leafy plants are much less abundant. Although explorers traveling by river often reported thick and impenetrable jungle, under the canopy away from the rivers it is possible to move about quite easily, as most branches and leaves are well off the forest floor.

Red-eyed tree frog.

The air here is calm even in strong storms, and at times completely still. The sound of insects is overpowering, as millions of unseen little creatures call to one another. At the bottommost level the leaves are very large; less than 5 percent of the sun's light actually reaches the jungle's floor.

BIODIVERSITY

It is this enormous variation of light, wind, and temperature that, together with the thousands of different species of plants, affords millions of different

Main Attractions

Pilpintuwasi Butterfly
  Farm
Iquitos
Traveling by riverboat
Staying in an eco-lodge
Reserva Nacional Pacaya-
  Samiria
Puerto Callao

Map on page 208

homes for animal and plant species. Whole communities of insects, birds, and other animals are specialized and adapted to different levels of the rainforest, so it is not surprising that it contains the highest species diversity in the world.

Parque Nacional del Manu in southeastern Peru, for example, covering an area roughly half the size of Switzerland, houses a staggering 1,000+ bird species (more than the whole of North America and one in nine of the whole planet), 20 percent of all the plant species found in South America, and more than 1,200 species of butterfly (Europe has just 400).

PUSH TOWARD CONSERVATION

Jungles have existed for hundreds of millions of years, but it is only within the past 100 years that they have been on the decline. The trend is in direct relation to the population of human beings. In the course of the past century humans have destroyed half of the world's rainforests. At the present rate of destruction, only 40 percent of the original Amazon rainforest will remain by 2025 or thereabouts.

Tampering with the jungles is not a modern phenomenon, of course. Europeans have long viewed the Amazon as a storehouse of raw materials. The

Northern Amazon

16th- and 17th-century search for gold was replaced by quests for other valuable commodities native to the Amazon jungle and found nowhere else in the world: quinine (which allowed British troops to conquer India without succumbing to malaria), cocoa (the basis of the world's chocolate industry), mahogany, vanilla, and others. No product made a bigger impact, however, than that which naturally exudes from three species of Amazonian tree: the sticky white latex called rubber.

THE RUBBER BOOM

The commodity had been known about for a very long time – Columbus reported tribes using strange "elastic" balls in their games – but its commercial use was limited due to the fact that natural rubber grew soft and sticky in hot weather and brittle and hard in cold. In 1844, however, Charles Goodyear invented the process of vulcanization, which allowed rubber to stay tough and firm at all temperatures. This revolutionized the rubber industry. With John Boyd Dunlop's later invention of the pneumatic tire, suddenly an enormous demand was created, which only the Amazon could satisfy.

The ensuing rubber boom was short-lived – it lasted from around 1880 to 1912 – but it transformed the Amazon's economy. Rubber trees in the most remote regions were soon being tapped, the latex gathered in cups, then coagulated into large balls that were cured over a fire. The tappers themselves were bankrolled by entrepreneurs who amassed enormous wealth and lived in luxury in newly burgeoning jungle cities such as Manaus in Brazil and Iquitos in Peru.

In the midst of the boom, however, an English adventurer named Henry Wickham quietly collected 70,000 rubber seeds and smuggled them out of the Amazon. First planted in Kew Gardens in England, and then transplanted to tropical Asia where they were safe from indigenous diseases, the seeds flourished. By 1912 the Amazon rubber boom was at an end.

In the latter half of the 20th century the largest destructive force on the Peruvian Amazon was the unmanaged influx of peasants from the Andes and the coast. Since the 1960s, successive governments, both military and civilian, have viewed the eastern Andean slopes and the Amazon basin as regions of unexploited natural resources, believing that their development would provide a politically painless solution to several urgent problems: land hunger in the Andes, the migration of masses of the rural poor to coastal cities, and the need to populate border regions in order to defend national sovereignty.

As a result the Belaúnde government financed the construction of a "marginal highway," a road paralleling the Andes to the east, which, it was hoped, would help open up the area to colonization and industry. But the idea of settling the Amazon ignored reality: less than 5 percent of the Peruvian Amazon's soil is

Wooly monkey.

Spiny bush cricket.

suitable for agriculture, and much of the region supports populations of indigenous peoples and settlers that are already large in relation to the exploitable resources.

As a consequence, agriculture that began on a few relatively fertile terraces in the eastern Andes has now spread to land ill-suited to continuous exploitation. With inadequate knowledge of better practices, many farmers work the land too long, allowing no time for it to renew itself. Once the soil has been drained of nutrients, poor farmers, unable to buy fertilizer, have no alternative but to move on, carving yet another plot from the forest.

The result has been extensive deforestation of Peru's cloud forest, where an estimated 50 percent of all neotropical plant species are found. Thus far over 70,000 sq km (27,000 sq miles) of the Peruvian Amazon have been deforested; 300,000 hectares (741,300 acres) are deforested every year.

An additional impact on Peru's rainforest has been the illegal cocaine industry, mostly concentrated in the north-central jungle's Huallaga Valley and Valle de los Ríos Apurímac, Ene y Antaro (VRAEM) in the south. Hundreds of thousands of hectares of virgin rainforest were destroyed in order to grow illegal plantations of coca shrubs – all to support the drug habits of, mainly, North Americans and Europeans. The US government pressurized Peru to use a major defoliant – Spike – on coca plantations, but protests by local and international conservationists about the effect such a chemical could have on the surrounding jungle prevented its use. In recent years, many hectares of coca-leaf plantations have been turned over to legal cash crops such as cocoa, coffee, or corn, and a government program has been initiated to help farmers find markets for their new crops. Nevertheless, a much more profitable drug production has hardly been dented.

SYSTEM OF PROTECTION

In spite of increasing rainforest destruction, however, a number of encouraging developments have taken place. Peru currently has roughly 5 percent of its

A caiman lying in wait.

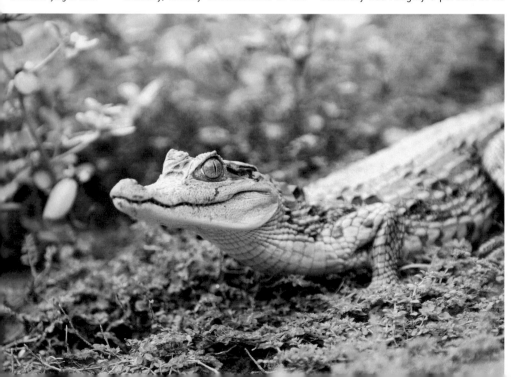

territory protected by a system of more than 50 national parks, reserves, sanctuaries, and other designated areas, a process that has thrived since it was begun in the 1960s. During the past few decades, considerable ecological awareness has developed and, as a consequence, there has been a proliferation of conservation organizations. In 1990 a giant 1.5 million-hectare (3.75 million-acre) "reserved zone" was declared in the Madre de Dios region – Peru's southernmost department, which contains some of the richest rainforest found anywhere in the world. This area – including almost the entire watershed of the Río Tambopata – is at the forefront of tropical rainforest conservation.

ECO-TOURISM DEVELOPS

The idea is to convert the zone not into a park but rather an "extractive reserve," which means an area of rainforest where renewable yearly harvests of Brazil nuts, rubber, and other rainforest products will create more revenue, in the long run, than the permanent destruction caused by unmanaged farming, logging, and cattle-ranching. The scheme was pioneered by the Brazilian rubber tapper turned environmentalist leader Chico Méndez (murdered in 1988 by Brazilian cattle-ranchers), but it still needs to compete with more damaging business. The global commodities boom has meanwhile led to a destructive influx of gold diggers to nearby areas.

The practice of so-called eco-tourism has also developed since the late 1980s. This "green" tourism is based on the belief that the rich natural rainforest cannot only be preserved, by using it as an extractive reserve, but can also attract tourist dollars. If the eco-tourism industry is managed responsibly, the income it generates, pumped into local economies and national-park infrastructures, may well prove to be one of the few counter-destructive economic forces currently available for preserving the jungle. Eco-tourism in Peru received another boost in 2014 when the first national EcoFest, an ecological festival aimed at raising consciousness, was held in Lima.

Paddling up the Amazon.

⊘ AYAHUASCA: THE SACRED VINE

Ayahuasca *(Banisteriopsis caapi)* is a rainforest vine with hallucinogenic properties that is used to promote knowledge and healing under the guidance of a shaman. The vine has been used for centuries by Amazon tribes as part of traditional celebrations and initiations. It has also been used to make predictions, in decision-making, and to aid the resolution of interfamilial and inter-tribal conflicts. Today, it is principally used as a key to self-knowledge and expanded consciousness.

Extract of the vine is prepared as a bitter-tasting drink which is administered by the shaman. After some time, this promotes vomiting – part of the cleansing process – and then a state in which visions are experienced, leading to a mental state of clarity, certainty, and self-awareness.

Courses in Ayahuasca are used in some Amazon clinics to treat alcoholism and drug addiction, and, in recent years, drinking Ayahuasca has become a popular activity for tourists. Some shamans conduct Ayahuasca ceremonies for groups, but if you are attracted by the idea, do your research carefully. While at its best, Ayahuasca is said to be profoundly enlightening, a bad experience can be very frightening.

Fact

A non-profit group dedicated to preserving these virgin forests is Pronaturaleza, contactable at Calle Doña Juana 137, Urb. Los Rosales – Santiago de Surco, Lima, or via their website (www.pronaturaleza.org).

THE NORTHERN JUNGLE

Some 3,200km (1,990 miles) upriver from the Amazon's mouth lies the bustling, jungle-locked city of **Iquitos** ❶. The capital of the department of Loreto, it is home to more than 420,000 people, and is linked to the exterior world only by air and riverboats. At one time the clearing-house for the millions of tons of rubber shipped to Europe, Iquitos still displays the vestiges of its former status as one of the most important rubber capitals in the world. Houses both near the main plaza and the river are still faced with *azulejos* (glazed tiles), which at the height of the rubber boom were originally shipped from Italy and Portugal along with other luxury goods such as early 20th-century ironwork from England, glass chandeliers, caviar, and fine wines.

On the Plaza de Armas stands the Casa de Fierro, or Iron House, which was designed by Gustave Eiffel for the Paris Exhibition in 1898. It is said to be the first prefabricated house in the Americas, and was transported unassembled from Paris by a local rubber baron. It is entirely constructed of iron trusses and bolted iron sheets. This sounds more impressive than it looks, and it is more interesting as a symbol of the town's short-lived affluence than architecturally.

Also on the plaza is the house of Carlos Fitzcarrald, the Peruvian rubber baron who dragged a steamship over the pass that bears his name, thus opening up the department of Madre de Dios. The German director Werner Herzog shot part of his film *Fitzcarraldo* here, and several of the refurbished steamships that he used are still in port. Hundreds of *iquiteños* were used as extras in the movie, which created a brief mini-boom of its own.

Iquitos today is a colorful, friendly city that seems to have a monopoly not on rubber but on three-wheeled taxis (charging approximately 50 cents a ride); motor scooters, with the consequent din as they are continually revved up; Amazon views; and a very special atmosphere. It is located some 80km (50 miles) downriver from where the Marañón and Ucayali rivers join to create the River Amazon.

Casa de Fierro, Iquitos.

The local dish is *paiche a la loretana*, a fillet of a huge primitive fish, served with fried manioc and vegetables. Exotic fruit juices are sold on the street corners, as are ice creams that are flavored with mango, papaya, *granadilla* (passion fruit), *guanábana* (soursop), and many other fruits.

You can take a taxi or simply walk down from the main plaza to the picturesque waterfront district of Belén, to the southeast of the town, where the houses float on rafts in the water. A primitive Venetian-style labyrinth of canals, canoes, and stores, Belén is the center for an incredible variety of Amazon products: exotic fruits, fish, turtles, edible frogs, herbal medicines, and waterfowl. Plowing the waterways are a plethora of small canoe-taxis paddled by *iquiteños*, some as young as five years old. A canoe tour of one of the most unusual waterfronts in the world costs just a few dollars.

Some 15km (9 miles) south of the city is the beautiful Lago Quistacocha, set in lush tropical jungle, which can be reached by bus. There is a small zoo, the Parque Zoológico de Quistacocha (daily 8am–5pm), where jaguars, ocelots, parrots, and anacondas can be seen, as well as the giant paiche fish, which are bred here in hatcheries. This makes it the place to sample paiche, as wild populations have been sadly overfished.

If you are spending a few days in Iquitos, it is worth taking a day trip to the **Animal Orphanage and Pilpintuwasi Butterfly Farm** (tel: 063-23-2665; www.amazonanimalorphanage.org; Tue–Sun 9am–4pm), just outside the city at Padre Cocha. On the banks of the Nanay river is a huge walk-through butterfly enclosure, with exhibits that explain the fascinating lifecycle of the butterfly. It is a delight to walk around surrounded by drifts of the colorful creatures. Located on the same site is the **Amazon Animal Orphanage**, a refuge for injured or previously caged animals. There is a magnificent jaguar and a giant anteater, as well as monkeys, tapirs, parrots, sloths, and a number of other denizens of the jungle, all rescued from unhappy captivity or recuperating from maltreatment.

The Butterfly Farm and the Animal Orphanage are a 20-minute boat ride from the Bella Vista sector in Iquitos (ask for Pilpintuwasi). In the dry season, there is a 15-minute walk from where the boat leaves you; in the wet, you are brought right to the front gate.

JUNGLE EXCURSIONS

Iquitos has long been a center for excursions into the surrounding jungle. It should be remembered, however, that because there are a lot of people in this area, and the Amazon here is a main waterway, you must travel well beyond a 60km (37-mile) radius of the city to see wildlife such as caiman, monkeys, macaws, or pink dolphins – in fact, the last are found only on remote tributaries of the upper Amazon and Orinoco rivers.

A good way to become acquainted quickly with the jungle is to visit one of a number of lodges that have been set up

⊘ **Eat**

A typical *iquiteño* specialty is *juanes*: rice, chicken, olive, and hardboiled egg, all wrapped in the leaf of a *bijao* plant. Served with a spicy *ají* condiment, they are delicious.

Giant waterlilies.

THE AMAZON BY RIVERBOAT

In Peru's Amazon regions, rivers are highways, and riverboat is the only way to get around and experience the slow-paced life of the Amazon.

Riverboats vary from *pequepeques* (small dugouts with outboard motors) to *lanchas* (larger cargo and passenger boats) and luxurious tourist boats with air conditioning and cocktails at sunset. Boats ply the tributaries of the Ucayali, Huallaga, Marañón, and Amazon rivers, and any number of lesser waterways in between.

To experience river life properly, buy yourself a hammock in Iquitos (for about US$10) and a ticket on a *lancha*. Locals travel on these boats, along with bags of bananas and mangoes, sacks of corn, cattle, pigs, chickens, dogs, and pet monkeys. You can string up your hammock in the middle of the friendly melee, opt for a private upper deck, or even pay for a cabin with a proper bed. The latter options offer more space and quiet, and provide you with somewhere secure to leave your belongings. If you can speak a bit of Spanish, hanging out with the locals can be a rewarding experience. As the boat churns its way along, you'll share snacks and jokes, and cement friendships.

Calipso riverboat.

LIFE ON BOARD

Meals are served three times a day, and the quality of the food depends on the boat and on which deck you choose. On the better boats, the upper-deck fare is good – meat and rice or river fish bought from settlements along the way. It is also worth sampling the wonderful array of tropical fruits sold by villagers en route. Depending on the amount of cargo to load and unload at different ports, there may be time to get off and explore.

Nights on the river are magical: hammocks sway gently as you drift through the jungle underneath a star-studded sky. Get up early and you'll be treated to an Amazon sunrise as the boat floats through the early morning mist. During the day, keep your eyes peeled for pink dolphins, which sometimes play around the boats as they dock. Traveling by riverboat is all about the journey – it's a time to stop and observe and become part of life here and, best of all, you might even be the only tourist on the boat.

BUYING TICKETS

Tickets can be bought from travel agencies in Iquitos, although it is best to buy them at the dock as this gives you a chance to see the boat you'll be traveling on. There are daily departures to Pucallpa, a journey of four to seven days (depending on water levels and cargo loading and unloading times), for which the Henry boats are recommended. The three- to four-day journey to Yurimaguas is best made on the Eduardo boats, of which Eduardo III is the most highly recommended. Tickets for this service must be reserved in person at the company's offices on the docks. Traveling to Manaus in Brazil takes around 10 days and requires a boat change at Santa Rosa on the border.

Boats leave from Puerto Masusa on Avenida La Marina, but don't expect them to stick to any schedule. To ply these routes in five-star style, contact Aqua Expeditions (www.aquaexpeditions.com), or Amazon Cruises, toll-free in the US: 1-866-725-3255; www.amazoncruise.net. Fares vary depending on the length of the trip and usually include meals and beverages, excursions, and transfers to and from Iquitos airport.

on nearby rivers. Although many of the two- or three-day lodge tours can be booked through a travel agent in Lima, they are much cheaper if arranged in Iquitos. Avoid the numerous individuals in the airport and the city who are keen to set up a "jungle lodge tour" on behalf of foreign visitors. Since these men are paid on a commission basis, you can buy the same package deal more cheaply by simply walking into a lodge's downtown office, most of which are clustered around Jirón Putumayo near the Plaza de Armas.

Explorama Lodges (www.explorama. com) is one of the largest companies, with four different lodges, all of them well run and efficient. One of the advantages of booking into one of the Explorama lodges is that they also provide access to the canopy walkway at the Amazon Conservatory of Tropical Studies (ACTS). First opened in 1992, it is now around 500 meters (1,640ft) in length, and reaching a height of up to 35 meters (115ft) it offers breathtaking views for birdwatching from a unique perspective. One of the most beautiful sights is that of mixed flocks of birds feeding in the early morning and late afternoon. Sloths, marmosets, and monkeys can also be spotted.

Other lodges in the area offer river trips to the beautiful Río Yarapa, where river dolphins can be seen, and interesting shamanic tours for more esoterically minded travelers.

SLOW BOATS

A commercial riverboat traveling either upriver toward Pucallpa or downriver toward Brazil is a great way to experience the Amazon. Although not much will be seen in the way of wildlife along the way (boats traveling upstream hug the banks, those in the opposite direction travel down the center of the river), the traveler will still see how people live along the Amazon and also enjoy beautiful sunsets and magnificent scenery.

Be warned that life along the Amazon is slow and leisurely – you should never travel by riverboat if you are in a hurry or have an inflexible schedule. Boats often break down, linger sometimes for days in port, and are generally unpredictable.

Another way to see the Amazon, and one highly recommended for those who have a little more time and want to get off the beaten path, is to hire a small boat and guide of your own. In every Amazon port there are boat-owners who are willing to rent you their services at only a fraction of the cost paid at a typical jungle lodge. If you make up a small group, it is even more economical. As with the commercial riverboats, the best way to locate a small boat and guide in Iquitos is simply to ask about on the wharves. With a boat, the entire Amazon suddenly opens up for your exploration.

Only 100km (62 miles) from Iquitos, for example, is the biggest national park in Peru, the 2 million-hectare (5 million-acre) **Reserva Nacional Pacaya-Samiria ❷**, a wildlife-packed lowland

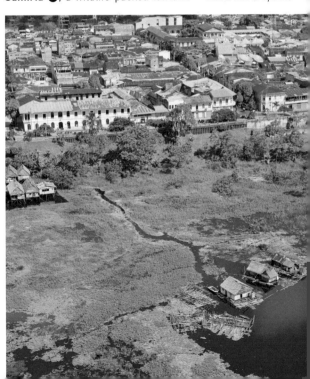

Aerial view of Iquitos.

jungle area bordered in the North by the massive Marañón and the Ucayali River in the south. The preserve is notable for its spectacular diversity of animal and plant life, including more than 520 bird species, over 100 mammal species – such as river dolphins, jaguars, and giant otters – and unknown numbers of insect and plant species. Conservation poses a challenge as close to 100,000 people live in the 200-odd villages on its fringes. Yet many are involved in protection efforts, ranging from repopulation of turtles to eco-tourism. Wildlife is best seen during the July–August dry season, while trips from February to May are inconvenient due to heaviest rains. Several options are available for visitors, including multi-day cruises and stays at rustic and luxury lodges inside the park. Individual trips are not permitted. International tour operators organize visits while local companies run trips from Iquitos, Tarapoto or Lagunas on the limit of the preserve, with several days the best option and some camping available. Entrance fees for the park must be paid in Iquitos.

Bananas en route to market in Iquitos.

THE CENTRAL JUNGLE

Seven days' travel upriver from Iquitos on the Río Ucayali is **Pucallpa**, a rapidly growing city of over 211,000 that can be reached from Lima by air – there are several flights daily – or on a 24-hour bus journey.

Most people arriving in the city prefer to stay at **Puerto Callao ❸** on the nearby Lago Yarinacocha, a 20-minute bus journey from the city, which is the main tourist attraction of the area. Based here are the Hospital Amazónico de Yarinacocha, which provides medical care for the local Indian population, and the Summer Institute of Linguistics (www.peru.sil.org), a non-denominational US missionary organization studying many of Peru's indigenous jungle languages, with the intention of concocting an alphabet so that the Bible can be translated into these hitherto unwritten languages. The latter organization, which can be visited by appointment only, has attracted a great deal of criticism from those who believe that through its influence indigenous peoples are in danger of losing their own culture and tribal identity.

In Puerto Callao you can visit the fascinating artisanal cooperative Maroti Shobo, where high-quality ceramics and weavings made by the Shipibo people from the surrounding villages are displayed and sold, and are sent to museums all over the world.

The Shipibo people have inhabited the area for at least the past 1,000 years, and trips can be arranged to some of their villages. There are a couple of lodges on the lake, and more wildlife than you might expect, considering the nearby population. The lodges will also organize jungle excursions, and private excursions by motor canoe into the surrounding jungle and canals are easy to arrange from Puerto Callao. While traveling on the canals, you may see numerous piranhas, caiman, and the occasional monkey.

Climbing the trees around Lago Yarinacocha.

Blue and yellow macaws
at a clay lick.

MANU TO MALDONADO

One of the truly pristine areas of the tropics, this southern corner of Peru is a birdwatcher's paradise. It can be reached from the gold-boom town of Maldonado.

Main Attractions
Parque Nacional del Manu
Manu Lodge
Reserva Nacional
  Tambopata
Colpa de Guacamayos
Puerto Maldonado

Map on page 222

The traditional hopping-off point for Peru's little-explored southern jungle is Cusco, where a variety of tours is available, along with a wealth of information on some of the national parks in the southern region, but the area has been included in this section of the book to offer continuity to readers who are interested in all aspects of travel in the Peruvian Amazon.

The adventurous traveler can go from Cusco by rail and truck to **Quillabamba** and **Kiteni** and from there hire a boat through the **Pongo de Manique**, a narrow gorge surrounded by lush jungle and waterfalls on the upper **Río Urubamba** as described in Peter Matthiesson's 1962 classic, *Cloud Forest*. It must be emphasized that transport and tours are infrequent in this area, and you should be flexible. There is a government air service that operates from the mission town of **Sepahua** (lower down on the Urubamba) to Pucallpa and then to Lima, but the flights are extremely unreliable. If you are highly adventurous and self-sufficient – only very basic food is available – you may find a boat to take you all the way to Pucallpa.

PARQUE NACIONAL DEL MANU

Also accessible from Cusco is one of the most bio-diverse rainforest parks in the world, located in Peru's southernmost jungle department of **Madre de Dios**. At 1.8 million hectares (4.5 million acres), the **Parque Nacional del Manu** ❶, one of the few truly pristine regions of the tropics, is perhaps the best area in the Amazon rainforest for watching wildlife. In many other jungle areas, because of the proximity of humans, you may be lucky to see anything other than birds, insects, or an occasional large animal, but in Manu you will see so many monkeys (there are 13 different species) that you may grow tired of them.

Paddling along an Amazon tributary.

JUNGLE LODGES

Whether it's to the northern Amazon from Iquitos or the southern rainforest from Puerto Maldonado, a visit to a lodge is an unforgettable experience.

Jungle lodges vary from basic to five-star, and accommodations are in the form of hammocks or individual cabins with comfortable beds. Food is generally simple, but includes plenty of river fish prepared in imaginative ways. However, it's what can be seen around the lodges that most visitors come for. Sightings of colorful macaws and chattering monkeys are almost guaranteed, and if you're lucky, you might see a caiman or pink river dolphin. Rainforest walks reveal rubber trees and Tarzan-style vines, while on the ground there are busy termites and frogs perfectly camouflaged as leaves. High up in the canopy you might glimpse a three-toed sloth or tiny lion-faced monkeys small enough to fit in your hand.

In some areas, there are opportunities for fishing for piranhas or peacock bass and spots where it's safe to swim. Where there are isolated jungle villages you may have a chance to meet the locals, and perhaps even trade for handicrafts.

Bookings can be arranged in Lima before you start your trip, or in Cusco or Iquitos. There are various tour companies, some of which run their own lodges. In Iquitos, **Explorama Tours** (www.explorama.com), one of the largest and most reliable companies, has three lodges, all well run and efficient. Ceiba Tops Luxury Lodge, 40km (25 miles) from Iquitos, has comfortable bungalows, hot water, good food, and attractive jungle walks. Explorama Lodge, 80km (50 miles) from Iquitos at Yanamono, has 40 rooms with private bathroom facilities and runs good jungle hikes. The third lodge is the ExplorNapo, 160km (100 miles) from Iquitos on the Río Napo, the most rustic of all, but facilities are good and you get a chance to explore primary forest, plus access to the canopy walkway at the Amazon Center for Environmental Education and Research. There is also the Amazon Conservatory of Tropical Studies (ACTS) field station where travelers may learn the secrets of medicinal plants.

There are numerous lodges in the southern jungle, including three in the Cultural Zone of Parque Nacional del Manu, for which you don't need a permit. These are the Manu Cloud Forest Lodge, near the Río Unin; the Amazonia Lodge (www.amazonialodgeperu.com) at Río Alto Madre de Dios; and the Albergue Pantiacolla Lodge (http://pantiacolla.com). The only accommodations in the Manu Reserve Zone are at the comfortable Manu Lodge (www.manu-peru.com). Overlooking a rainforest lagoon, it has both an expanding trail system and experienced (English-speaking) guides to help you spot the rarer bird species.

There are two very good agencies which will organize trips to the Manu lodges: the first is **Manu Nature Tours** (www.manuperu.com) in Cusco. The other is **Manu Expeditions** in Lima, run by English ornithologist Barry Walker. He specializes in camping trips with knowledgeable guides, but will also organize customized trips to most of the above lodges.

The best-known lodge in the Reserva Nacional Tambopata is Explorers' Inn, 60km (38 miles; http://www.explorersinn.com) from Maldonado. Newer lodges in Tambopata include the no-frills Tambopata Research Center (http://www.perunature.com) and the Ese'ejas community-run Posada Amazonas. Reserva Amazónica (www.inkaterra.com) and Tambopata Lodge (www.tambopatalodge.com) both offer good service and reasonably priced packages.

Refugio Amazonas Lodge in Reserva Nacional Tambopata.

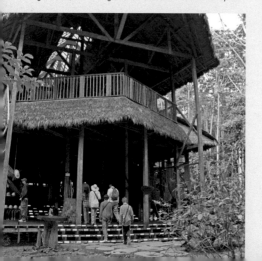

Besides an abundance of turtles, you'll have a great opportunity to see giant otters, peccaries, capybaras, tapirs, and even the occasional jaguar.

Manu is also an unparalleled place for birdwatching. Founded in 1973, the park was declared a Biosphere Reserve in 1977, and a Unesco World Natural Heritage Site 10 years later. It harbors over 1,000 species of bird – 300 more species than are found in the United States and Canada combined. The world record for the number of species seen and heard in one day was set in Manu in 1982, when 331 species were recorded in just a few square miles of forest.

MANU LODGE

Located right in the Reserve Zone is **Manu Lodge**, which overlooks a tranquil rainforest lagoon; its expanding trail system provides access to seasonally flooded forest, high-ground forest, and patches of bamboo. There are also experienced guides to help visitors find shy bird species. Large, rare game-birds such as razor-billed curassows and piping-guans have been hunted out of most areas, but are easy to see at Manu Lodge. Also seen are macaws, pale-winged trumpeters, the tall jabirú storks, roseate spoonbills, and five species of large eagle, including the majestic harpy eagle. New species are continually being discovered. The rare rufous-fronted ant-thrush, for example, was previously known from only one location, but has now also been found at Manu Lodge.

By far the easiest way to visit Manu is with one of the local tour operators such as Manu Expeditions or Manu Nature Tours, since all preparations for the trip must be made in advance and permits are required for entry into the reserve (although you don't need a permit for the Cultural Zone). The tour operator arranges permits, transport, equipment, gasoline, and food supplies for the trip. It can take up to two days to reach this isolated area by traveling overland from Cusco, down through the cloud forest, and later transferring to a boat – an unforgettable experience. There is also the option of chartering a small plane, which can fly to the junction of the Madre de Dios and Manu rivers. This is much more expensive, but necessary if your time is limited. Prices depend on the number of passengers.

RESERVA NACIONAL TAMBOPATA

There are yet more chances to see birds in Peru's second-largest reserve: the **Reserva Nacional Tambopata ❷**. Created by the Peruvian government in 1989, this 1.5-million-hectare (3.8-million-acre) zone has been set up both as an extractive reserve (for rubber, Brazil nuts, and other products) and for eco-tourism. The reserve encompasses the entire watershed of the Río Tambopata, one of Peru's most beautiful areas. Sadly, illegal gold mining is encroaching on this area at a troubling rate.

> **Tip**
> If you are on a low budget and can't afford the packages offered by the lodges, try staying with a local family. Arrangements can be made with contacts at Puerto Maldonado airport.

Jaguar on the lookout.

⊘ Eat

The harvesting of wild Brazil nuts is a major economy of the jungle and does not destroy its ecosystem. Fresh Brazil nuts are richer in flavor than processed ones, as they still contain many of their natural oils. Large bags of ready-shelled nuts can be bought very cheaply, either plain or with a sugar coating.

The river begins high in the Andean department of Puno; several tour companies lead kayak expeditions down the Tambopata, which offers a spectacular transition from the Andes to the low jungle. The reserve protects the largest macaw lick in South America, the Colpa de Guacamayos. Here birdwatchers can view one of the world's phenomenal avian spectacles, as hundreds of red, blue, and green parrots and macaws gather at the lick daily. Squawking raucously, they wheel through the air before landing together on the riverbank to eat clay. This breathtaking display can only be seen where there is undisturbed rainforest with healthy populations of wild macaws, as in southeast Peru.

Trails around the macaw lick offer birding in both floodplain and high-ground forest. Orinoco geese and large horned screamers can also be seen along clear streams near the Andean foothills. Comfortable accommodation is provided at the macaw lick by Tambopata Research Center

Lodge, run by Rainforest Expeditions. The only lodge in the uninhabited area of the reserve, it is about six hours from Puerto Maldonado in a speedboat, but twice that in one of the river boats known locally as *pequepeques*. Rainforest Expeditions, in conjunction with the Ese'ejas community, also runs Posada Amazonas, near Lago Chinbadas, where giant river otters and harpy eagles can be seen, and where mammals such as peccaries, tapirs, and a rodent known as a pacarana congregate at a nocturnal salt lick.

Also in the Tambopata Reserve is the Explorers' Inn lodge, around which some 500 bird species can be seen. These include quetzals, manakins, and many antbirds. The lodge trails also provide good access to patches of bamboo popular with bird species like the Peruvian recurve-bill, the white-cheeked tobey-flycatcher, and Goeldi's antbird.

The forests of southeast Peru offer the finest birdwatching experience. However, identifying all the different species, and finding elusive birds in the forest undergrowth, can prove overwhelming for an ornithologist inexperienced in tropical forests, which is why an expert guide is invaluable.

Birdwatching tours also help to support local families, who will conserve rainforest birds as if their livelihoods depend on it. Local people won't hunt macaws for trade or feathers if they can make more money by taking visitors to see them. By choosing such tours, visitors can make a positive conservation impact. However, the birds can't survive without the pristine rainforests in which they live, and conservation organizations and indigenous peoples are battling to preserve them.

BOOM TOWN OF THE SOUTH

From Cusco you can reach **Puerto Maldonado** ❸, the capital of the Peruvian department of Madre de Dios, either by air or along the 500km (310-mile) road, a trip that takes two and a half days; it's a bit uncomfortable, but worth it for the scenery. Long cut off from the rest of the world both by rapids on the **Río Madeira** and by the Andes, Puerto Maldonado, a thriving rubber town at the turn of the 20th century, lapsed into anonymity again until the discovery of gold in the 1970s, and the building of an airport in the early 1980s turned the city into a gold-rush boom town.

Set on a bluff overlooking the Madre de Dios and Tambopata rivers, Puerto Maldonado has a pleasant Plaza de Armas, and numerous hotels for miners, but not much to see or do. In 1897 the rubber baron Carlos Fitzcarrald traveled through here after having dragged his steamship, with the help of hundreds of Indians, over what is now known as the Fitzcarrald pass and down the Manu and Madre de Dios rivers on his way to Iquitos via Brazil. You can make an excursion, about half an hour from the city, to the site where locals will tell you Fitzcarrald's steamship is located, beached a little way inland. Actually, this isn't his boat at all; it is the remains of a German hospital ship which once plied the Madre de Dios.

Buy a bag or two of Brazil nuts while you are here. These rich, abundant, and inexpensive nuts will help encourage the preservation of Madre de Dios's rainforest, where around 30 percent of the population is employed in nut extraction.

Only an hour south of Puerto Maldonado is Lago Sandoval, a beautiful jungle lake that can be reached by boat from Puerto Maldonado's port. Three hours farther downriver, and well worth an overnight fishing expedition, is Lago Valencia, which is quite remote and relatively free of tourists. A several-day expedition can be mounted to the 100,000-hectare (250,000-acre) Reserva Nacional Pampas de Río Heath, a wild area of plains and swamps located on the Río Heath bordering Bolivia.

Giant otter.

Floating up the Madre de Dios river.

BIRDS OF THE AMAZON

For the keen amateur ornithologist, seeking out some of Peru's exotic birds may turn out to be the experience of a lifetime.

Nowhere in the world is there such a plethora of birdlife as in the Amazon rainforest. The Parque Nacional del Manu alone is home to over 1,000 different species. Their names are often as exotic as their appearance: from golden-headed quetzals to yellow-rumped caciques, roseate spoonbills to pale-winged trumpeters, they represent a birdwatcher's dream. Who wouldn't think their trip worthwhile if they spotted a paradise tanager, known as the *siete colores* because of its seven-colored plumage? Or a jabirú stork, one of the largest flying birds in the Americas, up to 1.4 meters (4.5ft) in length?

Many species fly in mixed flocks: insectivorous birds, such as woodcreepers and antbirds, will flock together, sometimes as many as 100 of them traveling in a great cloud. This makes individuals difficult to distinguish on first sighting, but they tend to stick to the same feeding areas so, if you identify their territory, you will have a great opportunity to spot a variety of species together.

The same applies to the mixed flocks of fruit-eaters, which include tanagers, fruitcrows, and parrots. Once you identify a food source you have an excellent chance of seeing a large number of birds. Not that rainforest birds are always easy for the uninitiated to spot, which is why an experienced guide is invaluable, and one usually accompanies visitors on organized tours.

The oxbow lakes of the Amazon are the habitat of herons, hoatzins, egrets, and wattled jacanas, species not difficult to spot as they forage for food on the shores. Raptors, flying high above the canopy, can present more of a problem, but the harpy eagle and the crested eagle, among other majestic creatures, can be spotted from vantage points at clearings or on riverbanks.

The harpy eagle is one of the most powerful raptors, with long talons designed to catch small mammals, such as howler monkeys and iguanas. They nest high in the forest canopy.

Hoatzins can manage only short, clumsy flights. They form mating groups, and share the rearing of their offspring. The young have clawed wing bends, to help them clamber about in trees.

Rufescent tiger herons are frequently spotted in and around the lakes and streams of Parque Nacional Manu. They can also be spotted flying over clearings.

The majestic golden macaw.

Stamping out the bird trade

One of the most spectacular sights in the Peruvian Amazon is that of macaws gathered at the huge salt licks in the Reserva Nacional Tambopata. But some people still regard exotic birds as interesting pets, and the macaws and parrots that inhabit the same part of the rainforest can be trapped, exported, and sold on the international market. Although the Convention on Trade in Endangered Species (CITES), signed in Washington DC in 1972, protects the species that are most under threat, it is not strictly adhered to, and doesn't affect birds whose numbers are high. The influx of tourists has helped to create an alternative source of revenue, making the trade less economically attractive to local trappers.

Blue-headed parrots have powerful beaks which they use for cracking nuts open. They are sociable birds, often seen in groups.

The wattled jacana is an unusual species in that the female takes more than one mate, lays several clutches of eggs, and leaves the males to rear the young.

The Paracas peninsula.

THE SOUTH COAST

The cryptic Nazca lines attract many people to the southern coast. For others, wildlife, sandboarding, and Afro-Peruvian music have an appeal that isn't at all mysterious.

⊙ Main Attractions

Pachacamac
Reserva Nacional de
  Paracas
Islas Ballestas
Ica bodegas
Laguna de Huacachina
Nazca Lines
Chauchilla Cemetery

📍

Map on page 230

Peru's southern desert coast, although inhospitable at first glance, is a historical and geographical encyclopedia of a handful of highly developed pre-Inca cultures known for their masterful pottery, fine weaving, medical advances, and for the enormous and mysterious drawings they left on the desert plain at Nazca.

The south coast is also where ancient indigenous peoples proved once again that they could at least adapt to the harsh physical reality of their environment even if they could not tame it. This time it was not the imposing Andean mountain chain that separated the different tribes, made agriculture difficult, and left the people subject to the subtle changes in climate. Rather it was the parched and desolate desert, among the driest on earth, which proved to be the obstacle.

SOUTH OF LIMA

Starting your southward journey from Lima, the first place of any interest you will come to is **Pachacamac ❶** (Tue–Sat 9am–5pm, Sun until 4pm; http://pachacamac.cultura.pe/tu-visita/informacion-general), some 32km (20 miles) south of the capital and normally visited on a day trip from the city. Although the more recent Inca culture has overshadowed much of the earlier development of this site, the artisan work left by the pre-Inca

civilizations proves that they were more sophisticated in terms of both ceramics and textiles. The ruins of the original settlement occupy a vast site on a low sand-hill overlooking the ocean. There is also a reconstruction of the Inca Templo de las Vírgenes (House of the Chosen Women), also known as *mamaconas*.

Heading south for another 35km (22 miles) you will come to **Pucusana ❷**. This coastal resort town, very popular with *Limeños*, is also a charming fishing village with panoramic views from its cliffs and good seafood in several

The mysterious Nazca lines.

of its restaurants. During the Peruvian summer, from January to April, the beaches at Pucusana, La Isla, Las Ninfas, and Naplo can get crowded on weekends. If you want peace and quiet, go on a weekday, when Pucusana reverts to being a fishing town and vacationers are fewer. Also, local fishermen ferry passengers around the island in the bay, and to other beaches, so you may be able to negotiate a ride to one of the more isolated stretches of sand, such as Naplo, first arranging to be picked up later in the day.

You may want to take a trip past the **Boquerón del Diablo**, literally the Devil's Big Mouth, which is a tunnel carved in the rock. If you decide to tempt fate by entering the tunnel either on foot or in a boat, do not be surprised if the astonishing din, described as "the groans of a thousand devils," makes you wonder if you will ever come out alive.

Some 75km (47 miles) down the coast is San Vicente de Cañete, from where a road goes inland to **Lunahuaná** ❸, a pretty village that has begun to attract *Limeños* and foreign visitors.

The village, with a colonial-era church, is set in a wine-growing valley; there are a couple of wineries that can be visited, including Los Reyes and La Reina de Lunahuaná, a *pisco* distillery. The Incahuasi (Incawuasi) ruins lie just outside the village, and river-rafting and kayaking on the Río Cañete centered in San Jerónimo have become popular, best in November through April. True to its two major claims to fame, in February, Lunahuaná hosts an adventure-sports festival, followed in March by the *Fiesta de la Vendimia*. Further upstream, the **Reserva Paisajística Nor Yauyos-Cochas** is a remote but spectacularly beautiful area for treks amid canyons and mountain lakes.

CHINCHA ALTA

Back on the coast, about 55km (34 miles) south of Cañete, lies **Chincha Alta** ❹, a city known for wine, fine-quality cotton, excellent athletes, and ferocious fighting cocks. Its name may be derived from *chinchay* – the Yauyo people's word for feline – although when the Spanish named it in 1571 it was more pompously called Pueblo Alto de Santo Domingo. Grapes and cotton flourish here, thanks to an elaborate system of irrigation and the re-routing of the Cochas River.

The city's fairly modern coliseum pays tribute to the long sporting tradition here. Chincha has turned out a number of the country's sports stars, principally in the fields of soccer (football) and boxing. The great Peruvian boxer Mauro Mina came from Chincha, and defeated a number of US boxers, including Floyd Patterson, before a detached retina prevented him from going for the world light heavyweight title. Another distinguished Chincha athlete, Fernando Acevedo, has held Peru's 100-, 200-, and 400-meter sprint records since the 1970s. His nickname was "The Harpoon of Chincha."

This town, and nearby El Carmen, are home to much of Peru's black

The pre-Inca pyramid at Pachacamac.

population, descendants of slaves brought here to work on coastal plantations. As such, it is the center for Afro-Peruvian dances, including the energetic and amusing *El Alcatraz*, in which a gyrating male dancer with a lighted candle in his hand attempts to ignite the cloth tail hanging from his partner's brightly colored skirt. Many of these dances are accompanied by rhythms supplied by the *cajón*, which is simply a hollow box pounded by open-palmed drummers to produce a reverberating rhythm. The *Fiesta Negra* in February and *Fiestas Patrias* in late July are the best and most atmospheric times to see and hear Afro-Peruvian music.

Close to Chincha is the **Hacienda San José** (http://casahaciendasanjose.com), a large country estate built in 1688. The estate was a rich sugar- and cotton-growing operation, and at its height owned 1,000 slaves. A fascinating but sinister feature of the hacienda is the labyrinth of catacombs under the house, which were once used for storing and punishing slaves. Tunnels are said to lead all the way to the port

of Pisco, where slave ships unloaded their human cargo.

Today, the hacienda is surrounded by colonnaded courtyards and cool terracotta floors, and is set in green gardens full of trees. It suffered major damage in the 2007 earthquake, but has since been restored and is now a luxury hotel.

PISCO

Continuing south on the Panamericana is **Pisco** ⑤, a port city that gave its name to the clear white-grape alcohol that is Peru's national drink, and is used to make the cocktail called *pisco sour*. Pisco is believed to have started out as a byproduct of grapes not considered good enough for wine production by the Spaniards, when they were introducing grapes and wine production to the dry coastal area of the New World. But once they tried this smooth yet potent version of brandy they decided it had merit in its own right – as many Peruvians and Chileans have gone on thinking ever since.

The city of Pisco (pop. 104,000) joined the bandwagon when revolutionary

Pelican on the beach at Paracas.

Preparing for the Fiesta Negra.

fever overtook the continent in the early 1800s. In Pisco's **Plaza de Armas** is a statue to General José de San Martín, the hero of the War of Independence against the Spanish. Originally, Pisco stood on another spot not far away, but an earthquake in 1687, and subsequent pirate attacks, badly damaged many of the structures in the city. This prompted the viceroy, Melchor Antonio Portocarrero, third Count de la Monclova, to order it moved to a safer spot. Construction of the opulent Baroque **Catedral** started shortly afterward, and was only completed in 1723. This was all but destroyed in August 2007 when the city was rocked by a devastating earthquake which laid waste to much of the city center and killed hundreds of people.

Reconstruction since the earthquake has been painfully slow amid widespread allegations of corruption and irregularities. Volunteer organizations like Pisco Sin Fronteras are trying to help local *pisqueños* rebuild their homes and lives, but many people continue to live in refugee shacks. Many tourism agencies have shifted away from downtown to where the Panamericana meets the main access to the center or to Paracas altogether. Pisco's small military airport, which used to serve as the emergency landing strip when heavy fog prevented planes from descending in Lima, was expanded in 2016 to become an important international hub.

PERU'S GALÁPAGOS

Some 15km (9 miles) down the coast lie the bay and peninsula of Paracas which, together with the Islas Ballestas, comprise the **Reserva Nacional de Paracas** ❻. The area, named after the Paracas winds – blustery sandstorms that sweep the coast – has a wide variety of sea mammals and exotic birds, among them the red-and-white flamingos that allegedly inspired General San Martín to design the red-and-white independence flag for the newly liberated country. A monument marks the spot where San

Martín, coming via Chile after liberating Argentina, set foot in Peru on September 8, 1820. Landing some 4,000 troops, within days he had taken over Pisco. The rebels' fleet, under the command of Scottish mercenary Lord Thomas Cochrane, then turned north to harass Spanish vessels, near Lima in particular. The British motivation was not to liberate a struggling people from their colonial masters, but to break Spain's monopoly on trade in the region.

The beach here is lovely, although craggy for swimming, and the waters contain jellyfish – some of them enormous and with a very unpleasant sting. There are a number of good jellyfish-free beaches around the isthmus: La Mina, Mendieta, La Catedral, and Atenas, the last very popular for windsurfing. The famous **Candelabro**, a candelabrum-shaped drawing scratched onto the highest point of a cliffside overlooking the bay, can be seen from the beach, although it is best viewed from a boat. Some scientists link the drawing to the Southern Cross constellation; others say it is actually a stylized drawing of a cactus – a symbol of power from the Chavín culture, which flourished farther north but whose influence has been found at great distances from its seat of power. The magic associated with the cactus is related to both its hallucinogenic powers and its use by high priests in ancient indigenous cultures.

TRIPS TO THE ISLAS BALLESTAS

A visit to the **Islas Ballestas** is highly recommended, and can be booked in Paracas or Pisco as you usually have to go with a group. Most of the trips start off quite early in the morning to avoid rough afternoon seas. For reasons of conservation visitors are not allowed to land on the island, but boats will take you close enough for a good view of the wildlife. Here sea lions, seals, penguins, guano-producing birds, and turtles rarely found at this latitude converge before photo-taking tourists. Dozens of bird species thrive here, among them albatrosses, pelicans, boobies, cormorants, and seagulls. Most Islas Ballestas tours also take in **Punta Pejerrey**,

> **⊙ Fact**
>
> The Humboldt penguin is one of the few species that lives far from the cold Austral southern zone. There are about 1,500 of them in and around Paracas.

Damage caused to Ica Cathedral by the 2007 earthquake.

⊘ THE PISCO EARTHQUAKE

On August 15, 2007, southern Peru was struck by one of the strongest earthquakes in the country's history. Measuring 7.8 on the Richter scale, the epicenter was very close to the city of Pisco and nearby Ica and Chincha also suffered extensive damage. The earthquake was even felt in Lima, 260km (156 miles) away.

In Pisco, the damage was most severe around the Plaza de Armas, where many beautiful colonial churches and buildings were brought down or damaged beyond repair. Many people had fled for protection into the 300-year-old cathedral, the roof of which subsequently collapsed, killing 150. Strong aftershocks continued through the night – one of the coldest on record. Only when dawn came could the damage be assessed: Pisco had been close to devastated. Over 500 people were killed and 80 percent of the city's homes were destroyed. Pisco's small hospital was overwhelmed with casualties and electricity and water were cut off for days.

While donations of tents and prefabricated houses came in from as far away as Turkey, the Peruvian government was criticized for doing little, and local people have since complained that they have seen none of millions of dollars in foreign donations intended for the earthquake victims. Despite the devastation, the people of Pisco remained positive: *Pisco se va a levantar*, said its citizens. "Pisco will rise again".

There are strict regulations regarding the type of grapes used to produce pisco.

Harvesting grapes at the Tabernero winery near Chincha.

nearly at the northernmost point of the isthmus and the best onshore spot for seeing the Candelabro. During the 19th century, this region was important for its guano – mineral-rich bird-droppings used as fertilizer in Europe – and guano collection still continues today, though on a smaller scale.

On the exact opposite side of the isthmus is **Punta Arquillo** and the *Mirador de Los Lobos*, or sea lion lookout point. This rough and rocky place can be reached by an hour's trek on foot, but take care, because the sun is very strong. It is far better to go by car, and if you are with a tour group transport may be provided. Looking down on the sea lion refuge you will find yourself almost face to face with a congregation of noisy sea mammals.

On lucky days, a look skyward is rewarded by the sight of a pair of condors soaring above. These majestic birds sweep down on sea lion carcasses, looking particularly for the seal's afterbirth during the breeding season, then use the intense coastal winds to wing themselves up to the high

altitudes they normally frequent. Extensive exploration of the peninsula is best done with the help of a guide, as paths are not clearly marked and it is easy to become lost. In June and August, Paracas is foggy – a reaction to the heat and extremely sparse precipitation combined with the water-laden ocean winds that caress the coast. A meteorological office here recorded only 36.7 mm (1.5 inches) of precipitation during a 20-year period, although the effects of the particularly harsh 1998 El Niño brought heavy rain to the area, and turned the desert green for a while.

The area has also seen important scientific discoveries, from giant fossil penguins of the Icadyptes and Perudyptes genus to the pygmy beaked whale *(Mesoplodon peruvianus)*, one of the smallest species of whale found.

DESERT BURIAL GROUNDS

Paracas is the name not only of the area but also of the ancient civilization founded here over 3,000 years ago, a pre-Columbian (and pre-Inca) culture that was uncovered in 1925 when archeologist Julio C. Tello found burial sites under the dunes. The sand and the extreme dryness of the desert protected the finely woven textiles around and inside the funeral bundles, which were buried when the Paracas culture thrived from 1300 BC to AD 200. The best examples of textiles and funeral bundles, and information about how the burial pits were arranged, can be found in several museums in Lima. Recommended are the Museo de la Nación, the Museo Nacional de Arqueología, Antropología e Historia del Perú (http://mnaahp.cultura.pe), and the private Museo Amano's collection of textiles in Miraflores (www.museoamano.org). The Museo Regional in Ica also has an interesting collection of pre-Columbian artifacts. The **Museo de Sitio Paracas Julio C. Tello** (tel: 056-234 383; Tue–Sun 9am–5pm), near the necropolis on the isthmus joining the Paracas peninsula to the mainland, has exhibits of artifacts discovered during the archeological dig, and although much of the collection was lost in a robbery it is well worth a visit.

The discovery of hundreds of so-called "funeral fards" – or burial cocoons – gave anthropologists and archeologists yet another small insight into this civilization. The fine weavings in both cotton and wool, with intricate and highly detailed embroidered designs, still astound modern-day textile experts, particularly those who are interested in how these people were able to develop permanent dyes with such brilliant tones.

The elaborately wrapped funeral bundles show that the Paracas culture performed skull trepanation, crude "brain surgery" designed to treat fractures and tumors, common injuries among a people whose battles were fought using stone-headed clubs and slingshots. The Paracas also practiced the intentional deformation or molding of infants' skulls for esthetic reasons. The results, akin to a conehead shape, were not only considered attractive but also clearly identified an individual's clan, since the molding differed significantly from tribe to tribe.

Heading some 48km (30 miles) inland from Pisco you will come to remains dating from another culture: the Inca **Tambo Colorado**. This adobe settlement, called *colorado* (colored) because of the red paint on many of the walls, is among the best Inca ruins on Peru's southern coast. Among the buildings still standing at this complex is one that is believed to have been a temple.

ICA WINE REGION

About 80km (50 miles) farther south from the ruins is **Ica** ❼, a bustling oasis amid one of the continent's driest deserts, and Peru's richest wine-growing region. Ica was hit quite badly by the El Niño flooding in 1998, but thanks to rapid clean-up and reconstruction work life got back to normal fairly fast. Ica however suffered again in the 2007

earthquake, and many buildings were damaged beyond repair. Once the city had rebuilt itself, it was hit yet again, this time by floods that damaged more than 1,500 homes in 2017; the situation was serious enough for President Kuczynski to introduce a state of emergency in town. Nevertheless, Ica remains the hub of Peru's wine and *pisco* industry.

Local vineyards and wineries can be explored all year round, but there is most to see during the grape harvest, from February to early April. The **Bodega El Carmelo** *pisco* distillery, which is open to the public (it is also a rustic hotel now; www.elcarmelohotelhacienda.com), has an ancient grape press made from a tree trunk. Tours (in Spanish) can be taken at the **Vista Alegre** (www.vistaalegre.com.pe) wine and *pisco* distillery in Ica, where there is a good shop. Peruvian wines tend to be very sweet, although the best ones, Ocucaje and Tacama, and Tabernero, are finer and drier. **Bodega El Catador** (www.elviejocatador.com) is also popular, in Ica's Subtanjalla district. **Bodega La Caravedo** (www.lacaravedo.com), which grows grapes organically, is

The intriguing sand drawing known as the Candelabro.

also directly on the Panamericana. This is also the case for the **Ocucaje Winery** (http://ocucaje.com), 30km (19 miles) south of Ica in the town of the same name. Wineries and distilleries can be visited individually or on day tours from the center of Ica. Peruvian wine and *pisco* production tends to be less industrial than that of their Chilean competitors.

Every March, the city goes all out with its annual wine festival, featuring grape-treading beauty queens and a flow of homemade wine that the locals swear is better than anything available for sale. The week-long event, called the *Fiesta Internacional de la Vendimia*, is punctuated by sports contests, cock fights, music, drinking, religious ceremonies, dancing, and general merrymaking.

Although the festival is the best time to experience the area's wine heritage, hotels fill up fast at fiesta time, and the rates rise steeply as well. The same problem arises during the week-long celebration of the town's foundation in mid-June, and at the festival of *El Señor de Luren*, on Maundy Thursday, when an image of the crucified Christ is paraded

around the city in all-night processions. A second procession in honor of the city's patron saint takes place on the third Monday in October. Sadly, remains of the original church were torn down in the wake of the 2007 earthquake.

The statue is believed to have arrived in Ica more than four centuries ago, carried to shore on a wave, then transported to the town. Records from the San Francisco monastery in Lima show that the image was purchased by a friar in 1570. A treacherous storm at sea, and the fear that the ship in which the statue was being transported would sink, apparently prompted the ship's captain to toss much of the cargo – including the wooden box containing the statue – overboard. Religious Ica residents took the icon's intact arrival as a miracle.

DISASTERS AND REVOLUTIONS

Although Ica was founded by the Spanish in 1536, European attempts to control the city were constantly fraught with problems. Local residents resisted the Spanish presence, and Ica was never granted a coat of arms, owing to its repudiation of attempts to make it a colonial center. Its current citizens remain proud of that rebellious image. The town has also suffered natural disasters: strong earth tremors caused damage in 1568 and 1571, and a devastating earthquake in 1664 completely leveled it, leaving 500 people dead – a phenomenal toll in those days.

Almost 300 years later, in 1963, floods seriously damaged much of the town, which explains why most of its colonial buildings have been replaced by more modern structures. Still, the city center retains its square-block layout, based on a chessboard design.

Churches worth visiting are **La Merced**, just off the Plaza de Armas, with its delicately carved wooden altars, and **San Francisco** (on the corner of Municipalidad and San Martín) with some admirable stained-glass windows. Competing with the

Colectivos vie for passengers on a street in Ica.

Christian importance of Ica is the city's widespread reputation for witchcraft, for which it is well known across the country.

One of the city's most famous sons was José de la Torre Ugarte, author of Peru's national anthem. He was born in Ica in 1786 and served as a local judge until he joined the revolutionary troops under General San Martín. After Peru's independence, he turned to politics, but found it an even more dangerous line of work than being a freedom fighter: in a power struggle between factions in the congress, he was condemned to death. When spared by the colonel commissioned to execute him, Torre Ugarte returned to a career in law.

The first civilian president of Peru was also from Ica, although Domingo Elías's tenure in office in 1844 was short-lived owing to political upheaval in the newly independent country. His attempts in 1854 to start a revolution of his own failed, and he retired to run his businesses after failing in a fresh bid to win the presidency four years later.

ICA'S REGIONAL MUSEUM

Today, just a 20-minute walk or a short bus ride from Ica's center, this region's revolutionary role is traced in a room at the **Museo Regional Adolfo Bermúdez Jenkins** (Av. Ayabaca block 8; Tue–Sun 8am–7pm), one of Peru's most interesting small regional museums. Even more interesting are exhibits of mummies, ceramics, and skulls from the Paracas, Nazca, and Inca cultures; and you will also see a number of *quipus* (also spelled *kipus*), the mysterious knotted strings believed to have been used to keep calculations, records, and historical notes for the Incas, who had no system of writing.

Since only selected members of the Inca civilization were permitted to "read" the *quipus*, the meaning of these knotted strings has been lost in intervening centuries, although most experts maintain that they were a sophisticated accounting system in which colored strings represented commodities and knots showed quantities. It is thought that the *quipus* may have been crucial in keeping food inventories in the Inca Empire.

Laguna de Huacachina.

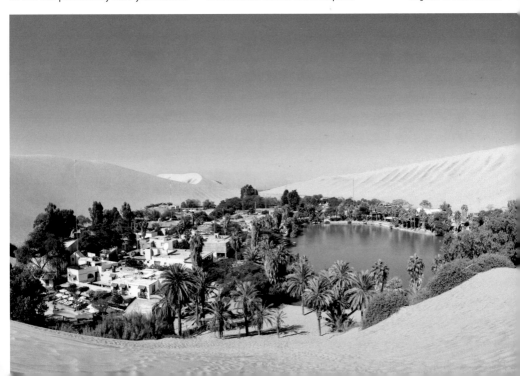

The regional museum also has an excellent collection of Paracas textiles and feather weavings. Most visitors find their curiosity piqued by the rehydrated mummy hand on exhibition – a must for those who think they have seen everything. Placed in a saline solution after being buried for centuries on the desert coast, this hand was part of an experiment by scientists who hoped that rehydration would provide medical information about the deceased individual.

On the **Plaza de Armas** is the **Museo Cabrera** (Bolívar 170; www.museocientificojaviercabrera.com; Mon–Sat 10am–1.30pm and 4–7.30pm), intriguing for the number (over 10,000) and variety of stones it contains.

DUNES AND LAGOONS

Outside Ica is **Las Dunas** (www.lasdunashotel.com), a full-scale resort and the most luxurious hotel complex of the area, with a restaurant, pool, sandboarding, and horses to hire. Las Dunas was at the forefront of the sandboarding frenzy that overtook this dune-covered coastal area. Principally attracting European sports fans, especially from Italy and France, the hotel has sponsored competitive sandboarding events on Cerro Blanco – a massive dune some 14km (8 miles) north of the town of Nazca, purportedly the world's biggest sand dune. The view from the top is fabulous. Sandboarders will get sand absolutely everywhere, and shouldn't forget water and sunblock. Wrist protectors are also helpful and, unless taking a tour with sandbuggies, don't expect the convenience of lifts back to the summit.

Also on the outskirts of Ica is **Laguna de Huacachina**, a green lagoon of sulfur waters that Peruvians claim has medicinal value. Since Angela Perotti, an Italian living in Ica, began espousing the curative properties of the waters in the 1930s, this spot has become a favorite pilgrimage center for people suffering from rheumatism and skin problems. This peaceful setting just 5km (3 miles) outside Ica also draws those just looking for sun, solitude, and sandboarding among the palm trees and dunes that ring the lagoon. Numerous smaller hostels have sprung up around the oasis, catering to the backpacking crowd.

THE NAZCA LINES

Thanks to irrigation, cotton fields and ribbons of orange trees mark the landscape on the voyage farther south, following the line of the coast, to **Nazca**, the home of the mysterious lined drawings that have prompted theories ranging from the fanciful to the scientific.

Sixty years ago Nazca was like any other small Peruvian town with no special claim to fame, except that it was necessary to cross one of the world's driest deserts to reach it from Lima. But it is that desert – a sketch-pad for pre-Hispanic peoples – that has since drawn thousands to this sun-bleached colonial town of 39,000 and made the *pampa*, or plain, north of the city one of the greatest scientific mysteries in the New World.

Pre-Columbian wooden idol in the Museo Regional, Ica.

The **Pampa de Nazca** ❽ (Nazca lines) is a series of drawings of animals, geometrical figures, and birds ranging up to 300 meters (1,000ft) in length, scratched onto the arid crust of the desert and preserved for about 2,000 years (it is estimated) owing to a complete lack of rain, and winds that cleaned – but did not erase – the surface of the *pampa*. The drawings were made by removing surface stones and piling them beside the lighter soil that was revealed beneath.

It wasn't until 1939 that Paul Kosok, a US anthropologist flying over the dry coast in a small plane, noticed the lines, then believed to be part of a pre-Inca irrigation system. A specialist in irrigation, he quickly concluded that this had nothing to do with water systems. By chance, the day of the flight coincided with the summer solstice and, in a second pass over the area, Kosok discovered that the lines of the sunset ran tandem to the direction of one of the bird drawings. He immediately dubbed the Nazca *pampa* "the biggest astronomy book in the world."

RIVAL THEORIES

It was not Kosok, but a young German mathematician who became the expert on the lines and put the backwater on the map. Maria Reiche was 35 years old when she met Kosok, serving as his translator at a seminar on the lines. After giving his speech the scientist encouraged her to study the *pampa*, and she dedicated the next half-century to the task.

Reiche concluded that the sketches corresponded to the constellations, and thought they were part of an astronomical calendar made by the people of the Nazca culture, and designed to send messages to the gods. She speculated that her favorite drawing, the monkey, was the ancient symbol for the Big Dipper, the constellation that was linked to rain. When rain was overdue – a common thing in this plain – the Nazca people sketched the monkey to remind the gods that the earth was parched.

There are, of course, many people who do not accept Reiche's theories, denying that the ancient people would have drawn something that they

Los Manos (the hands) can be seen from a viewing platform north of Nazca.

⊘ WRITING FROM THE PLANETS?

One well-known theory about the Nazca lines was put forward in 1968 when Swiss writer Erich von Däniken published his book *Chariots of the Gods*, in which he argued that the *pampa* was part of an extraterrestrial landing strip – an idea that Maria Reiche discarded impatiently and which has been scoffed at by other scientists. Erich von Däniken nevertheless became the public spokesperson for what became known as "paleocontact" and the book drew thousands of visitors to the lines. The newcomers set out across the *pampa* in search of the drawings on motorcycles, four-wheel-drive vehicles, and even horses – leaving ineradicable marks of their visits. Now it is illegal to walk or drive on the *pampa*, and Reiche used the profits from sales of her book, *Mystery on the Desert*, to pay guards to patrol the plain.

Other theorists say that the lines marked tracks for running competitions; that they were enlarged designs used in weaving and textiles; or that they are actually an enormous map of the Tiahuanaco civilization that once flourished near Lake Titicaca. Another idea that has gained a good many sensible adherents is that the lines were walkways linking sacred sites, and were kept clear for many years by the frequent passage of footsteps.

Tip

Flights over the Nazca lines can be organized with tour agencies in Lima and Nazca, or direct with the airlines at Nazca airport. It can be a bumpy ride, so it's best not to eat a large meal beforehand.

themselves could not see. Because the drawings can only be seen from the air, the International Explorers' Club set out in 1975 to prove a theory that the Nazca people had used balloons. The Explorers' Club made a cloth-and-reed hot-air balloon, the *Condor I*, and flew it for 60 seconds, reaching an altitude of 100 meters (330ft). But the flight, 14 minutes shorter than planned, hardly resolved the issue. It simply added another, rather wacky, theory to the many that surround the Nazca lines.

Maria Reiche used to live at the Nazca Lines Hotel (then called the Hotel Turistas), where she gave an hour-long talk on the lines every evening, until increasing age and infirmity made it impossible. Her last trip to the *pampa* was with Phyllis Pitluga, a US astronomer, whose initial computer-based research on the Nazca lines appeared to support their link to the constellations; and the idea that the drawings were some kind of message to the gods, appealing to them to send rain, is one that has recently been given backing by new scientific research – in this barren landscape it is certainly a believable theory. Other researchers have pointed to the vividly painted Nazca pottery, with its clock-shaped pieces and elaborate solar calendars, as further evidence of close links with the movement of the heavenly bodies.

Reiche died in June 1998. Children waving German and Peruvian flags joined the crowds that lined the streets on the day of her funeral.

VIEWING THE LINES

Some 20km (12 miles) north of Nazca, just off the Panamericana, there is a *mirador* (observation tower), although the only lines that can be seen clearly from here are the *árbol* (tree) and the *manos* (hands). By far the best way to capture the impact of the lines is to fly over them in small propeller planes or via helicopter, the latter being the most expensive option. The cheapest flight option takes about 30 minutes, and the best time to go is mid-morning: earlier in the day there is sometimes a haze over the *pampa*; while later on, the winds that buffet the

Aerial view of the Nazca desert.

plane leave observers more concerned about their stomachs than about the spectacle spread out beneath them. Shop around in Nazca before picking the flight as there are numerous different options. Some bookings are also available from Lima.

SKULLS IN THE SAND

Although the perplexing Nazca lines are what draw tourists to this area, they are by no means the only thing to see. Some 30km (18 miles) from Nazca is the fascinating **Cementerio de Chauchilla** ❾ (Chauchilla Cemetery; 8am–4pm), where sun-whitened bones and skulls, pottery shards, and mummies litter the plain, although some have been reburied. The cemetery otherwise remains as it was, in part to avoid further desecration of the area (most of the mummies were unearthed during tomb looting) and in part because there is not sufficient money available to fund proper storage or exhibition of the mummies and grave artifacts. Grave robbers, or *huaqueros*, are a major nuisance at all the archeological sites in Peru, despite a major crackdown by the authorities.

Local tours to the cemetery usually also stop at the **Paredones Ruins** in the grounds of the Hacienda Cantalloc beside the **Cantalloc Aqueducts**, an immense and complicated system built by the Incas and still supplying water to irrigate fields nearby, where cotton is grown. Further south at **Sacaco**, 90km (56 miles) south of Nazca, a site museum has been built over fossil whale remains. Nazca is also the starting point for tours to the **Reserva Nacional Pampa Galeras**, the best preserve to view wild vicuñas, and a rival to Ica as a center of sandboarding and other desert excursions.

FOLLOWING THE PANAMERICANA

The Panamericana continues down the coast from Nazca to **Camaná** ❿ (about 220km/135 miles), which has some good beaches and is a popular summer resort for Arequipa residents, as well as being the hometown of Peru's chess grand master, Julio Granda

Mummies in Chauchilla Cemetery.

Zúñiga. Buses from the town center head to La Punta (about 5km/3 miles) and the fine, although undeveloped, beach area. Camaná was, in colonial times, the unloading point for cargo headed to Arequipa and then on to the silver mines in Potosí in Bolivia.

From Camaná the highway goes inland, and after about 130km (80 miles) it divides, going farther inland to Arequipa, toward Moquegua, Tacna, and the Chilean border, or back to the coast to **Mollendo** . Mollendo and its sister resort, Mejía, 15km (10 miles) farther south, are popular with upper-class *arequipeños*. Mollendo was a principal port before being replaced by **Matarani**, 14km (8 miles) to the northwest. Now its attractions are three sandy beaches and its closeness to the **Santuario Nacional Lagunas de Mejía**, a nature reserve that is home to a variety of coastal birds and a stopping place for many migratory species. You can get a bus from the town to the reserve and to the agricultural lands of the Río Tambo Valley, where an ambitious irrigation project means that rice and sugar can

be grown. Mejía used to be a fishing village, and a few old fishermen's cottages still remain. There are only a few hotels, but *arequipeños* spend part of the summer in their holiday homes here.

The road from the valley rejoins the Panamericana, which continues south to **Moquegua** , a parched and dusty town on the banks of the Río Moquegua, at the spot where the Peruvian coastal desert reaches its driest point. Buildings here – even the cathedral – are roofed with sugar-cane stalks daubed with mud. Its streets are cobblestones, and its residents' topiary skills are evident on the **Plaza de Armas**, where most of the bushes are trimmed into the form of llamas. Wine and avocados are shipped out of this city, and both are worth sampling.

BORDER TOWN

Peru's southernmost city is **Tacna** , separated from Chile by a mined stretch of desert that marks the border between the two nations. The Atacama Desert region from Tacna as far as Antofagasta once belonged to Peru and

The Panamericana in southern Peru.

Bolivia, but the copper- and nitrate-rich territory was lost to Chile in 1880 during the War of the Pacific. The Treaty of Lima returned the Tacna department to Peru in 1929, and in the 1980s it was one of the main spots in the country for contraband activity. Government-subsidized milk and medicines were smuggled into Chile, while less expensive clothing and imported cosmetics were brought back into Peru.

Unlike other border cities on the continent, Tacna is fairly well developed and has some of Peru's best schools and medical facilities – perhaps owing to its importance as a military base. The downtown area has been refurbished, and its main boulevard is cut by an attractive flower-and-tree-studded promenade. A pedestrian mall passes by the shops, and here ice cream, or cold drinks such as *horchata*, the popular icy cinnamon-laced soy-milk beverage, help offset the intense heat during the Tacna summer. The tree-shaded **Plaza de Armas** is a welcome relief from the unrelenting sun. The centerpiece of the plaza is the huge arch that was built as a monument to the heroes of the War of the Pacific.

The **Museo Ferroviario** (Railway Museum; daily 6am–6pm) at the railway station has train engines from the turn of the 20th century when the British began constructing the complicated and, in some cases, rather reckless railway system in Peru. There is also a collection of railway-themed stamps.

WHERE TOURISTS ARE TARGETS

If you are in Tacna at all, it will be because you are on your way to or from Chile, and as Latin American border towns go, it's a very pleasant one. Even so, visitors should be on the alert in the train and bus station areas, and in the evening should avoid entirely the street where the bus companies are. Pickpockets and thieves work these areas, and tourists are an easy target. It would be a shame to leave Peru on a bad note. You can cross the border from Tacna to Arica by bus, train, or taxi; the train trip, while nostalgic, is slow and notoriously unreliable, although short.

Tacna's cathedral.

Arequipa's grand cathedral.

AREQUIPA

Arequipa, the intellectual capital of modern Peru, is a proud and prosperous city with some of the most beautiful colonial architecture in the country.

Far from Lima, isolated in a fertile valley tucked between desert and mountains and crowned by turquoise skies, **Arequipa** ❶ was a key stop on the cargo route linking the abundant silver mines of Bolivia to the coast. Built from the white sillar rock that spewed out from Volcán Misti, one of a trio of imposing volcanoes looming behind it, this is Peru's second-largest urban area and one of the country's most prosperous. In colonial days it had the largest Spanish population and the strongest European traditions; cattle and farming industries dating from that period remain principal sources of income for the region. *Arequipeños* are proud and fiercely independent people, and like to think of their city as a place separate from – and superior to – the rest of the country.

In 1541 the king of Spain granted this oasis at the foot of the snow-capped volcano the title "Most Noble, Most Loyal and Faithful City of the Assumption of Our Lady of the Beautiful Valley of Arequipa." Aymara people living here beside the Río Chili more concisely called it Ariquepa (sic), "the place behind the pointed mountain." Another legend has it that the Inca Mayta Capac was so moved by the beauty of the valley during one of his journeys that he ordered his entourage to stop. His exact words

were said to be "Ari quipay" – "Yes, stay" in Quechua. Whatever the truth, Arequipa has grown into a magnificent city and the intellectual capital of modern Peru.

There are many ways of getting here: frequent flights from Lima, Cusco, Juliaca, and Tacna (on the Chilean border); and buses from Lima, Nazca, Cusco, and Puno. How you travel will depend on your budget, timescale, the degree of comfort you require, and how much of the country you want to see.

Main Attractions

Plaza de Armas
La Compañía
Catedral
Monasterio de Santa
    Catalina
Museo Santuarios Andinos
Colca Canyon
Cotahuasi Canyon

**Maps on pages
245, 247**

Colonial balconies on the Plaza de Armas.

⊙ Tip

Calle Jerusalén, to the northeast of the Plaza de Armas, is a good place to change foreign currency as it has several exchange bureaux.

THE HEART OF THE CITY

Arequipa's **Plaza de Armas** Ⓐ is one of the most beautiful in Peru. Wander around it before you start your tour of the city, taking in the facade of the cathedral and the two-story arcades that grace the other three sides of the plaza, with its palm trees, old gas lamps, and a white stone fountain nestling in an English-style garden. *Arequipeños* congregate here for political rallies, protests, or fiestas. The plaza's thick stone buildings with busily carved portals, their Moorish touches evident, breathe 460 years of history. An earthquake in 2002 caused considerable damage, but most of the main historical buildings have been restored.

Head toward **La Compañía** Ⓑ (Mon–Sat 9.10am–1pm and 3.10–6pm, Sun 9.10am–1pm), on the southeast of the plaza. The frontispiece of this two-story Jesuit church is a compilation of columns, zigzags, spirals, laurel crowns, flowers, birds, and grapevines, into which are embroidered rock abbreviations of the Good Friday Masses, the city's coat of arms, and the date the

massive work was completed: 1698. But a careful look shows that the European influence had its limits. The angels have indigenous faces – one face is even crowned with feathers.

What lies inside La Compañía is equally impressive. The gilded main altar is the apogee of Peruvian Baroque, and the sacristy's ceiling is covered with miniature paintings and carvings of crimson and gold. The view from the steeple is fabulous, especially at sunset when the late light casts a pink, then mauve, glow on the city's gracious white buildings. On the Calle Morán side of the church is the cloister, where stark architectural lines are broken by detailed columns, demonstrating the high level that stone carving reached during the 17th century. The Capilla de San Ignacio (St Ignatius's Chapel) is also worth a look, but check the visiting hours because they are different from those of the church.

Now retrace your steps to the massive twin-towered **Basilica Catedral de Arequipa** Ⓒ (Mon–Sat 10am and 5pm; free), rebuilt (at least partially) a dozen

Refuse collector in the Plaza de Armas.

times since 1583 after it was damaged by fire, a volcanic eruption, and earthquakes – which La Compañía escaped. The cathedral's ornate exterior is misleading because the interior is unusually bare and simple, except for an elaborate chandelier. The church's organ hails from Belgium, and its elaborately carved wooden pulpit, the work of French artist Rigot in 1879, was brought to the city a century ago by a local aristocrat's daughter. Visitors can learn more about the cathedral's history and its valuable pieces of art at the Museo de la Catedral de Arequipa (www.museocatedralarequipa.org.pe; Mon–Sat 9am–5pm) inside the church (entrance on St. Catalina Street).

COLONIAL MANSIONS

Arequipa is a delight for those interested in secular colonial architecture, for this city is full of dignified patricians' homes built in the 18th century, which have somehow withstood the tremors that regularly shake this city (the latest major tremor was registered in 2017). The single-story structures are replete with massive carved wooden doors, French windows with ornate grilles, and high-ceilinged rooms clustered around spacious central patios.

To see some of the best of them, cross Calle San Francisco to **Casa Ricketts** . Built as a seminary in 1738, this is now the Banco Continental, but there is a small museum and art gallery inside (Mon–Fri 9.15am–12.45pm and 4–6pm, Sat 9.30am–12.30pm). Next, take the street round the back of the cathedral to the Casona Iriberry, built in the late 18th century, which houses the **Complejo Cultural Chaves la Rosa** ❺. There is often something on at the complex: films, art exhibitions, and concerts. A few meters away, on the corner of Moral and Bolívar, is the **Casa del Moral** ❻ (daily 9am–5pm), which is also a bank, the Banco Sur, and originally named, like the street, after the venerable mulberry tree on its patio. The carvings above the door depict pumas from whose mouths snakes are slithering – the same designs found on the ceramics and

Decorative arched ceiling in the Monasterio de Santa Catalina.

A tranquil plaza in the Santa Catalina monastery.

Strolling through the peaceful alleys of Santa Catalina.

Casa Ricketts, now home to the Banco Continental.

fabrics of the Nazca people. Another interesting colonial house that is open to the public is the Casa de Goyeneche (Goyeneche Palace), on the corner of La Merced and Palacio Viejo, Casa Irriberry, and Casa de la Moneda.

CONVENTS AND CHURCHES

From Casa del Moral turn right along Calle Moral, then left into Calle Santa Catalina to the 16th-century **Monasterio de Santa Catalina G** (daily 9am–5pm, until 8pm on Tue and Thu), the most astonishing site in Arequipa, which was opened to the public in 1970 after almost 400 years as a cloister. Despite the closed doors, little heed was paid to the vows of poverty and silence, at least in the early days. During its heyday this convent's sleeping cells were luxurious, with English carpets, silk curtains, cambric and delicate lace sheets, and tapestry-covered stools. As for silence, French feminist Flora Tristan, visiting the convent in 1832, said that the nuns – daughters of aristocrats – were nearly as good at talking as they were at spending

huge sums of money. Each had her own servants, and dined off porcelain plates, with damask tablecloths and silver cutlery.

Santa Catalina takes visitors back four centuries. Entering the cloister you see the spacious patios, the kitchen and slave quarters, and stone washtubs of this convent, where entrance requirements were among the strictest in Peru. Novices had to prove Spanish origin and come up with a dowry of at least 1,000 gold pesos. The narrow streets, arches, and gardens of the convent bear their original names: Calle Córdoba, its whitewashed walls stark against the pots of bright-red geraniums; Plaza Zocodober with a granite fountain; Calle Sevilla with archways and steps. There is also an impressive collection of paintings from the 17th and 18th centuries in what was formerly the community dormitory. About 30 nuns still live in the convent, which once housed up to 500.

When the convent opened its doors to the public, its anecdotes and

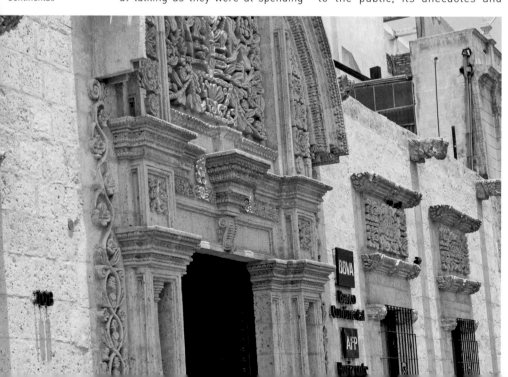

scandals were resurrected, among them the story of Sister Dominga, the 16-year-old who entered the convent when her betrothed left her for a rich widow. The religious life did not agree with this beautiful young woman, and she staged her own death to escape. Dominga really did place the body of a deceased Indian woman in her bed one night and set the room on fire, but it actually happened in the Convento de Santa Rosa, seven blocks from Arequipa's main square, which remains cloistered. It was founded in 1747 by four nuns from Santa Catalina; nearly two dozen members of the religious Order still reside there.

Close to Santa Catalina is the **Museo Histórico Municipal** ⊕ (Mon–Sat 9am–5pm), which is interesting for an overview of the city's history. From here it is only a few yards to the **Iglesia de San Francisco** ⓘ (daily 7–10am and 4–8pm), the focus of attention every December 8 during the Feast of the Immaculate Conception. A fairytale coach topped with the image of the Virgin Mary surrounded

by angels and saints, usually stored in the small chapel of the Sorrowful Virgin, is paraded through the streets in a colorful procession of pilgrims carrying flowers and candles.

To reach another highlight among Arequipa museums, the **Monasterio de la Recoleta** ⓙ (Mon–Sat 9am–noon and 3–5pm), you must cross the Río Chili, by either the Puente Grau or the Puente Bolognesi. The monastery has a vast library of 20,000 books, many of them very old, and a collection of religious art. There is also the **Museo de Arte Contemporáneo** (Tacna y Aríca 201; Tue–Fri 10am–4.45pm), showing 20th-century art and housed in the old railway manager's house opposite the train station.

SECEDING FROM THE NORTH

Arequipeños are a proud, even haughty lot, and their perennial attempts to secede from the rest of the country are a source of entertainment for *Limeños*. They once designed their own passport and flag in a futile attempt at separatism. From Arequipa's well-educated

Best served chilled: Arequipa's local brew.

Colca Canyon and the view toward Ampato, Sabancaya, and Hualca Hualca volcanoes.

Around Arequipa

Domesticated alpacas in the Colca Valley.

and politically passionate ranks have come two of the country's best-known figures: the former President Fernando Belaúnde Terry, and the internationally known novelist and failed presidential hopeful, Mario Vargas Llosa who donated his private collection of books (some 30,000 volumes) to Arequipa's regional library.

This regionalist passion peaks at the annual celebrations marking the anniversary of the city's foundation. Every August 15, arequipeños cut loose with parades, bullfights, and night-time revelry highlighted by fireworks. The birthday celebration is accompanied by a week-long handicrafts and folk festival. The other important festival in Arequipa is a more solemn one – the traditional religious processions of Semana Santa, at Easter.

To unwind in Arequipa in the evening, do what the locals do: head to a picantería for a cold arequipeña beer and some spicy food – stuffed peppers, pressed rabbit, or marinated pork. If you opt for the peppers (*rocoto relleno*), take care – they are scorchingly hot. Tourist reactions to this spicy dish are a source of amusement for other diners and concern for restaurant owners. The beer will be accompanied by a dish of *cancha* or salty fried corn which, like potato crisps, makes you even thirstier. There is no shortage of restaurants, with something to suit all pockets, serving a wide variety of food, from the local specialties already mentioned, to good ceviche (the typical, marinated seafood dish – Arequipa is less than two hours from the ocean), to vegetarian dishes and good pizzas.

EXCURSIONS FROM AREQUIPA

There are some interesting trips to be made outside Arequipa. One is to Sabandía, about 7km (4 miles) from the city, near the pleasant suburb of Paucarpata. Here stands a flour mill, made of volcanic rock, which was built in the 17th century and restored, stone by stone, in 1973. In 1966, architect Luis Felipe Calle had restored an old mansion in Arequipa (now the main

⊙ JUANITA THE ICE MAIDEN

In September 1995 a fascinating discovery was made at the summit of the volcano Ampato (6,314 meters/20,750ft), near Arequipa. The heat from the eruption of a nearby volcano melted Ampato's normally ice-bound peak, which allowed a team of archeologists from Arequipa's Catholic University of Santa Maria (UCSM) to look for the remains of human sacrifices ritually made by the Incas to their apus (mountain gods).

These high-altitude sacrifices were the culmination of lengthy ceremonies made every few years, and through their sacrifice, the victims were thought to attain divinity. A child would be chosen at birth to be raised as an offering to the gods. For the parents, it was the ultimate honor. When the child reached the age of about twelve, he or she was dressed up in fine clothes and jewelry and led by an entourage of priests and assistants to the peak of a high mountain. Once the summit was reached, the victim was given coca leaves and *chicha* and instructed to sit on a blanket. Approaching from behind, a priest would then deal a deadly blow to the head with a sharp instrument. Afterwards the body would be buried on the summit along with funeral offerings.

The number of sacrificial sites in the Peruvian Andes likely runs into the hundreds. So far, more than 110 high-altitude sites have been discovered on Peruvian, Argentine and Chilean peaks, all above 3,000 meters (15,000ft) and all involving young victims. The archeologists found a perfectly preserved 550-year-old sacrifice, mummified by the aridity and cold. Dressed in finely worked ceremonial robes, and surrounded by spiritually significant objects, this victim turned out to be a delicate 12-year-old girl who soon became known to researchers as Juanita the Ice Maiden. For research and preservation, Juanita was brought down to the University of Arequipa, where she and her retinue of ceremonial objects have since shed much light on Inca beliefs. Juanita, frozen to below zero and encased in glass, is now the centerpiece of a captivating exhibition mounted by the **Museo Santuarios Andinos** at the UCSM, which elaborates on the Inca rituals of sacrifice to the mountain gods (Calle La Merced 110; www.ucsm.edu.pe/museo-santuarios-andinos; Mon–Sat 9am–6pm, Sun until 3pm).

branch of the Central Bank) when he was given the task of restoring this old ruined mill outside the city. He set up a tent beside the mill and lived there for the two and a half years it took him to finish the project, which he did by referring to old documents and conducting interviews with residents who remembered when the mill had last operated, nearly half a century earlier. After the restoration the bank put the *molino* up for sale – and Calle himself purchased it. "Architecture of Arequipa is a fusion. The big stone houses are humble but at the same time vigorous, a faithful reflection of the spirit of their people," said Calle, whose 17th-century property – open to visitors – is set in some of the area's most beautiful countryside.

A little farther out from the city are the thermal springs of Yura, 30km (18 miles) from Arequipa in the foothills of the extinct Volcán Chachani. Crude cement pools fed by the sulfurous waters are open for bathing. Two hours from the city, on the road to Lima, are the **Petroglifos de Toro Muerto** ❷ (Toro Muerto petroglyphs), hundreds of volcanic rocks believed to have been engraved and painted more than 1,000 years ago by Wari (Huari) people living in the region. The petroglyphs show realistic depictions of llamas, condors, pumas, guanacos, dancers, and warriors.

PERU'S GRAND CANYON

Four hours away from Arequipa, and drawing almost as much tourist attention these days, is the **Cañón del Colca** ❸, one of the world's deepest gorges, cut 3,182 meters (10,607ft) into the earth's crust. Far deeper than the Grand Canyon, the Colca is shadowed by snow-topped peaks – many of them volcanoes – and sliced by the silvery Río Colca. The base of this canyon is cold and windy and draws only daredevil kayak enthusiasts and researchers. Above, at the brink of the chasm, Quechua-speaking farmers irrigate narrow terraces of rich volcanic earth in much the same way as their ancestors did centuries ago.

Ⓘ Tip

Tours of the Colca Canyon usually go to the Cruz del Cóndor from Chivay, which has thermal springs. If you are trekking rather than going on a tour, Chivay has a choice of accommodations and can be used as a base.

Colonial church in the town of Pinchollo.

Women in local traditional dress, wearing Cabana hats, which are painstakingly embroidered.

Cruz del Condor, famous look-out spot into the Colca valley.

Though isolated, the Colca was a productive farming area even before the Incas claimed it, and when the Spanish reached the 64km (40-mile) long valley where this canyon lies, they found terraced fields and herds of llamas and alpacas. When the canyon became part of the route between the silver mines of Bolivia and the coast, the Colca farmers were snatched from their homes and forced to work in the mines. Later, when the railroad reached as far as Arequipa, the Colca Valley was forgotten.

When a multinational consortium began investigating the possibility of diverting the Río Colca for a desert irrigation project, eyes turned once again to this valley and its gorge. From a lost chasm trapped in a time warp, the Colca has become one of the hottest tourist attractions in southwestern Peru. There has been a modification in the valley's crops as it has more contact with the outside world. One innovation is barley, which is now grown on some terraces for use in the brewery that makes some of the rather good Arequipeña beer.

The canyon is an average of 900 meters (3,000ft) deep. Perhaps the most popular section of the canyon is the Cruz del Cóndor (Condor Crossing), where visitors scan the skies for a glimpse of the majestic birds soaring above in pairs. They use the thermal air currents produced in the early morning or the early evening, and few who visit at those times in the hope of spotting them are disappointed.

The Cruz del Cóndor is included in a variety of one- and two-day trips, which can be organized in Arequipa. En route, many of the tours take in the Reserva Nacional Salinas y Aguada Blanca (at 3,900 meters/12,800ft you'll notice how thin the air seems), where groups of shy vicuñas can often be seen. Even more remote than Colca, the **Cañón de Cotahuasi** ❹ (Cotahuasi Canyon) has only recently been exposed to tourism. Now believed by many to exceed Colca in depth, making it the world's deepest canyon, it is a pristine area of great natural beauty ideal for adventurers and nature-lovers. Accommodations can be found in the small town of Cotahuasi.

COLONIAL ART AND ARCHITECTURE

Once the Spaniards laid aside the sword and the musket, they began building. Wonderful examples of their architecture still grace Peru's oldest cities.

After subduing the indigenous peoples, one of the conquistadors' first acts was to start building splendid churches. This symbolized their power and confidence, glorified God, and provided places of worship for new converts. The earliest churches were built by the Franciscans: the first cathedral in Lima was completed in 1555, but only a decade later they considered it too small and began another. In Cusco, the Renaissance church of El Triunfo was begun in 1536. The first stones for Cusco's cathedral were laid in 1559. Not to be outdone, the Dominican Order founded Santo Domingo on the site of the Inca Temple of the Sun, which the Spaniards had stripped of its vast wealth.

When the Jesuits, the most zealous of the missionaries, arrived, they started their own building program, taken from the Counter-Reformation emanating from Rome. La Compañía in Cusco, begun in 1571, rivaled the cathedral in splendor. It was virtually destroyed by an earthquake less than a century later, but rebuilt with an ornate Baroque facade. La Compañía in Arequipa was initiated only in the late 17th century. It was pre-dated by the cathedral and the exquisite Monastery of Santa Catalina. Italian and German builders joined Spaniards and mestizos in erecting the churches. Many were built in imitation of the great churches of Rome, with massive towers and cupolas, and arched, shady cloisters, and had strong Mudéjar influences while incorporating paintings from the Schools of Cusco and Quito. Churches flanked at least one side of the great Plazas de Armas – the one in Cusco is a magnificent example – and in the late 17th and the 18th century elegant townhouses were constructed in the colonial Baroque style in all the major cities.

A statue in the Chapel of Saint Anne in Lima Cathedral.

The beautifully preserved Santa Catalina monastery in Arequipa. Its shady streets and cloisters were built in imitation of Mudéjar buildings in 17th-century Spain.

The cathedral in Cusco contains several ornate altars, including this one which is covered with gold leaf and features paintings by artists from the School of Cusco.

School of Cusco painting in the Museo de Arte Virreinal de Santa Teresa, Arequipa.

The School of Cusco

The innovative School of Cusco was a 17th-century movement which blended European and indigenous motifs to create a New World art form. Paintings were religious in nature, and the costumes worn by the archangels were in the sumptuous style of the Spanish court. The colors were rich and dark, and the themes had their dark side too, depicting martyrs' horrific deaths. But despite the typically somber backgrounds, the school's works very frequently displayed strong shades of red and blue. Master of this school was the *indígeno* artist Diego Quispe Tito, examples of whose work hang in the Museo de Arte Religioso and Cusco's cathedral, where his *Signs of the Zodiac* series can be seen. Each painting in the series depicts a scene from the life of Christ. Cusco School paintings can be found in churches as far south as Santiago, Chile.

The town of Julí on Lake Titicaca is home to several colonial churches, including San Juan Bautista, which contains paintings depicting the life of Saint John the Baptist.

San Francisco is one of the best-preserved colonial churches in Lima. There are extensive catacombs underneath the church, and its interior has strong Mudéjar influences mingled with the Baroque.

CUSCO

The ancient capital of the Inca Empire is the city most tourists want to visit, a jewel of Inca and colonial architecture standing 3,330 meters (10,900ft) above sea level.

Main Attractions

Plaza de Armas
Catedral
Calle Hatunrumiyoc
Artisans' stores, Cuesta
  San Blas
Iglesia Santo Domingo/
  Qoricancha
La Compañía de Jesús
Museo de Arte
  Precolombino
Planetarium Cusco

**Maps on pages
256, 270**

Indigenous vendors speak Spanish to tourists and Quechua to each other. Catholic nuns live in buildings once inhabited by Inca "chosen women." The Marcos Zapata painting of the Last Supper in the cathedral shows Christ and his Apostles dining on Andean cheese, hot peppers, and roast guinea pig. **Cusco** ❶ is a city where past and present collide in an intriguing mix.

When Francisco Pizarro and his soldiers arrived nearly five centuries ago, Cusco, the capital of the Inca Empire, served as home to an estimated 15,000 nobles, priests, and servants. Where now daily rail, plane, and bus services connect this city to the rest of the country, long-distance relay runners called *chasquis* once linked it to the rest of Tahuantinsuyo, as the empire was called. Today, local residents have attempted to recall those glory days, relabeling streets with their original Quechua names and even calling the city Qosqo, a pronunciation closer to its original Inca name.

CENTER OF THE WORLD

For the Incas, Qosqo meant "navel of the world," and they believed their splendid city was the source of life. Legend has it Cusco was founded by Manco Capac and his sister-consort Mama Ocllo, sent by the sun god Inti with the divine task of finding a spot where the

gold staff they carried would sink easily into fertile ground. That place was Cusco, and there Manco Capac taught the men to farm and Mama Ocllo taught the women to weave.

The Inca Empire came into being during the reign of Inca Pachacutec Yupanqui, who began a great expansion, imposing Quechua as the common language, conquering other native nations, creating a state religion, and turning Cusco into a glittering capital able to rival many European cities. It was Pachacutec who transformed Cusco from a city of

Colonial street.

A water fountain in the Plaza de Armas.

clay and straw into a thriving metropolis with grand stone buildings in the second half of the 15th century.

A modern stone statue of Pachacutec on the south side of Cusco pays tribute to the king who ruled for 40 years and was one of the empire's greatest warriors, innovators, and unifiers of Andean civilizations. His son, Inca Tupac Yupanqui, continued his work, expanding the empire's boundaries even farther.

A BRIEF MOMENT OF GLORY

At its peak, Cusco, built in the shape of a puma, was a city with sophisticated water systems, paved streets, and no poverty. But it had been an imposing urban center for only about 70 years before the Spanish arrived. Of course, since the Incas left no written records, and the Spanish explanations of what they found are contradictory, theories about Cusco's design are numerous. One specialist in archeology and astronomy even speculates that one city boundary was warped to make it coincide with the midpoint in the Milky

Way, reflecting the Indian sensitivity to astronomy and the movements of the heavenly bodies.

The Spaniards were certainly impressed by the order and magnificence of Cusco, and wrote back to Spain that it was the most marvelous city of the New World. But the Incas' cultural achievements were merely a minor distraction in comparison with the lure of their treasures: conquistadors greedily pushed their way into ancient temples and seized their gold and silver artworks, which they promptly melted into bullion.

In addition to palaces and gold-filled temples, indestructible foundations, and advanced medical techniques, the Spanish soldiers found the Inca society full of skilled artisans. A storehouse of delicate, brightly colored feathers from tropical birds was used solely for the weaving of fine capes for the Inca and his priests. Rescued examples of the capes or *mantas*, which reflect the most extreme test of patience and handiwork, are found in museums in Lima. These survived because the

Spanish thirst for gold was so great that they overlooked many of the empire's other treasures.

Cusco retained a level of importance for the first few decades after the Spanish conquest. It was here that Diego de Almagro's faction of Spanish soldiers attempted to wrest control from Pizarro, and for his treachery the leader was executed on the city's main plaza. It was also here that the Spanish struggled against Manco Inca as the Indians made an ill-fated attempt to stop the European conquest through gallant guerrilla warfare. But by 1535 the capital of this new Spanish colony had been set up in Lima, Cusco's wealth had been stripped, and silver from Bolivia had turned attention away from this valley.

After centuries of provincial obscurity, Hiram Bingham's discovery of Machu Picchu in 1911 and the subsequent construction of a road up to that mountaintop citadel in 1948 transformed Cusco into the jumping-off point for visits to one of South America's best-known tourist attractions.

THE ARCHITECTURE OF CUSCO

The most startling and curious characteristic of Cusco at first glance is its architecture. Huge walls of intricately laid stone pay testimony to the civilization that 500 years ago controlled much of this continent. The Spaniards ended up putting their own buildings on the mammoth foundations of the Inca ones, often using the same stones that had been cut and rounded by Inca masons. When a massive earthquake shook the city in March 1650, the colonial walls came crashing down but the Inca foundations remained intact. The Inca remains and Spanish reconstruction make the city an unparalleled Andean jewel.

PLAZA DE ARMAS

Before you start to explore this picture-perfect city, remember that it is more than 3,330 meters (10,900ft) above sea level, so take it easy until you get acclimatized. Also, don't forget to buy a Cusco Visitor Ticket, which is essential for visits to historic sites in Cusco and the Sacred Valley. Bearing these two

The Twelve-Angled Stone on Calle Hatunrumiyoc.

Plaza de Armas.

Virgin of Carmel Saving Souls in Purgatory by Diego Quispe Tito (Brooklyn Museum, New York).

Flying the Inca flag in the Plaza de Armas.

things in mind, the **Plaza de Armas** is a perfect place to start. In Inca times it was not only the exact center of the empire known as Tahuantinsuyo – or The Four Quarters of the Earth – but was also twice as large as it is now. Samples of soil from each of the conquered areas of the empire were joined at this spot, and the plaza itself, flanked by Inca palaces, was surfaced with white sand mixed with tiny shells, bits of gold, silver, and coral.

This was the spot where important Inca religious and military ceremonies were staged. Some claim the section that remains today was a portion of Aucaypata, the Square of War, featuring a stone covered in sheets of gold where offerings were made before military actions. However, other experts disagree, and suggest it was called Huacaypata – or Weeping Square – because it was here that deceased Incas were mourned. During the early days of Spanish control, the plaza was the scene of much violence and bloodletting, such as the execution of the rebel leader Tupac Amaru II in 1781. Captured while trying to flee with his pregnant wife, Tupac Amaru was a mestizo whose real name was José Gabriel Condorcanqui.

These days, things are quieter on the plaza, which is one of the most superb colonial squares in Latin America. Tourists study the handicrafts for sale as insistent local women sitting under blankets beneath the colonial arcades chant "cómprame," or "buy from me." Quality varies, but good bargains can be found. However, don't believe it when vendors claim their rugs and weavings are antique: wool does not endure indefinitely in the damp highlands. In any case, it is forbidden to buy antique textiles or take them out of the country.

CUSCO'S CATHEDRAL

The most spectacular view of the plaza comes after nightfall, when dramatic lighting transforms the square. But while the night is best for outside photos, the interior of Cusco's magnificent **Catedral** can only be seen during the day (daily 10am–6pm, Mass Mon–Thu 6.30am, 7am, 8am, 8.30am,

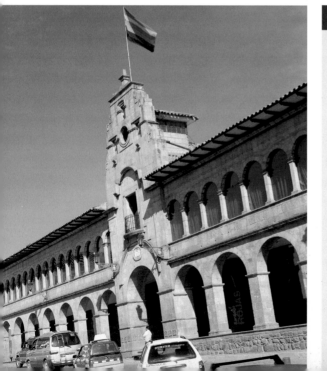

⊘ PERUVIAN THEATER

Some of the best-loved Inca legends have been transferred to the Peruvian theater. Among them is *Ollantay* – the story of Pachacutec's most famous general, granted any wish for services rendered. Ollantay boldly asked for the hand of Kusi Kuyur, the monarch's daughter. But Pachacutec, the son of the sun, could not allow a member of the monarchy to marry a commoner even though the daughter professed her love for the military leader. Ollantay rebelled against Pachacutec and was eventually imprisoned for life. Kusi Kuyur refused to marry anyone else and was sent to be a Chosen Woman, dedicating her life to serving the sun god, but years later an unforeseen event brought the couple together again. The play is frequently staged in Cusco and Lima, and is worth seeing if you understand some Spanish.

Fri 6.30am, 7.15am, 8am, 9am, Sun at 6am, 7am, 8am, and 9am). It is flanked by the church of Holy Family, to the right – also known as the Iglesia de la Sagrada Familia– and El Triunfo to the left. Jesús María was built in the mid-18th century, which makes it one of the newer structures.

Built on what once was the palace of Inca Wiracocha, and made in part from stones hauled from the fortress of Sacsayhuamán outside the city, the cathedral mixes Spanish Baroque architecture with Inca stonework. Begun in 1559, it took a century to build. The altar is of solid silver.

The cathedral also contains magnificent examples of Escuela Cusqueña (School of Cusco) paintings, including some by Diego Quispe Tito, the 17th-century Indian painter widely regarded as the master of the school. In the corner next to the sacristy is a painting by Marcos Zapata of the Last Supper, with Christ and his Apostles dining on roast guinea pig (cuy), hot peppers, and Andean cheese. A painting of Christ's crucifixion is the subject of many

theories: some believe it is a 17th-century work by a member of the Cusco School; others hold that it is the work of Flemish painter Sir Anthony van Dyck; still others believe it was by a Spanish artist, Alonzo Ocano; while a final theory proposes that it is the work of various artists, because the head is out of proportion with the body. The third side-altar from the left contains a curious painting of a pregnant Virgin Mary.

The city's most venerated statue is the crucified Christ known as *Nuestro Señor de los Temblores* (Our Lord of the Earthquakes), which is depicted in a painting beside the main altar. The statue was paraded around the city during the 1650 earthquake, and after the tremors eventually stopped it was credited with miraculously bringing about the end of seismic activity. Borne on a silver litter, this gift to the New World from Spain, sent by Holy Roman Emperor Charles V, is still paraded around Cusco during Easter. For the rest of the year it remains in an alcove inside the cathedral. It is blackened by the smoke of candles perpetually burning beneath it.

⊘ Tip

The **Cusco Visitor Ticket** covers many of the must-see sites in Cusco and the Sacred Valley and is valid for 10 days. It's good value for money if you intend to visit several sights, and can be purchased at the COSITUC office (Av. Sol 103; www.cosituc.gob.pe/tarifario.html). A separate **Religious Circuit Ticket** (http://ticketmachupicchu.com/buy-ticket-religious-circuit-cusco) allows entrance to some of Cusco's most important churches.

Cusco's imposing cathedral.

The Chapel of the Holy Family, next to the cathedral.

The cathedral's María Angola bell in the north tower can be heard up to 40km (25 miles) away. Made of a tonne of gold, silver, and bronze, the bell, which is more than 300 years old, is reportedly the continent's largest. But when it was cast it had a partner – the Magdalena, which was dropped by workers during a storm at the edge of Lake Titicaca, where the bells were made. *Cusqueños* now say that the echoes from the first peals of the María Angola each morning are actually the tolling of the Magdalena on the bottom of the lake.

CUSCO'S FIRST CHURCH

Renaissance **El Triunfo** (opening hours as for the cathedral) means "the triumph," and it was built in honor of the Spanish victory over the Indians in the great rebellion of 1536, when Cusco was under siege for many months. The uprising was led by Manco Inca, a descendant of an Inca leader, who the Spaniards assumed would be their political puppet. They were surprised, then, to find Manco surrounding the city with some 200,000

Chatting on the cathedral steps.

followers – against the Spaniards' 200 men and loyal Indians.

The turning point of the siege was a great attack on the city, with Manco's men slinging red-hot stones to set the thatched roofs alight. The Spaniards were gathered in the old Inca armory of Suntur Huasi when it was pelted with fiery rocks. When the building did not catch fire, priests declared that the Virgin of the Assumption had appeared to put out the flames and inspire the Spaniards to defend the city. El Triunfo – the city's first Christian church – was built on the site. The tomb containing the ashes of the indigenous historian Garcilaso de la Vega, who died in Spain in 1616 but whose remains were returned to Cusco a few years ago, can be found in this church.

RELIGIOUS ART

If you turn left when you emerge from El Triunfo and walk one block up to the corner of **Calle Hatunrumiyoc**, literally "the Street of the Big Stones," and Calle Palacio, you will come to the **Museo de Arte Religioso del**

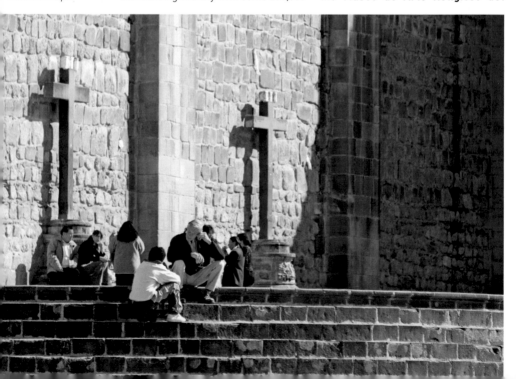

Arzobispado ⑩ (Mon–Sat 8am–6pm). This Moorish building with complicated carvings on its doors and balconies was constructed on the site of the 15th-century palace of Inca Roca, under whose rule Cusco's schools were initiated. It used to be the Archbishop's Palace, and that is what people sometimes still call it. Just outside is the famous **Twelve-Angled Stone**. A "fitting" tribute to the skill of Inca masons, this masonry masterpiece was left by Inca architects seemingly anxious to prove that no piece of granite was too irregular to be fitted without mortar. The museum houses an impressive collection of religious paintings of the Cusco School, including some by Diego Quispe Tito.

Head straight up Calle Hatunrumiyoc, and on your right you will find the **Iglesia de San Blas** ⓔ. Apart from its ornate altar, San Blas is a simple church by Latin American standards, and has a beautifully carved pulpit, said to be one of the world's finest pieces of woodwork. There is some dispute about who produced it; some say it was an Indian leper who initiated the work after he was miraculously cured (daily 8am–6pm). The streets around San Blas, notably the Cuesta San Blas, form Cusco's artists' quarter, with galleries, studios, and small shops, *hostales* and restaurants, and the workshops of the prolific Mendival family.

TEMPLE OF THE SUN

Take any of the streets leading southeast from the Plaza de Armas and you will find your way to the most important place of worship in the Inca Empire. Now a church, the **Iglesia Santo Domingo** ⓕ (Mon–Sat 8.30am–5.30pm, Sun 2–5pm) was once **El Templo del Qoricancha** – the Temple of the Sun, and the most magnificent complex in Cusco. Walls there were covered in 700 sheets of gold studded with emeralds and turquoise, and windows were constructed so the sun would enter and cast a nearly blinding reflection off the precious metals inside.

The mummified bodies of deceased Inca leaders, dressed in fine clothing and adornments, were kept on thrones of gold, tended by women selected for that honor. In the same room, a huge gold disk representing the sun covered one full wall while a sister disk of silver, to reflect the moonlight, was positioned on another.

Spanish chronicles recall the Europeans' astonishment when they saw Qoricancha's patio filled with life-size gold and silver statues of llamas, trees, flowers, and handcrafted butterflies. According to legend, Atahualpa's ransom included 20 of Qoricancha's life-size golden statues of beautiful women.

The Spanish historian Pedro de Cieza de León wrote a description of the patio "in which the earth was lumps of fine gold... with stalks of corn that were of gold-stalks, leaves and ears... so well planted that no matter how hard the wind blew it could not uproot them. Aside from this there were more than 20 sheep of gold with their lambs and

☉ **Drink**

Most bars on or near the plaza offer 2 for 1 drinks during "happy hour." Many of them also show free films, usually in English with Spanish subtitles.

A busy backstreet.

⊙ Eat

Just two blocks from the Plaza de Armas, chocolate lovers should make for the ChocoMuseo (www.chocomuseo.com, museum daily 9am–7pm, shop 8am–8pm), which offers an insight into the history of chocolate as well as putting on a selection of workshops.

the shepherds who guarded them, all of this metal."

Although the temple's wealth can only be imagined, its Inca architecture can still be appreciated. Visible from inside is the perfectly fitted curved stone wall that has survived at least two major earthquakes.

Spanish chronicles also describe a fabulous Hall of the Sun in Qoricancha and four chapels dedicated to lesser gods, including the moon, stars, thunder, and the rainbow. The rainbow had special significance for the Incas, and it remains a good omen today. Any Peruvian child asked to draw a picture of the Sierra will invariably sketch a house with mountains in the background and a rainbow arching the sky – even if the use of its colors in a supposed Inca flag is, however, a myth. Current excavations at the Temple of the Sun promise to reveal more of its mysteries.

MONASTERIO DE SANTA CATALINA

Retrace your steps toward the Plaza de Armas, and on Calle Arequipa you will find another Christian enclave that was formerly an Inca holy place. This is the **Museo de Arte y Monasterio de Santa Catalina ⑥** (Mon–Sat 8.30am–5.30pm; Sun 2–5pm), which centuries ago housed a different group of cloistered females: some 3,000 Chosen Women who dedicated their lives to the sun god. Foremost among these were the *mamaconas*, consecrated women who taught religion to selected virgins – called *acllas*. The *acllas* were taught to prepare *chicha* for use in religious ceremonies, to weave, and to pray. They made the fine robes that the Inca wore – only once – out of vicuña, alpaca, and even a silky fabric that was made from bat skins.

Attached to the convent is a museum containing works of religious art. An important contribution to the art world grew out of Cusco's mixing of the Indian and Spanish cultures in the often violent and bloody paintings of the School of Cusco. In many of these paintings archangels are dressed as Spaniards carrying European guns, but surrounded by cherubs with

Iglesia Santo Domingo.

Indian faces, or Christ is accompanied by indigenous Apostles. The Virgin Mary wears local Peruvian dress, and Christ hangs on a cross decorated with Indian symbols.

Just round the corner, at Calle Santa Catalina Ancha, there is **Museo de Machu Picchu de la Casa Concha** (www.museomachupicchu.com; Mon–Sat 9am–5pm), situated in a beautiful colonial building dating from the end of the 18th-century. It contains Hiram Bingham's collection of archeological artifacts from Machu Picchu.

THE MOST BEAUTIFUL CHURCH

In a city with so many churches, it is an honor to be dubbed the "most beautiful." That distinction belongs to **La Compañia de Jesús** ❶ (Mon–Sat 8–11am and 1–5pm, Sun 9–10.30am and 1–5pm), sitting on the southeast corner of the Plaza de Armas where Inca Huayna Capac's palace once stood. The Jesuit church, with its Baroque facade, intricate interior, finely carved balconies, and altars covered in gold leaf, was started in 1571 and took nearly 100 years to complete, in part because of damage in the 1650 earthquake. During its construction, the building drew so much attention that the bishop of Cusco complained it outshone the cathedral. But by the time Pope Paul III had been called in to mediate, and had ruled in favor of the cathedral, La Compañia de Jesús was all but finished.

To the right of La Compañía, also on the main plaza, is the university-owned **Museo de Historia Natural** (Mon–Fri 8.30am–5pm, subject to change), with good examples of local fauna.

A few yards down the street, just past the Plaza de Armas, is the **Iglesia de la Merced** ❶ (Mon–Sat 7am–7.30pm and 5–8pm, Sun 6am–1pm, 6–8pm), one of the most important churches in the city. Destroyed by the massive earthquake in 1650, this church was erected for a second time four years

later. It contains the remains of Francisco Pizarro's brother Gonzalo, and of Pizarro's fellow conquistador Diego de Almagro, who returned to Peru after an unsuccessful search for riches in Chile, and was executed here after his failed coup attempt.

There is a connected monastery **Museo del Convento de la Merced** ❶ (Mon–Sat 8am–12.30pm, 2–5.30pm). This one contains several fine paintings, including a Rubens, and gold and silver altarpieces, the most ostentatious of which is a jewel-studded, solid gold monstrance.

GARDEN SQUARE

Continue a couple of blocks down the same street – Calle Marqués – and you will come to the **Plaza San Francisco**. This square has been planted entirely with Andean flora, including amaranth grain. Here, too, is Cusco's coat of arms, featuring a castle surrounded by eight condors. The castle represents Sacsayhuamán, and the emblem refers to the bloody battle fought there in 1536 as

The recently refurbished Teatro Garcilaso on Calle Unión 117 is a good place to see contemporary Peruvian theater.

La Compañía de Jesús.

⊙ Fact

You may be surprised to see some signs in Cusco's tourist areas translated into Hebrew. This is because so many young Israelis travel to Peru when they come out of the army.

the Incas tried to defeat the Spanish conquerors. The condors flying over the castle vividly recall the scores of flesh-eating birds that, according to legend, circled over the Inca fort as the bodies of the dead piled up.

Flanking one side of the plaza is the 16th-century church and monastery, the **Iglesia de San Francisco ⓛ** (church Mon–Sat 6.30–8am, 5.30–7.30pm, Sun 6.30am–noon, 5–8pm, museum Mon–Fri 9am–noon and 3–5.45pm, Sat 9am–noon). Simple in comparison with other houses of worship in the city, it has an extensive collection of colonial art, including a painting – said to be one of the largest canvases in South America – showing the family tree of St Francis of Assisi.

There are two more churches that are well worth seeing, but rather difficult to get into, because both are the homes of closed orders of nuns. To see the first, turn down Calle Santa Clara, leading from the Plaza San Francisco, and you will find the 16th-century **Iglesia de Santa Clara ⓜ** (daily for Mass 7pm). The tiny mirrors

The five-star Libertador hotel.

that cover the interior are the most impressive sight in this building. In order to see the second beautiful but usually inaccessible church, the **Iglesia de Santa Teresa ⓝ** (daily for Mass 7am and 7pm), you must go a couple of blocks past the Plaza San Francisco, then turn right on Calle Siete Cuartones. The cloistered nuns sit at the back of the church, behind a grille, and form the church's choir. The exterior of this lovely building is also worth seeing.

Circling round behind the Plaza de Armas, on the corner of Calle Tucumán and Calle Ataúd you will find the **Museo Inka ⓞ** (Mon–Fri 8am–6pm, Sat–Sun 9am–4pm), also known as the **Admiral's Palace** because it was once the home of Admiral Francisco Aldrete Maldonado. A coat of arms over its doorway belongs to a subsequent owner, the arrogant and self-important Count of Laguna, who died in mysterious circumstances. His body was found hanging in the mansion's courtyard shortly after he mistreated a priest who had complained about the

⊙ INTI RAYMI

Many travelers come to Cusco for *Inti Raymi* (the Festival of the Sun) on June 24. *Inti Raymi* was the Inca winter solstice celebration held on June 21 or 22, which the Spanish moved to June 24, the Catholic feast of St John the Baptist. In the 1940s a group of Cusco intellectuals revived *Inti Raymi*, basing their fiesta on colonial accounts of the Inca festival. *Campesinos*, townspeople, and travelers follow the Inca's procession from Qori-cancha, via the Plaza de Armas, to the fortress of Sacsayhuamán. The regal Inca-for-a-day is borne on a litter, dressed in aluminum foil and glittering gold, his guard consisting of costumed Peruvian army troops. The fires of the empire are ceremonially relit, a llama is "sacrificed" to the sun, and music and dance groups perform.

count's behavior. In the same courtyard are miniature profiles of Pizarro and Spain's Queen Isabela.

There are some strange architectural features: an optical illusion is found in a corner window column, which looks like a bearded man from the inside and a nude woman from the outside, and there are mythical creatures guarding the main stairway. The building is well worth seeing for itself, as well as for the museum's collection of pottery, textiles, and gold artifacts. Another splendid museum can be found at the Casa Cabrera in Plaza Nazarenas, the **Museo de Arte Precolombino** ❶ (daily 9am–10pm). It contains 403 carefully selected pieces of pre-Columbian art chosen from the vast collection of the Museo Larco in Lima (see page 157).

PLANETARIUM

Before leaving Cusco and heading for landmarks outside the city, it's worth visiting the modest, private, and family-run **Planetarium Cusco** ❶ (www. planetariumcusco.com; Mon–Sat tours 5.40–8pm). Here you'll get a splendid view of the southern night sky (on a clear evening you can see Jupiter and its four large moons) and an interpretation of Inca astronomy. The Planetarium is located on the road to Sacsayhuamán, but tours leave from 5.40pm at the Plaza Regocijo.

TRAVELERS' REST

The Cross Keys Pub is located near the Plaza de Armas. In this city of contrasts, what could be more natural than a British-owned watering hole for travelers, cartographers, self-styled pioneers, eccentric scientists, and birdwatchers? The owner, ornithologist Barry Walker, who also acts as the British Consul in Cusco, runs Manu Expeditions, which organizes nature tours in Manu National Park.

There is a wide selection of restaurants in Cusco, serving both Peruvian and international food. If you are looking for nocturnal entertainment as well as food, it can be found at the restaurants from which lively Andean music emanates. One of the finest floorshows takes place nightly at El Truco (also known as Inka Wasi Restaurant), where the *pisco* sours pack a hefty punch and the musicians and dancers are first-rate. Eating a plate of *anticuchos*, a delicious shish kebab of beef heart, while watching the traditionally garbed performers singing in Quechua and playing reed flutes, will make visitors temporarily forget that the Incas lost their showdown with the Spanish.

Eventually the dance songs will be replaced by much quieter mountain music. Locals will tell you that it was when the Spanish killed the last Inca and the sun god turned his back on his children that Andean songs became melancholic. If you are looking for something more contemporary, there are several video bars in Cusco where tourists can enjoy American or other foreign movies.

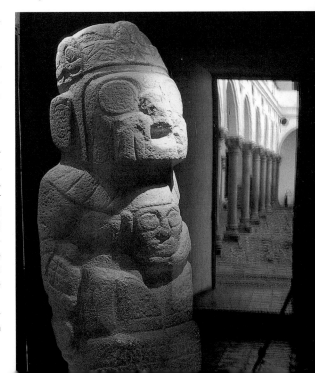

One of the many fascinating artifacts in the Museo Inka.

CUSCO'S FIESTAS

Cusco holds a number of very colorful festivals; the best known of them are in June, but there are several exceptions. One is the Christmas Eve festival called *Santorantikuy* (which means the buying of saints), when crafts and Nativity sets are sold in the Plaza de Armas. Another is the celebration in Easter when *Nuestro Señor de los Temblores* (Our Lord of the Earthquakes), the image of Christ on the cross that is credited with saving the city from destruction during the earthquake of 1650, and which stands in the cathedral, is paraded through the streets on a silver litter. Red flower petals are thrown in its wake, symbolizing the blood of Christ, and thousands of *cusqueños* turn out along with the civic, religious, and military hierarchies of the city.

A third exception is International Workers' Day (May 1), when workers parade through the square, each group lined up behind its respective banners – from the organization of transportation workers to the union of

Drummers at Inti Raymi.

informal street vendors (*ambulantes*), which is made up mostly of women with their babies. Like many ceremonies in Cusco, it opens with the raising of both the red-and-white Peruvian flag and the 1970s rainbow-colored standard of the city.

Corpus Christi (in honor of the Eucharist) is a movable feast, held on the Thursday after Trinity Sunday – usually in early to mid-June. Effigies of St Sebastian and St Jeronimo race into Cusco from the little towns named after them, borne on enormous litters by their devotees and led by a brass band and people carrying banners and candles. Accompanied by other statues of saints and the Virgin, brought from Cusco's barrios and suburbs, they are taken to the church of Santa Clara. The Plaza de Armas comes alive: large altars decorated with flowers, tin, mirrors, crosses, and images of the sun are erected, and vendors set up booths with food prepared especially for Corpus Christi. These treats, well worth sampling, include *chiriuchu*, made with guinea pig, chicken, corn, cheese, eggs, and peppers; and baked *achira*, a variety of Peruvian tuber.

After High Mass, the statues are paraded around the plaza, stopping to bow at each altar – no mean feat when some of the gilded and silver-covered figures weigh up to a tonne. Each parish has its own brass band, costumed dance groups, and devotees, and the plaza is a mélange of color and sound. At the end of the procession comes the priest bearing the Eucharist, almost forgotten in the crush. Slip inside the cathedral if you can, because some of the elderly women remain there to sing Quechua hymns in the high, bird-like voices typical of traditional music. The day gets livelier as it goes on: generous quantities of alcohol are consumed, and masked devil-dancers frolic among the shrubberies.

View along the Sacred Valley.

THE SACRED VALLEY

The heartland of the last Incas, the Sacred Valley is home to the awe-inspiring fortresses of Sacsayhuamán and Ollantaytambo, and the colorful Sunday market at Pisac.

Lima

Above Cusco – in walking distance for those willing to brave the altitude – still stands the overwhelming fortress of **Sacsayhuamán ❷**, a bold demonstration of Inca construction skills. Made of massive stones weighing up to 17,000kg (125 tons), this military complex overlooking Cusco has a double wall in a zigzag shape – some say to imitate the teeth of the puma figure whose head the fort may have formed. Others say it represents the god of lightning. The fort also once had at least three fabulously huge towers, and a labyrinth of rooms large enough for a garrison of 5,000 Inca soldiers. It marks the birthplace of the river that runs under Cusco, channeled through stone conduits cut to give the city an invisible water supply.

Sacsayhuamán was the focus of the Great Rebellion led by Manco Inca against the Spanish in 1536. From here, the Incas besieged Cusco for 10 months. Historians say that if Manco Inca had defeated the Spanish in Cusco, he might have saved the empire. But, no matter how valiantly his troops fought and died, the Spanish eventually wrested back control of the fort and thus the Inca capital of Cusco.

Archeologists estimate that tens of thousands of workers labored on this massive structure for up to seven decades, hauling the immense stone blocks that make up its double outside walls,

and erecting the nearly indestructible buildings that transformed the complex into one of the most wondrous in all the empire. Although the outer walls remain intact, the buildings in the complex have been destroyed – in part to provide building stones for many of Cusco's structures. Even so, visitors to the fortress can still see the so-called **Inca's Throne** from which it is said parading troops were reviewed.

This is one of the area's most spectacular spots at which to take dawn photos, and, like much of Cusco, it provides

◎ Main Attractions

Sacsayhuamán
Qenko
Tambo Machay
Chinchero
Pisac Market
Urubamba
Ollantaytambo

◉

Map on page 270

Market day in Pisac.

The Inca fortress of Sacsayhuamán, the scene of bloody battles between the Incas and the Spanish.

a startling contrast of Indian and Christian cultures. Beside this complex, built during the reign of Inca Pachacutec, is a giant white statue of Christ, his arms outstretched over Cusco in the valley below, donated to the city in 1944 by grateful Palestinian refugees. It's a good place for a picnic lunch, too: perched on almost any stone you'll have an amazing view of the red-tiled roofs of Cusco and the lush fields of the surrounding valley. The gaily decorated llamas wandering through the ruins are smelly but harmless, and the giggling children tending them will almost certainly ask you to take a photograph in exchange for a tip.

In response to claims by Peruvian archeologists and Inca scholars who said that Sacsayhuamán was in danger from the 100,000 tourists and Peruvians who annually attend the colorful *Inti Raymi* festival to celebrate the winter solstice, the celebrations were moved to the esplanade facing the great walls. The move has satisfied conservationists and those who insist that Cusco's largest celebration each year must be held inside the Inca stronghold.

QENKO AND PUCA PUCARA

Some 7km (4 miles) from Sacsayhuamán is **Qenko ❸**, an Inca shrine with a circular amphitheater and a 5-meter (18ft) stone block that is said to represent a puma. Its name means "zigzag," and this ceremonial center – dedicated to the worship of Mother Earth (Pacha Mama) – includes water canals cut into solid rock, and a subterranean room. Unlike Sacsayhuamán, which is a complex made up of huge stone blocks transported to the spot and assembled there, Quenko was carved from a huge limestone formation found at the site. Into its walls were carved typical Inca-style niches and alcoves used to display gold and holy items in pre-Hispanic times. The shrine also contains drawings etched laboriously into its stone, among them a puma, a condor, and a llama.

Farther along the road to Pisac is a smaller fortress, **Puca Pucara ❹**, believed to have guarded the road to the Sacred Valley of the Incas. Like Machu Picchu, this pink stone

The Sacred Valley

0 — 10 km
0 — 10 miles

complex has hillside terraces, stairways, tunnels, and towers. To the north is **Tambo Machay** ❺, the sacred bathing place for the Inca rulers and the royal women. A hydraulic engineering marvel, its aqueduct system still feeds crystalline water into a series of showers where water rituals were once held. The ruins now consist of three massive walls of Inca stonework tucked into a hillside. There are Peruvian historians who say that this was used by Inca Tupac Yupanqui as a hunting lodge, in addition to being a shrine. Some claim that it was where Pachacutec received a prophetic vision of the Incas as conquerors. Others say that the water running through the aqueduct came from a holy spring, and that this may have been one of the rare spots where child sacrifices were made.

There are a handful of pre-Hispanic and colonial sites worth visiting east of Cusco, toward Urcos. There are frequent buses that leave from near the Puno railway station. **Tipón**, 15km (9 miles) away and a worthwhile hike

north of the main highway, has fine terracing and the largest remaining Inca channeling of any known site cascading down its walls. Farther onward, **Pikillacta** ❻, some 30km (18 miles) from Cusco, pre-dates the Incas by centuries: it is a large, only slightly restored Wari (or Huari) ruin, probably constructed early in the 12th century, with rough stone walls more than 3 meters (10ft) high. About 1km (0.6 miles) farther on is **Rumicolca**, the Inca gateway to the Cusco Valley. In order to control access to the city, the Incas built, on Wari foundations, a wall of stone at the point where the valley narrows.

About 8km (5 miles) farther on is **Andahuaylillas** ❼, a little village with some interesting colonial houses and a 17th-century Jesuit church (daily 7.30am–5.30pm) – so extraordinarily ornate the locals call it "Peru's Sistine Chapel"– which contains some particularly fine murals. **Huaro**, a little farther on, is another tiny village whose church has some marvelous 17th-century murals (daily 8am–5.pm).

The church at Andahuaylillas.

Tip

Many of the Sacred Valley ruins, including Sacsayhuamán, Pisac, and Ollantaytambo, are covered by the Cusco Visitor Ticket (see page 259), which can be purchased in Cusco.

MARKET VILLAGE

Chinchero 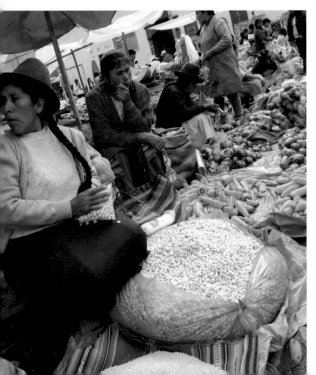 is an attractive village with Inca ruins, which can be visited by bus from Cusco. It has a lively market on Tuesday, Thursday, and Sunday. It is said that Chinchero was one of the favorite spots of Inca Tupac Yupanqui, who built a palace and had agricultural terraces cultivated here at the mouth of the Río Vilcanota. Other historians say it was an important population center in Inca times and that Tupac Inca, the son of Pachacutec, had an estate here. If the Inca royalty were lured to Chinchero, it might have been by the view of snowcapped mountains and the river below. If you are here for the Sunday market, the best day to go, you will notice that local people use it as an opportunity to socialize as much as to buy goods. This "town of the rainbow," as it was known in pre-Hispanic days, has kept many of its ancient customs and traditional ways.

PISAC

Pisac ❾ makes a good base for exploring the Sacred Valley. The valley is a delightful place: the climate is pleasant, the people are agreeable, the agricultural terracing is a marvel, and there are a number of welcoming little *hostales* in which to spend the night. Pisac is a friendly village known for its good fishing, busy Sunday market, and the ruins above the town; and it lies about 32km (20 miles) from Cusco on a curving but decent road. There is a road up to the ruins, and you can sometimes get a ride in a taxi, but otherwise you can climb there past the mountainside terraces (local children will serve as guides for a small fee) or hire a horse from beside the village church. At this high altitude, even the fittest travelers find themselves winded and their hearts pounding, so they are grateful when they round the bend on an isolated trail to find themselves face to face with one of the many Inca Kola vendors at the site.

Steep terraces and dramatic architecture mark this one-time fortress city, whose many features include ritual baths fed by aqueducts and one of the largest known Inca cemeteries. The stones making up Pisac's buildings are smaller than those at Sacsayhuamán, but the precision with which they are cut is amazing.

In fact, in some respects the stonemasonry is more awesome than that of the more famous ruins at Machu Picchu. There are residential buildings and towers that some scientists say may have been astronomical observation spots. Higher up is a second set of ruins whose style – smaller stones more haphazardly arranged – has given rise to a number of theories as to the origin of this section. Some say that it was used by servants or other community members with low social standing; a less likely theory is that it pre-dates the main part of the complex.

Pisac's **Sunday market** is a riotous affair in a town where the people

Fresh produce at Pisac.

work hard and – apparently – play hard. The beer tent is the favorite haunt of the motley brass band that adds an increasingly out-of-tune touch to the town's festivities. Sometimes it seems that the beer tent is the favorite stop for most of the other villagers, too. For that reason, the later in the day visitors arrive, the better their chances for some congenial bargaining for the fine alpaca blankets and sweaters available. There is a less touristy market held on Tuesday and Thursday.

URUBAMBA

From Pisac, follow the road and the river about 40km (25 miles) through the picturesque village of Yucay to **Urubamba ⑩**, which lies at the center of the valley. In recent years this has become a popular place to stay. The weather is milder than in Cusco, it is closer to Machu Picchu, and it makes a good center for visiting other places of interest. There are a number of hotels, cheap and not so cheap, in Urubamba itself and

scattered along the valley. Urubamba is a bustling place with a strong indigenous flavor. The coat of arms on the City Hall is sufficient evidence of this; no Spanish symbols are found in the emblem, which bears pumas, snakes, and trees. It was the beauty and calm of this village in former times that prompted the 18th-century naturalist Antonio de León Pinelo to expound on his theory that Urubamba was the biblical Eden. From here you can make trips to the saltpans at **Salinas** and the circular Inca agricultural terracing at **Moray**. You can take a bus for the first part of the way, but after that it's a hike.

OLLANTAYTAMBO

West of Pisac further along the valley, you come to the great fortress of **Ollantaytambo ⑪**, a place of great sacred and military importance to the Incas. Here, travelers find themselves facing an elegant and intricate walled complex containing seven rose-colored granite monoliths that puzzle scientists, who say that the stone

Market trader wearing a traditional embroidered skirt at the Pisac market.

Cusco and the Sacred Valley attract huge numbers of backpackers each year.

☉ TOO MUCH TOURISM?

Cusco, the Sacred Valley, and Machu Picchu see more tourists than any other part of Peru. While people have certainly benefited greatly from tourism, the rise in tourist numbers has its downsides, too. Huge numbers of tourists mean a huge demand for resources such as water, and there has been a surge in road traffic. Thousands of feet walk on the Sacred Valley ruins each day, and Machu Picchu itself is considered one of the most endangered Unesco World Heritage Sites. At its worst, tourism here can feel exploitative for both sides of the equation, a trend that could be disastrous for a region that depends so heavily on the tourist dollar. You can help by picking your guides and tours carefully, patronising grassroots tourist operators, and those that give something back.

The Princess's Bath at Ollantaytambo.

is not mined in the valley. A steep stairway enters the group of buildings, among which the best known is the so-called **Temple of the Sun** – an unfinished construction in front of a wall of enormous boulders. Portions of the original carvings on these huge worn stones can still be seen, although it is unclear if they really are pumas, as some claim. Specialists say that the unfinished condition of the temple has less to do with the Spanish destruction of Ollantaytambo than with the fact that it was simply never completed.

Ollantaytambo, strategically placed at the northern end of the Sacred Valley, also has plazas with sacred niches, shrines, an area of stone stocks where prisoners were tied by their hands, and ritual shower areas, including the **Princess's Bath**, or Baño de la Ñusta.

The village's military fortification was so well planned that it took the Spanish by surprise when they arrived in search of Manco Inca during the 1536 uprising. Hernando Pizarro (a brother of Francisco) led a contingent of about 100 Spaniards and a number of local Indians to the fort with the intention of capturing and executing the rebel leader. Chronicles say that as the Spaniards sneaked up to the fort just before dawn, they looked up to see the silhouettes of Inca warriors ready to take them on. It is even said they saw Manco Inca himself, directing troops from inside the Ollantaytambo complex, mounted on a captured horse. In fact, Manco Inca's men had diverted the Patacancha River through some canals, and now they opened barriers that allowed the water to flood the plain that the Europeans were crossing. However, the Spaniards managed to escape to Cusco, where they recruited a force of 300 cavalrymen to return and confront Manco Inca. Outnumbered, he abandoned the walled city and fled to Vilcabamba, where he was killed.

Ollantaytambo is nowadays the best preserved of all the Inca settlements. The old walls of the houses are still standing, and water still runs through original channels in narrow streets that are believed to date from the 15th century. In the nearby river stand the remains of an Inca bridge, and *campesinos* around the settlement live in houses that have changed very little since Pizarro's arrival. The museum in the **Centro Andino de Tecnología Tradicional y Cultural de las Comunidades de Ollantaytambo (CATCCO) Museum** has information about local history, culture, and architecture (Tue–Sun 10am–1pm, 2–4pm).

After exploring the Sacred Valley, most visitors head for the **Inca Trail** and **Machu Picchu**. You can get a train from Ollantaytambo (either the tourist train or the local one), or take a train from Cusco and get off at Aguas Calientes (Machu Picchu Pueblo). Machu Picchu, of course, merits a chapter all to itself.

The imposing ruins of Ollantaytambo.

The Inca terracing at Moray.

The lost city of the Incas.

MACHU PICCHU

Hidden from the world until 1911, this Inca refuge in the mountains is breathtaking in every sense. Trekkers can choose the hard way up, via the Inca Trail; others must opt for the train.

Of all the popular treks in South America, the three- to five-day **Inca Trail** is the one the most travelers want to do. The adventure begins with a four-hour train ride along the Río Urubamba, a region known to the Incas as the Sacred Valley. Legions of early-rising *campesinos*, loading and unloading their marketable goods at every station along the way, crowd together in what begins to look more like a cattle car than a passenger train. At Qorihuayrachina, **Kilometer 88**, the hikers' trail begins. It is no longer possible to walk the Inca Trail independently; you must prearrange the trip at home (book at least 6 months in advance). (If you want to avoid several days of arduous trekking, the train leaving from Cusco also stops at Chalcabamba, **Kilometer 104**, 8km/5 miles from the lost city, and you can get off there, but you will miss out on some stunning scenery.)

The first 11km (7 miles) meander through easy terrain of dusty scrub bushes, low-lying hills, and a few rustic huts. Conserve your strength on this stretch, because it will soon get tougher. The first barrier is the **Warmiwañusqu pass,** beyond which lies a wealth of Inca ruins. Reaching the top of this 4,000-meter (13,000ft) pass is no small challenge: laboring up the seemingly endless trail, the hiker soon identifies with its name – literally, "Dead Woman's" pass.

From here, Inca history begins to unfold. The small guard-post of **Runku-raqay**, overlooking the valley and often shrouded in morning mist, is the first reward offered by the Inca Trail. Farther along, the more elaborately constructed site of **Sayaj-marka** (Dominant Town) perches atop a narrow cliff. The fine stonework for which the Incas were justly famous is apparent here. Snaking along the valley below is an incredible "paved highway" made of neatly fitted stone, a fine example of the Inca road network

◉ **Main Attractions**
Puyapatamarka
Huiñay Huayna
Intipunku
Machu Picchu
Huayna Picchu

Map on page 282

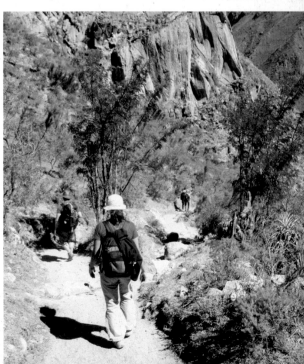
Hiking the Inca Trail.

invariably compared with the great Roman roads of Antiquity.

STUNNING RUINS

As the trek progresses, the archeological sites become more stunning and complex. **Puyapatamarka** (Cloud-Level Town) is fascinating for its circular walls and the finely engineered aqueduct system, which still provides spring water to the ancient ceremonial baths. Below, the trail offers up yet another delight.

Huge steps, a virtual stone stairway almost 1km (0.6 miles) in length, lead down into high jungle vegetation where wild orchids and other exotic flowers bloom. Curiously, this section of the trail lay undiscovered until 1984. Until then, a modern footpath connected this interrupted section of the Inca highway.

Tenaciously clinging to the side of a steep ravine is the last set of ruins, and the most stunning. **Huiñay Huayna** presents an unbelievable picture when first seen in the distance. The ability of the Incas to construct something so complex in an area so vertical defies

comprehension, yet the series of ritual baths, long stretches of terracing, and intricate stonework prove what would appear to be impossible.

About two hours away lies the jewel in the crown – **Machu Picchu**. From the high pass of **Intipunku**, the Sun Gate, you get the first glimpse of the fabled city. This is the culmination of days of walking; the immersion into an ancient culture is complete. Arriving as the Incas did centuries ago, the trekker begins the final descent into Machu Picchu, sharing a path with history.

DISCOVERING THE RUINS

When Hiram Bingham and his party discovered **Machu Picchu** in July 1911, Bingham was actually searching for the ruins of Vilcabamba, the remote stronghold of the last Incas. Today we know that he had almost certainly found Vilcabamba, without realizing it, when he stumbled across the jungle-covered ruins of Espíritu Pampa, some 100km (60 miles) west of Machu Picchu, two months before making his spectacular find on the Urubamba gorge. But Bingham saw only a small section of Espíritu Pampa, and dismissed it as insignificant. It was left to Gene Savoy, another American explorer, to investigate Espíritu Pampa when he came looking for the lost city of the Incas more than 50 years later.

Bingham was a Yale graduate, later a US senator, who became fascinated with Inca archeology in 1909 while in Peru studying Simón de Bolívar's independence struggle. He returned with the Yale Peruvian expedition in 1911, and took the narrow mule trail down the Urubamba gorge in July of that year. Melchor Arteaga, a local *campesino* whom he met by chance while camping on the riverbanks, led him to the jungle-covered ruins.

Machu Picchu – Ancient Peak – was what the local people called the mountain above the saddle-ridge where the ruins were located, and its sister mountain was Huayna Picchu – Young Peak.

A bridge on the Inca Trail.

Not only did Bingham want to call these ruins Vilcabamba, because he believed he had discovered Manco Capac's gilded city, but he also speculated that the mountain refuge was Tampu Tocco, the mythical birthplace of the Ayar brothers, the first of the Incas.

Bingham's mistake in thinking that he had found the location of Vilcabamba is understandable. Who would have imagined that there were not one, but two, lost cities in the jungle north of Cusco? But overwhelming evidence against the Machu-Picchu-as-Vilcabamba hypothesis emerged, and Bingham was presented with an enigma: if Machu Picchu was not the last refuge of the Incas, then what on earth was it?

OUTPOST IN A LOST PROVINCE

Bingham carried out further explorations between 1911 and 1915, discovering a string of other ruins and a major Inca highway (now known as the Inca Trail) to the south of Machu Picchu. Later still, in 1941, the Viking Fund expedition led by Paul Fejos discovered the important ruins of Huiñay Huayna above the Urubamba gorge, about 4.5km (3 miles) due south of Machu Picchu. This proved that Machu Picchu was not merely a lost city, but part of an entire lost region – a fact generally ignored by popular histories. The usual account portrays Machu Picchu as a secret refuge known only to a select few, and concealed from the Spaniards. But this would have been impossible; the location of an entire active and populated region could not have been concealed from the Spaniards, who had many allies among the Indian peoples.

And yet the Spaniards did not know of Machu Picchu's existence. The only possible conclusion is that the Incas and Indians at the time of the conquest did not know of it either. Somehow the city and its region were abandoned and depopulated before the conquistadors arrived, and the memory was lost even to the Incas themselves. Perhaps the area

was devastated by plague, or overrun by the Antis, the hostile jungle tribesmen. But why would there be total amnesia about its location? This cannot have been accidental. The Incas had a caste of *quipucamayocs* – oral history recorders – who kept detailed accounts of the Inca past, but this was official history, and the Incas were notorious for wiping inconvenient details off the record. Perhaps this was Machu Picchu's fate: a province that rebelled and was dealt with so ruthlessly that its existence was erased from official memory.

That is merely one theory that fits the known facts. Here is another: according to new evidence unearthed from Spanish colonial archives, and recently presented by the archeologist J.H. Rowe, there was a "royal estate" (a rather Western concept, but the most intelligible way to put it) of the Inca Pachacutec at a place called "Picchu," north of Cusco. This leads to an interpretation that Machu Picchu was built and populated by the *panaca* (royal house) of Pachacutec, and that the eventual disappearance of the *panaca*,

House of the Terrace Caretakers.

Onboard the train from Ollantaytambo to Machu Picchu.

Huiñay Huayna.

a generation or so after the ninth Inca's death, led to the depopulation and abandonment of the whole region.

Signs of a pre-Inca occupation at Machu Picchu, going back 2,000 years, have been discovered, but there was certainly no pre-Inca city of any consequence here. If we accept that Machu Picchu was built for Pachacutec, we can speak of the construction dates of Machu Picchu with reasonable confidence. According to a widely accepted chronology, the Inca expansion began in the year 1438, after Pachacutec had defeated the Chanca invasion from the north. Various chronicles tell us that for strategic reasons (mainly to keep the retreating Chancas out) this mountainous area was the first to be settled in the headlong rush toward empire.

The building style of Machu Picchu is "late imperial Inca," which supports this thesis, and there are no signs of post-conquest occupation. So the whole settlement was built, occupied, and abandoned in the space of less than 100 years. The rest is speculation. And who can resist speculating when faced with something as affecting and impenetrable as the mystery of these silent stones?

PIECING TOGETHER THE PAST

What kind of settlement was Machu Picchu? John Hemming, author of *The Conquest of the Incas* – probably the best book on the subject – states that the site has only 200 habitation structures, leading him to estimate a permanent population of about 1,000 people. It is interesting that the agricultural output of the area would have greatly exceeded the needs of the population, for, beside the large extension of agricultural terracing at Machu Picchu itself, there were also much larger terraced areas at Inti Pata (just behind Machu Picchu peak to the southwest), and Huiñay Huayna, along the Inca Trail. More than one archeologist has proposed that the principal material function of the Machu Picchu region was to create a reliable supply of coca leaves for the priests and royals of Cusco.

Hiram Bingham called the ruin a "citadel," existing for strategic and defensive purposes. But beside its outer walls and moat, Machu Picchu contains an unusually high proportion and quality of religious architecture. Modern opinion leans more to the view that Machu Picchu was essentially a site of spiritual and ceremonial significance, with important agricultural functions. Its strategic purposes, if any, were secondary.

Bingham's fortress idea did not prevent him from speculating that the city was a refuge of Cusco's Virgins of the Sun, an idea inspired by the revelation that more than 75 percent of the skeletal remains found there were female. This exciting piece of news has been on the lips of tour guides ever since. Yet there is one difficulty with this hypothesis: the Yale expedition found only skulls, the other bones having disintegrated in the humid climate. It is hard to pronounce on the gender of a skull, particularly if, like the expedition's medical authority George Eaton, you are not very familiar with bones of the racial subgroup it comes from. Dr Eaton pronounced most of the skulls "gracile," and therefore, he assumed, female. But they could as easily have been young men, or men of small stature. The skulls still exist, and could be studied again by modern experts, but so far no one has done so.

It is alleged that the terms of Bingham's permission to excavate at the site of Machu Picchu were unclear. This led to vague accusations of smuggling after he shipped all the relics back to Yale University. In late 2007, following negotiations with the Peruvian government, Yale finally agreed to return the majority of the artifacts to Peru and they are now housed in the **Museo de Machu Picchu de la Casa Concha** in Cusco. The Manuel Chávez Ballón Museum (Mon–Sat 10am–4pm) near the ruins is a short walk from Aguas Calientes, the last stop on the train. It displays 250 objects excavated at Machu Picchu.

NEW DISCOVERIES

Since 1985 an astonishing number of new discoveries have been made around Machu Picchu. Taken as a whole they support and expand the emerging view of Machu Picchu as the ceremonial and possibly administrative center of a huge and quite populous region. The alluring myth of Machu Picchu as some kind of Andean Shangri-la perched alone on its remote crag must now be laid to rest.

The most extensive finds have been made across the river to the northeast, on a sloping plateau known as Mandorpampa about 100 meters (330ft) above the railroad. Its outstanding feature is an enormous wall about 3.5 meters high by 2.5 meters wide (11.5 by 8.5ft), and more than a kilometer (0.6 miles) long, which runs straight up the mountainside toward a pointed peak known as Yanantin. It was apparently built to protect the adjacent agricultural terraces from erosion, and may also have served to demarcate two areas with separate functions.

A road running along its top heads off northeast into densely forested mountains toward Amaybamba, or perhaps some other Inca settlement as yet undiscovered. Other finds on the *pampa* include quarries, circular buildings, a

⊙ Tip

The best way to buy tickets for Machu Picchu is from the official site, www.machupicchu.gob.pe. Booking in advance is advisable as there is a limit of only 2,500 persons per day. There are different options available: Machu Picchu only or Machu Picchu and the mountain, plus Huayna Picchu or/and the Museo Manuel Chávez Ballón.

The train to Machu Picchu.

⊙ RIDING THE RAILS

Unless you hike the Inca Trail or an alternative route, your journey to Machu Picchu will be by train (to the station in Aguas Calientes). Trains from Poroy, near Cusco, are run by Perurail (www.perurail.com) and these include the Expedition, the Vistadome, the Sacred Valley, and the Belmond Hiram Bingham. Prices range from US$73 to US$397 one way. From Ollantaytambo, 89km (56 miles) from Cusco, you can travel with two companies: Perurail (from US$59 one way) and Inca Rail (Calle Portal de Panes 105, Plaza de Armas, Cusco; tel: 084-581 860; www.incarail.com; from US$50 one way). Tickets are available at the stations, Lima's international airport, travel agencies, and online. There is huge demand for a small number of tickets, so be sure to book well in advance.

Machu Picchu

Uña Huayna Picchu

I Sacred Rock

Central Plaza

Common District

H Intihuatana

Sacristy ★

G Principal Temple

F Temple of the Three Windows

rocks

Mortar Building ★

Temple of the Condor **J** **K** Intimachay

Royal Sector **E**

Main Fountain **B**

Fountain Caretaker's House **D**

★ Fountains

C Temple of the Sun

Palace of the Princess ★

Dry Moat ★

Agricultural Terraces

Agricultural Sector **A**

House of the Terrace Caretakers ★

Agricultural Terraces

Main entrance

Funeral Rock ★

Inca Trail

Hotel, train & bus stations

large number of stone mortars, and a big observation platform.

Closer to Machu Picchu itself, the sector on the north slope of Huayna Picchu, which is known as the "Temple of the Moon," has been cleared to reveal a subterranean temple, a fine wall with an imposing gateway, and an observatory directed toward the Yanantin peak.

Farther upriver, two important burial sites known as Killipata and Ch'askapata have been discovered, and the ruins of Choquesuysuy, just upstream from where the hydroelectric power station used to stand, now appear to be much larger than had been previously believed. Of all these sites only the Temple of the Moon has been opened to the public so far.

Every year archeologists are making new discoveries in Machu Picchu itself, as well as in its surroundings.

In the years following Bingham's discovery the ruins were cleared of vegetation, excavations were made, and later a railroad was blasted out of the sheer granite cliffs of the imposing canyon. Visitors began to arrive. Chilean Pablo Neruda came in 1942, and was inspired to write one of his most famous poems, *The Heights of Machu Picchu*. In 1948 a sinuous 12km (7-mile) road from the riverbanks to the ruins was inaugurated by Hiram Bingham himself.

A WALKING TOUR OF THE RUINS

To understand the ruins best, you can hire one of the certified multilingual guides who offer their services at the entrance to the ruins. Otherwise, use this walking tour as an interpretive aid. Bingham classified the ruins into sectors, naming some of the buildings. Some of his conclusions appear wide of the mark to modern archeologists; others seem too arbitrary, resting on minimal evidence. However, since nobody has come up with a better system than Bingham's and for the sake of clear directions, we

will use the following sector names. Enter the ruins through the **House of the Terrace Caretakers**, which flanks the **Agricultural Sector Ⓐ**. This great area of terracing was undoubtedly for agricultural purposes, and may have made the city self-sufficient in crops. The terraces end in a **Dry Moat**, beyond which lies the city itself.

If you continue straight ahead you come to the **Fountains**, which are actually small waterfalls, in a chain of 16 little "baths," varying in the quality of their construction. These were probably for ritual, religious purposes relating to the worship of water. Bingham speculated that Machu Picchu might have been abandoned because this water supply dried up, or became inadequate to irrigate the terraces. The hotel near the ruins consumes most of this spring water today. The **Main Fountain Ⓑ**, just above you to the left as you arrive from the terraces, is so called because it has the finest stonework and the most important location.

Here, too, is the **Temple of the Sun Ⓒ**. This round, tapering tower features the

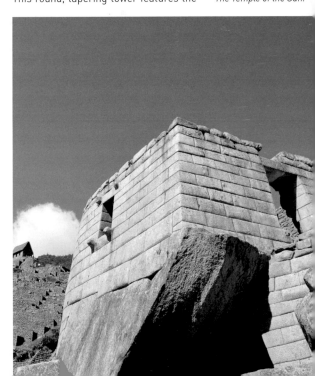

The Temple of the Sun.

most perfect stonework to be found in Machu Picchu. It contains sacred niches for holding idols or offerings, and the centerpiece is a great rock, part of the actual outcrop on which the temple is built. The base of this rock forms a grotto casually referred to as the Royal Tomb, although no bones were found there.

Recent archeo-astronomical studies have demonstrated how this temple would have served as an astronomical observatory. The rock in the center of the tower has a straight edge cut into it. This is precisely aligned through the adjacent window to the rising point of the sun on the morning of the June solstice. The pegs on the outside of the window may have been used to support a shadow-casting device, which would have made observation simpler.

The temple's entrance doorway has holes drilled about the jamb, less complex than those on a similar doorway at the Coricancha in Cusco. The adjacent building has two stories and was obviously the house of someone important. Bingham named it the **Palace of the Princess**.

View from Huayna Picchu.

Next to the Sun Temple, just above the main fountain, is a three-walled house, which has been restored and had its roof thatched as an example of how these structures looked in Inca times. It is usually called the **Fountain Caretaker's House** ⑩ – but it is unlikely to have been a house at all, since it is open to the elements on one side. The thick stone pegs fixed high up in the wall are thought to have served as hangers for heavy objects.

Students of the more esoteric aspects of the Inca culture have suggested that this complex of adjacent structures forms a temple to the four elements: the Temple of the Sun (Fire), the "Royal Tomb" (Earth), the open-fronted Fountain Caretaker's House (Air), and the Principal Fountain (Water).

The structures directly opposite the Sun Temple, across the staircase, have been classified as the **Royal Sector** ⓔ because of the roominess of the buildings, and also for the huge rock lintels (weighing up to 3,050kg/3 tons) that in Inca architecture generally characterized the homes of the mighty.

At the top of the agricultural terraces, standing high above the city, is a lone **hut**, which is a great place for an overall view of the ruins. It backs onto a gently sloping area known as the cemetery, because Bingham discovered numerous bones and mummies at this spot. Just a few meters from the hut lies a curiously shaped carved rock, called the **Funeral Rock**. Bingham speculated that this had been used as a place of lying-in-state for the dead, or as a kind of mortician's slab, on which bodies were eviscerated and then left to be dried by the sun for mummification.

MYSTERIOUS STONE

At the top of the staircase leading up from the fountains you come to a great jumble of **rocks** that served as a quarry for the Inca masons. There is a fascinating discovery in this sector – a partially split rock that seems to show precisely how the builders cut stone from the quarry. The rock bears a line of wedge-shaped cuts where tools were hammered in to form a crack. The problem with this rock, though, is that it was reportedly cut by 20th-century Peruvian archeologist Manuel Chávez Ballón.

Follow the ridge away from the quarry with your back to the staircase, and you come to one of the most interesting areas of the city. Here is the **Temple of the Three Windows ❻**. Its east wall is built on a single huge rock; the trapezoidal windows are partly cut into it. On the empty side of this three-walled building stands a stone pillar that once supported the roof. On the ground by this pillar is a rock bearing the sacred step-motif common to many other Inca and pre-Inca temples.

Next to this site stands the **Principal Temple ❼**, another three-walled building with immense foundation rocks and artfully cut masonry. It is named for its size and quality, and also because it is the only temple with a kind of sub-temple attached to it. This is generally called the **Sacristy**, because it seems a suitable place for the priests to have prepared themselves before sacred rites. The stone that forms part of the left-hand door jamb has 32 corners in its separate faces.

Ascending the mound beyond this temple leads you to what was probably the most important of all the many shrines at Machu Picchu, the **Intihuatana ❽**, the so-called "Hitching Post of the Sun." This term was popularized by the American traveler Ephraim Squier in the 19th century, but nobody has ever unraveled the mystery of how this stone and others like it were used. Every major Inca center had one. It seems likely that the stones somehow served for making astronomical observations and calculating the passing seasons. There was at least one other "Intihuatana" in the vicinity, located near the site of the old hydroelectric

power station in the valley below, to the west. The second stone was probably situated to make a specific astronomical alignment with the main one. The main Intihuatana is a sculpture of surpassing beauty. It is the only one in all Peru to have escaped the diligent attention of the Spanish "extirpators of idolatry," and luckily has survived in its original condition.

The group of buildings across the large grassy plaza below forms another, more utilitarian sector of the city. At the north end, farthest from the entrance to the ruins, you find two three-sided buildings opening onto a small plaza, which is backed by a huge rock generally called the **Sacred Rock ❶**. An intriguing aspect of this plaza is that the outline of the great flat rock erected at the northeast edge is shaped to form a visual tracing of the mountain skyline behind it. Then, if you step behind the *masma* (three-sided hut) on the southeast edge and look northwest, you find another rock that echoes in the same way the skyline of the small outcrop named **Uña**

Tip

The Salcantay to Santa Teresa trek (see page 120) is a good alternative to the "classic" Inca Trail, which is often fully booked.

Climbing Huayna Picchu.

Visitors climbing the steps toward the Sacred Rock.

A resident llama.

Huayna Picchu. In 2000, an enormous scandal broke out in Peru after a lighting crane being used during the filming of a commercial fell and broke part of the sacred stone. Since then, all visitors must visit the site with an official guide.

Walking back toward the main entrance along the east flank of the ridge, you pass through a large district of cruder constructions that has been labeled the **Common District**. At the end of this sector you reach a building known as the **Mortar Building**, with two curious disk shapes cut into the stone of the floor. Each is about 30cm (1ft) in diameter, flat, with a low rim carved around the edge. Bingham thought these were mortars for grinding corn, but this is doubtful. True, he did find some pestle stones in the same building, but the normal mortar used by the Quechua people today is much deeper and more rounded within; also it is portable, not fixed in one spot. These "mortars" would not have served well for that function. However, nobody has suggested a more plausible explanation for these enigmatic cavities.

Just across the next staircase you come to a deep hollow, surrounded by walls and niches, which is known as the **Temple of the Condor ❶**. Bingham called this the Prison Group, because there are vaults below ground, and man-size niches with holes that might have been used for binding wrists. But the concept of "prison" probably did not exist in Inca society; punishments tended to involve loss of privileges, or physical suffering, or death. Some early Spaniards reported pits full of snakes or pumas into which offenders were dropped to see if they would survive, but that is hardly a prison. The complex was probably a temple. A rock at the bottom of this hollow bears a stylized carving, apparently a condor, with the shape of the head and the ruff at the neck clearly discernible.

There is a small cave known as **Intimachay ❻** above and to the east of the Condor Temple, which has been identified as a solar observatory for marking the December solstice. The cave is faced with coursed masonry and features a window carved out of a boulder that forms part of the front wall. This window is precisely aligned with the winter solstice sunrise, so that morning light falls on the back wall of the cave for 10 days before and after that date.

THREE WALKS

If you arrived at Machu Picchu via Aguas Calientes rather than by the Inca Trail, there are three walks that are worth attempting. First, above the ruins to the southeast you can see a pass scooped out of the ridge, with a small ruin at the center. This is **Intipunku**, the Sun Gate. You can actually see the sun rise in this gateway from the western heights of the ruins at certain times of year. The trail traversing the mountainside from this point was the main Inca highway from

Huiñay Huayna and other sites farther south. It is well preserved, and makes for a fairly easy climb, taking about an hour and a half there and back. The view of Machu Picchu from Intipunku is magnificent.

The second walk is to the **Inca Drawbridge**. A trail winds back from the heights of the ruins, by the cemetery, leading along the west flank of the mountain behind Machu Picchu. This trail grows narrower until it is cut into the side of a sheer precipice, and you find yourself taking each step with care. Follow it until you come to a spot so steep that the ancients had to build a huge stone buttress to create a ledge for the path to cross. They left a strategic gap in the middle of the buttress, bridged by logs that could be withdrawn. Beyond this point the trail quickly peters out, becoming unstable and extremely dangerous. The path has been fenced off shortly before the bridge, ever since one walker tried to hike beyond it and fell to his death. To the bridge and back is an exciting one-hour walk demanding a cool head for heights.

Hardy visitors also like to climb **Huayna Picchu**, the towering granite peak that overlooks Machu Picchu from the north. It is the original Inca path, very steep, and stepped in places. Approach it with caution, particularly when wet, but don't be put off by the peak's fearsome appearance. You don't have to be a mountaineer, just reasonably active and healthy, to get to the top – and back. Everyone planning to climb Huayna Picchu must buy a ticket together with the Machu Picchu entrance(see page 281).

As you near the top, you pass through ancient terraces so inaccessible and so narrow that their value for agricultural purposes would have been negligible. It is thought that they were probably ornamental gardens. About an hour and a half gets the average person to the peak for a stupendous view.

The **Temple of the Moon** stands inside a cavern halfway down the north face. It was discovered in 1936 and contains some of the finest stonework of the entire Machu Picchu complex. The Inca pathway that leads to the temple forks off the main trail to the left about one third of the way up to the peak of Huayna Picchu.

HUIÑAY HUAYNA

Physically active people staying overnight at Machu Picchu can also take the **Inca Trail** to **Huiñay Huayna**. The round-trip takes about four hours, including some time to look at the ruins, a miniature Machu Picchu. Note that the Inca Trail fee, minus the entrance fee to Machu Picchu, is charged for this hike.

The journey itself is rewarding and well worth the effort since the trail passes through exotic tropical forest. It is also possible to spend the night at the basic hostel at Huiñay Huayna, and return to Machu Picchu the next morning.

> **⊙ Tip**
>
> The climb to Huayna Picchu is a great way to see the famous ruins from a different angle. Only the first 400 people are allowed up in turns at 7am and 11am. Make sure you book your tickets well in advance (see page 281). It is not possible to purchase them on site.

Train arriving at Aguas Calientes.

Candelaria festival, Puno.

LAKE TITICACA

The highest navigable lake in the world is the legendary birthplace of the first Inca and the site of fascinating island communities.

Lake Titicaca is the world's highest navigable lake and the center of a region where thousands of subsistence farmers eke out a living fishing in its icy waters, growing potatoes in the rocky land at its edge, or herding llama and alpaca at altitudes that leave Europeans and North Americans gasping for air. It is also where traces of the rich pre-Hispanic past still stubbornly cling, resisting in past centuries the Spanish conquistadors' aggressive campaign to erase Inca and pre-Inca cultures and, in recent times, the lure of modernization.

The turquoise-blue lake was the most sacred body of water in the Inca Empire, and is now the natural separation between Peru and Bolivia; it has a surface area exceeding 8,000 sq km (3,100 sq miles), not counting its more than 30 islands. At 3,856 meters (12,725ft) above sea level, it has two climates: chilly and rainy or chilly and dry. It gets cold in the evenings, dropping below freezing from June through August. During the day the sun is intense and sunburn is common, so take care.

BIRTHPLACE OF THE INCAS

According to legend, this lake gave birth to the Inca civilization. Before the Incas, the lake and its islands were holy places for the Aymara people, whose civilization was centered at Tiahuanaco, now a complex of ruins on

the Bolivian side of Titicaca but once a revered temple site with advanced irrigation techniques. Geologically, Titicaca's origins are disputed, although it was probably a glacial lake. Some scientists claim that it had a volcanic start; a century ago, it was popularly believed to be an immense mountaintop crater. There are a few diehards today who stick to the notion that the lake was part of a massive river system from the Pacific Ocean – but then, there are those who insist that the earth is flat.

◉ Main Attractions
Puno Cathedral
Yavari steamship
Uros Islands
Taquile Island
Amantaní Island
Juli

Map on page 290

Navigating Lake Titicaca.

One of the elaborate flower carpets created for Puno's Virgen de la Candelaria festival.

Indian legend says the sun god had his children, Manco Capac and his sister-consort Mama Ocllo, spring from the freezing waters of the lake to found Cusco and the beginning of the Inca dynasty. Later, during the Spanish conquest, the lake allegedly became a secret repository for the empire's gold. Recent aquatic expeditions have found gold figurines and other items, most notably around the Islands of the Sun and Moon in Bolivia, but these were most probably thrown into the lake as ritual sacrifices.

In 1961, the oceanographer Jacques-Yves Cousteau used mini-submarines to explore the depths of the lake, but found no gold. What he did discover, to the amazement of the scientific world, was a 60cm (24in) tri-colored frog that apparently never surfaces. Visitors today find a region unlike anywhere else: a place of floating reed islands, ancient lifestyles, and crumbling churches, where women wear bowler hats and the men knit their own brightly colored headgear.

URBAN BASE

If you are approaching the area from Cusco as an independent traveler you will probably take the bus to **Juliaca**. Luxury Train service is also available, but with the disadvantage that you will not be able to make stops at individual locations such as Raqchi. Be fore-warned also that flights from Cusco are sometimes discontinued for no apparent reason. Juliaca is a busy town, with the largest railway terminus in the country, a good airport, and plenty of places to eat, but not much else going for it except for a lively Sunday market.

CAPITAL OF THE ALTIPLANO

From here you can continue by train or minibus to **Puno ❶**, a commercial center settled as a Spanish community in 1668 by the Count of Lemos. During the colonial period it was one of the continent's richest cities because of its proximity to the Laykakota silver mines discovered by brothers Gaspar and José Salcedo in 1657. The mining boom drew 10,000 people to an area not far from what is now Puno. It also brought a bloody rivalry that ended only when the count ordered José Salcedo to be executed, and transferred Laykakota's residents to Puno.

At an altitude of 3,830 meters (12,630ft), Puno is the capital of Peru's Altiplano – the harsh highland region much better suited to roaming vicuñas and alpacas than to people. It is also Peru's folklore center, with a rich array of handicrafts, costumes, fiestas, legends, and, most importantly, more than 300 different ethnic dances. Among the latter, the most famous is the *Diablada* (Devil Dance), performed during the feast of the Virgen de la Candelaria during the first two weeks in February. Dancers compete fiercely to outdo one another in this dance, notable for its profusion of costly and grotesque masks. The origins of the dance have become lost over the centuries, but it is believed to have started with pre-Inca cultures, surviving through the Inca conquest and the Spanish takeover of the country, with the costumes being modified each time.

The lavish outfits the dancers wear are as varied as the dances themselves.

They range from multi-hued *polleras* (layered skirts), worn by barefoot female dancers, to the short skirts, fringed shawls, and bowler hats used in the highland version of the *marinera* dance. For centuries people living in the Altiplano were accustomed to working hard, then celebrating their special days with gusto. Many of the dances incorporate features of the most repressive times, with dancers dressed as mine overseers or as cruel landowners – characters who are mocked during the festivities.

PUNO'S SIGHTS

Little of Puno's colonial heritage is visible, but there remain a handful of buildings worth seeing. The **Catedral San Carlos Borromeo** is a magnificent stone structure, dating back to 1757, with a weather-beaten Baroque-style exterior and a surprisingly spartan interior – except for its center altar of carved marble, which is plated in silver. Over a side altar to the right side of the church is the icon of The Lord of Agony, commonly known as El Señor de la Bala (Lord of the Bullet). Beside

⊘ Tip

Taking the Andean Explorer train from Cusco is a wonderful way to arrive in Puno. Trains depart three times a week and tickets can be purchased at Huanchac (Wanchac) station in Cusco or from Perurail (tel: 51-84-581 414; www.perurail.com). The luxurious first-class service includes meals and entertainment.

The imposing cathedral on the Plaza de Armas.

the cathedral is the Balcony of the Count of Lemos, found on an old house on the corners of Deústua and Conde de Lemos streets. It is said that Peru's Viceroy Don Pedro Antonio Fernández de Castro Andrade y Portugal stayed here when he first arrived in the city he later named "San Carlos de Puno."

On the **Plaza de Armas** are the **Biblioteca** (Library) and the municipal **Pinacoteca** (Art Gallery), and half a block off the plaza is the **Museo Carlos Dreyer** (Mon–Sat 9.30am–7.30pm), displaying a collection of Nazca, Tiahuanaco, Paracas, Chimu, and Inca artifacts bequeathed to the city on the death of their owner, for whom the museum is named. One of the museum's most valuable pieces is an Aymara *aribalo*, the delicate pointed-bottomed pottery whose wide belly curves up to a narrow neck, as well as the "Treasure of Sillustani," including 501 golden pieces, found in an archeological site near Lago Umayo.

Three blocks uphill from the plaza is the **Parque Huajsapata**, a hill that figures in the lyrics of local songs,

and an excellent spot for a panoramic view of Puno. Huajsapata is topped by a huge white statue of Manco Capac gazing down at the lake from which he sprang. Another lookout point is found beside **Parque Pino**, at the city's north side, in the plaza four blocks up Calle Lima from the Plaza de Armas, in which stands the Arco Deústua, a monument honoring those killed in the decisive independence battles of Junín and Ayacucho.

The park is also called Parque San Juan, after the San Juan Bautista church within its limits; at its main altar is a statue of the patron saint of Puno, the Virgin of Candelaria. Also in the park is the Colegio Nacional de San Carlos, a grade school founded by a decree signed by Simón de Bolívar in 1825. It was later converted into a university and then used as a military barracks.

PUNO'S MARKET

Two blocks down Calle F. Arbul from Parque Pino is the city market, a colorful collection of people, goods, and food. Tourists should keep their eyes on their money and cameras, but it is worth a stop to see the wide selection of products – especially the amazing variety of potatoes, ranging from the hard, freeze-dried *papa seca* that looks like gravel to the purple potatoes and yellow-and-orange-speckled *olluco* tubers. Woolen goods, colorful blankets, and ponchos are on sale here, along with miniature versions of the reed boats that ply Lake Titicaca. Among the more intriguing trinkets are the *Ekekos*, the ceramic statues of stout jolly men laden with good luck-charms, ranging from fake money to little bags of coca leaves. Believers say that the *Ekekos* like to smoke, and they are often found with lit cigarettes hanging from their mouths. It is also said that these images only bring luck if they are received as gifts – not purchased.

Making handicrafts on the Uros Islands.

EXPLORING THE LAKE

The real reason for coming to Puno is that it is the stepping-off point for exploring Lake Titicaca and its amazing array of islands, Indian inhabitants, and colorful traditions. Small motorboats can be hired for island visits or fishing trips – although fish stocks have declined in recent years and most lake trout is now farmed. Another fascinating relic of a different era is the **Yavari steamship**. Built by the British in 1862, it plied the lake until 1975, and is now a floating B&B (www.yavari.org; temporarily closed for 2017 season), moored by the Sonesta Posada del Inca.

FLOATING ISLANDS

The best known of the islands dotting Titicaca are the **Islas de los Uros ❷**, artificial floating islands of reed named after the natives who inhabited them, but often known as the Islas Flotantes. Legends described the Uro islanders as people incapable of drowning, "like the fish and the birds of the water." Their original language is practically extinct, with most now speaking Aymara. They are believed to have originally stemmed from the Oruro area in Bolivia and to have developed their unique way of life in resistance against the conquering Incas.

Poverty has prompted more and more of the people to move to Puno, and has caused those who remain to take a hard-sell approach to tourists on those islands that are most visited. But why not? They certainly need the money. Take some fresh fruit as gifts when you visit, as the islanders' diet is very basic. There is some criticism that tourism has not only opened the Uros Islands to the stares of insensitive tourists but has also destroyed much of the culture, as the islanders modify their handicrafts to appeal to outsiders, or abandon traditional practices to dedicate more time to the influx of outsiders; but in fact, most of the close to 50 floating islands are not visited, and therefore remain untouched by tourism.

Many traditional customs and crafts stay unchanged, and the islanders are

The Yavari steamship still has many of its original features.

The Yavari steamship.

A Taquile woman wearing a traditional black shawl.

Terraced fields on Isla Amantaní.

still quite different from other Peruvians. They fish, hunt birds, and live off lake plants, and the most important element in their lives is the lake reeds they use to make their houses and boats and even as the base of their islands – the largest of which are **Toranipata**, **Huaca Huacani**, and **Santa María**. The lower layers of the reed islands decay in the water and are replaced from the top with new layers, making a spongy surface that is a bit difficult to walk on. Even the walls of the schools on the bigger islands are made of *totora*. The soft roots of the reed are eaten, too, making it a pretty handy thing.

A solid island that lures tourists is **Isla Taquile** ❸, the home of skilled weavers and a spot where travelers can buy well-made woolen and alpaca goods, as well as colorful garments whose patterns and designs bear hidden messages about the wearer's social standing or marital status. Prices of these goods may be higher than on the mainland, but the quality is very good. The residents of this island run their own tourism operations in the hope of maintaining a degree of control over tourism and ensuring that the visits of outsiders do not destroy their delicate culture. There are no hotels on Taquile, but the Quechua-speaking islanders open their homes to tourists interested in an overnight stay. Arrangements for such accommodations can be made with local people, who wait at the top of the steep stone staircase where the boats dock. You will find several places to eat, mostly serving simple but tasty fish and rice dishes. You can visit Taquile in one day, combined with a trip to the Uros, but it means spending much of the day on a boat; an overnight stay is recommended.

ISLA AMANTANÍ

Handicrafts also play an important role in life on **Isla Amantaní** ❹, a lovely, peaceful island at a similar distance from Puno as Taquile, but less visited. Amantaní was once part of the Inca Empire, as attested to by local ruins, and was reputedly once a prison island, before the Spanish invaded and slaughtered the islanders. The Spaniard who was granted a concession to the island used the native population in forced labor, and his descendants were still in control after Peru's independence from Spain. But eventually an island fiesta turned violent, and the islanders attacked their landlord with hoes and subsequently split up the island into communally held fields.

Amantaní has opened its doors to outsiders who are willing to live for a few days as the Aymara-speaking islanders do – and that means sleeping on beds made of long hard reeds and eating potatoes for every meal. There is no running water, and nighttime temperatures drop to freezing even in the summer. But those happy to rough it catch a glimpse of an Andean agricultural community that has maintained the same traditions for centuries. Some Amantaní residents live and die without ever leaving the island.

Journeys to Amantaní and Taquile commence at the Puno docks aboard spluttering wooden motorboats that are operated by the islanders. At the end of the three-hour trip, visitors are registered as guests and then assigned to a host family, which shows the way to its mud-brick or reed home set around an open courtyard decorated with white pebbles spelling out the family's name. The socializing begins when a family member who may speak a little English offers a guided walk around the island, from where the views are absolutely spectacular. Women from the island wearing traditional black-and-white lace dresses pass by with slingshots in their hands to kill scavenging birds.

Another island, **Isla Esteves**, is connected to Puno by a causeway and is best known for the luxurious but ugly Hotel Libertador Isla Esteves (www.libertador.com.pe), which stands out like a sore thumb. It is a far cry from what used to be the main construction on the island – a prison that accommodated the patriots captured by the Spanish during Peru's War of Independence. James Orton, a naturalist and explorer who died crossing Titicaca on a steamship in 1877, is buried here; his memorial sits alongside one honoring the liberation fighters who perished in the war with Spain. Orton, a professor of natural history from Vassar University, was on his third expedition to explore the Beni River in the Amazon area. The Beni's link to the Mamore River – both crucial conduits during the jungle's 19th-century rubber boom – was named the Orton in honor of the great explorer.

EXCURSIONS FROM PUNO

Some 35km (20 miles) from Puno is **Sillustani ⑤**, with its circular burial towers or *chullpas* overlooking **Lago Umayo**. The age of the towers, which are up to 12 meters (40ft) high, remains a puzzle. They were built by people of the Colla civilization, who spoke Aymara, and whose architecture was considered more sophisticated than that of the Incas, but who had been conquered by the Incas about a century before the Spanish arrived. The *chullpas* were apparently used as burial chambers for members of the nobility, who were entombed together with their entire families and possessions. In 2011, near the tallest one, *chullpa lagarto* (lizard chullpa), the remains of 44 children sacrificed in the 14th century were found surrounded by offerings, including animals, food, and ceramic pots. The site is a stunningly beautiful spot with a wealth of birdlife, and guinea pigs scuttling across the paths.

Not far away (about 20km/12 miles from Puno) is **Chucuito ⑥**, an Altiplano village that sits upon what was once an Inca settlement and which has an Inca sundial in the

A stone archway on Isla Amantaní.

On the island of Taquile, men can be seen knitting wherever they go.

plaza. Close to the village stands the ancient fertility temple of the same name, whose most notable feature is an enclosure of giant stone phalluses. Have a look at the **Iglesia Santo Domingo** with its small museum; the church of **La Asunción** is also worth visiting.

Juli ❼ (about 80km/50 miles southeast of Puno), once the capital of the lake area, has four beautiful colonial churches. Although it now appears a little strange to see so many large churches so close together, at the time when the Spanish had them built they were hoping to convert huge numbers of natives to Catholicism. In addition, the Spanish were accustomed to providing one church for Europeans, one for mixed-race Christians, and yet another for Indians. The largest – and oldest – of Juli's ornate churches is **San Juan Bautista**, with rich colonial paintings tracing the life of its patron saint, John the Baptist.

From the courtyard of the **Iglesia La Asunción** there is a captivating view of the lake. The other churches

Ruined church, Juli.

in the city are **San Pedro**, once the principal place of worship, in which a 400-strong Indian choir used to sing on Sunday, and **Santa Cruz**, which is just beside the city's old cemetery, and is currently in the worst state of repair. Santa Cruz was originally a Jesuit church upon the front of which indigenous stonemasons carved a huge sun – the Inca god – along with more traditional Christian symbols. From Juli, the Transturin hydrofoils leave for Bolivia. The timetable is a bit erratic, and it is best to make arrangements in Puno, rather than wait until you get to Juli.

The road from Juli hugs the shore, and about 25km (15 miles) farther on you come to the little village of **Pomata**, with its granite church of **Santiago Apóstol**.

PILGRIMAGE SITE

Copacabana ❽, a pleasant and friendly little town on the Bolivian side of the lake, can be reached by taking a minibus ride from Puno (via Yunguyo) around the side of the lake,

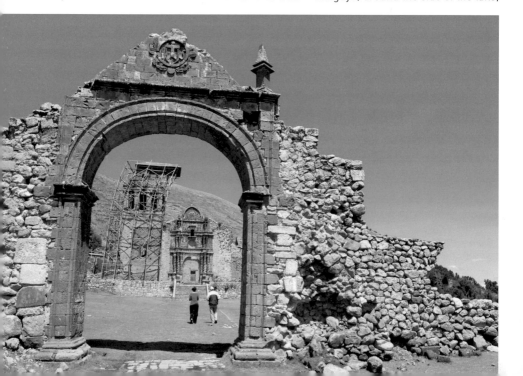

passing the reeds waving in the wind, shy but curious children at the bends in the road, and the ever-present brilliant blue of Titicaca. This pleasant trip sometimes involves a short ferry ride at the **Strait of Tiquina**. As a pilgrimage site, Copacabana is accustomed to tourists and has a number of modest but clean restaurants and hotels, and a couple of very comfortable ones, newly built by the lakeside. It is most famous for its basilica devoted to the Virgin Mary containing a 16th-century carved wooden figure of the Virgin of Copacabana, the Christian guardian of the lake. The statue, finished in 1853, was the work of native sculptor Francisco Tito Yupanqui, nephew of Inca Huayna Capac. Except during Mass, the statue stands with its back to the congregation – but facing the lake so that it can keep an eye out for any approaching storms and earthquakes. One of the loveliest outings in Copacabana is a dawn or dusk walk along the waterfront, watching the sky explode into color with sunrise, or slip into the blue-black of night at sunset.

GETTING TO BOLIVIA

From Copacabana, launches can be hired to visit the Bolivian islands on Lake Titicaca – the **Isla del Sol** and the **Isla de la Luna** (the Island of the Sun and the Island of the Moon). The former (also accessible via a public ferry) has a sacred Inca rock at one end and the ruins of Pilko Caima, with a portal dedicated to the sun god, at the other. The Island of the Moon, which is also known as Coati, has ruins of an Inca temple and a cloister for Chosen Women.

The bus from Puno to La Paz takes about eight hours on a paved road via Copacabana in Bolivia: an impressive route with great views of snowy peaks over the lake. Most buses stop for lunch in Copacabana, allowing for a peek into the beautiful basilica. You can also reach Bolivia by taking a bus from Puno around the other side of the lake, via Desaguadero, a scruffy border town. This route is shorter, but is not as scenic as going via Copacabana.

Baroque stonework on the Iglesia Santa Cruz in Juli.

Copacabana on Lake Titicaca.

📷 TAQUILE ISLAND

Lake Titicaca's Taquile Island is a harshly beautiful place whose people have retained their traditional lifestyle and values.

In the 16th century Taquile was a colonial hacienda that set the clothing style of the people, adapted from southern Spain. After Peru's independence in 1821 it became a prison island, but the people of Taquile gradually regained control of their lands and today they are a closely integrated community. Their language sets them aside from other Titicaca Amerindians: they speak Quechua rather than the more common Aymara.

Taquile is a very special place: the earth is a rich, reddish brown, a color that predominates in the women's clothes, and the lake a glorious vivid blue. Life seems to have changed little over the centuries: the earth is farmed with traditional implements, and crop diversification is almost unknown. Plenty of potatoes but few fresh vegetables or fruits are grown. Trout, the best in Peru, are fished from the lake and served in the few basic restaurants. On the hillsides stand the remains of Inca terracing.

The Taquile weaving cooperative is renowned for the quality of its garments, and the people habitually look as if they are dressed for a fiesta. The women wear layers of multi-colored skirts and embroidered blouses; the men sport smart waistcoats and black trousers along with the little pointed hats that they knit themselves.

The islanders have a passion for fiestas, too, and whether they are celebrating Santiago (St James), which falls on July 25, or Pacha Mama (Mother Earth) in early August, high spirits, music, and plenty of *chicha* are always very much in evidence.

Music is one of the ways in which islanders preserve their heritage. The men's embroidered belts contain coded calendars giving information about crops and marriage dates.

Island agriculture is largely based on fishing and terraced horticulture. Small herds of cattle can be seen grazing on the steep slopes of the island.

Wherever you go on Taquile, you will see men knitting the brightly colored stocking hats they wear. Colors denote marital status and social standing.

Boats to Taquile Island leave at regular intervals from Puno.

Controlling the flow

When visitors first arrived on Taquile during the early 1970s, the islanders decided that if change was on the way they wanted to control it. They began operating their own passenger boats, and regulating the number of people who visit the island. In 2009 they set up their own community-based travel agency, Munay Taquile (tel: 051-351 448; www.taquile.net/es/).

There are no hotels on the island, but some families open their homes to visitors, who can spend the night and share their meal for a very reasonable charge. If you want to sample their hospitality, remember that the accommodations will be pretty basic. Realizing that their woven goods are also of interest to outsiders, the islanders now sell them on the main plaza. Prices are higher than on the mainland, but the quality is superb. It seems that the people of Taquile are making a very good job of managing tourism: enjoying the economic benefits without allowing it to erode their culture.

Children growing up on Taquile today will inevitably find their lives affected – for good and ill – by the influx of foreign tourists. However, their parents' generation is trying hard to make tourism work while preserving the traditional ways.

Musicians and dancers celebrate the festival of Santiago on 25 July.

Vivid scenes on woven tapestries.

PERU

TRAVEL TIPS

TRANSPORTATION

Getting there **302**
    By air...................................**302**
    Travel agents **302**
    Overland...............................**302**
    By boat **303**
Getting around **303**
    From the airport **303**
    Orientation in Lima..............**303**
    By bus **304**
    By car **304**
    By air....................................**305**
    By rail...................................**305**
    By boat **305**

A – Z

Accommodations **306**
Addresses **306**
Admission charges **306**
Budgeting for your trip **306**
Business travelers...................**306**
Children....................................**306**
Climate.....................................**307**
Crime and security...................**307**
Customs regulations................**308**
Disabled travelers....................**308**
Electricity **308**
Embassies and
    consulates...........................**308**

Etiquette...................................**309**
Health and medical care...........**309**
Internet **310**
LGBTQ travel **310**
Maps...**310**
Media..**310**
Money.......................................**310**
Opening hours..........................**312**
Photography.............................**312**
Postal services........................**312**
Public holidays.........................**313**
Religious services **313**
Shopping **313**
Student travelers **313**
Telephones...............................**313**
Time zones **314**
Toilets......................................**314**
Tourist information **314**
Visas and passports.................**314**
Weights and measures **314**
Women travelers.......................**314**

LANGUAGE

Language **315**
Pronunciation...........................**315**
    Vowels **315**
    Consonants **315**
Basics.......................................**315**
Greetings..................................**315**
Telephone calls **316**

Finding your way **316**
In the hotel...............................**316**
In the restaurant **317**
Menu decoder **317**
    Entremeses/Primer Plato
    (First Course)....................**317**
    La carne (Meat)....................**317**
    Pescado/Mariscos (Fish/
    Seafood)............................**317**
    Vegetales (Vegetables)..........**317**
    Frutas (Fruit)........................**317**
    Bebidas (Drinks) **318**
    Miscellaneous......................**318**
Shopping **318**
Tourist attractions....................**318**
Airport/travel agency **318**
Transportation **319**
Driving......................................**319**
Road signs................................**319**
Emergencies **320**
Health.......................................**320**
Months of the year **320**
Seasons....................................**320**
Time **320**

FURTHER READING

General......................................**321**
History......................................**321**
Amazon Jungle **322**
Other Insight Guides................**322**

TRANSPORTATION

GETTING THERE

By air

Peru is well connected by international flights, which arrive at the Jorge Chávez International Airport in Lima.

Flights from Europe

Direct flights to Lima are available from Amsterdam with KLM and Air France, from Madrid with British Airways, Iberia, LATAM, and Air Europa, and from Paris with Air France. There are numerous connecting flights from other European cities to these airports. Other non-direct flights to Lima make connections in Brazil, Chile, or the US.

Flights from the US and Canada

American Airlines, Avianca, Delta, Jet Blue, LATAM, Spirit Airlines, and United Airlines fly direct to Lima from major US cities including Miami, Houston, Fort Lauderdale, Los Angeles, and New York. Delta operates direct flights from Atlanta. Air Canada flies direct from Toronto to Lima.

Flights from Australasia

The best route from Australia or New Zealand is probably with LATAM to Santiago de Chile, and then continuing with LATAM to Lima.

Flights from South Africa

Flights from South Africa require connections in Buenos Aires, Argentina, or São Paulo, Brazil.

Flights within Latin America

There is no shortage of flights to Peru from other South American countries. LATAM operates an extensive network of flights across the continent, including direct flights from Lima to Buenos Aires, Argentina; Santiago de Chile; Quito, Ecuador; and Caracas, Venezuela. Avianca operate flights from Lima to numerous cities in South and Central America.

For travel to and from Mexico, Aeroméxico operates regular flights.

Travel agents

The following travel agents specialize in travel to South America and can arrange flights, accommodations, and transportation. They may also be able to provide information on air passes, offered by airlines such as LATAM, for travel within the continent.

UK

Audley Travel
Monsoon Building, 1 Nicholas Road, London W11 4AN
Tel: 01 993 838 650
www.audleytravel.com
Journey Latin America
401 King Street, London W6 9NJ
Tel: 020-3811 6079
www.journeylatinamerica.co.uk
Select Latin America
3.51 Canterbury Court, 1-3 Brixton Road, London SW9 6DE
Tel: 0207 407 1478
www.selectlatinamerica.co.uk

USA

Yampu Tours
673 South Main St, Stove, VT 05672
Tel: 802-760 6546
www.yampu.com
Exito
108 Rutgers Av., Fort Collins, Colorado, CO80525
Tel: 800-655 4053/970 482 3019
www.exitotravel.com

Canada

Inti Travel
Box 1586, Banff, AB, T1L 1B5
Tel: 1-403-760 3565
www.discovergalapagos.com/intitravel/

Australia

World Expeditions
Level 5, 71 York Street, Sydney, NSW 2000
Tel: 02-8270 8400
www.worldexpeditions.com

Overland

Peru has borders with Chile, Bolivia, Colombia, Brazil, and Ecuador. The border crossing with Chile is at Tacna on the Peruvian side, and Arica on the Chilean; taxis regularly

Keeping the traffic moving in Trujillo.

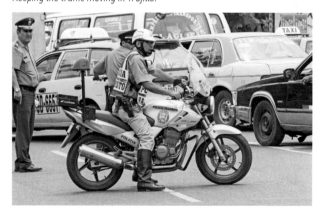

make the crossing, and some long-distance buses operate between Lima, Quito, Santiago de Chile, São Paulo via Iñapari, and Buenos Aires. Tickets for such marathon journeys sometimes include food and overnight accommodations.

From Bolivia, there are two crossings at Desaguadero and Kasani for those traveling from La Paz and Copacabana respectively. The journey from Ecuador is also straightforward: take a bus to the border at Huaquillas and walk through to Tumbes. Other buses operate from there, but note that the "international service" advertised in Quito still requires a change of bus at the border, unless you are traveling with the Ormeño bus company (see page 304), so it is actually more expensive and occasionally much less convenient than doing the trip in stages. Less traveled options include crossings at La Tina–Macará and La Balsa–Zumba. Arica–Tacna is the sole cross-border rail option.

By boat

Few people arrive at Lima's port of Callao by ocean liner or freight ship. The limited services available are expensive and inconvenient in comparison to flying. It is possible to enter Peru by boat from Guaqui in Bolivia, which docks at Puno on the shore of lake Titicaca.

On the Amazon, passengers may enter Iquitos in Peru from Colombia (Leticia) or Brazil (Tabatinga).

GETTING AROUND

From the airport

Jorge Chávez International Airport lies around 16km (10 miles) from the center of Lima.

The most reliable bus service to and from the airport is the Airport Express (tel: 51 1 446 5539, www.

✈ Airline offices in Lima

Aerolíneas Argentinas
Calle Dean Valdivia 243, of. 301, San Isidro
Tel: 0800-52 200/51 1-513 6565
www.aerolineas.com
Aeroméxico
Av. Alfredo Benavides 1579, Edificio Park II, Of. 405, Miraflores
Tel: 0800-53 407/51-1-705 1111
www.aeromexico.com
Air Canada
Calle Italia 389, Of. 101, Edificio Mar Azul, Miraflores
Tel: 0800-52 073/51-1-626 0900
www.aircanada.com
Air France
Av. Álvarez Calderón 185, Of. 601, San Isidro
Tel: 0800-539-91/51-1-213 0200
www.airfrance.com
American Airlines
Av. Pardo 392, Miraflores
Tel: 1-211 7000
www.aa.com
United Airlines
Víctor Andrés Belaúnde 147, Via Principal 110, Of. 101, San Isidro
Tel: 0800 70030/51 1 712 9230
www.united.com
Copa Airlines
Los Halcones, 105, San Isidro
Tel: 51 1-709 2600
www.copaair.com
Delta
Av. Víctor Andrés Belaúnde 147, Via Principal 180, Of. 701 San Isidro
Tel: 01-800 241 4141
www.delta.com

Iberia
Av. Camino Real 390, Of. 902, Torre Central, Of. 902 San Isidro
Tel: 51-1-705 7285
www.iberia.com
KLM
Av. Álvarez Calderón 185 piso (floor) 6, San Isidro
Tel: 51-1-213-0200
www.klm.com
LAN
Av. José Pardo 513, Miraflores
Tel: 01-213 8200, from abroad: 51 1 213 8200
www.latam.com
LC Perú
Av. José Pardo 269, San Isidro
Tel: 01-204 1313
www.lcperu.pe/
Lufthansa
Hansaperú Travel, Av. Jorge Basadre 1330, San Isidro
Tel: 51-1-748 0770
www.lcc-hansaperu.com
Peruvian Airlines
Av. José Pardo 495, Miraflores
Tel: 51-1-716 6000/715 6122/748 0111
www.peruvianairlines.pe
Star Perú
Av. Comandante Espinar 331, Miraflores
Tel: 01-705 9000/213 8813
Av. José Pardo 485, Miraflores
Tel: 01-213 8813
www.starperu.com
Avianca
Av. José Pardo 811, Miraflores
Tel: 51-1- 511 8222
www.avianca.com

✈ Flight information

For general information about **Jorge Chávez International Airport** in Lima, or to check international and domestic flight times, visit their website, www.lima-airport.com, or call the flight center on 511-511 6055

airportexpresslima.com). It operates 365 days a year, and runs every half hour (hourly between noon and 6pm) from 7am to midnight, linking the airport with 7 stops in Miraflores, where most hotels are located. All buses have reclining seats, free Wi-Fi, USB cable ports, toilets, and large baggage storage areas (no weight limit). At the time of writing, a return ticket cost US$15 (single US$8).

There are several official taxi and van services from the airport. Check the list at www.airportexpresslima.com. You may try the Quickllama (http://quickllama.com/esp/index.htm) airport shuttle, which operates around the clock. See website for details. Otherwise, once past the Arrivals barrier, there are plenty of

taxi drivers waiting, but be prepared to bargain. Alternatively you can pre-book a taxi (see page 305, for a list of recommended taxi companies) . A fare to the center of Lima is US$15–20. *Ejecutivo* taxis charge a little more.

In Cusco and other cities, taxis from the airport into the center are very cheap, but make sure you agree on a price before starting your journey.

Orientation in Lima

Lima is divided into districts, each with its own character. Downtown Lima has grandiose plazas, mansions, and the restored historical Plaza Mayor, although there is a certain amount of street crime.

In the more glitzy suburbs of Miraflores and San Isidro, there is better security. New shopping complexes and landscaped gardens make this a complete contrast to the rest of the city.

Barranco is an upmarket beach suburb where some artists have their workshops, giving it a bohemian reputation. Open-air cafés and restaurants have live jazz and Creole music, while the crumbling old mansions give the tree-lined streets a relaxed ambience.

By bus

Local transport

For foreign visitors, local buses and minibuses will be very cheap, but slow and confusing. Much easier to use is the modern Metropolitano bus service which whisks users between the center, San Isidro, Miraflores, and Barranco on dedicated bus lanes. It approaches long-distance bus stations at the Javier Prado and Grau stops. The Metro de Lima currently has one line (Linea 1), running east of the main areas of interest, but two more (lines 2 and 4) are due for completion by 2021. As for taxis, they are relatively cheap. Just make sure you agree on the fare before entering the taxi.

Between small towns and villages in Peru there are regular local buses. You can also travel by *taxi colectivo*: a car acting as a taxi service for four or five passengers. *Colectivos* leave whenever they are full. In more remote parts, most travel is by pick-up truck. If you have a long journey ahead, insist on a seat inside. It's standing room only on top

Rush hour in the capital.

and you'll be smothered by the dust – or drenched in the rainy season.

Long-distance buses

Between cities, there are excellent, comfortable bus services. Numerous companies operate morning and evening departures from Lima to most cities. There is no central bus station in Lima, as each company has its own terminal. Always check the departure point for the journey you are making when buying tickets. Reliable bus companies include:

Civa
Av. Paseo de la Republica 575, La Victoria
Tel: 51 1-418 1111
Cruz del Sur
Jr. Quilca 531
Av. Javier Prado Este 1109, San Isidro
Call center tel: 51-1-311 5050/toll free: 72-0444 or 0801 11111
www.cruzdelsur.com.pe
Free delivery for tickets purchased through the call center. Luxury buses leave from the San Isidro terminal.
Ormeño
Av. Javier Prado Oeste 1057, La Victoria
Call center tel: 51-1-472 1710
Free delivery for tickets purchased through the call center.
Tepsa
Av. Javier Prado Este 1091, La Victoria
Call center tel: 51-1-617 9000

By car

Driving in Lima is a nightmare: road conditions are chaotic, the local style

⊙ **On departure**
Don't forget to hang on to the tourist card that you fill out when you arrive in Peru. You'll need to hand it in to immigration when you leave. The airport departure tax on international flights is now included in the ticket price.

of driving is aggressive, signposting is rare, and theft from cars is a constant danger, particularly at night. Taking all of this into consideration, the best way to travel is by taxi. However, outside the capital driving gets easier, and the main hazard is the state of the roads – apart from the main highways, many are unpaved. Certain regions are better appreciated with your own mode of transport, such as the Callejón de Huaylas. The town of Huaraz is a 6-hour drive from Lima on well-surfaced roads.

For stays of up to 30 days, you don't need an international driving license to rent a car, just a valid driving license from your own country, a passport, and a credit card. For longer stays, contact your home automobile license authority to obtain an international driver's license, valid for 12 months.

Car rental agencies

In addition to their branches in Lima (listed below), most car rental companies have branches in Arequipa and Cusco, and at some regional airports.
Avis
28 de Julio 587, Miraflores
Tel: 51-1-444 0450
Jorge Chávez International Airport
Tel: 51-1-517 1847 (24 hours)
www.avis.com
Budget
Av. Francisco Bolognesi 808, Barranco
Tel: 51-1-204 4400
Av. Larco 998, Miraflores
Tel/mob: 981 248 595
Jorge Chávez International Airport
Tel:55-1-1517-1880 (24 hours)
www.budgetperu.com
Hertz
Pasaje Tello 215, Miraflores
Tel: 51-1-447 2129
Jorge Chávez International Airport
Tel: 51-1-517 2402 (24 hours)
www.hertz.com
National Car Rental
Av. Costanera 1380, San Miguel
Jorge Chávez International Airport

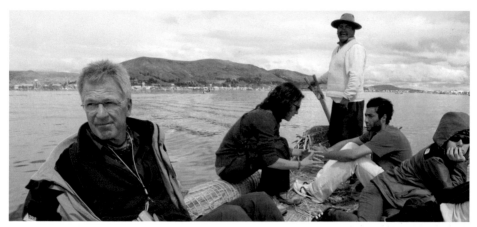

Crossing Lake Titicaca on a totora boat.

Tel: 55-1-574 1374 (24 hours)
www.grupoanc.com/

By air

Lima is the gateway to the rest of the country, although there are a handful of international flights to Cusco and Iquitos. There are domestic flights between all major cities and several domestic airlines, including Avianca Peru, Viva Air Peru, Star Perú, LC Perú, and Peruvian Airlines, providing daily services to most cities. LATAM Perú operates domestic flights to destinations throughout the country.

It's best to book in person at the reservations office, or through a good travel agent who will confirm your tickets. Some online booking is available. Tales of travelers being bumped off flights are legion:

it is best to reconfirm your ticket 72 hours in advance.

By rail

Train journeys in Peru are spectacular, but tend to be expensive. The trips provide valuable glimpses of rural life and views of magnificent landscapes.

The 10-hour journey between Puno and Cusco, which goes via Juliaca, is a wonderful experience. The Belmond Andean Explorer service, operated by PeruRail, runs once a week in both directions, and also offers services to/from Arequipa. (See page 291 for information on tickets.) Perurail and Incarail have counters at Lima airport.

The Lima–Huancayo passenger service (see page 203), the world's

second-highest train journey, runs approximately twice a month. It is operated by Ferrocarril Central Andino (FCCA), tel: 01-226 6363 ext. 222/235, www.ferrocarrilcentral.com.pe.

To reach the ruins at Machu Picchu by train, there are several trains that make the journey from Cusco to Aguas Calientes, from where you catch a shuttle bus to the ruins. A good option for travelers wishing to explore the Sacred Valley rather than traveling directly to Machu Picchu from Cusco is to take a morning train from Ollantaytambo. There are several types of train to choose from, including the Vistadome and Expedition trains, and the five-star Hiram Bingham service. (See page 281).

By boat

From Puno, there are tranquil excursions by boat across Lake Titicaca to the islands of Taquile and Amantaní, and the floating islands of Uros, which are made entirely of reeds. Simply go to the dock, where boats leave at regular intervals. It is a 3-hour boat ride to Taquile or Amantaní and boats usually depart between 8 and 9am. Boats return from Taquile in the late afternoon, although many visitors choose to stay overnight. Boats to Amantaní are less frequent, so visitors usually stay at least one night on the island.

In the Amazon, passenger and cargo boats, and motorized canoes are the only way to travel along the winding, muddy waterways. (See page 214 for details of Amazon riverboats.)

⊘ Taxis

Taxis in Peru have no meters – you flag a car down and simply bargain on a rate, preferably before even getting in. There have been some incidents of hijacking involving taxis in the past, so it is best to use a registered one where possible. In smaller cities you may prefer to walk, but in Lima taxis are often essential and very cheap.

Note that your hotel will arrange taxis for you if you ask. This is more expensive, but very secure. If you don't speak much Spanish, this can be the best option.

Reliable taxi services in Lima

include the following:
CMV Taxi Remisse Ejecutivo
Tel: 511-219 0266/ 219 0277
Mitsoo Taxi Remisse Ejecutivo
Tel: 511-517 1893
www.mitsoo.net/
Taxi Green
Tel: 511 484 4001
www.taxigreen.com.pe
Taxi Directo
Tel: 511 711 1111
www.taxidirecto.com
Taxi 365
Tel: 511 219 0271
Taxi Seguro
Tel: 01-200 2000
www.taxiseguro.com.pe

A

Accommodations

Accommodations in Peru can be as sophisticated or as simple as you wish. There's everything from the smartest five-star hotels imaginable to village home-stays where your bed is a mattress on an earthen floor. In between there's a plethora of sleeping options, from colonial mansions to simple and welcoming hostels. For longer stays, many cities now offer rental apartments. Some of the loveliest places to stay in Peru are the country haciendas and lodges, away from the big towns. These often offer activities such as trekking and horseback riding, and are sometimes built near hot springs.

Addresses

The following will help you find your way around the addresses listed in this book:
Av. *(Avenida)* = avenue
Calle = street
Crta *(Carretera)* = highway
Edificio = building
Esq. *(Esquina)* = corner
Hostal = cheap hotel (not a hostel)
Jr. *(Jirón)* = way/street
Of. *(Oficina)* = office
Pasaje = passage/alley
Piso = floor/story
s/n *(sin numéro)* = no number
Urb. *(Urbanización)* = area/neighborhood

Admission charges

All tourist attractions, apart from some churches and a handful of museums, charge admission. Most expensive of all is Machu Picchu, but when you've come all this way, it's worth the price. There are usually discounts for children and students, and family tickets are sometimes available. If you're claiming a student discount, be sure to carry your International Student Identity Card. Entrance fees are usually quoted in soles, although larger attractions may give them in dollars as well. Be sure to keep your ticket after you enter a site, as it may be checked. In Cusco, the Cusco Tourist Ticket (www.cosituc.gob.pe) is the way to see the city's main attractions (see page 259).

B

Budgeting for your trip

You can manage in Peru on US$20 a day – but that would be just getting by at rock-bottom prices, and why would you want to stint when there's so much enjoyment to be had? A more reasonable budget is US$40–60 per day for a comfortable and enjoyable holiday. This includes decent accommodations at US$20–40 per night and meals at less touristy restaurants which are amazingly cheap. The best value is the daily lunch *menú*, which often costs less than 15 soles.

Children are often doted on in Peru.

If you stay in four- and five-star hotels and eat in restaurants designed for tourists, your budget will need to be several hundred dollars per day. Long-distance transport by bus is cheap, and taxis in town likewise. Handicrafts are more expensive in the big city craft markets; try to buy in the villages instead.

Business travelers

All of the five-star hotels, and many of the four-star hotels, have business centers. Most hotels have computers with internet connection for guests' use, and a large number now have a wireless internet connection too. Mobile phone SIM cards can be bought in any telecommunications shop. Most of the better hotel rooms have phones, and the rates are often reasonable, but check at reception before you dial.

C

Children

Peruvians love children, and your child will receive much positive

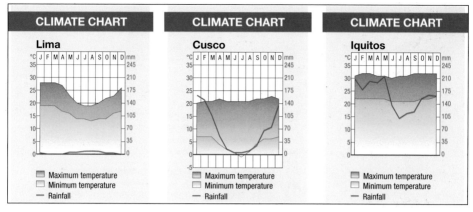

CLIMATE CHART
Lima

Maximum temperature
Minimum temperature
— Rainfall

CLIMATE CHART
Cusco

Maximum temperature
Minimum temperature
— Rainfall

CLIMATE CHART
Iquitos

Maximum temperature
Minimum temperature
— Rainfall

attention while traveling in Peru. In Lima and the bigger cities there are parks with children's playgrounds, and older children will enjoy many of the regular tourist attractions.

Shops sell babies' diapers (nappies), baby food, and formula milk. Be very careful with the food your children eat. Avoid uncooked vegetables, salads, and unpeeled fruits. Make sure all water is bottled, filtered, or at least well boiled. Children become especially tired at high altitude: take it easy. Bring a child seat if you are renting a car, as these are hard to come by. Better restaurants have children's high chairs. Peruvian children's clothes and shoes are beautiful and cheap: make sure your children's suitcases are just half full when you leave home!

Climate

Peru has wet and dry seasons, although on the coastal desert strip it is always dry. However, Lima suffers a bizarre weather condition prevailing from April to November called the *garúa*, a damp, cold mist which obliterates the sun and sours everyone's mood. August is the worst month for this, with temperatures around 13–17°C (55–62°F). The rest of the year, Lima enjoys sunshine and moderate temperatures from 21–26°C (69–79°F).

Towns like Nazca on the western slopes of the Andes are dry and hot all year round, but the central Andes experience distinct wet and dry seasons. Snow is uncommon in inhabited highland areas, although the highest Andean peaks are snow-covered throughout the year. The best time to visit the highlands is between May and September, when

views of the mountains are crystal-clear. Although the days are bright and clear, nights can be bitterly cold, and temperatures can fall to 0°C (32°F). During the rest of the year, the weather is warmer but wetter, and the Andes are often obscured.

In the Amazon basin, the wet season lasts from January to April, when landslides and flooding are a constant problem. During the dry season, May to October, it might not rain for weeks at a time (although there might be short showers every day). Daytime temperatures average 27–32°C (81–90°F), with nighttime lows averaging 21–26°C (69–79°F).

However, unexpected cold fronts called *friajes*, which come up from the south, are unique to the southern rainforests and can bring a few days of wind and rain with spring-like daytime temperatures of 13–18°C (55–65°F) and nighttime lows of 10°C (50°F). Although this weather condition is unusual, it is said to have a beneficial effect on the wildlife of the region.

When to go

It is possible to visit Peru all year round, but the most popular time of year is between May and September, as this coincides with the dry season in the highlands and the jungle.

What to wear

Good traveling clothes should be comfortable and durable and preferably made of natural fiber, although one or two synthetics in the form of evening wear that won't wrinkle in your suitcase come in handy for those formal nightspots. Take some good walking shoes that won't look too out of place in a casual restaurant.

One rarely regrets traveling light, especially in a land where clothes shopping is a dream. Remember all those alpaca sweaters and leather goods – you can buy as many warm clothes as you like when you arrive. However, it is almost impossible to get shoes in large sizes.

Bring warm clothes for the Sierra, light clothes for the jungle, and a combination for the coastal deserts, which are warm by day and cool at night. The most appropriate clothing for a jungle trip is a long-sleeved shirt and trousers of close-woven material. These protect the wearer from most biting insects. A hat gives valuable protection while traveling on the river or birdwatching on the lakes. Mountaineers and hikers should not forget to bring good walking shoes, warm clothes, and equipment, because there is a shortage of trekking supplies in Peru. Avoid olive-green trousers and military-style jackets: Peruvians could get the wrong idea.

Crime and security

As Peru's urban centers have swollen, so has petty crime. Pickpockets and thieves have become more and more common in Lima, Cusco and other major cities. It is recommended that tourists do not wear costly jewelry and that watches be covered by a sleeve. Thieves are amazingly adept at slitting open shoulder bags, camera cases, and knapsacks; keep an eye on your belongings. Beware of bogus taxi drivers at Lima airport.

All kind of confidence tricksters pull ever more imaginative ruses; some pose as policemen, others work together with bus and taxi

Tourist police on patrol in Arequipa's main square.

drivers or use diversionary tactics to get hold of your valuables. Special care is needed at railway stations and airports and when withdrawing cash from ATMs. Should you have anything stolen, you will need to fill out a report with the Tourist Police (see page 308). There have also been cases of people being drugged and sexually abused, so buy your own drinks and never lose sight of them in bars, discos, and nightclubs.

Go out at night in small groups if possible. Visits to the shantytowns (pueblos jóvenes) on the outskirts of the cities are very dangerous without a guide.

Officials also warn against dealing with anyone calling your hotel room or approaching you in the lobby or on the street, claiming to represent a travel agency or specialty shop. Avoid contact with over-friendly strangers who may want to get you involved in criminal deals. Be aware that drug-dealing is a crime that results in a long prison sentence.

Driving alone and after dusk is not advisable. Don't hitchhike. For journeys overland choose only well-known and established bus companies and take care that you are always able to identify yourself: carry your passport at all times.

There is little or no activity by rebel groups these days, and incidents of violence involving foreign tourists are few and far between. There is army activity in the coca-growing regions of the Andes, but these are extremely remote.

Expeditions and trekking tours should ideally be undertaken in larger groups and accompanied by a local and experienced mountain guide. It is a good idea to notify a reliable third party of your destination and home address before leaving for a long trekking tour. For more specific inquiries, contact your embassy or the **South American Explorers' Club** (see page 313).

Tourist police

Peru's tourist police, known as DIRTUR (Dirección de Turismo Ecología) can be found in downtown Lima and other tourist centers. Recognizable by their white shirts, they are very helpful, and have special English speakers on duty. Their general number is 01-460 1060. They can also be contacted at the following addresses:

Lima: Jr. Moore 268, Magdalena del Mar, tel: 01-462 2899.

Cusco: Plaza Tupac Amaru, s/n, tel: 084-223 701.

Arequipa: Calle Jerusalén 315, tel: 054-201 258.

Iquitos: Calle Sargento Lores 834, tel: 065-242 081.

Customs regulations

Visitors of 18 and older are allowed to bring in up to 400 cigarettes or 50 cigars or 250 grams of tobacco and up to 3 liters of liquor.

Visitors may bring along one set of sporting goods, such as windsurfing or diving equipment.

Regarding electronics, one digital camera, two mobile phones, portable computer and non-professional video camera may be imported duty-free per person of 7 years of age and older.

Gifts worth up to US$500 may be imported duty-free. Foreign currency worth up to US$10,000 or equivalent in other currencies may also be brought in free of charge.

D

Disabled travelers

Unfortunately, there isn't much in the way of facilities for disabled travelers in Peru. Hotels, except for the more upmarket, five-star variety, tend not to have accessible rooms or bathrooms. However, the following companies offer tours for disabled travelers:

Mosoq Huayra Travel Agency
Quewarpay F1 Arco Tica tica, Cusco
Tel: 084-634 699/984263781
www.mosoqhuayratravel.com

⏱ Emergencies

In case of an accident, attack, or other emergency, call: **General emergency** 105/911; fire emergencies 116; medical emergencies 106 (SAMU, Sistema de Atención Médica Móvil de Urgencia). *See also page 309 for medical services.*
Policía Nacional del Perú (National Police), tel: 431 3040.
Policía de Careteras (Traffic Police), tel: 110
Dirección Nacional Contra El Terrorismo (DINCOTE; terrorism and hijacking), tel: 475 2995.
Tourist Police (DIRTUR). In Lima and other tourist centers, tel: 01-460 1060 (24-hour emergency line).
Comisaría de Mujeres de Lima (Women's police station – Lima), tel: 427-9006 / 428-2700

View Peru & Signatures
Jiron Iquitos 1006, Dpto 100, Urbanización Cusco, Fideranda
Tel: USA 1 518 643 4205, UK 020 32399404 and worldwide: 084 232 205
www.disabledtravelperu.com

E

Electricity

Peru uses 220 volts, 60 cycles AC, except Arequipa which is on 50 cycles. The major hotels provide 110-volt outlets in bathrooms for the use of shavers only.

Embassies and consulates

Foreign embassies and consulates in Peru

Argentina
Av. Las Flores 326, San Isidro, Lima 27
Tel: (511) -441 4444/3065/3257;
http://eperu.cancilleria.gov.ar/

Australia
Av, La Paz 1049, Piso 10 Miraflores, Lima 18,
Tel: (511) 630 0500; http://peru.embassy.gov.au/lima/home.html

Bolivia
Los Castaños 235, San Isidro, Lima 27
Tel: (511) -440 2095; http://boliviaenperu.com/

Brazil
Av. José Pardo 850, Miraflores

Tel: (511) -512 0830; http://lima.itama raty.gov.br/es-es/

Canada
Bolognesi 228, Miraflores, Lima 18
Tel: (511) -319 3200; www.canada international.gc.ca/peru-perou/index. aspx?lang=spa

Chile
Av. Javier Prado Oeste 790, San Isidro
Tel: (511) -710 2211; http://chile.gob. cl/peru/en/

Colombia
Av Víctor Andrés Belaúnde 340 Of. 602, San Isidro Lima 27
Tel: (511) -201 9830; http://peru.emba jada.gov.co/

Ecuador
Las Palmeras 356, San Isidro
Tel: (511) -212 4161/5502/4171; http://peru.embajada.gob.ec/es/

Ireland (honorary consulate)
Av. Camino Real 390, Torre Central, Oficina 801, San Isidro, Lima 27
Tel: (511) 222 5252; www.dfa.ie/ embassies/irish-embassies-abroad/ south-america/peru/

South Africa
Víctor A. Belaúnde 147, Edificio Real 3, Of. 801, San Isidro
Tel: (511) -612 4848

UK
Torre Parque Mar (22nd Floor), Avenida José Larco 1301, Miraflores
Tel: (511)-617 3000; www.gov.uk/world/ organisations/british-embassy-peru

US
Av. La Encalada s/n, cuadra 17, Urb. Monterrico, Surco, Lima
Tel: (511)-618 2000; https://pe.us embassy.gov/
US Consulate, Cusco
Avenida El Sol 449 Office #201
Tel: 084-231 474

Peruvian embassies abroad
Australia
40 Brisbane Avenue, Ground Floor
Barton ACT 2600
Tel: (02)-6273 7351/2

☼ Heat of the sun

The tropical sun might feel very gentle, but it can burn you to a crisp. Ultraviolet rays are particularly powerful at high altitudes; wearing a brimmed hat as well as sunglasses, and using a high-factor sunscreen will all help protect you from the glare. High humidity dehydrates the body; drink plenty of liquid and add salt to your food.

---

www.embaperu.org.au
Canada
130 Albert Street, Suite 1901
Ottawa, Ontario K1P 5G4
Tel: (613)-238 1777
www.embassyofperu.ca

South Africa
200 Saint Patricks Rd, Muckleneuk Hill, 0183 Pretoria
Tel: (012)-440 1030

UK
52 Sloane Street, London SW1X 9SP
Tel: (020)-7235 3802
www.peruembassy-uk.com

US
1700 Massachusetts Avenue N.W., Washington D.C. 20036
Tel: (202)-833 9860; www.embassyof peru.org

Etiquette

Peruvians are polite and call each other *Señor* (Sir), *Señora* (Madam), or *Señorita* (Miss). Say *joven* to attract the attention of a young boy or young man.

Always greet someone with *buenos días* (good morning), *buenas tardes* (good afternoon/evening), or *buenas noches* (good night) before starting a conversation. Men shake hands when meeting for the first time and women usually kiss when they are introduced to men or women for the first time. Say *mucho gusto* (pleased to meet you) when you first meet someone. Men usually open doors for women or stand aside to let them go first.

Before starting a meal, wish others *buen provecho* (bon appétit). Toast others with *salud* – and you can also say this when someone sneezes.

H

Health and medical care

The most serious illnesses to guard against are **yellow fever** and **malaria**, which both occur in jungle areas of the North and South Amazon, and malaria on parts of the coast. Visitors are advised to consult their physician about anti-malarial drugs before leaving home. Malarial mosquitoes only bite at night, so always use a mosquito net when sleeping in jungle towns and keep covered up as much as possible between dusk and dawn. **Cholera** is not a great threat to tourists. It is

---

caused by the bacterium Vibrio cholerae; the main symptom is diarrhea and the best treatment is rehydration. Vaccination is possible, but the best protection is to take elementary hygiene precautions such as avoiding unclean water and raw or poorly cooked food (particularly seafood), and steering clear of dirty accommodations and swimming pools. UK health authorities warn there is a risk of **Zika virus** transmission in Peru. For up to date information consult the National Travel Health Network and Centre website (https:// travelhealthpro.org.uk/country/177/ peru#Other_risks).

Hepatitis A is caught by ingesting contaminated food or water. Be cautious about seafood; stick to bottled drinks, peeled fruit, and good-quality restaurants, thereby ensuring your standard of hygiene. Two shots taken six months apart should protect against Hepatitis A for 10 years (one shot works for six months).

A less serious and much more common condition for travelers in Peru is upset stomach and **diarrhea** – often caused by a change in diet and unclean water or utensils. Traveling itself places extra pressure on the immune system, so take it easy until you feel stronger. In most cases, the symptoms will improve after a day or so of fasting and drinking plenty of fluids (hot tea without milk is ideal). If the more serious condition of dysentery develops (ie any blood or pus in the stool), you should see a doctor.

Don't be surprised if your exultation at flying into Andean mountain cities is followed by a less pleasant sensation called *soroche* or **altitude sickness**. In most cases the symptoms are mild – fatigue, shortness of breath, slight nausea, and headache. The best prevention and cure is to lie down for a few hours upon arrival at your hotel and then slowly introduce yourself to physical activity. Coca tea, available in all highland hotels and restaurants, is also said to help. If it doesn't, medication (which among other things contains aspirin and caffeine) is available without prescription at pharmacies. If the symptoms are severe – vomiting, rapid irregular pulse, insomnia – take it very seriously and descend immediately to a lower altitude as it can be deadly (although this usually happens only to mountain climbers).

Travel insurance which covers the cost of an air ambulance should be taken out before you start your trip.

Medical services

Good hotels will have reliable doctors on call. The following clinics in Lima have 24-hour emergency service and an English-speaking staff member on duty:

Clínica Anglo Americana
Alfredo Salazar 350, San Isidro
Tel: (511)-616 8900, www.angloamericana.com.pe

Clínica Internacional
Av. Inca Garcilaso de la Vega 1420, Lima
Tel: (511)-619 6161, www.clinicainternacional.com.pe

Clínica Javier Prado
Av. Javier Prado Este 499, San Isidro
Tel: (511)-211 4141, www.clinicajavierprado.com.pe

Clínica San Felipe
Gregorio Escobedo 650, Jesús María, Lima
Tel: (511)-219 0000, www.clinicasanfelipe.com

Clínica Tezza
Av. El Polo 570, Monterrico, Surco
Tel: (511)-610 5070, www.clinicatezza.com.pe

Emergency Hospital Casimiro Ulloa
Av. Roosevelt 6355, San Antonio, Miraflores
Tel: (511)-204 0900
A recommended dental clinic is **Smiles Peru** (www.smilesperu.com), 575 Jose Pardo Avenue, Miraflores, Lima, tel: (511)-242 2152.

Internet

There are hundreds of internet cafés and telephone *cabinas* all over Peru where you can surf the internet and make cheap international phone calls. Wi-Fi has also become widespread in cafes, restaurants and hotels.

LGBTQ travel

Homosexuality is rarely openly talked about or revealed in Peru. Gay men are derisively called *maricón* or *mariposa* (butterfly), and lesbian women are barely heard of. The rainbow Inca flag should not be confused with the gay-friendly rainbow seen in other parts of the world. That said, there is a gay community, particularly in Lima, and information on gay venues in the city can be found at www.gayperu.pe (in Spanish). The same organization runs a travel agency operating tours to major tourist destinations in Peru: www.gayperutravel.pe.

Maps

The **Touring y Automóvil Club del Perú (TACP)**, Av. Trinidad Morán 698, Lince, Lima, tel: 611 9999, www.touringperu.com.pe (in Spanish), is the best source for maps and information. General maps are available from the **Instituto Geográfico Nacional** (www.ign.gob.pe), Av. Aramburú 1198, Surquillo, tel: 01-475 9960; Mon–Fri 8.30am–4.45pm. Maps and street plans can also be bought at kiosks and bookshops. Telefónica's Yellow Pages *(Páginas Amarillas)* includes street maps of Lima Metropolitana and Callao.

The tourist offices of iPeru (see page 314) give out good maps of Peru, Lima, and other cities for free. Bookshops, particularly Ibero Librerías (www.iberolibrerias.com) in Lima and Huancayo, stock useful driving maps of Peru.

Media

Peru has an enormous, unbridled, and ever-changing media scene. Newspapers and magazines – mostly of the tabloid variety – come and go, and there's a large television network with nine terrestrial channels and dozens of cable channels. TVs and satellite dishes are ubiquitous, even in the remotest settings, while radio is the medium of choice for local news. Panamericana is Peru's top TV and radio station (the radio found at 101.1FM on the dial).

Of the Peruvian print media, Lima-based *El Comercio* (www.elcomercio.pe; in Spanish) is the largest and most serious. *Expreso* (www.expreso.com.pe; in Spanish) is considered right-leaning and has a good listings section for goings-on in Lima. Another leading daily is the high-circulation sensationalist tabloid *La República* (in Spanish; http://larepublica.pe/). The weekly news magazine *Caretas* (www.caretas.com.pe; in Spanish) has excellent in-depth features on current affairs.

Outside the capital, there's the well-regarded *El Diario del Cusco* (www.diariodelcusco.com), the Arequipa-based weekly news magazine *El Búho*, (http://elbuho.pe) which is thought of as an independent voice for the nation, and a wide range of small regional papers.

For travelers, most of the better hotels have cable TV with English-language news networks. English-language newspapers are available in some news agencies in Lima and Cusco, but not always reliably. With the wide availability of internet connections, the web is your best bet for up-to-date news. The *Living in Peru* website (http://www.livinginperu.com) provides up to date information in English on anything regarding life in Peru including politics, economics, and travel.

Money

Since 1986 Peru has twice introduced a new currency to stop depreciation. In 1991 the nuevo sol (s/) replaced the shrinking inti at a ratio of 1 to 1 million. The annual inflation rate steadied during the 1990s after the hyperinflation of the 1980s.

There is no shortage of money-changing facilities in Lima, formal and otherwise – if you don't mind haggling on street corners. On the Plaza San Martín, in downtown Lima, hundreds of outdoor bankers run alongside the traffic – the rate is usually a little better than in the banks. It is legal to change with these *cambistas*, who generally wear a blue jacket and carry a calculator, and usually quite safe – although if you don't feel comfortable with it, there are plenty of alternatives. Banks will change your currency at the slightly inflated "official" rate, and good hotels have exchange services or will send a hotel courier to one of the *casas de cambio* for a better rate (remember to give him a tip). Travel agents accept payment in some foreign currencies and exchange small amounts.

◷ Calendar of festivals and holidays

January

January 1 New Year's Day (national holiday).
January 18 Official anniversary of the founding of Lima by the Spanish conquistador Francisco Pizarro on January 18, 1535.
End January *Festival de la Marinera*, Trujillo. Annual traditional dance competitions.

February

February 1–15 *Cruz de Chalpon*, Chiclayo. Handicraft and commercial fair in the nearby pilgrimage center of Motupe.
Early February. "La Mamita Candicha," the patron of Puno, is honored with folklore demonstrations. Thousands participate in the parades, dances, fireworks, and music of this important religious event.
Mid-February Carnival, Puno, Cajamarca, Ayacucho, and Huarás. Pre-Lent carnival is celebrated throughout Peru, but especially in these cities, with *La Pandilla* dancing and traditional festivities.

March/April

Early March *Fiesta de la Vendimia*, Ica. The grape harvest of the Ica Valley is celebrated with parades, dances, and revelry.
March Playa Rock Fest. A feast of the best Peruvian punk rock and ska at the Playa Conchan, about 40 minutes away from Lima.
March/April *Semana Santa* (Easter/Holy Week). Among the nationwide commemorations is the spectacular procession in Cusco in honor of *El Señor de los Temblores*, held on Holy Monday and Maundy Thursday. The people of Tarma make carpets of flowers to cover the streets for their evening processions. (Full-day holiday on Maundy Thursday and Good Friday).
Third week April National Contest of *Caballos de Paso*, Lima. This exhibition and contest in Mamacona, 30km (18 miles) south of Lima, involves horse breeders from the most important regions of Peru.

May

May 1 Labor Day and *San José* (St Joseph's Day) (national holiday).
May 2 *Cruz Velacuy*, Cusco. The crosses in all the churches of Cusco are veiled, and festivities take place.
May 2–4 *Las Alasitas*, Puno. Important exhibition and sale of miniature handicrafts.

June

First week Mountaineering Week in the Andes, particularly in Huaraz. The Callejón de Huaylas and the Cordillera Blanca provide the majestic settings for the National and International Ski Championships, as well as many other adventurous activities.
Mid-June Corpus Christi, Cusco. One of the most beautiful displays of religious folklore, the Procession of the Consecrated Host is accompanied by statues of saints from churches all over Cusco.
June 24 *Inti Raymi* (Festival of the Sun), Cusco. This ancient festival is staged at the Sacsayhuamán fortress, and involves Inca rituals, parades, folk dances, and contests. *San Juan* (St John's Day) is also celebrated throughout the Andes.
June 29 *San Pedro y San Pablo* (St Peter's and St Paul's Day; national holiday).
End of June Selvámonos. A music, craft and food festival (www.selvamonos.org) held in in the jungle of Oxapampa.

July

July 15–17 *La Virgen del Carmen*, Cusco. Festivities are held throughout the highlands and are especially colorful in Paucartambo, 255km (160 miles) from Cusco.
July 28–9 Peru's Independence celebrations (national holiday).

August

August 15 Arequipa Day, the city's most important annual event. Festivities include folkloric dances and handicraft markets, and climax with a fireworks display in the Plaza de Armas.
August 30 Santa Rosa de Lima (national holiday).

September

Sept–Oct Trujillo Spring Festival featuring spring parade, beauty queen contest, and the Peruvian Paso Horse contest.

October

October 8 Commemoration of the Battle of Angamos (national holiday).
October 7–20 *El Señor de Luren*, Ica. Thousands of pilgrims pay homage to the town patron, with the main procession on the 17th.
October 18, 19, and 28 *El Señor de los Milagros*, Lima. A massive procession in honor of Lima's patron saint, on the 18th.
October 19 Unu Urco Festival, Urcos and Calca (near Cusco). Ceremonies, Andean music, dancing, and parades.

November

November 1 *Día de Todos los Santos* (All Saints' Day; national holiday).
November 1–7 Puno Jubilee Week. Puno celebrates its founding by the Spanish, followed by a re-enactment of the emergence of the legendary founders of the Inca Empire, Manco Capac and Mama Ocllo, from the waters of Lake Titicaca. This week sees the best of Puno's folkloric festivities.
November 29 Zaña Week, Chiclayo. Week of celebrations for the foundation of Zaña include folklore shows, sporting events, and exhibitions of *Caballos de Paso*.

December

December 8 *La Concepción Inmaculada* (Immaculate Conception; national holiday).
December 24 Festival of *Santu Rantikuy*, Cusco. Andean toy and handicrafts fair in the main plaza.
December 24–5 Christmas (half-day national holiday on 24th, full day on 25th).

The Banco de Crédito and the Banco de la Nación are recommended for any international banking business, such as receiving US dollars from overseas. Ask for a *liquidación por canje de moneda extranjera* (cash in exchange for foreign currency).

It is convenient to carry some US cash as well as your travelers' checks, credit cards, or cash advance card (although Lima, Cusco, Arequipa, and Iquitos have every money-changing facility). It is not always possible to change checks, and cash dollars get a better rate, although you run the risk of theft. American Express will replace lost travelers' checks only in Lima.

Make sure that you don't carry more cash than your insurance policy covers you for, or you will be penalized for being under-insured in the event of a claim.

Local currency can be obtained using Visa, Cirrus, Plus, and Master-Card at the ATM machines of most banks, including Banco de Crédito, BBVA Continental, Banco de la Nación, Interbank, and Scotiabank.

Credit cards

Credit cards such as Diners Club, Visa, American Express, and MasterCard are accepted by good hotels and restaurants. There are branches of Diners, MasterCard, and Visa in Lima.

To report credit card loss in Lima, call:

Visa: 800-890 0623
Diners Club: 615-1111 option 1
MasterCard: 800-5 0587
American Express: 801-449-4019

Counterfeit money

Peru has become a hub of the global counterfeit money trade. Most of the fake cash churned out in clandestine printing shops takes the form of dollars and euros; however, the risk of being conned with phony nuevos soles is still something visitors should be aware of. The Central Bank recommends that you "look, touch, and turn" for the modern security features of Peruvian paper currency. These include a watermark of the main characters on the bills and circles that create a complete image, both features visible when held up to the light. Twist bills to see the color switch in a box below the circle, revealing the denomination, and below the coat of arms. Security threads with "Peru" and the bill's denomination run vertically, slightly off center. Among the coins, bi-metallic 2 and 5 soles coins were introduced in late 2010 with the hummingbird and frigate bird from the Nazca lines running across both metals, to make them harder to forge. Choose these where possible.

Tipping

At some of the smartest hotels and restaurants, service charges are sometimes included, and this will be stated on the bill. Otherwise tipping is up to the customer. Peruvians themselves rarely leave tips in restaurants, and tipping is not routinely expected, but you can leave a few soles. Tipping seems to be most customary in Cusco, where there are the most tourists. It's not customary to tip taxi drivers, but you should tip people who help you with your luggage. If you stay any length of time in a hotel, you can, if you are happy with the service, leave a tip for the people who have serviced your room. On the conclusion of trekking, climbing, and other outdoor adventure activities, it's usual to leave a generous tip for your guide.

O

Opening hours

In Lima office hours are Mon–Fri 9am–5pm with a lunch break at noon. Shops are generally open from 9 or 10am until about 8 or 9pm. Larger shopping centers open earlier and stay open later. Banks are generally open Mon–Fri 9am–6pm (and some until 7 or even 10pm). Weekend banking hours depend on the bank, although most are open on Saturday from 9am to 1pm. Outside Lima and the larger cities, shops and banks usually close for lunch between 12 or 1pm and 3.30 or 4pm. Money changers are on the streets, especially in Lima, almost 24 hours a day.

P

Photography

There are so many wonderful things and interesting-looking people to photograph in Peru, you'll want to just keep clicking. But do be respectful about photography and ask people before taking pictures of them, unless it's from a good distance. People usually oblige, often for a tip. Taking pictures of airports and military installations is prohibited. If you are shooting film, you can get this developed in most of the larger towns and cities, and most photographic shops and even hotels will download digital photos to disk for a fee. Take care to protect your camera from dust in the highlands in the dry season, and from the extreme humidity of the rainforest.

Postal services

The central Post Office in Lima, operated by Serpost (www.serpost.com.pe), at Jr. Camana no 157, opens Mon–Sat 9am–9pm and Sun 8am–4pm.

To have mail sent to you in Lima or any other city, it should be addressed, with your surname in capital letters, to Poste Restante, Lista de Correos, Correo Central, followed by the name of the city. Take your passport for identification when you go to collect it. There are branch post offices throughout Lima, including:

Airport office: Jorge Chávez International Airport; 24 hours.
Cercado de Lima: Avde la Republica 170; Mon–Sun 7am–3 pm and 3.30–11pm.
Miraflores: Av. Petit Thouars 5201; Mon–Sat 8am–8.30pm, Sun closed.

Courier services

DHL International
Calle 1, Mz A, Lt 6 Bocanegra, Callao Lima
Tel: 01-575 4433
www.dhl.com.pe

Federal Express
Pasaje Mártir José Olaya 260, Miraflores
Tel: 01-242 2280/242 16
www.fedex.com/pe

OLVA Courier
Av. Paseo de la República 1415, Miraflores
Tel: 01-714 0909 (ext. 4540)
www.olvacourier.com

SkyNet
Av. Benavides 4408, Santiago de Surco, Lima
Tel: 01-311 8800
www.skynetlim.com.pe

TNT International Express
Av. Libertadores 199, San Isidro
Tel: 01-222 0555 (Lima); Tel: 01-619 5900 (call center)
www.tnt.com

UPS
Av. de Ejército 2107, San Isidro
Tel: 01-264 0105
www.ups.com

World Courier
Av. Camino Real 390, Of. 1002, San Isidro
Tel: 01-442 8080
www.worldcourier.com

Public holidays

Peru has numerous national holidays, as well as some regional ones.

R

Religious services

Catholic services are held daily in larger churches and on Sundays in most smaller parishes. The conveniently located Iglesia de La Virgen Milagrosa in Miraflores, Lima, has regular daily services. Visitors of other Christian denominations will now find churches of most persuasions in Peru, but other religions are less well served.

S

Shopping

What to buy

In Lima, as well as in the many regional market places, the best quality and value lies in handcrafted products. This particularly applies to gold, silver, and copper work, as well as Peru's rich textile goods – such as alpaca garments and woven tapestries. Many tourists also take home reproductions of pre-Columbian ceramics, with gourds being a great favorite.

Visitors to the jungle may have the opportunity to purchase traditional handicrafts, including adornments (necklaces worn for tribal dances), utensils (baskets, food bowls, hunting bags), and weapons (bows, arrows, spears). However, never be tempted to buy skins, live animals, or arrows decorated with parrot feathers. In the Andes, this applies also to unlicensed vicuña fibers and trinkets made with condor feathers. This trade is largely illegal and has direct consequences in destroying wildlife populations.

Apart from *artesanías*, quality shopping goods can only be found in the commercial streets of Miraflores and San Isidro, where suppliers for international brands keep a limited stock at very high prices. South America isn't a region to look for bargains in electronics or cameras.

Where to shop

Each region has its own distinctive crafts, but if your time is limited, you'll find that many cultures are well represented in Lima. Two recognized centers of quality merchandise are El Mercado Artesanal on Av. Petit Thouars, Miraflores, and El Suche, Av. La Paz 646 also in Miraflores.

Markets

Outside Lima and Cusco, the best places to purchase crafts are usually cooperatives or outdoor markets. The latter offer the best bargains – and you are usually expected to bargain – although quality varies and one needs to be wary of pickpockets. The best ones in Lima are to be found on the first four blocks of Avenida Petit Thouars. There is also a pleasant artists' market with canvases of varying quality on Parque Kennedy in the heart of Miraflores.

Outside Lima, Pisac market is renowned for its woolen rugs, blankets, bags, and beautifully soft alpaca sweaters. The Sunday market in Huancayo is packed with stalls selling woven blankets and knitted jumpers, hats and bags, and is also known for its carved pumpkin gourds.

Depending on the size and vitality of the town, the markets may last only from pre-dawn to mid-morning once a week, or they may go on for days.

Student travelers

Full-time students traveling in Peru are eligible for many discounts if they produce their International Student Identity Card (ISIC). See the Peru section of the website (www.isic.org) for details of

☉ Fine alpaca

Alpaca products are well worth buying, as long as you are prepared to hand-wash them with great care. Vendors will often tell you their goods are made from alpaca "bebé." This does not mean baby alpacas, but refers to the wool taken from the throat of the animal, where it is at its finest and softest.

Most woolen jumpers sold as alpaca are usually a more hard-wearing mix of llama wool and synthetic fibers.

discounts on attractions in Peru and recommended points of interest for student travelers.

T

Telephones

There are public phone boxes on just about every corner in Lima, charging varying rates. You can call from these using coins, telephone cards, and in some cases credit cards. A disproportionately high number of phone boxes in Peru seem to swallow coins without letting you call, so it's better to use one of the many *locutorios* found in cities, towns, and even small villages throughout Peru. Here there is a series of phone booths for local, long-distance, and international calls, as well as calls to mobiles. Show the number you want to call and you will be directed to a glass-walled booth. Charges are calculated on the central computer, and you pay after you have made your calls. It's convenient, cheap, and private.

There are also mobile *locutorio* services in the street: people dressed in an apron bearing the logo of the mobile service provider offer calls which are charged by the minute. There are a variety of phone cards *(tarjetas telefónicas)* available from corner stores and supermarkets for cheap local, national, and international calls.

Mobile phones *(cellulares)* are ubiquitous in Peru, and signal coverage is good. SIM cards can be purchased at booths in the airport on arrival, or phone shops in major towns and cities. Alternatively, buy a new handset and SIM card: both the hardware and the calls are extremely cheap.

Calls from hotel phones range from reasonable to expensive. Check before you call – phone cards can sometimes be used in conjunction with hotel phones.

Telephone codes

Dial 103 for general information. The international code for Peru is 00 51. Below are the codes for the principal cities. You only need to include the area code when dialing between areas (long-distance calls).
Arequipa: 054
Ayacucho: 066
Cajamarca: 076

Chachapoyas: 041
Chiclayo: 074
Cusco: 084
Huancavelica: 067
Huancayo: 064
Huaraz: 043
Ica: 056
Iquitos: 065
Lima: 01
Piura: 073
Puerto Maldonado: 082
Puno: 051
Tacna: 052
Trujillo: 044
Tumbes: 072
Ucayali: 061

Time zones

Lima is five hours behind Greenwich Mean Time and therefore coincides with Eastern Standard Time in the US.

Toilets

Unfortunately, toilets in Peru leave much to be desired. Apart from in the smarter parts of Lima and at the main tourist attractions, it's rare to find public toilets. Outside these areas, you often have to use a restaurant or bus station toilet, and in smaller towns toilets are often of the squat variety. Carry your own toilet paper as this is rarely provided, but remember to dispose of it in the bin provided, as the drains are not built to cope with toilet paper. When trekking in areas where there are no drop toilets, dig a 20cm (8-inch) deep hole at least 100 meters (330ft) away from water and bury your waste. Burn toilet paper if you can.

Tourist information

Peru has an excellent tourist information infrastructure provided by iPeru. Their offices and information booths are in central locations in all the bigger towns and tourist attractions of Peru. iPeru staff provide general (though comprehensive) information, but cannot recommend particular companies' services. For this there are travel agencies in all the major tourist areas that can advise on activities and book hotels. The 24-hour number for enquiries is 01-574 8000. See also www.peru.info.
Lima: Jorge Chávez International Airport, main hall, tel: 01-574 8000.
Jorge Basadre 610, San Isidro, tel: 01-421 1627/1227.

Larcomar Entertainment Center, La Rotonda, nivel 2, Stand 211/212, Miraflores, tel: 01-234 0340.
Arequipa: Rodríguez Ballón Airport, 1st floor, main hall, tel: 054-444 564.
Portal de la Municipalidad 110, Plaza de Armas, tel: 054-223 265.
Ayacucho: Municipalidad de Huamanga (town hall), Plaza Mayor, tel: 066-318 305.
Coronel FAP Alfredo Mendívil Duarte Airport.
Chachapoyas: Jr. Ortiz Arrieta 582, Plaza Mayor, tel: 041-477 292.
Chiclayo: Siete de Enero 579, tel: 041-205 703.
Av. Juan Pablo Vizcardo y Guzmán s/n, Museo de Tumbas Reales de Sipán.
Cusco: Velasco Astete Airport, main hall, tel: 084-237 364.
Av. Pachacutec s/n, Of. 4 (Edificio INC), Machu Picchu, tel: 084-211 104.
Portal de Harinas 177, Plaza de Armas, tel: 084-252 974.
Huaraz: Pasaje Atusparia, Of. 1, Plaza de Armas, tel: 043-428 812.
Iquitos: Francisco Secada Vignetta Airport, main hall, tel: 065-260 251.
Centro de Iquitos, Calle Napo 161, tel: 065-236 144.
Puno: Calle Lima y Deustua (on the north corner of Plaza de Armas), tel: 051-365 088.
Tacna: San Martín 491, tel: 052-425 514.
Tumbes: Jr. Bolognesi 194, Municipalidad Provincial de Tumbes – Centro Cívico, tel: 979 968 897.

Websites

http://www.peru.travel/
Official Peru tourism website, including practical information for tourists.
www.peru-travel.net
Online hotel bookings, and an excellent range of articles on places of interest. In English.
www.andeantravelweb.com/peru
Full of useful information about tour companies, adventure activities, hotels, and the best destinations.
www.go2peru.com
Good travel planning website in English and Spanish with hotel, transport and flight information.
www.livinginperu.com
Local website geared at expats in Peru with up-to-date travel suggestions and news in English.
www.enperublog.com
Interesting blog about Peru's culture, history, news, and travel.
www.expatperu.com
A comprehensive expat guide to Peru with a good travel forum.

http://perudelights.com/
All about Peruvian food with lots of recipes and interesting descriptions of what to eat and drink during your trip.

Visas and passports

Visas are not required by citizens of most other South American countries, the EU, the US, Canada, Japan, South Africa, Australia, or New Zealand.

All visitors, however, must have a valid passport (and in some cases may be asked for evidence of return or onward travel). They are issued with an entry stamp (make sure you get it when traveling overland) and tourist card (Andean Immigration Card or Tarjeta Andina de Migración – TAM) on arrival. These are valid for 183 days (cannot be extended), and the card must be surrendered on departure. If you lose your tourist card, go to the Superintendencia Nacional de Migraciones, Av. España 734, Breña, Lima, tel: 200 1000; www.migraciones.gob.pe.

Weights and measures

The metric system is used to calculate distances and weights.

Women travelers

Apart from the usual precautions, lone female travelers can feel safe in Peru. Don't walk alone late at night in questionable areas, watch out for your handbag, and keep money in inside pockets or a body pouch. Peruvians are generally very polite, helpful, and respectful of women: you will be helped with bags and have doors held open for you. If you are traveling alone, the most common reaction amongst Peruvians is a welcoming and protective one. They may ask you if you're single or married, which is not meant to be any kind of advance, they are just intrigued to see a woman unaccompanied. If you do have to fend off unwanted advances, say *soy casada* (I'm married) or you could consider putting a ring on your left ring finger. You'll find feminine hygiene products in most supermarkets and chemists.

LANGUAGE

Understanding a little Spanish will help you get the most out of your stay in Peru. There are a few local variations of the European Spanish (castellano) familiar to many. An expression you will hear everywhere, and which is difficult to translate, is no más. Siga no más for example, means "Go ahead." Come no más means "Just eat it (It'll get cold/it's nicer than it looks, etc)." You will soon get the hang of it. There are also slight differences between the Spanish spoken along the coast, in the Andes, and in the Amazon region. However, Spanish spoken in Peru is for the most part quite clearly spoken, making this an excellent country to learn the language.

In the Andes, most indígenas speak Spanish, but you will hear Quechua (also spelled Kechwa) words that have crept into the language: wambras translates as "adolescents," and cuy means "guinea pig." Another indigenous language, Aymara, is spoken around Lake Titicaca.

Berlitz publishes an excellent Latin American Spanish Phrase Book and Dictionary, containing vocabulary and phrases for every situation.

It would be impossible for us to give a complete language guide here, but the following are some useful words, phrases, and tips that will hopefully ease understanding.

PRONUNCIATION

Vowels

a as in apple
e as in bed
i as in police
o as in got
u as in rude

Consonants

Consonants are approximately like those in English, the main exceptions being:

c is hard before **a**, **o**, or **u** (as in English), and is soft before **e** or **i**, when it sounds like **s** (as opposed to the pronunciation of **th** as in think used in Spain). Thus, censo (census) sounds like senso.

g is hard before **a**, **o**, or **u** (as in English), but where English **g** sounds like **j** – before **e** or **i** – Spanish **g** sounds like a guttural **h**. **g** before **ua** is often soft or silent, so that agua sounds more like awa, and Guadalajara like Wadalajara.

h is silent.

j sounds like a gutteral h.

ll sounds like y.

ñ sounds like ni, as in onion.

q is followed by u as in English, but the combination sounds like k instead of like kw. *¿Qué quiere usted?* is pronounced: Keh kee-ehr-eh oostehd?

r is normally rolled.

x between vowels sounds like a guttural h, e.g. in México or Oaxaca.

y alone, as the word meaning "and", is pronounced **ee**.

Note that **ch** and **ll** are each a separate letter of the Spanish alphabet; if looking in a phone book or dictionary for a word beginning with **ch**, you will find it after the final **c** entry. A name or word beginning with **ll** will be listed after the final **l** entry.

BASICS

yes sí
no no
thank you gracias
you're welcome de nada
okay está bien
please por favor
Excuse me (to get attention) ¡Perdón! ¡Por favor!

Excuse me (to get through a crowd) ¡Permiso!
Excuse me (sorry) Perdóneme
Wait a minute! ¡Un momento!
Can you help me? ¿Me puede ayudar?
Do you speak English? (formal) ¿Habla inglés?
Please speak more slowly Hable más despacio, por favor
Could you repeat that please ¿Podría repetírmelo, por favor?
I (don't) understand (No) entiendo
Show me the word in the book Muéstreme la palabra en el libro
I'm sorry Lo siento/Perdone
I don't know No lo sé
No problem No hay problema
Where is...? ¿Dónde está...?
I am looking for... Estoy buscando
That's it Eso es
Here it is Aquí está
There it is Allí está
Let's go Vámonos
At what time? ¿A qué hora?
late tarde
early temprano
yesterday ayer
today hoy
tomorrow mañana

GREETINGS

Hello ¡Hola!
good morning buenos días
good afternoon buenas tardes
welcome bienvenido
How are you? (formal/informal) ¿Cómo está?/¿Qué tal?
Very well Muy bien
And you? (formal/informal) ¿Y usted?/¿Y tú?
What is your name? ¿Como se llama?
My name is... Me llamo...
Mr/Miss/Mrs Señor/Señorita/Señora
Pleased to meet you ¡Mucho gusto!
I am British/American Soy británico(a)/norteamericano(a)
See you tomorrow Hasta mañana
See you soon Hasta pronto
See you later Hasta luego

Some basic Spanish comes in very handy when traveling in Peru.

goodbye *adiós*
good night *buenas noches*

TELEPHONE CALLS

The area code *El código de área*
Where can I buy telephone cards? *¿Dónde puedo comprar tarjetas telefónicas?*
May I use your telephone to make a local call? *¿Puedo usar su teléfono para hacer una llamada local?*
Of course you may *¡Claro!*
Hello (on the phone) *¡Hola!*
May I speak to...? *¿Puedo hablar con... [name], por favor?*
Sorry, he/she isn't in *Lo siento, no se encuentra*
Can he/she call you back? *¿Puede devolver la llamada?*
Yes, he/she can reach me at... *Sí, él/ella puede llamarme a* [number]
I'll try again later *Voy a intentar más tarde*
Can I leave a message? *¿Puedo dejar un mensaje?*
Please tell him/her I called *Por favor avisarle que llamé*
Hold on *Un momento, por favor*
Can you speak up, please? *¿Puede hablar más fuerte, por favor?*

FINDING YOUR WAY

Where is the lavatory (men's/women's)? *¿Dónde está el baño (de caballeros/de damas)?*
Where is the (tourist office)? *¿Dónde está la (oficina de turismo)?*
I am lost *Estoy perdido/a*

Is it near/far from here? *¿Está cerca/lejos de aquí?*
on the right *a la derecha*
on the left *a la izquierda*
straight ahead *derecho*
near *cerca de*
in front of *en frente de/frente de/frente a*
beside *al lado de*
above *arriba*
below *abajo*
behind *atrás de*
around *alrededor de*
in, on, at *en*
between *entre*
avenue *avenida (Av.)*
street *calle*
main street *calle principal*
corner *esquina (Esq.)*
building *edificio (Edif.)*
penthouse *PH – penthouse*
ground floor *PB – planta baja*
upper floor (of two) *PA – planta alta*
mezzanine *mezanina*
basement *sótano*
small pension *residencia (Res.)*
a block *una cuadra*
town square *plaza*
bank *banco*
post office *correos*
library *biblioteca*
town hall *ayuntamiento*
theater *teatro*
cinema *cine*
disco *discoteca/boliche*
sports ground *polideportivo*
stadium *estadio*
bus stop *parada de autobús*
bus station *estación de autobuses*
train station *estación de tren*
taxi stand *parada de taxi*
pharmacy *farmacia*
hospital *hospital*
police station *estación de policía*
hotel *hotel*
youth hostel *albergue*
camping *camping*
parking *playa de estacionamiento*

IN THE HOTEL

Do you have a vacant room? *¿Tiene una habitación disponible?*
I have a reservation *Tengo una reserva*
I'd like... *Quisiera...*
a single/double (with double bed)/a room with twin beds *una habitación individual (sencilla)/una habitación matrimonial/una habitación doble*
for one night/two nights *por una noche/dos noches*
with a sea view *con vista al mar*
Does the room have a private bathroom or shared bathroom? *¿Tiene la habitación baño privado o baño compartido?*
Does it have hot water? *¿Tiene agua caliente?*
Could you show me another room, please? *¿Puede mostrarme otra habitación, por favor?*
What time do you close (lock) the doors? *¿A qué hora se cierran las puertas?*
I would like to change rooms *Quisiera cambiar la habitación*
How much is it? *¿Cuánto cuesta?/¿Cuánto sale?*
Do you accept credit cards/travelers' checks/dollars? *¿Se aceptan tarjetas de crédito/ cheques de viajeros/dólares?*
What time is breakfast/lunch/dinner? *¿A qué hora es el desayuno/el almuerzo/la cena?*
Please wake me at... *Por favor despertarme a...*
Come in! *¡Pase!/¡Adelante!*

☉ The alphabet

Learning the pronunciation of the Spanish alphabet is a good idea. In particular, learn how to spell out your own name. Spanish has three letters in its alphabet that don't exist in English: the "ñ", the "ch", and the "ll".

a = *ah*
b = *bay*
c = *say*
ch = *chay*
d = *day*
e = *ay*
f = *effay*
g = *hay*
h = *ah-chay*
i = *ee*
j = *hotah*
k = *kah*
l = *ellay*
ll = *ell-yay*
m = *emmay*
n = *ennay*
ñ = *enyay*
o = *oh*
p = *pay*
q = *koo*
r = *erray*
s = *essay*
t = *tay*
u = *oo*
v = *oovay*
w = *oovay doe-blay*
x = *ek-kiss*
y = *ee gree-ay-gah*
z = *say-tah*

I'd like to pay the bill now, please *Quisiera cancelar la cuenta ahora, por favor*

IN THE RESTAURANT

I'd like to book a table *Quisiera reservar una mesa, por favor*
Do you have a table for...? *¿Tiene una mesa para...?*
breakfast *desayuno*
lunch *almuerzo*
dinner *cena*
I'm a vegetarian *Soy vegetariano(a)*
May we have the menu? *¿Puede traernos la carta/el menú?*
wine list *la carta de vinos*
What would you recommend? *¿Qué recomienda?*
fixed-price menu *el menú fijo*
special of the day *plato del día/sugerencia del chef*
waiter *mozo*
What would you like to drink? *¿Qué quiere tomar?*
a bottle of... *una botella de...*
a glass of... *un vaso/una copa de...*
Is service included? *¿Incluye el servicio?*

MENU DECODER

Entremeses/Primer Plato (First Course)

sopa/crema *soup/cream soup*
sopa de ajo *garlic soup*
sopa de cebolla *onion soup*
ensalada mixta *mixed salad*
ensalada de palta con tomate *avocado and tomato salad*
pan con ajo *garlic bread*

La carne (Meat)

crudo *raw*
jugoso(a) *rare*
término medio *medium rare*
a punto *medium*
bien hecho *well done*
a la brasa/a la parrilla *charcoal grilled*
a la plancha *grilled*
al horno *baked*
ahumado(a) *smoked*
alas *wings*
albóndigas *meat balls*
asado(a)/horneado(a) *roasted*
ave *poultry*
cerdo/chancho/puerco *pork*
chivito *goat*
chorizo *Spanish-style sausage*
chuleta *chop*

☉ Money

money *dinero*
credit card *tarjeta de crédito*
bank *banco*
cash machine/atm *cajero automático*
currency exchange bureau *casa de cambio*
I'd like to change some dollars/pounds into soles *Quisiera cambiar unos dólares/libras esterlinas por soles*
I'd like to change some traveler's cheques *Quisiera cambiar unos cheques de viajero*
What is the exchange rate? *¿Cuál es la tasa de cambio?*
How much commission do you charge? *¿Cuál es la comisión?*

conejo *rabbit*
cordero *lamb*
costillas *ribs*
empanizado(a) *breaded*
frito(a) *fried*
guisado(a) *stewed*
hamburguesa *hamburger*
hígado de res *beef liver*
jamón *ham*
lechón *piglet*
lengua *tongue*
lomito *tenderloin*
milanesa *breaded and fried thin cut of meat*
morcilla *blood sausage*
muslo *thigh*
pato *duck*
pavo *turkey*
pechuga *breast*
pernil *leg of pork*
piernas *legs*
pollo *chicken*
rebozado(a) *batter-fried*
salchichas/panchos *sausages or hot dogs*
ternera *veal*
chicharrón de pollo *chicken cut up in small pieces and deep fried*

Pescado/Mariscos (Fish/Seafood)

almejas *clams*
anchoa *anchovy*
atún *tuna*
bacalao *cod*
calamares *squid*
camarones *shrimp*
cangrejo *crab*
centolla *kingcrab*
langosta *lobster*
langostinos *prawns*
lenguado *sole or flounder*

mariscos *shellfish*
mejillones *mussels*
mero *grouper, sea bass*
ostras *oysters*
pulpo *octopus*
salmón *salmon*
sardinas *sardines*
trucha *trout*
vieiras *scallops*

Vegetales (Vegetables)

ajo *garlic*
alcaucil *artichoke*
arvejas *peas*
batata *sweet potato*
berenjena *eggplant/aubergine*
brócoli *broccoli*
calabaza *pumpkin or yellow squash*
cebolla *onion*
chauchas *green beans*
choclo *corn (on the cob)*
coliflor *cauliflower*
espárrago *asparagus*
espinaca *spinach*
hongos, champiñones *mushrooms*
lechuga *lettuce*
papa *potato*
pepino *cucumber*
pimentón *green (bell) pepper*
porotos *Lima beans*
puerro *leeks*
remolacha *beets/beetroot*
repollo *cabbage*
zanahorias *carrots*
zapallito *green squash*
zapallito largo *zucchini/courgette*
zapallo *yellow squash*

Frutas (Fruit)

banana *banana*
cereza *cherry*
ciruela *plum*
dátil *date*
durazno *peach*
frambuesa *raspberry*
fresa *strawberry*
guayaba *guava*
higo *fig*
lima *lime*
limón *lemon*
mandarina *tangerine*
manzana *apple*
melón *cantelope/melon*
naranja *orange*
palta *avocado*
papaya *papaya*
parchita *passion fruit*
pera *pear*
piña *pineapple*
plátano *green banana*
pomelo *grapefruit*
sandía *watermelon*
uvas *grapes*

Bebidas (Drinks)

agua mineral con gas/sin gas *carbonated/non-carbonated mineral water*
café *coffee*
cerveza *beer*
chocolate caliente *hot chocolate*
coca *cola*
jugo de fruta *fruit juice*
jugo de naranja *orange juice*
limonada *lemonade*
mate de coca *coca-leaf tea*
pisco *wine brandy*
té (con leche) *tea (with milk)*
té manzanilla *camomile tea*
tónica con ginebra *gin and tonic*
vino blanco *white wine*
vino tinto *red wine*
vodka *vodka*
whisky *whisky*

Miscellaneous

arroz *rice*
azúcar *sugar*
empanada *savory turnover*
fideos *spaghetti*
huevos (revueltos/fritos/hervidos) *eggs (scrambled/fried/boiled)*
helado *ice cream*
manteca *butter*
margarina *margarine*
mermelada *jam*
mostaza *mustard*
pan *bread*
pan integral *wholewheat bread*
pan tostado/tostadas *toast*
pimienta negra *black pepper*
queso *cheese*
sal *salt*
salsa picante *spicy sauce*
sandwich *sandwich*
panceta *bacon*
tortilla *omelette*

SHOPPING

I'd like... *Quisiera...*
I'm just looking *Sólo estoy mirando, gracias*
How much is this? *¿Cuanto cuesta/sale?*
Do you have it in another color? *¿Tiene en otro color?*
Do you have it in another size? *¿Tiene en otro talle/número?*
smaller/larger *más pequeño/más grande*
trousers *pantalones*
skirt *falda*
dress *vestido*
shirt *camisa*
jacket *chaqueta*
suit *traje*

coat *abrigo*
underpants *calzoncillos*
socks *calcetines*
shoes *zapatos*
hat *sombrero*
swimsuit *traje de baño*
I would like some of that... *Quisiera un poco de eso...*
I would like a kilo of... *Quisiera un kilo de...*
I would like half a kilo of... *Quisiera un medio kilo de...*
A little more/less *Un poco más/menos*
That's enough/no more *Está bien/nada más*
Would you like anything else? *¿Quiere algo más?*
expensive *caro*
cheap *barato*
clothes store *tienda de ropa*
bookstore *librería*
hairdressers *peluquería*
bakery *panadería*
cake shop *pastelería*
butcher's *carnicería*
fishmonger's *pescadería*
green grocery *verdulería*
market *mercado*
supermarket *supermercado*
grocery store *tienda de abarrotes*
newsstand *kiosco*
shopping center *centro comercial*

TOURIST ATTRACTIONS

tourist office *oficina de turismo*
postcard *postal*
handicrafts *artesanía*
market *mercado*
winery *bodega*
museum *museo*
art gallery *sala de exposiciones*
indigenous community *comunidad indígena*
old town *ciudad vieja*
ruins *ruinas*
bridge *puente*
tower *torre*
monument *monumento*
statue *estatua*
fort *castillo/fuerte*
palace *palacio*
chapel *capilla*
church *iglesia*
cathedral *catedral*
convent *convento*
park *parque*
playground *parque infantil*
botanical garden *jardín botánico*
zoo *zoológico*
cable car *teleférico*
viewpoint *mirador*
hill *cerro*
mountain *montaña*

(mountain) peak *pico*
stream *quebrada*
river *río*
lagoon *laguna*
lake *lago*
sea *mar*
Pacific Ocean *Océano Pacífico*
island *isla*
glacier *glaciar*
beach *playa*
hot springs *aguas termales*
swimming pool *piscina*

AIRPORT/TRAVEL AGENCY

airport *aeropuerto*
airline *línea aérea*
flight *vuelo*
arrivals *llegadas*
departures *salidas*
connection *conexión*
customs and immigration *aduana y migraciones*
travel/tour agency *agencia de viajes/de turismo*
ticket *boleto pasaje*
I would like to purchase a ticket for... *Quisiera comprar un boleto (pasaje) para...*
When is the next/last flight/departure for...? *¿Cuándo es el próximo/último vuelo/para...?*
How long is the flight? *¿Cuánto tiempo dura el vuelo?*
What time do I have to be at the airport? *¿A qué hora tengo que estar en el aeropuerto?*
Is the tax included? *¿Se incluye el impuesto?*
What is included in the price? *¿Qué está incluido en el precio?*
departure tax *el impuesto de salida*

☉ Colors

light *claro*
dark *oscuro*
red *rojo*
blue *azul*
sky blue *celeste*
green *verde*
yellow *amarillo*
brown *marrón*
cream *color crema*
beige *beige*
gray *gris*
orange *naranja*
pink *rosado*
purple *púrpura*
white *blanco*
black *negro*
silver *plateado*
gold *dorado*

I would like a seat in first class/business class/tourist class *Quisiera un asiento en primera clase/ejecutivo/clase de turista*
I need to change my ticket *Necesito cambiar mi boleto*
lost-luggage office *oficina de reclamos*
on time *a tiempo*
late *atrasado*

TRANSPORTATION

luggage, bag(s) *equipaje, valija(s)*
bus *colectivo* (urban), *micro* (long-distance)
bus stop *parada (de colectivo/micro)*
bus terminal *terminal de pasajeros*
first class *primera clase*
second class *segunda clase*
tourist class *clase de turista*
one-way ticket *boleto de ida*
round-trip, return ticket *boleto de ida y vuelta*
What time does the bus/boat/ferry [leave/return?] *¿A qué hora [sale/regresa] el autobús/la lancha/el ferry?*
Which is the stop closest to...? *¿Cuál es la parada más cerca de...?*
Is this seat taken? *¿Está ocupado este asiento?*
Could you please advise me when we reach/the stop for...? *¿Por favor, puede avisarme cuando llegamos a/a la parada para...?*
Is this the stop for...? *¿Es ésta la parada para...?*
Next stop please *La próxima parada, por favor*
subway *metro/subterráneo*
train station *estación de tren*
platform *el andén*
sleeping car *coche cama*
taxi *taxi*
car *coche/automóvil*
car rental *alquiler de coche*
dock for small boats/large boats *embarcadero/muelle*
ferry *ferry*
sailboat *velero*
yacht *yate*
ship *barco*

DRIVING

Where can I rent a car? *¿Dónde puedo alquilar un coche?*
Is mileage included? *¿Está incluido el kilometraje?*
comprehensive insurance *seguros comprensivos*
spare tire *goma de repuesto*
jack *gato*

⊙ Numbers

1 *uno*		100 *cien*	
2 *dos*		101 *ciento uno*	
3 *tres*		200 *doscientos*	
4 *cuatro*		300 *trescientos*	
5 *cinco*		400 *cuatrocientos*	
6 *seis*		500 *quinientos*	
7 *siete*		600 *seiscientos*	
8 *ocho*		700 *setecientos*	
9 *nueve*		800 *ochocientos*	
10 *diez*		900 *novecientos*	
11 *once*		1,000 *mil*	
12 *doce*		2,000 *dos mil*	
13 *trece*		10,000 *diez mil*	
14 *catorce*		100,000 *cien mil*	
15 *quince*		1,000,000 *un millón*	
16 *dieciséis*		2,000,000 *dos millones*	
17 *diecisiete*		first *primer(o)/a*	
18 *dieciocho*		second *segund(o)/a*	
19 *diecinueve*		third *tercer(o)/a*	
20 *veinte*		fourth *cuart(o)/a*	
21 *veintiuno*		NOTE	
25 *veinticinco*			
30 *treinta*			

21 *veintiuno*
25 *veinticinco*
30 *treinta*
40 *cuarenta*
50 *cincuenta*
60 *sesenta*
70 *setenta*
80 *ochenta*
90 *noventa*

NOTE
In Spanish, in numbers, commas are used where decimal points are used in English and vice versa. For example:
English > Spanish
$19.30 > $19,30
1,000 m > 1.000 m
9.5 % > 9,5 %

emergency triangle *triángulo de emergencia*
Where is the registration document? *¿Dónde está el carnet de circulación?*
Does the car have an alarm? *¿El coche tiene alarma?*
a road map *un mapa vial*
a city map *plano de la ciudad*
How do I get to...? *¿Cómo se llega a...?*
Turn right/left *Gire a la derecha/izquierda*
at the next corner/street *en la próxima esquina/calle*
Go straight ahead *Siga derecho*
You are on the wrong road *Esta no es la calle*
Please show me where I am on the map *Por favor, indíqueme dónde estoy en el mapa*
Where can I find...? *¿Dónde hay...?*
Where is the nearest...? *¿Dónde está el/la... más cerca?*
How long does it take to get there? *¿Cuánto tiempo lleva para llegar?*
driver's license *licencia de conducir/manejar*
service/gasoline station *gasolinera/estación de servicio*
I would like to fill the tank *Quisiera llenar el tanque*
My car won't start *Mi coche no arranca*

My car is overheating *Mi coche está recalentando*
My car has broken down *Mi coche se rompió/no anda*
tow truck *una grúa*
Where can I find a car repair shop? *¿Dónde hay un taller mecánico?*
Can you check the...? *¿Puede revisar/chequear...?*
There's something wrong with the... *Hay un problema con...*
gasoline *gasolina*
diesel *diesel*
oil *aceite*
water *agua*
air *aire*
lubricant *lubricante*
brake fluid *líquido de frenos*
light bulb *bombita*
trunk *maletín*
hood *capó*
door *puerta*
window *ventana*

ROAD SIGNS

autopista *freeway*
bajada/subida peligrosa *dangerous downgrade/incline*
calle flechada/de una sola mano *one-way street*

⊘ Days of the week

Note that the Spanish form takes a lower-case initial letter.
Monday *lunes*
Tuesday *martes*
Wednesday *miércoles*
Thursday *jueves*
Friday *viernes*
Saturday *sábado*
Sunday *domingo*

calle sin salida *dead-end street*
carril derecho *right lane*
carril izquierdo *left lane*
carretera *highway, road*
cede el paso *yield/give way*
circunvalación *by-pass road/ringroad*
conserve su carril *do not change lanes*
conserve su derecha *keep to the right*
cruce de ferrocarril (sin señal) *railway crossing (without signal)*
despacio *slow*
desvío *detour*
distribuidor *freeway interchange*
doble vía *two-way traffic*
enciende luces en el túnel *turn on lights in the tunnel*
encrucijada *crossroads*
entrada prohibida *no entry*
estacionamiento *parking lot*
fuera de servicio *not in service*
gomería *tire repair shop*
hundimiento *sunken road*
intercomunal *interconnecting freeway between two close towns*
lomo de burro/reductor de velocidad/obstáculos en la vía/muros en la vía/policía acostada *speed bump(s)*
no estacione/prohibido estacionar *no parking*
no gire en U *no U-turn*
no hay paso/vía cerrada *road blocked*
no pare *no stopping here*
no toque la bocina *no horn honking*
¡ojo! *watch out!*
pare *stop*
paso de ganado *cattle crossing*
paso de peatones *pedestrian crossing*
peaje *toll booth*
peligro *danger*
pendiente fuerte, curva fuerte *steep hill, sharp curve*
rotonda *traffic circle/roundabout*
resbaladizo al humedecerse *slippery when wet*
ruta *highway*
salida *exit*
semáforo *traffic light*
sin salida *no exit*
sólo tránsito local *local traffic only*

tome precauciones *caution*
un solo carril *single lane*
velocidad controlada *speed controlled or restricted*
vía en reparación/en recuperación *road under repair*
zona de construcción *construction zone*
zona de derrumbes *landslide zone*
zona de niebla (neblina) *fog zone*
zona de remolque *tow zone*
zona escolar *school zone*
zona militar *military zone*

EMERGENCIES

Help! *¡Socorro! ¡Auxilio!*
Stop! *¡Pare!*
Watch out! *¡Cuidado! ¡Ojo!*
I've had an accident *He tenido un accidente/Sufrí un accidente*
Call a doctor *Llame a un médico*
Call an ambulance *Llame una ambulancia*
Call the... *Llame a...*
...police *la policía* (for minor accidents)
...transit police *la policía de tránsito* (for traffic accidents)
the fire brigade *los bomberos*
This is an emergency, where is a telephone? *Esto es una emergencia. ¿Dónde hay un teléfono?*
Where is the nearest hospital? *¿Dónde queda el hospital más cercano?*
I want to report an assault/a robbery *Quisiera reportar un asalto/un robo*
Thank you very much for your help *Muchísimas gracias por su ayuda*

HEALTH

shift duty pharmacy *farmacia de turno*
hospital/clinic *hospital/clínica*
I need a doctor/dentist *Necesito un médico/dentista (odontólogo)*
I don't feel well *Me siento mal*
I am sick *Estoy enfermo(a)*
It hurts here *Duele aquí*
I have a headache/stomachache/cramps *Tengo dolor de cabeza/de estómago/de vientre*
I feel dizzy *Me siento mareado(a)*
Do you have (something for)...? *¿Tiene (algo para)...?*
cold *resfrío*
flu *gripe*
cough *tos*
sore throat *dolor de gargantua*
diarrhea *diarrea*

constipation *estreñimiento*
fever *fiebre*
heartburn *acidez*
aspirin *aspirina*
antiseptic cream *crema antiséptica*
insect/mosquito bites *picaduras de insectos/mosquitos*
insect repellent *repelente contra insectos*
sun block *bloqueador solar*
toothpaste *pasta de dientes*
toilet paper *papel higiénico*
tampons *tampones*
condoms *condones*

MONTHS OF THE YEAR

Note that the Spanish form takes a lower-case initial letter.
January *enero*
February *febrero*
March *marzo*
April *abril*
May *mayo*
June *junio*
July *julio*
August *agosto*
September *septiembre*
October *octubre*
November *noviembre*
December *diciembre*

SEASONS

spring *primavera*
summer *verano*
fall (autumn) *otoño*
winter *invierno*

TIME

Note that times are usually followed by *de la mañana* (in the morning) or *de la tarde* (in the afternoon). Transport schedules are often given using the 24-hour clock.
at nine o'clock *a las nueve*
at a quarter past ten *a las diez y cuarto*
at half past one/one thirty *a la una y media*
at a quarter to two *a las dos menos cuarto*
at midday/noon *a mediodía*
at midnight *a medianoche*
it is five past three *son las tres y cinco*
it is twenty-five past seven *son las siete y veinticinco*
it is ten to eight *son las ocho menos diez*
in five minutes *en cinco minutos*
does it take long? *¿tarda mucho?*

GENERAL

The novels of Peru's high-profile writer and former presidential candidate, Mario Vargas Llosa, provide an interesting insight into the country's psyche. **Aunt Julia and the Scriptwriter, Captain Pantoja and the Special Service** – which have also been made into movies – and **The Time of the Hero** are among the most easily readable. **The Green House** is set in Peru's Amazon, and **Death in the Andes** explores the effects of terrorism on various rural communities. Vargas Llosa has also tackled foreign subjects, including **The Feast of the Goat** on the Trujillo dictatorship in the Dominican Republic, and a late 19th-century uprising in Brazil in **The War of the End of the World**.

A World for Julius: A Novel, by Alfredo Bryce Echenique. The best-known Peruvian author after Vargas Llosa, his most famous novel portrays Lima in the 1950s through the eyes of a boy, from the lower to the upper classes and fusing humor with moral criticism of a racist oligarchy in decay.

Eight Feet in the Andes, by Dervla Murphy. Describes Murphy's extraordinary journey from Cajamarca to Cusco.

The Dancer Upstairs, by Nicholas Shakespeare. A fascinating account of Shining Path leader Abimael Guzmán's final attempt to avoid capture.

Inca Kola, by Matthew Parris. Entertaining account of backpacking in Peru.

Touching the Void, by Joe Simpson. Gripping account of an ill-fated ascent of Siula Grande.

Exploring Cusco, by Peter Frost. Comprehensive coverage of the Cusco region by a longtime resident. Frost's **Machu Picchu Historical Sanctuary** makes for a beautiful companion piece.

Martín Chambi: 1920–1950, by Martín Chambi. A collection of pictures by Peru's most famous photographer.

The White Rock, An Exploration of the Inca Heartland, by Hugh Thomson. How the lost cities of the Incas have been rediscovered.

The Bridge of San Luis Rey, by Thornton Wilder. First published in 1927, it netted its US author a Pulitzer Prize. The novelist includes historic Peruvian figures in his analysis of fate and the human will tied to the collapse of an Inca rope suspension bridge.

The Peru Reader: History, Culture, Politics, by Orin Starn, Carlos Degregori, Robin Kirk (eds). A collection of essays and extracts that gives a portrait of Peru's social history through the 20th century.

Turn Right at Machu Picchu, by Mark Adams. The wonderfully told story of the author's quest to retrace the steps of Hiram Bingham, the legendary discoverer of Machu Picchu.

Eat Smart in Peru: How to Decipher the Menu, Know the Market Foods and Embark on a Tasting Adventure, by Joan Peterson. A helpful guide to navigating the wealth of tastes in Latin America's most exciting cuisine.

⊘ Send Us Your Thoughts

We do our best to ensure the information in our books is as accurate and up-to-date as possible. The books are updated on a regular basis using local contacts, who painstakingly add, amend and correct as required. However, some details (such as telephone numbers and opening times) are liable to change, and we are ultimately reliant on our readers to put us in the picture.

We welcome your feedback, especially your experience of using the book "on the road". Maybe you came across a great bar or new attraction we missed.

We will acknowledge all contributions, and we'll offer an Insight Guide to the best letters received.

Please write to us at:
**Insight Guides
PO Box 7910
London SE1 1WE**

Or email us at:
hello@insightguides.com

HISTORY

Corrupt Circles: A History of Unbound Graft in Peru, by Alfonso Quiroz. A unique and in-depth investigation that tracks Peru's history of corruption and sets the standard for similar research in Latin America.

Chavin: and the Origins of Andean Civilization, by Richard Burger (ed.). A thorough study by British archeologists of one of Peru's most fascinating pre-Inca cultures.

In Search of an Inca, by Alberto Flores Galindo. Famous Peruvian historian Galindo's take on 500 years of Andean history and the Inca's impact on the regional inhabitants' identity.

The Incas and Their Ancestors, by Michael E. Moseley. Fascinating research into how the Inca Empire flourished.

The Ancient Kingdoms of Peru, by Nigel Davies. Peru's ancient civilizations, from the Moche to the Incas.

Antisuyo, by Gene Savoy. Fascinating book, long out of print, by a man with an incredible nose for lost cities.

Lost City of the Incas, by Hiram Bingham. Classic account of Bingham's explorations. Outdated theories, but a great read.

The Conquest of the Incas, by John Hemming. Excellent, encyclopedic account of the fall of the Inca Empire. Extremely readable style, brings the conquest of Peru to life. Hemming has also written a coffee-table book called **Monuments of the Incas**, with black-and-white photography by Edward Ranney. Both are classic introductions to understanding Peru.

Everyday Life of the Incas, by Ann Kendall. A comprehensive description of life in Peru before the conquest, recommended by John Hemming.

The Incas: New Perspectives, by Gordon F. McEwan. This accessible book offers interpretations of Inca culture, religion, and politics.

Bourbon Peru, 1750–1824, by John Robert Fisher. The Spanish Crown's attempt at reforming a weakened empire and Peru's reluctant march to independence in an accessible historical description.

The Last Days of the Incas, by Kim MacQuarrie. Captivating account of the conquest written by an Emmy-award winning author and anthropologist. A fine, more contemporary alternative or complement to Hemming's book.

Peru: Society and Nationhood in the Andes, by Peter Klarén. A balanced overview of Peruvian history from before the Incas to the return of democracy.

The Shining Path: A History of the Millenarian War in Peru, by Gustavo Gorriti. The distinguished Peruvian journalist who covered the terrorist uprising since the late 1970s offers the critically acclaimed, best English-language account of the rise of the violent guerrilla.

The Fujimori File: Peru and Its

President 1990–2000, by Sally Bowen. A UK reporter's balanced and very readable account of the controversial presidential strongman and a long-running bestseller in Peru itself.

Voice and Vote: Decentralization and Participation in Post-Fujimori Peru, by Stephanie L. McNulty. A thoughtful study of democracy in Peru.

AMAZON JUNGLE

The Cloud Forest, by Peter Matthiesson. Account of travel on the Amazon and through the cloud forest of Peru.

Birds of Peru: Revised Edition, by Thomas S. Schulenberg et al. The definitive, abundantly illustrated guide to one of the world's most important birding destinations.

At Play in the Fields of the Lord, by Peter Matthiesson. Matthiesson's novel of uncontacted tribes and missionaries set in the department of Madre de Dios.

The Jivaro: People of the Sacred Waterfall, by Michael Harner. A celebrated ethnography of the head-shrinking Shuar in northeast Peru.

The Wizard of the Upper Amazon, by Ralph Lamb. His true account of a boy captured by natives in northern Peru and his apprenticeship as a shaman.

Neotropical Rainforest Mammals: A Field Guide, by Louise Emmons. A popular guide to 315 species in the Amazon rainforest, including 195 maps in its revised, second edition.

OTHER INSIGHT GUIDES

Insight Guides cover nearly 200 destinations, providing information on culture and all the top sights, as well as superb photography. *Insight Guide: South America* covers the whole subcontinent, from Colombia to Tierra del Fuego. Other Insight Guides on South America include: Argentina, Brazil, Chile and Easter Island, and Ecuador and the Galápagos.

CREDITS

INSIGHT GUIDE CREDITS

Distribution
UK, Ireland and Europe
Apa Publications (UK) Ltd;
sales@insightguides.com
United States and Canada
Ingram Publisher Services;
ips@ingramcontent.com
Australia and New Zealand
Woodslane; info@woodslane.com.au
Southeast Asia
Apa Publications (SN) Pte;
singaporeoffice@insightguides.com
Worldwide
Apa Publications (UK) Ltd;
sales@insightguides.com
**Special Sales, Content Licensing and
CoPublishing**
Insight Guides can be purchased in
bulk quantities at discounted prices.
We can create special editions,
personalised jackets and corporate
imprints tailored to your needs.
sales@insightguides.com
www.insightguides.biz

Printed in China by CTPS

All Rights Reserved
© 2018 Apa Digital (CH) AG and
Apa Publications (UK) Ltd

First Edition 1991
Eighth Edition 2018

Every effort has been made to provide
accurate information in this
publication, but changes are
inevitable. The publisher cannot be
responsible for any resulting loss,
inconvenience or injury. We would
appreciate it if readers would call our
attention to any errors or outdated
information. We also welcome your
suggestions; please contact us at:
hello@insightguides.com

www.insightguides.com

Editor: Helen Fanthorpe
Author: Maciej Zglinicki
Head of Production: Rebeka Davies
Update Production: Apa Digital
Picture Editor: Tom Smyth
Cartography: original cartography
Berndtson & Berndtson, updated by
Carte

CONTRIBUTORS

This new edition was commissioned
and edited by **Helen Fanthorpe**. It was
updated by **Maciej Zglinicki**, a Latin
American specialist who has traveled
extensively in the region. It builds on
earlier editions produced by **Nick
Caistor**, **Mary Dempsey**, **John Forrest**,
Peter Frost, **Jane Holligan**, **Stefan

Küffner**, **Kim MacQuarrie**, **Lynn
Meisch**, **Julia Meyerson**, **Gabi Mocatta**,
Robert Randall, **Mike Reid**, **Katherine
Renton**, **Michael Smith**, **Simon Strong**,
Lesley Thelander, **Betsy Wagen-
hauser**, **Barry Walker**, **Adriana von
Hagen**, and **Diana Zileri**. The index was
compiled by **Penny Phenix**.

ABOUT INSIGHT GUIDES

Insight Guides have more than 45
years' experience of publishing high-
quality, visual travel guides. We
produce 400 full-colour titles, in both
print and digital form, covering more
than 200 destinations across the
globe, in a variety of formats to meet
your different needs.
   Insight Guides are written by local
authors, whose expertise is evident in
the extensive historical and cultural

background features. Each destination
is carefully researched by regional
experts to ensure our guides provide
the very latest information. All the
reviews in **Insight Guides** are
independent; we strive to maintain an
impartial view. Our reviews are
carefully selected to guide you to the
best places to visit, so you can be
confident that when we say a place is
special, we really mean it.

Legend

City maps

- Freeway/Highway/Motorway
- Divided Highway
- Main Roads
- Minor Roads
- Pedestrian Roads
- Steps
- Footpath
- Railway
- Funicular Railway
- Cable Car
- Tunnel
- City Wall
- Important Building
- Built Up Area
- Other Land
- Transport Hub
- Park
- Pedestrian Area
- Bus Station
- Tourist Information
- Main Post Office
- Cathedral/Church
- Mosque
- Synagogue
- Statue/Monument
- Beach
- Airport

Regional maps

- Freeway/Highway/Motorway (with junction)
- Freeway/Highway/Motorway (under construction)
- Divided Highway
- Main Road
- Secondary Road
- Minor Road
- Track
- Footpath
- International Boundary
- State/Province Boundary
- National Park/Reserve
- Marine Park
- Ferry Route
- Marshland/Swamp
- Glacier
- Salt Lake
- Airport/Airfield
- Ancient Site
- Border Control
- Cable Car
- Castle/Castle Ruins
- Cave
- Chateau/Stately Home
- Church/Church Ruins
- Crater
- Lighthouse
- Mountain Peak
- Place of Interest
- Viewpoint

INDEX

A

accommodations
Gran Hotel Bolívar (Lima) 154
Hacienda San Vicente
(Cajamarca) 180
home-stays 294
Hotel Libertador Trujillo
(Trujillo) 163
jungle lodges 213, 220, 222
Laguna Seca (Cajamarca) 181
Manu Lodge 221
Accommodations 306
Acevedo, Fernando 228
activities 117
climbing and trekking 8, 10,
117, **118**, 123, 185, 188, 192,
249, 277, 285
freshwater fishing 202, 220,
272, 293
horseback riding 117, 124
kayaking 8, 117, 222, 228, 249
marlin fishing 170
mountain bike rentals 123
mountain biking 8, 117, 123
paragliding 117, 124, 157
rafting 8, 117, 125, 228
sandboarding 122, 236
skiing and paraskiing 185
snowboarding 185
spectator sports 228
surfing 8, 117, 122, 170
windsurfing 231
Acurio, Gastón 112
addresses 306
admission charges 306
agriculture 22, 81, 87, 88, 156,
190, 210, 240, 243, 250, 289
coffee 115
corn 190
dairy farms 175
Hacienda La Colpa 182
potatoes 88, 113
sugar 167
wild Brazil nuts 222, 223
Aguas Verdes 170
Alegría, Ciro
El Mundo Es Ancho y Ajeno (The
World is Wide and Alien) 163
La Serpiente de Oro (The
Serpent of Gold) 163
alluvions 185
Altiplano 291
Alva, Dr Walter 169
Amantaní island 10
Amaru, Tupac 56
Amazon 21, 80, 125, 139
deforestation 208
pharmaceutical exploitation 95
recommended reading 322
riverboat trips 214, 305
Amazon Animal Orphanage 213
Amazon Center for
Environmental Education and
Research 220

Amazon Conservatory of Tropical
Studies (ACTS) 215
Andahuaylas 74
Andahuaylillas 271
Andes 8, 19, 22, 31, 81, 79, 125
Animal Orphanage and
Pilpintuwasi Butterfly Farm
213
archeology 57, 248. *See*
also historic sites
visiting digs in progress 179
architecture 243, 245, 257
Arequipa 22, 23, 122, 123, 125,
139
Basilica Catedral of Arequipa
244
Calle Jerusalén 244
Casa de Goyeneche 246
Casa del Moral 245
Casa Ricketts 245
Complejo Cultural Chaves la
Rosa 245
festivals and events 248
Iglesia de San Francisco 247
La Compañía 244
Monasterio de la Recoleta 247
Monasterio de Santa Catalina
246
Museo de Arte Contemporáneo
247
Museo Histórico Municipal
247
nightlife 248
Museo Santuarios Andinos 11,
248
Plaza de Armas 244
restaurants 248
art and crafts 81, 291, 293
Artesanías del Perú 100
basketry 100
engraved pumpkin gourds 200
fine art 253
gold and silver 97, 98
jewelry 98
metalwork 34, 35
pottery 34, 35, 94, 97, **101**
retablos 100
School of Cusco 253, 259
shopping for 97, 98, 99, 100,
158, 181, 200, 201, 216, 258,
313
textiles 94
textiles and knitwear 33, 34, 97,
99, 294
Aspero 31
Atahualpa 44, 47, **48**, 175, 177,
180
Ayacucho 9, 197
Arco de San Francisco de Asis
198
Casona Boza y Solis 200
Casona Jáuregui 199
Casona Vivanco 199
Catedral A, Nuestra Señora de
las Nieves 198

Iglesia de San Francisco de
Paula 199
Instituto Nacional de Cultura
199
Museo Hipólito Unanue 199
Museo Joaquín López Antay 199
Museo Mariscal Cáceres 199
Santa Ana 200
Santo Domingo church 199
Semana Santa celebrations 10
shopping 200
Templo de la Compañía 198
Ayllón, Eva 107

B

Baca, Susana 107
Baños Intihuatana 201
beaches 21
Lima 158
north coast 169, 170
south coast 228, 231, 239, 240
Belaúnde Terry, President
Fernando 66, 69, 248
Bingham, Hiram 57, 257, 278
Bolívar, Simón 63, 147, 162
Boquerón del Diablo 228
border crossings 170
Brea Tarpits 170
budgeting for your trip 306
business travelers 306

C

caballitos de totora (reed boats)
167
Cabanaconde 122
Cabo Blanco 122, 170
Cáceres, Andrés 199
Cajamarca 9, 63, 99, **175**
accommodations 176, 181
Baños del Inca 8, 180
carnival 177
Catedral Santa Catalina 176
ceramics 181
Cerro Apolonia 180
Complejo Belén 177
El Cuarto del Rescate (Ransom
Room) 175, 177
Hacienda San Vicente 180
Iglesia San Francisco 176
Museo de Arte Religioso 176
Museo Etnográfico y de
Arqueología 179
nightlife 180
Pinacoteca 179
Plaza de Armas 176
Restaurante Salas 176
restaurants 176
Teatro Cajamarca 177
transportation to 175
Cajamarquilla 35
Cajatambo 121
Caleta La Cruz 170
Callao 64

Callejón de Conchucos 121
Callejón de Huaylas 10, 121, 125, **185**
Calle, Luis Felipe 248
Camaná 239
camping 170
Campos Ríos, Victor 177
Candelabro 231, 232
Cañón de Cotahuasi 22, 117, 122, 123, 250
Cañón del Colca 22, 122, 123, 124, 125, **249**
Cañón del Pato 185
Cantalloc Aqueducts 239
Caral 161
Caraz 189
Castilla, President Ramón 107, 203
Catac 187
Catacaos 98
Central Sierra 197
Cerro Blanco 236
Chachapoyas 19, 122, 182
Chan Chan 19, 37, 139, 163, **166**
Chancos 189
Chauchilla 172, 239
Chavín 193
Chavín de Huantar 33, 168, 186, **191**
Chicama 122
Chiclayo 19, 167
    Mercado de Brujos (Witchcraft Market) 169
children 306
Chincha 23
    Fiesta Negra 107, 229
    Fiestas Patrias 229
    Hacienda San José 229
Chincha Alta 228
Chinchero 272
Chiquián 121
Chivay 249
    hot springs 8
Choquequirao 120
Chosen Women 41, 262
Chucuito 295
    Iglesia Santo Domingo 296
    La Asunción 296
churches
    architecture 252
    Basilica Catedral of Arequipa (Arequipa) 244
    Capilla de la Merced (Huancayo) 203
    Catedral A, Nuestra Señora de las Nieves (Ayacucho) 198
    Catedral (Cusco) 258
    Catedral de San Juan Evangelista (Lima) 149
    Catedral (Pisco) 230
    Catedral San Antonio (Huancavelica) 202
    Catedral San Carlos Borromeo (Puno) 291
    Catedral Santa Catalina (Cajamarca) 176
    Catedral Santa María (Trujillo) 163
    Complejo Belén (Cajamarca) 177
    El Triunfo (Cusco) 260

Iglesia de la Merced (Cusco) 263
Iglesia de la Merced (Lima) 153
Iglesia de La Merced (Trujillo) 164
Iglesia de San Agustín (Trujillo) 164
Iglesia de San Blas (Cusco) 261
Iglesia de San Francisco (Arequipa) 247
Iglesia de San Francisco (Cusco) 264
Iglesia de San Francisco de Paula (Ayacucho) 199
Iglesia de San Francisco (Huánuco) 204
Iglesia de San Pedro (Lima) 153
Iglesia de Santa Clara (Cusco) 264
Iglesia de Santa Teresa (Cusco) 264
Iglesia de Santo Domingo (Lima) 152
Iglesia La Asunción (Juli) 296
Iglesia San Cristóbal (Huánuco) 204
Iglesia San Francisco (Cajamarca) 176
Iglesia San Francisco (Trujillo) 163
Iglesia Santo Domingo (Chucuito) 296
Iglesia Santo Domingo (Cusco) **261**
Jesuit church (Andahuaylillas) 271
La Asunción (Chucuito) 296
La Compañía (Arequipa) 244
La Compañía de Jesús (Cusco) 252, 263
La Compañía (Trujillo) 165
La Merced (Ica) 234
Monasterio de San Francisco (Lima) 151
San Francisco (Huancavelica) 202
San Francisco (Ica) 234
San Juan Bautista (Juli) 296
San Pedro (Juli) 296
Santa Clara (Trujillo) 164
Santa Cruz (Juli) 296
Santiago Apóstol (Pomata) 296
Santo Domingo (Ayacucho) 199
Santo Domingo (Huancavelica) 202
Santuario y Monasterio de las Nazarenas (Lima) 153
Templo de la Compañía (Ayacucho) 198
Cipriani, Archbishop Juan Luis 83
climate **307**, 22, 23, 88, 117, 289
    El Niño 22, 23, 35, 69, 232, 233
    Lima microclimate 146
    south coast 232
cloud forest. See jungle, rainforest an cloud forest
Coastal Desert 19, 21, 227, 240
coca 60, 61, 80, **88**, 178, 210
    Coca-Cola 178
Cochas Chico 200, 203

Colca Canyon. See Ca—n del Colca
Colpa de Guacamayos 222
conservation 23
Copacabana (Bolivia) 296
Cordillera Blanca 120, 123, 124, 185
Cordillera Huayhuash 121, 192
Cordillera Huaytapallana 203
Cordillera Negra 185
Cordillera Occidental 197
Cordillera Urubamba 124
Cotahuasi Canyon 125. See Cañón de Cotahuasi
Cousteau, Jacques-Yves 290
Covered Ones 67
credit cards 312
crime 85, 166, 170, 188, 241, 273, 292, 304, **307**
    cocaine industry 178, 210
    cocaine-related violence 178
    in Lima 150
    smuggling of antiquities 173
    tourist police 308
Cruz del Cóndor 250
Cumbemayo 182
Cusco 19, 40, 41, 19, 52, 53, 54, 118, 123, 124, 139, 219, 269
    airport transportation 303
    Calle Hatunrumiyoc 260
    Catedral 258
    Cross Keys Pub 265
    Cusco Visitor Ticket 257, 272
    El Triunfo church 260
    festivals 266
    Iglesia de la Merced 263
    Iglesia de San Blas 261
    Iglesia de San Francisco 264
    Iglesia de Santa Clara 264
    Iglesia de Santa Teresa 264
    Iglesia Santo Domingo **261**
    Inti Raymi (Festival of the Sun) 9, 108, 270
    La Compañía de Jesús 252, 263
    Museo de Arte Precolombino 265
    Museo de Arte Religioso 253
    Museo de Arte Religioso del Arzobispado 261
    Museo de Arte Religioso, Merced 263
    Museo de Arte y Monasterio de Santa Catalina 262
    Museo de Historia Natural 263
    Museo Inka 264
    nightlife 261, 265
    Nuestro Señor de los Temblores (Our Lord of the Earthquakes) 109
    Planetarium Cusco 265
    Plaza de Armas 99, 252, 258
    Plaza San Francisco 263
    restaurants 265, 266
    South American Explorers' Club 118
    Twelve-Angled Stone 261
Cusi, Titu 56
customs and immigration formalities. 304. See also visas and passports
customs regulations 308

D

dance. *See* music and dance
Darwin, Charles 64
de Almagro, Diego 48, 51, 55, 257
de Croix, Teodoro 62
de la Gasca, Pedro 55
de la Mar, President José 64
de la Vega, Garcilaso 146, 260
de Orellana, Francisco 92
de San Martín, General José 63, 147
de Soto, Hernando 50
de Toledo, Francisco 59, 61
de Valverde, Friar Vicente 49
disabled travelers 308
driving 304
  Carretera de Huallanca 185
  Panamericana highway 139
  road conditions 87, 304
  Trans-Oceanic highway 119
Durand, Óscar 201

E

earthquakes 23, 79, 146, 149, 164, 185
  of 1650 257
  of 1664 234
  of 1687 230
  of 2002 244
  of 2007 230, 231, 233
economy 64, 66, 69, 71, 72, 73, 74, 81, 82
  black market 85
  US free-trade treaty 84
education 79, 82, 156
Eiffel, Gustave 212, 239
electricity 308
Elías, Domingo 235
El Mirador 188
El Señor de Sipán tomb 169
embassies and consulates 308
emergencies 308
environmental issues 192
  alternative energy 181
  animal product goods 215
  conservation 22, 223
  destruction of the rainforest 208
  ecological awareness 211
  illegal hunting 128
  water pollution 125
Escuela Cusqueña. *See* art and crafts, School of Cusco
Espíritu Pampa 57
etiquette 309

F

Ferrañave
  Museo Sicán 169
festivals and events 108, **311**
  adventure sports festival (Lunahuaná) 228
  at Marcahuasi 204
  Carnival 108
  carnival (Cajamarca) 177
  El Señor de los Milagros procession (Lima) 108, 153
El Señor de Luren festival (Ica) 234
Festival de la Marinera (Trujillo) 107, 165
Festival de la Primavera (Trujillo) 165
Fiesta de las Cruces (Huancayo) 203
Fiesta de la Vendimia 233
Fiesta de la Vendimia (Lunahuaná) 228
Fiesta Internacional de la Vendimia (Ica) 234
Fiesta Negra (Chincha) 107, 229
Fiestas Patrias 108
Fiestas Patrias (Chincha) 229
foundation anniversary (Arequipa) 248
  in Callejón de Huaylas 190
  in Cusco 266
  in Huánuco 204
  in the Central Sierra 198
  Inti Raymi (Cusco) 108, 264, 270
  La Virgen de la Candelaria 108
  Nuestro Señor de los Temblores (Cusco) 109
  on Taquile island 298
  Puno Week (Puno) 292
  saints' days 89
  Virgen de la Candelaria feast (Puno) 291
Fitzcarrald, Carlos 212, 223
food and drink 10, **111**, 169
  Arequipeña beer 250
  Cartavio rum 167
  cheese 175
  corn beer (chicha) 89, 190
  food markets 10
  guinea pig 33, 114
  mate de coca 115
  pachamanca 202
  pisco 228, 233
  pisco sour 115, 229
  ponche (punch) 200
  regional specialties 213, 216, 248
  wine industry 115, 228, 233, 240
fossils 232
Fujimori, President Alberto 70, 75
further reading 321

G

García, President Alán 69, 74, 84
gas 23, 94
  Camisea pipelines 95
geography and geology 19, 79, 117
Gocta waterfall 183
gold 49, 91, 98
Granda Zúñiga, Julio 240
Gran Pajatén 57
Gran Sapososa 37
Grau, Admiral Miguel 170
guano 64, 65, 232
Guzmán, Abimael 71, 197

H

Hacienda La Colpa 182
Haya de la Torre, Víctor Raúl 66, 162
health 79, **309**
  altitude sickness 115, **118**, 190
  herbal remedies 169, 211
  Medical services 310
  street food hazards 146
  sulfur water treatments 236
  traditional healers 170
  traditional healing ceremonies 168, 211
Hemingway, Ernest 170
Hemming, John
  The Conquest of the Incas 49, 280
Herradura 122
Heyerdahl, Thor 57
historic sites 161
  along the Inca Trail 277
  Aspero 31
  Baños Intihuatana 201
  Cajamarquilla 35
  Candelabro 231, 232
  Cantalloc Aqueducts 239
  Caral 161
  Chan Chan 19, 37, 139, 163, **166**
  Chauchilla 172, 239
  Chavín de Huantar 33, 186, **191**
  Choquequirao 120
  Chucuito temple 296
  Colla burial chullpas 19
  Cumbemayo 182
  El Señor de Sipán tomb 169
  Espíritu Pampa 57
  Gran Pajatén 57
  Gran Sapososa 37
  Huaca del Dragón 166
  Huaca de los Reyes 32
  Huaca el Brujo 167
  Huaca La Esmeralda 166
  Huaca Pucllana (Lima) 158
  Huacas del Sol y de la Luna 35, 166
  Huari 202
  Huaricoto 33
  Huchuy Cusco 120
  Kuélap 19, 37, 57, **181**, 183
  Laguna de los Cóndores 57
  Machu Picchu 19, 45, 57, 117, 119, 139, 168, 257, 273, 274
  Marca Huamachuco 35
  Monte Peruvia (Purunllacta) 57
  Moray 42
  Moxeke-Pampa de las Llamas 32
  Nazca lines 19, 34, 139, **236**
  Ollantaytambo 273
  Pachacámac 146, 227
  Paracas 172, 232
  Paraíso 31
  Paredones 239
  Pikillacta 35, 271
  Pisac 272
  Puca Pucara 270
  Qenko 270
  Rumicolca 271

Sacsayhuamán 45, 53, 54, **269**
Santuario Warivilca 203
Sechín 32, 161
Sicán 36
Sipán 35, 169
Tambo Colorado 233
Tambo Machay 271
Templo de las Manos Cruzadas (Kotosh) 204
Tipón 271
Toro Muerto 125, 249
Túcume 169
Ventanillas de Otuzco 182
Vilcashuamán 201
Wari 35
Willkawain 188
history 31, 69, 91
  1996 hostage crisis 73
  ancient civilizations 31
  Chachapoyas culture 37
  Chavín culture 33, 191
  Chimú culture 36, 37
  colonial era 59
  Ecuadorean hostilities 71
  Inca culture 37, 37, 47, 255, 289
  independence 63, 162
  Moche culture 23, 35
  Nazca culture 34
  Paracas culture 232
  recommended reading 321
  Sicán culture 36
  Spanish conquest 19, 39, 91, 256
  Wari culture 35
  War of the Pacific (1879–83) 22, 65, 147
horses
  caballos de paso 165
  paso breed 124
hotels. See accommodations
hot springs 119, 120, 189, 249
  Baños del Inca (Cajamarca) 180
Huaca del Dragón 166
Huaca de los Reyes 32
Huaca el Brujo 167
Huaca La Esmeralda 166
Huacas del Sol y de la Luna 35, 166
Huallaga Valley 178
Huamán Poma de Ayala, Felipe 103, 105
Huancavelica 202
  Catedral San Antonio 202
  San Francisco 202
  Santo Domingo 202
Huancayo 99, 203
  Capilla de la Merced 203
  Museo del Colegio Salesiano 203
  Sunday market 200
  Torre Torre 203
Huanchaco 100, 122, 167
Huánuco 204
  festivals and events 204
  Iglesia de San Francisco 204
  Iglesia San Cristóbal 204
Huaraz 118, 120, 123, 125, **186**
  accommodations 187
  earthquake of 1970 186

Museo Arqueológico de Ancash 187
  nightlife 187
  restaurants 187
  shopping 187
  street food 187
  transporation to 186
Huaricoto 33
Huari (Wari) 35, 202
Huaro 271
Huascar 44, 48
Huascarán 8
Huayllapa 192
Huayna 44
Huchuy Cusco 120
Huiñay Huayna 278, 287
Humala, Antauro 74
Humala, Ollanta 74
human rights issues 73
Humboldt Current 23, 35

I

Ica 23, 233
  Bodega El Carmelo 233
  Bodega El Catador 233
  Bodega La Caravedo 233
  El Señor de Luren 234
  Fiesta Internacional de la Vendimia 234
  La Merced 234
  Las Dunas 236
  Museo Cabrera 236
  Museo Regional 232
  Museo Regional Adolfo Bermúdez Jenkins 235
  San Francisco 234
  Vista Alegre 233
Inca Trail 117, 118, 119, 274, **277**, 281
  daily trekker limits 278
industry 66, 69
infrastructure 139, 147
International Explorers' Club 238
Internet 310
Intipunku pass 278
Iquitos 139, 209, 212
  Belén 213
  Plaza de Armas 212
Islas Ballestas
  boat trips to 9, 231

J

Jauja 52, 204
Jorge Chávez International Airport 303
Juanita the Ice Maiden 248
Juli 296
  Iglesia La Asunción 296
  San Juan Bautista 296
  San Pedro church 296
  Santa Cruz church 296
Juliaca 290
jungle, rainforest and cloud forest 8, 19, 21, 22, 93, 131, 139, 179.
  See also Amazon
  climate 23
  deforestation 208
  hardwood extraction 92
  illegal logging 95

K

Kiteni 219
Kosok, Paul 34, 237
Kotosh
  Templo de las Manos Cruzadas 204
Kuélap 37, 57, **181**, 183

L

Lago Parón 189
Lago Quistacocha 213
Lago Sandoval 223
Lago Umayo 295
Lago Valencia 223
Lago Yarinacocha 216
Laguna Calcacocha 186
Laguna Churup 188
Laguna de Huacachina 236
Laguna de los Cóndores 57
Lagunas de Llanganuco 189
Lake Titicaca 10, 21, 99, 100, 139, 168
  boat rentals 293
  boat trips 295, 305
  Bolivian islands 297
  islands 293
  transportation to 290, 291
  Yavari steamship 293
Lamay 120
Lambayeque 63
  Museo Brüning 98, 169
  Museo Tumbas Reales de Sipán 169
language 315, 19, 21, 40, 45, 66, 79, 80, 93
  pronunciation 315
  quipus 45
  Summer Institute of Linguistics (SIL) 94
  useful words and phrases 315
La Oroya 65
La Perrichola 153
La Pimentel 169
Lares 120
Lares pass 123
Las Pocitas 170
Lee, Vincent 45
Leimebamba 122
LGBTQ travel 310
Lima 53, 54, 61, 81, 97, 123, 139
  airport shuttle bus 303
  Alameda de los Descalzos 153
  Avenida Nicolás de Piérola 148
  Avenida Petit Thouars 158
  Barranco 159
  beaches 158
  boat trips 159
  cafés 158
  Callao 159
  Casa de Osambela 152
  Catedral de San Juan Evangelista 149
  Chinatown 154
  Chorrillos 147, 158
  Circuito Mágico del Agua 154
  Club de la Unión 150
  Club Nacional 155

Costa Verde 158
Desamparados Station 151
El Señor de los Milagros
    procession 9, 153
Enrico Poli 157
Fuente Mágica 154
Gran Hotel Bolívar 154
Huaca Pucllana 158
Iglesia de la Merced 153
Iglesia de San Pedro 153
Iglesia de Santo Domingo 152
Jirón de la Unión 154
Jirón Ocoña 155
La Casa del Oidor 151
La Herradura beach 158
La Punta 159
L'Eau Vive Restaurant 154
Miraflores 98, 100, 147, 148,
    158
Monasterio de los Descalzos
    (Monastery of the Barefoot
    Friars) 153
Monasterio de San Francisco
    151
Municipalidad de Lima (City
    Hall) 150
Museo Amano 158
Museo de Arte de Lima 155
Museo de Arte Italiano 155
Museo de la Inquisición y del
    Congreso 154
Museo de la Nación 32, 33,
    157
Museo de Oro 157
Museo Larco 101, 157
Museo Nacional de Arqueología,
    Antropología e Historia 194
Museo Nacional de Arqueología,
    Antropología e Historia 157
Museo Taurino 153
nightlife 158, 159
orientation 303
Palacio de Gobierno
    (Government Palace) 150
Palacio del Arzobispo
    (Archbishop's Palace) 150
Palacio Torre Tagle 153
Parque de La Reserva 154
Parque de las Leyendas zoo 155
Parque Kennedy 158
Paseo Colón 148
Paseo de Aguas 153
Plaza de Acho 153
Plaza Mayor 148, **149**
Plaza San Martín 99, 148, 154
population 21
Puente de Los Suspiros 159
Puente de Piedra (Stone Bridge)
    152
Real Felipe Fort 159
restaurants 158
Rímac 152
San Isidro 157
Santuario de Santa Rosa 152
Santuario y Monasterio de las
    Nazarenas 153
shantytowns 148, 156
shopping 80, 158
Surquillo No. 1 market 146
transportation 304
Villa El Salvador 156

Llamac 192
llamas 33, 250, 270
    trekking with 194
Llanganuco 189
Los Frailones (The Friars) 182
Los Incas. See Urubamba
Lunahuaná 125, 228
    adventure sports festival 228
    Fiesta de la Vendimia 228

M

Macará 170
Machu Picchu 19, 45, 57, 117, 119,
    139, 168, 257, 273
    trains to 274, 281
Madre de Dios 94, 219, 223
Málaga pass 123
Manco 40, 41, 49, 53, 255, 269
Máncora 8, 122, 170
mangrove swamps 170
Mantaro Valley 203
maps 310
Maras plateau 124
Marca Huamachuco 35
Marcahuasi 168, 197, 204
**Martínez de Compañón y Bujanda,
    Don Baltasar Jaime** 62
Matarani 240
Matthiesson, Peter
    Cloud Forest 219
media 310
Melville, Herman 145
Méndez, Chico 211
Mina, Mauro 228
mining 60, 65, 75, 94, 95, 192
    copper 197
    gold 23, 223
    illegal gold mining 221
    silver 202
Misti volcano 139
Mollendo 240
money 310
Monte Peruvia (Purunllacta) 57
Monterrey 189
Montesinos, Vladimiro 72, 73, 74
Moquegua 240
    Plaza de Armas 240
Morales Bermúdez, Francisco
    66
Moray 42, 273
mountaineering. See activities,
    climbing and trekking
Mount Ausangate 119
Mount Huanacauri 120
Mount Huascarán 21, 121, 123,
    188
Mount Humantay 119
Mount Mama Simona 120
Mount Nevado Lasuntaysuyo 204
Mount Nevado Pisco 123
Mount Picol 120
Mount Salcantay 120
Mount Senca 120
Mount Siulá Grande 124
Mount Yerupajá 121, 192
movies 321
    Fitzcarraldo 212
Moxeke-Pampa de las Llamas 32
Moyano, María Elena 156
Murra, John 81

museums and galleries
    Casa de los Leones (Trujillo)
        163
    Casona Jáuregui (Ayacucho)
        199
    Centro Andino de Tecnología
        Tradicional y Cultural de las
        Comunidades de
        Ollantaytambo (CATCCO)
        Museum 274
    Enrico Poli (Lima) 157
    Manuel Chávez Ballón Museum
        (Machu Picchu) 281
    Museo Amano (Lima) 158
    Museo Arqueológico (Huaraz)
        187
    Museo Brüning (Lambayeque)
        98, 169
    Museo Cabrera (Ica) 236
    Museo Carlos Dreyer (Puno)
        292
    Museo Catedralicio (Trujillo)
        163
    Museo de Arqueología (Trujillo)
        164
    Museo de Arte Contemporáneo
        (Arequipa) 247
    Museo de Arte de Lima (Lima)
        155
    Museo de Arte Italiano (Lima)
        155
    Museo de Arte Precolombino
        (Cusco) 265
    Museo de Arte Religioso
        (Cajamarca) 176
    Museo de Arte Religioso (Cusco)
        253
    Museo de Arte Religioso del
        Arzobispado (Cusco) 261
    Museo de Arte Religioso,
        Merced (Cusco) 263
    Museo de Arte y Monasterio de
        Santa Catalina (Cusco) 262
    Museo de Historia Natural
        (Cusco) 263
    Museo de la Inquisición y del
        Congreso (Lima) 154
    Museo de la Nación (Lima) 32,
        33, 157
    Museo del Colegio Salesiano
        (Huancayo) 203
    Museo del Juguete (Trujillo)
        164
    Museo de Oro (Lima) 157
    Museo Etnográfico y de
        Arqueología (Cajamarca)
        179
    Museo Ferroviario (Tacna) 241
    Museo Hipólito Unanue
        (Ayacucho) 199
    Museo Histórico Municipal
        (Arequipa) 247
    Museo Inka (Cusco) 264
    Museo Joaquín López Antay
        (Ayacucho) 199
    Museo Julio C. Tello (Paracas)
        232
    Museo Larco (Lima) 101, 157
    Museo Mariscal Cáceres
        (Ayacucho) 199
    Museo Militar (Lima) 159

Museo Nacional de Arqueología, Antropología e Historia (Lima) 157, 194
Museo Naval Miguel Grau (Piura) 170
Museo Pedro de Osma (Lima) 159
Museo Regional Adolfo Bermúdez Jenkins (Ica) 235
Museo Regional (Ica) 232
Museo Sicán (Ferrañave) 169
Museo Taurino (Lima) 153
Museo Tumbas Reales de Sipán (Lambayeque) 169
Museo Zoológico (Trujillo) 165
Pinacoteca (Cajamarca) 179
Pinacoteca (Puno) 292
religious art collection (Monasterio de San Francisco, Lima) 151
Sechín museum 161
Musho 188
music and dance 103, 266
  African influences 107
  chica 106
  dance 107
  El Alcatraz dance 229
  El Cóndor Pasa 103
  folk dances 291
  Hispanic influences 104
  the tondero 169
  traditional music 103
  traditional music revival 105
  wayno (huayno) 105

N

national anthem 235
national parks and reserves 211
  Bahuaja-Sonene 94
  Cordillera Azul 179
  Cordillera Huayhuash 192
  Huascarán 190
  Junín 204
  Lagunas de Mejía 240
  Manu 22, 139, 208, 219, 220
  Otishi 94
  Pacaya-Samiria 215
  Paisajística Nor Yauyos-Cochas 228
  Pampa Galeras 127, 239
  Pampas de Río Heath 223
  Paracas 230
  Salinas y Aguada Blanca 250
  Tambopata 23, 220, 221
Nazca 34, 139, 236
  Maria Reiche Center 237
Nazca lines 19, 34, 139, **236**
  flights over 238
Nazca Valley 34
Neruda, Pablo
  The Heights of Machu Picchu 283
nightlife
  Cajamarca 180
  Huaraz 187
  Lima 158, 159
North Amazon 207
north coast 161
northern sierra 175

O

Ocucaje
  Ocucaje Winery 234
Offenbach, Jacques
  La Périchole 67
oil 23, 75, 94, 95
Ollantaytambo 273
  Centro Andino de Tecnología Tradicional y Cultural de las Comunidades de Ollantaytambo (CATCCO) Museum 274
opening hours 312
Ortiz, Friar Diego 56
Orton, James 295

P

Pacasmayo 122
Pachacámac 146, 227
Pachacutec 39, 41, 44, 255, 280
Pacllon 192
Pampa de Nazca. See Nazca lines
Pampa Galeras reserve 127
Paniagua, Valentín 74
Paracas 63
  Museo de Sitio Paracas Julio C. Tello 232
  necropolis 232
Paraíso 31
Paredones Ruins 239
Parque Nacional Bahuaja-Sonene 94
Parque Nacional Cordillera Azul 179
Parque Nacional del Manu 22, 139, 208, **219**, 220
Parque Nacional Huascarán 190
Parque Nacional Otishi 94
Parque Zoológico de Quistacocha 213
people 19, 21, 179, 183
  Afro-Peruvians 80, 229
  Amazonian 91
  Andean 87
  land rights 95
  mestizo 79
  of Arab descent 80
  of Asian descent 80
  of European descent 80
  Q'eros 83
  uncontacted tribes 92, 94, 95
Peruvian flag 63
photography 312
Pikillacta 35, 271
Pisac 272
  Sunday market 10, 99, 272
Pisco 23, 229, 231
  Catedral 230
  Plaza de Armas 230, 231
Pitec Trail 188
Pitluga, Phyllis 238
Piura 63, 101, 169
Pizarro, Francisco 21, 47, 145, 175, 255
Pizarro, Gonzalo 55
Pizarro, Hernando 53
Pizarro, Juan 54
plantlife
  ayahuasca 211

biodiversity 207
rare species 187
police corruption 170
politics and government 94
  Alianza Popular Revolucionaria Americana (APRA) 66, 69
  American Popular Revolutionary Alliance (APRA) 162
  Cambio 90 Party 71
  corruption 72, 74
  labor unions 66
  La Cantuta murders 72
  Movimiento Revolucionario Tupac Amaru (MRTA) 70, 73
  separatist attempt (Arequipa) 247
  Truth and Reconciliation Commission 74
Pomata 296
  Santiago Apóstol church 296
Pongo de Manique 219
population 21, 79, 148, 162, 211
postal services 312
Prado de Bellido, María 200
Prado, President Mariano 64
public holidays 313
Pucallpa 216
  Summer Institute of Linguistics 216
Puca Pucara 270
Pucusana 227
Puerto Callao 216
  Maroti Shobo artisan cooperative 216
Puerto Maldonado 125, 223
  Plaza de Armas 223
Puerto Pizarro 170
Puno 139, 290, 305
  Biblioteca 292
  Catedral San Carlos Borromeo 291
  city market 292
  La Virgen de La Candelaria festival 9
  Museo Carlos Dreyer 292
  Parque Huajsapata 292
  Parque Pino 292
  Pinacoteca (Art Gallery) 292
  Plaza de Armas 292
  Puno Week 292
Punta Arquillo 232
Punta Hermosa 122
Punta Pejerrey 231
Punta Sal 8, 170
Puyapatamarka 278
pyramids. See historic sites

Q

Qenko 270
Quillabamba 219
Quinua 201
Quispe Tito, Diego 253, 259

R

Raimondi, Antonio 194
rainforest. See jungle, rainforest and cloud forest

Ramos, Edilberto 156
Reiche, Maria 34, 57, 237, 238
  Mystery on the Desert 237
religion 21, 168
  Catholicism 61, 83
  evangelical sects 83
  of the Incas 41
  saints' days 89
  traditional ceremonies 89
religious services 313
Reserva Nacional de Junín 204
Reserva Nacional de Paracas 230
Reserva Nacional Pacaya-Samiria 215
Reserva Nacional Pampa Galeras 239
Reserva Nacional Pampas de Río Heath 223
Reserva Nacional Salinas y Aguada Blanca 250
Reserva Nacional Tambopata 221, 23, 220
Reserva Paisajística Nor Yauyos-Cochas 228
restaurants 112
  Lima 154
Rímac Valley 145
Río Apurímac 117, 125
Rio Cañete 117
Río Cañete 125, 228
Río Chili 125
Río Chillón 145
Río Colca 249, 250
Río Lurín 145
Río Madeira 223
Río Majes 125
Río Marañón 212
Río Napo 220
Río Rímac 145
Río San Lucas 176
Río Santa 125
Río Tambopata 117, 125, 211, 221
Río Ucayali 212
Río Urubamba 219
Río Yarapa 215
Robles, Daniel Alomías 103
Rowe, J.H. 279
rubber 65, 92, 208, **209**
Rumicolca 271
Runku-raqay 277

S

Sabandía 248
Sacaco 239
Sacred Valley 42, 120, 124, 168
Sacsayhuamán 45, 53, 54, **269**
Salazar Bondy, Sebastián 145
Salcantay 119
Salinas 273
Santa Barbara
  mine visits 202
Santa Cruz 189
Santa Rosa 169
Santa Teresa 119
Santuario Nacional Lagunas de Mejía 240
Santuario Warivilca 203
Savoy, Gene 57, 278

Sayajmarka 277
Sechín 32, 161
Sepahua 219
shamans 83, 168, 169, 211, 215
shopping 313. See also art and crafts
  art and crafts 313
  bargaining 158
  forbidden goods 100
Sicán 172
Sierra 22, 79
  climate 23
Sillustani 295
Simpson, Joe 124
  Touching the Void 192
Sipán 35, 169
  Lord of Sipán tomb 35
society 79
  Andean communities 87
  traditional dress 87
  Villa El Salvador 156
  women's role 83, 190
South American Explorers' Club 118
south coast 227
sport. See activities
Strait of Tiquina 297
student travelers 313
Sucre, Antonio José de 201
Summer Institute of Linguistics (SIL) 94
Survival International 95

T

Tacaynamo 37
Tacna 240
  Museo Ferroviario (Railway Museum) 241
  Plaza de Armas 241
Talara 170
Tambo Colorado 233
Tambo Machay 271
Taquile island 99, 294
telephones 313
Tello, Julio C. 194, 232
terrorism 69, 73, 74, 85, 197
  Sendero Luminoso (Shining Path) 66, 69, 70, 71, 81, 83, 94, 139, 148, 156, 192, 197, 201
theater 258
time zones 314
Tingo María 178
Tipón 168, 271
tipping 312
tips 11
toilets 314
Toledo, Alejandro 73, 74
Toro Muerto 125
  Petroglifos 249
Torre Ugarte, José de la 235
tourism 273, 294, 293
  eco-tourism 211, 221
tourist information 314
transportation 302
  air travel 305
  arriving by boat 303
  boats 305
  buses 161, 303, 304
  pick-up trucks 181, 304

scenic train journeys 203
  taxis 85, 305
  trains 9, 305
  trains to Machu Picchu 119
travel agents 302
trekking. See climbing and trekking
Tres Cruces 123
Trujillo 19, 60, 63, 139, 161, **162**
  caballos de paso (dancing horses) 165
  Casa de los Leones 163
  Casa de Urquiaga 164
  Casona Orbegoso 164
  Catedral Santa María 163
  Festival de la Marinera 107, 165
  Festival de la Primavera 165
  Hotel Libertador Trujillo 163
  Iglesia de La Merced 164
  Iglesia de San Agustín 164
  Iglesia San Francisco 163
  La Casa de la Emancipación 164
  La Compañía 165
  Museo Catedralicio 163
  Museo de Arqueología 164
  Museo del Juguete (Toy Museum) 164
  Museo Zoológico 165
  Palacio Iturregui 164
  Plaza de Armas (Plaza Mayor) 163
  Santa Clara church 164
Trujillo Valley 35
Túcume 169
Tumbes 8, 48, 170, 303
Tupac 37, 44
Tupac Amaru II 61, 258

U

Unesco biosphere reserves
  Parque Nacional del Manu 221
  Parque Nacional Huascarán 190
Unesco world natural heritage sites
  Parque Nacional del Manu 221
Urteaga, Mario 177
Urubamba 103, 273
Urubamba Valley 125, 139

V

Vargas Llosa, Mario 70, 248
Velasco, General Juan 66
Ventanillas de Otuzco 182
Vilcashuamán 201
Villegas, Micaela (La Perrichola) 67
visas and passports 314
Volcán Ampato 248
Volcán Chachani 249
Volcán Misti 21, 122, 243
volcanoes 243, 248, 249
  Misti 122, 139
von Däniken, Erich 34, 236, 237
von Humboldt, Alexander 93

W

Wari. See Huari
Warmiwañusqu pass 277

water
  purification 119
websites 314
weights and measures 314
wildlife 22, 125, 125. *See*
    also national parks and reserves
  Andean cat 129
  Andean condor 131
  Andean fox 129
  Andean huemul (taruka) 129
  birds 131, 170, 208, 215, 221,
    222, 240, 295
  birds of prey 130
  butterflies 208
  caiman 213, 216, 220
  capybaras 221
  condors 131, 232, 250
  deer 129, 131
  endangered species 127
  flamingoes 295
  flamingos 230
  giant otters 221
  guanacos 127, 128
  guinea pig (cuy) 130
  guinea pigs 295

hog-nosed skunk 130
Humboldt penguins 231
jaguars 221
macaws 213, 222, 223, 220
marine mammals 230, 231
marmosets 215
monkeys 131, 213, 215, 216,
  219, 220
mountain vizcacha 130
pampas cat 128
parrots 222
peccaries 221, 222
pink dolphins 213, 214, 220
piranhas 216
puma (mountain lion) 128, 190
river dolphins 215
rodents 130, 222
sea birds 231
sea lion refuge (Punta Arquillo)
  232
sloths 215, 220
spectacled bear 130, 131
tapirs 221, 222
turtles 221, 231
vicuñas 127, 190, 250

Willkawain 188
witchcraft 235
women travelers 314

Y

Yates, Simon 124
Yungay 189
  earthquake of 1970 186
Yura 249

Z

Zapata, Marcos
  Last Supper 255, 259
Zevallos, Andrés 177
zoos and animal parks
  Amazon Animal Orphanage 213
  Animal Orphanage and Pilpin-
    tuwasi Butterfly Farm 213
  Parque de las Leyendas (Lima)
    155
  Parque Zoológico de
    Quistacocha 213
Zorritos 170

INSIGHT ⊙ GUIDES

OFF THE SHELF

Since 1970, **INSIGHT GUIDES** has provided a unique perspective on the world's best travel destinations by using specially commissioned photography and illuminating text written by local authors.

Whether you're planning a city break, a walking tour or the journey of a lifetime, our superb range of guidebooks and phrasebooks will inspire you to discover more about your chosen destination.

INSIGHT GUIDES

offer a unique combination of stunning photos, absorbing narrative and detailed maps, providing all the inspiration and information you need.

PHRASEBOOKS & DICTIONARIES

help users to feel at home, when away. Pocket-sized with a free app to download, they go where you do.

CITY GUIDES

pack hundreds of great photos into a smaller format with detailed practical information, so you can navigate the world's top cities with confidence.

EXPLORE GUIDES

feature easy-to-follow walks and itineraries in the world's most exciting destinations, with our choice of the best places to eat and drink along the way.

POCKET GUIDES

combine concise information on where to go and what to do in a handy compact format, ideal on the ground. Includes a full-colour, fold-out map.

EXPERIENCE GUIDES

feature offbeat perspectives and secret gems for experienced travellers, with a collection of over 100 ideas for a memorable stay in a city.

www.insightguides.com